THE CLAY
WE ARE
MADE OF

CRITICAL STUDIES IN NATIVE HISTORY
ISSN 1925-5888

THE CLAY WE ARE MADE OF

HAUDENOSAUNEE LAND TENURE ON THE GRAND RIVER

Susan M. Hill

UNIVERSITY OF MANITOBA PRESS

Clay We Are Made Of: Haudenosaunee Land Tenure on the Grand River
© Susan M. Hill 2017

21 20 19 18 17   2 3 4 5 6

University of Manitoba Press
Winnipeg, Manitoba, Canada
Treaty 1 Territory
uofmpress.ca

Cataloguing data available from Library and Archives Canada
Critical Studies in Native History, ISSN 1925-5888 ; 20
ISBN 978-0-88755-717-0 (PAPER)
ISBN 978-0-88755-457-5 (PDF)
ISBN 978-0-88755-458-2 (EPUB)

Cover design by Mike Carroll
Interior design by Karen Armstrong
Cover image (background): Thomas Connon, Stereograph of Grand River,
c. 1860, C 286-2-0-5, Archives of Ontario, 10011441.
Frontispiece: Richard W. Hill, Sr., *Four Beings*. Used by permission.

Printed in Canada

The University of Manitoba Press acknowledges the financial support for
its publication program provided by the Government of Canada through
the Canada Book Fund, the Canada Council for the Arts, the Manitoba
Department of Sport, Culture, and Heritage, the Manitoba Arts Council,
and the Manitoba Book Publishing Tax Credit.

Funded by the Government of Canada | Canadä

CONTENTS

ILLUSTRATIONS

List of Illustrations

List of Maps

List of Tables

ACKNOWLEDGEMENTS

This book would not have been possible without the assistance and support of many people, and to each of you I am forever grateful. These include librarians, archivists, students, fellow researchers, and members of the Six Nations and other Haudenosaunee communities. In particular, I would like to acknowledge the following:

Staff from the University of Manitoba Press, expressly Glenn Bergen and Jill McConkey. Your patience and persistence have made all the difference.

The Woodland Cultural Centre, most notably Keith Jamieson—your assistance in accessing the Council records was invaluable, in addition to your historical knowledge of our community.

For language advice and cultural/political insights: Brian Owennatekha Maracle, David Kanatawakhon, Jordan Brant, Winnie Thomas, and particularly Tom Deer.

For assistance with editing and other contributions: M. Sam Cronk, Evan Habkirk, Aroha Harris, Mary Jane Logan McCallum, Sabrina Saunders, Raymond Skye, and Danielle Soucy.

My most trusted teachers and advisors: Paul Williams, John Milloy, Kiera Ladner, Rick Hill, and especially Carol and the late Norman Jacobs. Your guidance and belief in my abilities made all the difference.

My family, particularly my parents Wilfred and Anita Hill, my sister Billie Spencer, my brother Bill Hill, and my husband, Rick Powless—each of you has contributed to my ability to do this work.

Finally, I dedicate this book to my children, Spencer and Anita Powless, and for all those yet unborn.

THE CLAY WE ARE MADE OF

Akwekon enskat entitewawenonni ne Onkwanikonhra.
Tahnon onen teyethinonhweraton ne Yethinihstenha
Onhwentsya akwekon skennen akenhake. Tho niyotonhak ne
Onkwanikonhra.
All of us, we will make our minds as one. And now we send
greetings to our Mother, the Earth, all is peaceful and well.
And our minds are one.

This passage from the Haudenosaunee Thanksgiving Address, the Ohenton
Karihwatehkwen, is part of the greetings spoken each morning and evening
by traditional Haudenosaunee to greet the rest of the natural world, to address
all of creation.[1] It is also spoken before and after all ceremonies and official
government meetings. In addition to recognizing our dependence as humans
upon the natural world—all of which can survive without humans and none of
which humans could survive without—in group settings, it serves to unify the
assembled individuals and bring about skanikonhra (one mind).[2] It also con-
nects the Haudenosaunee of today with all the generations who came before
and all those who will come after and recalls the lessons of Haudenosaunee
cultural history.

Haudenosaunee Historical Consciousness

One cannot be truly Haudenosaunee without a historical consciousness of
the collective experiences of our ancestors. The very core of our existence is
formed around the historic inheritance passed down through the generations.
This inheritance was meant to guide the Haudenosaunee for all time, as established at the time of creation. The lessons contained within our historical
consciousness constitute the roadmap for a sustainable, balanced life for the

current generation and the "coming faces" of our future. But our historical consciousness—and cultural base—suffered greatly in the process of European colonization of the Americas, the land we know as Turtle Island. Our lifestyles were greatly altered by epidemic diseases, warfare, environmental degradation, and territorial encroachment. Our traditional processes for conveying historical knowledge were impeded as a result. And, for many, the once effective roadmap seemed to lack the necessary direction for handling the drastic changes of the colonial period.

Many Haudenosaunee people drifted away from honouring the knowledge and lessons of our collective past; however, they often did try to preserve and perpetuate parts of it. But others were still able to see the paths to the future contained within the original map. They took on the task of perpetuating the historical knowledge of our ancestors and showed others how those lessons provided a means to survive in the face of colonial onslaught. In the spirit of those who have perpetuated the historical consciousness of the Haudenosaunee, this book seeks to honour that knowledge and use it as a framework for interpreting contemporary Haudenosaunee history. In this, it serves two purposes. First, it is a call to those Haudenosaunee people who have drifted away from the collective knowledge of our ancestors to reconsider their current direction and regain an understanding of our shared past. Second, it provides a window for non-Haudenosaunee to reconsider the history they have previously been taught about the Haudenosaunee and our shared history with Europeans and other peoples who have come to our territory.

Haudenosaunee history is examined here through the stories of our land, under the framework of our cultural history. Western history has typically painted Native history through the eyes of explorers, conquistadores, missionaries, and traders. Native peoples in North America (and other colonized lands) are typically depicted as background scenery to the "real" history of the continent. The only exception to this depiction is the "Big Chief" method of analysis, wherein one Native man (or a few) is represented as the sole Native worthy of historical discussion. In short, these depictions focus on individuals or small groups of male leaders and their interactions with Europeans. In many cases, these "chiefs" are only marginal leaders, and the chroniclers fail to comprehend the larger collective leadership of the community or nation in question. Instead, they focus on one man, and often discuss ideas of nobility or evidence of acculturation. The Western historical depiction of the Haudenosaunee often falls into this category, with the representation of Haudenosaunee men such as the Four Kings, Joseph Brant, and Red Jacket.

Like many "others," women and internal events and relationships have been left out of these histories, leading to a gross misrepresentation of Haudenosaunee society and history. In their defence, if one is to rely on written historical sources it is difficult to construct any alternative to the "Big Chief" depiction. However, that is reason enough to move beyond those limitations and consider other ways to write about Native history. Furthermore, while Haudenosaunee history has always been in the hands of the Haudenosaunee people, the published history of the Haudenosaunee has rarely been in our control or informed by our thought and philosophy.

Haudenosaunee historical knowledge does record the names of important leaders—male and female—and important events, but the emphasis is always placed on the constant elements of the Haudenosaunee world. A human lifespan is extremely limited, not to mention self-centred, but other parts of the natural world provide a better guide and better perspective for examining the past. For the Haudenosaunee, land is possibly the best point of reference for considering history. Historical knowledge and lessons embodied in the Haudenosaunee cultural history demonstrate land and territory as the prime determinants of Haudenosaunee identity. So if one seeks to understand Haudenosaunee history one must consider the history of Haudenosaunee land. Therefore, in this written account of Haudenosaunee history, the focus has been placed upon the land and away from individual persons. With the understanding that we are born from the land and our bodies will return to it when our time on the earth is done, land serves as the primary focus of our identity. In this, if we are to understand where we have been as a people—to understand our history—we must look to the history of our land and our relationship to her. In characterizing the Haudenosaunee relationship to our territory, we can also point to the perpetuation of original thought and philosophy despite drastic changes in physical lifestyle.

Land as Mother or Land for Sale

Yethi'nihstenha Onhwentsya is the Kanyen'keha (Mohawk) name for the earth. "She-to-us-mother provides-[for our]-needs" describes the relationship between Onkwehonwe (humans) and the earth. The name for the earth, along with the history of how that name came into being, explains Haudenosaunee land philosophy. Everything a person could possibly need to know is there. Yet sometimes our minds wander and fancy "knowing more." We convince ourselves that it is possible to discover deeper meaning. But, really, what deeper meaning can there be than the realization that humans cannot survive without the earth and what she provides for us? This book does not attempt to reach a higher understanding of the Haudenosaunee relationship to the earth. Instead, it is a journey through historical records related to the Grand River Haudenosaunee and their territory. It contemplates how a 55,000-acre plot of land along the banks of the Grand River came to be known as Six Nations. And it considers the legacy of the past generations and that legacy's impact on the contemporary relationship between the Grand River Haudenosaunee and our territory.

Despite the belief in a familial relationship with the earth, the Haudenosaunee—as groups and individuals—have participated in land-sharing deals, initially through treaties and later through leases and direct sales, for over four centuries—actions that appear to contradict the philosophical understanding of responsibility to the land. This book examines that apparent contradiction, focusing upon a discussion of land relationships and policies established by the Haudenosaunee of Ohswe:ken, that is, the Grand River Territory. It draws upon the written record of the Confederacy Council from the late eighteenth century to the early twentieth century, including the speeches and decisions of this governing body. Their words, as the official spokesmen of their respective clan families and nations, demonstrate the collective values of the community in regard to land, treaty obligations, and sovereignty. This book seeks to retell Grand River Haudenosaunee history in a manner that privileges Haudenosaunee knowledge and records in order to fill in many of the gaps within the existing published record.

The records of the Confederacy Council illustrate how the Grand River Haudenosaunee used their traditional teachings to develop land tenure policies in the face of their interactions with European peoples. The policies they created flowed out of the beliefs that land was intended to provide for the people, as a mother does for her child. Coupled with that belief, people have an obligation to respect the earth and to maintain a sustainable relationship with their land. The Haudenosaunee land tenure policies were framed within the parameters of land providing for the people, especially children, and people not being allowed to over-harvest the resources of the territory, including the individual holdings they had been allocated. While many of the land policies for the Grand River Territory were developed in reaction to negative interactions with their non-Native neighbours, they were structured in a manner consistent with original Haudenosaunee teachings. These policies demonstrate a continuity of thought and philosophy and a persistence of Haudenosaunee values regarding land that stem from the time of creation.

Studying Haudenosaunee Land Tenure

In order to examine the history of land tenure on the Grand River Territory, several questions must be considered. First, how did we get from Yethi'nihstenha Onhwentsya—that is, continually recognizing our responsibility to and dependence upon the land—to "Land for Sale"? Is this the complete contradiction that it appears to be, or is there another way to look at it? What do our traditional teachings say about our relationship to the land? What effect did migration have on our settlement on the Grand River? How has the political relationship with Canada changed the process of land tenure as well as the way the people view land? In order to examine these questions, an approach different from previous scholarly studies of the Haudenosaunee was necessary.

One of the Kanyen'keha words for clan is Otara; when one asks another what clan they belong to, the question literally translates to "what clay are you made of?"[3] Many Indigenous knowledge holders talk about the idea that the land does not belong to Native people, but rather Native people belong to the land.[4] The Haudenosaunee share in this philosophy. Examples of this can be found in the names the Haudenosaunee nations call themselves within their languages, all of which refer to a specific characteristic of their original national territory (see Table 1).

Table 1. Haudenosaunee Nation Names.

Onkwehonweneha	English	Translation
Kanyen'kehaka	Mohawk	People of the flint
Onyota'a:ka	Oneida	People of the standing stone
Onönda'gega'	Onondaga	People of the hills
Gayogohono	Cayuga	People of the marshy area
Onöndowága'	Seneca	People of the great hills

I do not believe that it is only by chance that we identify ourselves in relationship to the land we come from, the land we belong to. The land—the territory—defines who we are and how we relate to the rest of the world. James Sákéj Youngblood Henderson has described this aspect of Indigenous philosophies as *ecological contexts*, wherein Indigenous peoples are integrally connected to the territory from which they originate and their interactions with that territory define their relationship to the rest of the world.[5] In discussing Haudenosaunee philosophy, many people have explained ecological contexts through the teachings of the Ohenton Karihwatehkwen.[6] In this, they have asserted that this expression of thanksgiving links the Haudenosaunee people to the rest of creation—their ecological context.

Changes in territory have changed the day-to-day Haudenosaunee inter-actions with their land, but despite these changes the philosophical basis of how the Haudenosaunee see their relationship to land has persisted. Despite enormous territorial change, there are important elements of continuity that have persisted and resisted great pressures to conform to Western views of land relationships.

The writing herein builds upon the work and theories put forward by several Indigenist thinkers within the field of decolonization. I have drawn particularly from Indigenous theory, postcolonial theory, Amerindian autohistory, and decolonizing methodologies. Each of these theories or methodologies really comprises a multitude of approaches to research and takes on different forms depending on the research topic and the researcher. The general commonality found across the theories is a basis within Indigenous thought and research goals related to Indigenous autonomy and sovereignty. In this vein, this book looks at how these theories relate to the concepts of territory and Indigenous knowledge. In order to do this, territoriality and Haudenosaunee knowledge are combined as a means of examining the history of the Grand River Territory. Linda Tuhiwai Smith writes that this combination is essential for Indigenous scholarship (and more importantly for Indigenous peoples):

> Coming to know the past has been part of the critical pedagogy of decolonization. To hold alternative histories is to hold alternative knowledges. The pedagogical implications of this access to alterna-tive knowledges is that they can form the basis of alternative ways of doing things. Transforming our colonized views of our own history (as written by the West), however, requires us to revisit, site by site, our history under Western eyes. This in turn requires a theory or approach which helps us to engage with, understand and then act upon history. . . . Telling our stories from the past, reclaiming the past, giving testimony to the injustices of the past are all strategies which are commonly employed by indigenous peoples struggling for justice.[7]

Using a similar approach, I have revisited the historical record and identified key aspects of the Haudenosaunee record that have been dismissed in the published literature in order to re-present Grand River Haudenosaunee land history. Our cultural history documents how the Haudenosaunee developed philosophies about their land based upon their experiences. Furthermore, Onkwehonweneha (Haudenosaunee languages) and the visual records of the Haudenosaunee Confederacy document the connection between identity, land, and responsibilities of the Onkwehonwe to the earth.

In developing my analysis of the history of Indigenous land relationships, George Sioui's *Amerindian Autohistory*—which is both a theory and a methodology of how to reconstruct Native history through themes of continuity—was especially relevant. Sioui describes this approach as "a technique that aims, through a varied set of sources and categories of informers, to establish the constant cultural traits of one or more culturally related peoples."[8] I use the tools of autohistory to examine the historical relationship of the Haudenosaunee and the Grand River Territory. Some people might look at the Grand River community today and think the people are very assimilated. On the other hand, within the Confederacy, Grand River is recognized as the strongest repository of traditional Haudenosaunee knowledge. In reconstructing the history of the territory that produced the people of Grand River of the twenty-first century, I attempt to reconcile the contradictions that exist within the truths of both of these assessments. Sioui refers to this process as "a new history to match the image of themselves that people have always had, or should have."[9] I believe the themes of continuity—as articulated in Sioui's *Amerindian Autohistory*— regarding relationships to land are a means of finding that reconciliation.

An eclectic mixture of methods is necessary to conduct this type of research. Similar to the representation of the Circle Wampum (see Figure 4), we need to look from many angles in order to get a better picture of what has happened over time. The first step in achieving these multiple views is taken by placing the research within Haudenosaunee epistemology—the way the Haudenosaunee understand the world. In that vein, history begins with creation and unfolds from there. I have drawn from the teachings about land found within four epics of the Haudenosaunee: the Creation Story, the Kayeri Niyorihwai:ke (Four Ceremonies), the Kayaneren'kowa (Great Law of Peace), and the Karihwiyo[10] (Good Message of Handsome Lake). These represent some of the most critical aspects of Haudenosaunee cultural history and inform the Haudenosaunee world view. They are often referred to collectively as the "Original Instructions," but this designation is also used to describe the Creation Story in solitary form as well. While many other epic-like stories exist within Haudenosaunee cultural history, these four are typically referred to as the major accounts that have shaped critical aspects of Haudenosaunee philosophy. They also all have important messages about land and the intended relationship that the Creator expected to exist between humans and the land. To examine these teachings, I chose sources for their respect and integrity as viewed by Haudenosaunee knowledge holders, including those sources originally gathered from Grand River Haudenosaunee knowledge holders. I also chose sources that were published in both English and Haudenosaunee languages. These tend to have a more direct translation into English, and while they are often difficult to read for an English speaker they retain much of the spirit of the words from their original languages.

In an attempt to ground this research within Haudenosaunee thought, I have used aspects of Onkwehonweneha to discuss the philosophical relationship with land. These languages are the products of Haudenosaunee interaction with their lands, with the other beings of creation, and with human beings. They hold the key to understanding the Haudenosaunee mind (skanikonhra). Kanyen'keha examples are usually given (I am most familiar with that Haudenosaunee language) and when possible Cayuga language examples are also noted, as Cayuga and Mohawk are the two most widely spoken Haudenosaunee languages in the Grand River Territory. While there are six distinct Haudenosaunee languages, they are similar in terms of basic word structure patterns, with many words sharing a common root among two or more of the languages.

In order to discuss the impacts of contact between the Haudenosaunee and Europeans, one needs to consider what Haudenosaunee life was like before contact. The sources consulted in this endeavour were numerous. First, I reviewed available Haudenosaunee historical records. These include oral sources such as (recorded) stories and aspects of the Great Law, as well as wampum documents recorded in strings and belts. Because these sources were recorded mostly by non-Haudenosaunee scholars, decolonizing lenses had to be applied in many instances to discern what was actually being said rather than simply accept a Western interpretation. For example, in his article on Iroquois women, J.N.B. Hewitt translates the name of Jigonsaseh[11] to mean "The Most Pure Person." In reality, the name translates as "the one with a fresh, new face." There is nothing in the name that states that her face is "more" or the "most" of anything. While Hewitt's meaning is close to the actual translation of the name, it infers something quite different about Haudenosaunee names and the historical legacy of this particular woman. This type of reinterpretation is necessary in order to get a more accurate representation of history and Haudenosaunee philosophy.

The next area I explored in regard to "pre-contact" times was archeological evidence. While much of the archeological discussion of this era focuses upon evolutionary theories of development, I focussed on the physical locations and descriptions of Haudenosaunee villages as a means of looking at the actual territories of the Confederacy and various territorial boundaries (as discussed in Chapter 3). I have used pre-contact archeological sources sparingly, as many of these are not directly relevant.

Finally, I looked at early historical sources that addressed life before European presence, based upon statements made by Haudenosaunee people to the European newcomers. Some of these are found within travel narratives; others are in early missionary accounts. Again, many of these sources need to be reinterpreted in order to get a clearer picture of what was being told, but there is a great deal of useful information to be found in these records.

As one could expect, there are many more sources available to examine the "post-contact" world of the Haudenosaunee than that of the "pre-contact" era. In studying this aspect of Haudenosaunee history I reviewed a variety of sources, including Haudenosaunee records (oral, wampum, etc.), travel narratives and other written sources, treaty records, the papers of various colonial officials, and written Haudenosaunee documents. Again I applied decolonizing approaches to the sources such as "reading between the lines" in travel narratives. For example, Harmen Meyndertsz van den Bogaert mentions Oneida[12] women trading salmon in a Mohawk village he was visiting in 1634.[13] Several things can be inferred from this occurrence beyond his commentary, including the fact that women were actively participating in the trading economy of the day, not only on the home front but also across territorial borders.

Using sources such as travel narratives and missionary journals presents a very slippery slope in historical research. Oftentimes the authors embellish their "observations" in order to fit their own personal agendas. In the case of missionaries, there was a need to "demonize" Native spiritual practices in order to justify their imposition of Christianity at every turn. Furthermore, they often portray resistant nations, villages, and individuals as "evildoers" who took every opportunity to brutalize the faithful followers of the Church. Sources such as the *Jesuit Relations* are full of such biased portrayals, written to help justify the presence of the missionaries in New France as they waged a spiritual battle against "pagan" beliefs of the unconverted (especially the Haudenosaunee). As a result, these references have to be used very carefully and preferably in the context of critical analysis.

Similarly, the collections of government officials such as Sir William Johnson (the first imperial superintendent general of Indian Affairs for the northern superintendency of North America) present a wealth of information but must take into account the political desires of their authors as well. Related to that, the official records of treaty councils also contain critical information but require the application of cultural lenses to interpret the events they chronicle. For example, treaty council records often report that meetings began "with the typical pageantry." This "pageantry" would regularly take several days. When the recorders made such comments they failed to recognize the critical openings of the treaty councils, which typically centred on the principle of condolence—essential in the Haudenosaunee mind for respectful relations and decision making.

An examination of the move from the Haudenosaunee homelands to the ancient hunting grounds along the Grand River in 1784 brings the researcher to additional sources. In this period we find the first examples of written political records that were created by and for the Haudenosaunee. While the written treaty council records of the previous era represent Haudenosaunee political history, they were recorded by Euro-Americans who viewed events through the lens of their own experiences. In addition to traditional recording methods, the Haudenosaunee began writing more extensively in this time period. The most active of these chroniclers was Joseph Brant. His letters (many of which were written long before the migration to the Grand River) typically served as calls to action for the Crown to uphold their promises and responsibilities to their staunch allies, the Haudenosaunee. The writings of other leaders such as John Norton, Isaac Hill, and John Brant often had a similar purpose. The Grand Council also began keeping written minutes of some of their meetings at this time. It appears that most of these records were made of meetings with external bodies (usually Crown representatives), but they exist as a window into the political workings of the Confederacy in the early nineteenth century. It is important to note, however, that clearly there were internal meetings, which happened regularly, that were not recorded in written form. This is true throughout time, to the present day.

Starting in the 1870s, the Confederacy Council at Grand River began employing their own secretary to keep the records of their meetings. The minutes were written in English, although the council proceedings were held in the Haudenosaunee languages. The purpose of these written records was to support the memories of the chiefs regarding the numerous decisions required of them during that time. The secretary also had the responsibility of providing a copy of the minutes to the visiting superintendent (Indian agent) for the purposes of his reports to the Department of Indian Affairs. Notations within the minute books show what sections were included in the superintendent's copy and what was left out. Corresponding records from the Department of Indian Affairs (held by Library and Archives Canada) match up with the notations found within the minute books. I was able to gain access to microfilmed copies of all the minute books from 1880 to 1924, the majority of which were written by Chief Josiah Hill (Nanticoke and Tuscarora[14] representative to the council), who served as secretary from 1876 until his death in 1915. These sources provide the majority of information for Chapters 5 and 6 and were especially useful in examining the development of community land policies as well as providing evidence of continuity in regard to land philosophy and the assertions of land claims and sovereignty.

Other sources from this time period include aspects of legal history such as the Haldimand Proclamation, the Simcoe Deed, and court decisions regarding squatter cases. The sources for this era are primarily archival in nature, requiring typical research methods. My analysis of such records is not typical, however. Instead, I employ techniques such as those of Sioui to determine themes of continuity in philosophy and relationships to land and territory.

Finally, in assessing the current relationship of the Grand River Haudenosaunee to our territory, I employ key aspects of our cultural thought and historic relationships with the Crown. First, the Haudenosaunee have a responsibility to future generations, "the coming faces." I analyze the current land tenure practices and land situation within that framework of future considerations. Next, I frame the discussion of the Haudenosaunee relationship to the Crown and Canada within our historic relationship, utilizing the analogy of "polishing the Covenant Chain" as laid out in the treaty agreements of the seventeenth and eighteenth centuries. Lastly, I assess the implications of the treaty rights accorded to the Haudenosaunee and citizens of the British Crown in accordance with the Two Row Wampum Belt and the Covenant Chain. These principles represent those aspects of the relationship created by the ancestors of the Haudenosaunee and Canadians. As a conclusion, I consider the contemporary Crown-Haudenosaunee relationship within the Canadian calls for reconciliation.

PART I
Haudenosaunee Cultural History and Relationship to Land

CHAPTER 1

Karihwa'onwe—The Original Matters

My people, the Haudenosaunee, have always shared stories about our land. We told these stories long before a 55,000-acre plot of land along the Grand River in present-day southern Ontario became known as Six Nations. We told them before the Haudenosaunee people moved their homes to that land, part of our traditional hunting territory, in the upheavals following the American Revolution. And we told them even earlier, before written history recorded the arrival of Europeans to Turtle Island.

Haudenosaunee thought and philosophy is rooted in these stories. Of these, there are four major elements, or epics, that express our cultural history: the Creation Story, the Kayeri Niyorihwa:ke (Four Ceremonies), the Kayaneren'kowa (Great Law of Peace), and the Karihwiyo (Good Message of Handsome Lake).[1] All four of these epics were recorded through traditional means, including oral texts (stories), speeches, songs, wampum belts, and other visual images. They are represented throughout Haudenosaunee culture in a multitude of ways, including the greetings of the Ohenton Karihwatehkwen ("the words before all else"/Thanksgiving Address). Through the Thanksgiving Address the speaker reminds all present that the earth is our mother and that she supports all life as we know it. This echoes the Haudenosaunee Creation Story, which teaches that the first person born on this earth was buried under the ground, and from her body the plants that sustain life grew and continue to grow to this day. The Four Ceremonies recall the gifts of creation and remind us of our dependence upon the earth. Through the establishment of the Great Law, the Peacemaker taught the Haudenosaunee how to live in balance with each other as human beings of a collective territory. And the Karihwiyo reminds us of our responsibilities to all of creation and the manner in which we are to care for the earth so she can continue to provide for us, as set out within creation.

Onkwehonweneha[2] were the original languages of these texts, and the stories remain intact within those languages to the present time. Since the early days of European contact, however, these texts have been translated into English and French, often for the purposes of ethnographic study by non-Haudenosaunee individuals, including those working within missionary efforts. There are, of course, dangers in segmenting and compartmentalizing aspects of Haudenosaunee knowledge. The Haudenosaunee knowledge base exists as a complete entity, and the various parts of it are interconnected and dependent upon each other in order to understand the whole. When one removes a segment of it, that portion ceases to be what it is within the context of the whole. It is still useful for studies such as these, but the ensuing discussions of those pieces are limited representations of the original. Due to the limitations of translating between languages that are based within very different world views, as well as the frequent biases of the European-speaking interpreters, the texts produced through these translations have many shortcomings. Even later translations—often conducted in close collaboration with or solely by Haudenosaunee people—cannot make up for the concepts that exist in one culture but not in the other. Yet, the product of these translations becomes a representation of the original and can be very useful when its limitations are considered. For the purposes of this discussion, the sources cited are representations of the original texts that have been written in the English language; in certain cases there is a directly corresponding Onkwehonweneha text accompanying the English.

The Creation Story

As with most cultures in the world, the Haudenosaunee Creation Story serves as the basis for our understanding of the world and our place within it. The Creation Story holds many of our beliefs regarding the relationship intended to exist between humans and the rest of the natural world. This story has been recorded in a multitude of ways within cultural practices. Representations of it exist not only in the retelling of the story but also in elements such as beadwork designs[3] and social dances and songs. Through these various elements of cultural expression the Creation Story remains an active part of everyday life. A striking difference between the Creation Story and the other three epics is the lack of formal procedures to maintain the story as a single entity. Instead, the story of how this world came to be has been recorded and maintained in many forms. Considering the overarching themes of creation and the belief that creation is a constantly occurring and recurring process rather than something that happened once in the long-ago past, it is understandable that the story of creation cannot be expressed in a single form.

Still, Europeans (and their descendants) have sought to record the "definitive version" for centuries. Missionaries were the first to undertake this task,[4] although their interests were limited and, therefore, did not produce an in-depth representation of the story. Brief mention of the Haudenosaunee Creation Story, as well as those of other Native peoples, can be found within the *Jesuit Relations*, a compilation of North American Jesuit records from the seventeenth century, and in other early missionary accounts. Perhaps the missionaries' interests in studying Native views of creation focussed upon their ability to develop effective means through which to convert the Natives and "save their souls." Their religious fervour clouded their ability to recognize other views of creation on the same footing as their own idea of creation—the one for which they were sacrificing themselves in order to convert the "New World pagans." Their religious elitism guided their depictions of Indigenous cultures and practices, often leading them to compare what they saw and heard to "devil worship."[5] In these accounts, issues also arise around translation as well as the Christianization of recorded stories.

The first academic undertaking to study Haudenosaunee views of creation came through the anthropological studies of Lewis Henry Morgan, who generalized his work with the Tonawanda Seneca to be representative of the entire Confederacy.[6] While Morgan's *League of the Ho-de-no-sau-nee* (1851) was a major undertaking in Haudenosaunee cultural study, it only briefly addresses the Creation Story. His only real reference to the story is as follows: "The Iroquois, also, believed that the Great Spirit was born; and tradition has handed down the narrative, with embellishments of fancy which Hesiod himself would not have disdained."[7] In contrast, he described aspects of Greek origin stories in the three pages that preceded this lone statement. Other anthropologists who followed in Morgan's footsteps in the late nineteenth century, including Horatio Hale and Alexander Goldenweiser, also made only limited mention of the Creation Story. Instead, they tended to focus upon the governance structures of the Great Law and ceremonial rites practised in different communities.

In contrast to his ethnographic peers, J.N.B. Hewitt began collecting versions of the Creation Story in 1889 as he travelled to several Haudenosaunee communities while working as an ethnographer with the Bureau of American Ethnology (BAE), a division of the Smithsonian Institution. Hewitt is often represented as a Tuscarora who happened to be an anthropologist.[8] I would argue, however, that through his writings it is clear that he was an anthropologist who happened to be of Haudenosaunee descent. His personal identification as an ethnographer first and foremost is telling in the manner in which he depicted the culture of the Haudenosaunee. For example, in the introduction to his 1903 publication, "Iroquois Cosmology, Part 1," he discusses the differences between Iroquoian and English languages: "It is no ready task to embody in the language of enlightenment the thought of barbarism. The viewpoint of the one plane of thought differs much from that of the other."[9] While he did have a certain respect for the Haudenosaunee, he clearly did not see them as equals of American society—where he placed himself. Despite his own identification as an American ("civilized"), his Tuscarora descent is often heralded as a mark of "insider authenticity,"[10] glossing over the fact that his representations of culture are external to Haudenosaunee society and contain many of the same pitfalls found in the work of non-Native anthropologists.

Hewitt collected five versions of the Creation Story over an eleven-year period (1889 to 1900) and proceeded to publish four of them—the first three in 1903 and the last one in 1928[11]—in annual reports of the BAE. All of the versions begin with an English narrative translation and conclude with a word-by-word translation from the Haudenosaunee languages into English. The first three vary in length but all are relatively short compared to the final publication of an Onondaga language version[12] collected from John Arthur Gibson (who held the title of Skanyatariyo, or Handsome Lake), the Seneca Royaner (chief) from Grand River.[13]

Following Hewitt's publications of the Creation Story, many others have documented portions of the story in different forms. Some of these versions represent the ethnographic research of anthropologists.[14] Others are the products of people from Haudenosaunee communities, whose primary focus was the perpetuation of this epic within the Confederacy.[15] Others yet have taken Hewitt's writings and reworked them using various techniques. For example, Seneca historian John Mohawk focuses much of his dissertation on reframing and re-presenting many of the versions of the Creation Story that Hewitt had recorded and published. Mohawk recognized the value of Hewitt's work both for Haudenosaunee people—"Hewitt's work provides some record of how things got to be the way they are, and why"[16]—and for the academy. Furthermore, Mohawk points out not only the complexities of Hewitt's "versions" of the Creation Story but also the shortcomings of all of the written forms of Haudenosaunee cultural history: "The essays contained here are not an attempt to penetrate or comment on the linguistics of the piece, nor is there an attempt to provide the definitive version of this story. This is one version of many. The actual story, a classic myth with a powerful ritual tradition, contains nuances buried within the languages which defy unambiguous translation, a characteristic which I tried to leave intact."[17] In this, Mohawk affirms the common Haudenosaunee understanding of the limitations of translating Onkwehonweneha narratives into English. Oneida educator Carol Cornelius also uses Hewitt's documentation of the Creation Story for her educational text *Iroquois Corn in a Culture-Based Curriculum*. She says this about the varying "versions" of the story:

> There are many versions of the Creation story which differ because in the oral tradition some speakers provide a long, detailed narrative of the Sky World, while others place emphasis on the section of the narrative about twin forces here on earth. Although the emphasis or details change depending on the speaker, the basic story remains the same. The English version [Hewitt's] uses terminology that is cumbersome in many respects. It uses archaic language such as "verily," "ye," "thee," and "thou," which one must suspect was used in the early 1900s to enable Hewitt to publish this manuscript for the general public.[18]

As Mohawk and Cornelius point out, there are many complications with Hewitt's work—such as outdated English terminology, less-than-accurate and culturally incorrect translations, and the limitations of writing in general—but it does serve as an important resource, especially in terms of the Onkwehonweneha renderings included in the accounts. Many Haudenosaunee people continue to study this source for key information regarding older forms of Haudenosaunee languages that are no longer in common use. Furthermore, its availability to the public allows for its use in this study without compromising more private Haudenosaunee texts.[19] Hewitt's Creation Story texts have proven very useful in finding evidence of Haudenosaunee land philosophy. The discussion of the story that follows is primarily informed by Hewitt's published versions (as noted), with the overall framework and occasional direct references to my own (English) understanding of the oral record.

Land in the Creation Story

When we look at the Creation Story, several themes appear relevant to a discussion of land and territory. The story begins in the Sky World with the interaction of two villages. One is the domain of the "Earth Grasper" (De'haonhwendjiawa'khon) and the other is that of Mature Flowers (Awen'ha'i'); these two are destined to marry. The uncle of Mature Flowers instructs her to travel to the village of the Earth Grasper (who is the leader there) and announce herself to him. Her uncle tells her that she will be asked to explain where she came from, and she is to reply, "the place where my uncle has a standing tree."[20] This description of her community alludes to a matrilineal village identity (her uncle is her mother's brother) denoted through a male name (similar to the clan family lineages that are confirmed under the Great Law). In other words, territory is connected to kinship and identity.

After Earth Grasper and Mature Flowers were married, Earth Grasper dreamed of uprooting the tree, which was under his stewardship. Because of the type of dream it was and the recurrence of the images, it was decided that the dream must be realized. Many of the beings of the Sky World (including Wind, the Fire Dragon, and various game animals) were called upon to collectively uproot the tree. Then Earth Grasper and Mature Flowers sat on the edge of the hole where the roots once were. At that moment, Earth Grasper pushed his pregnant wife into the hole, fulfilling the final part of his dream. As he had the tree replanted, she made her descent to the world of water below. She was met by large waterfowl (some versions mention ducks, others mention geese) who broke her fall and placed her on the back of a giant sea turtle who had offered his back to support her. The muskrat died in his attempt to bring dirt from under the water to place on the turtle in order to help Mature Flowers feel more at home, but through the sacrifice of his life, earth was placed on the back of the turtle. As a result of the combination of the retrieved earth, the footsteps of Mature Flowers, and the power of the turtle, the world began to grow. From this we learn that soil has transformative powers.[21] We learn that because of great sacrifices such as those of the turtle and the muskrat, life in this world had a chance to start because they assisted in the creation of land. Additionally, Mature Flowers's descent through that hole in the earth of the Sky World allowed for the creation of this world.

Shortly after being placed on the turtle's back, Mature Flowers gave birth to her daughter, Gaende'so'k, also known as Zephyr. Together they travelled about the turtle's back, which continued to grow as they walked about. Zephyr grew rapidly and soon became a young woman. She was courted by many beings who sought marriage, but her mother declined each of the suitors until her daughter told her of a Turtleman who sought her for a wife. Mature Flowers selected the Turtleman for her daughter.

Hewitt attributed her choice to the fact that she understood the turtle to have transformative powers, and although he was a being of this world he was worthy of a woman who was the product of the Sky World.[22] Furthermore, while none of the written versions of the Creation Story reviewed directly make this connection, I believe this Turtleman may have been the same turtle who gave his back to carry the earth. Later in the story one of the offspring of this union jumped in the water in search of a mis-shot arrow and landed at the doorstep of the Turtleman (his father).[23]

The Turtleman visited the home of Mature Flowers and Zephyr only once. He laid two arrows over Zephyr's abdomen and told her he would return for them in the morning, which he did. She never saw him again, but it soon became apparent that she was pregnant. She realized that she carried twins because she could hear them arguing inside of her. When it came time for them to be born, the two argued over who would be born first. Mature Flowers was away from the house and Zephyr was left to deliver her children alone. One of the boys was in position to be born first but his brother did not want to wait and be born second, despite his brother's warnings that he should be patient. So as one entered this world through the birth canal, the other pushed his way out through his mother's armpit and, in so doing, killed her. When Mature Flowers returned, she was shocked to find her daughter dead and questioned the twins as to who was responsible. The one who caused her death, Flint,[24] accused his brother, Sapling—also known as Skyholder and later as the Creator—and this set the stage for the grandmother's distrust of the latter boy. The three then took Zephyr's body and placed it in the earth.[25] She became the first person buried in this world, and on top of her grave Mature Flowers planted seeds of corn, beans, squash, tobacco, and strawberries.[26] Because her body was placed in the earth, allowing her remains to nourish growing things, the Creator instructed humans to refer to the earth as Yethi'nihstenha Onhwentsya—our mother, the earth—in honour of his mother. The grandmother was then left to raise the twins.

Mature Flowers challenged Skyholder to a contest to determine who would control the earth—this great gamble was about the control of land. The grandmother and Flint believed the earth should be a cold place, free of the life forms created by Skyholder. Skyholder, of course, advocated for the continuation of the world he had brought forth. In a game of chance with the sacrifice of six chickadees and the support of the rest of the beings he created, Skyholder won the challenge. This competition was not only for control but also for life itself. In other words, in order to have life continue, Skyholder had to win control of the land.[27]

As mentioned previously, the Creation Story alludes to a special power held within the earth. This power is the combination of all the things that brought the earth into existence, including the power of Mature Flowers as a being of the Sky World, the great sacrifices of the muskrat and the turtle, and the nutrients provided by the body of the twins' mother. Skyholder used the power of the earth in creating various living beings of this earth. These include the deer, bear, various birds, and other game animals. In order to create these beings, he first took soil (clay) and formed it into the physical shape of the being. Once the body was complete, he breathed into the form, giving it life. The following passage from John Arthur Gibson and J.N.B. Hewitt[28] depicts the words of Skyholder: "[I say] that indeed this earth is alive, be it known, so therefrom I took up earth by which I made all the things I have planted and I have finished living bodies, so that is the reason all they are severally alive and that in their bodies severally they will die, that earth they will become again, not as to their lives."[29] In this statement, Skyholder determined the cycle that life would take in this world. This demonstrates the view that life comes from the earth and once it is completed it returns to the earth, allowing for future life. Further, Gibson and Hewitt recall Skyholder's words about the creation of humans:

> He took up earth and he said, "This earth which I have taken up is really alive. Thus also is it as to the earth present here, and verily the body which I shall make from that kind of thing shall continue to live."
>
> Then at that time he made the flesh of the human being. As soon as he had completed it he then meditated and then said, "That verily, perhaps, will result in good that thus it shall continue to be that he shall have life as much as that is wherein I myself am alive." Now at that time he took a portion of his own life and he put it into the inside of the body of the human being; so also he took a portion of his own mind and he inclosed it in his head; so also he took a portion of his own blood and he inclosed it inside of his flesh; so also did he take a portion of his power to see and

he inclosed it in his head; so also he took a portion of his power to speak and he inclosed it in the throat of the human being. Now at that time, too, he placed his breath in the body of the human being. Just then the human being came to life, i.e., the flesh, and he also arose and he stood up on the earth here present.[30]

This excerpt demonstrates the Haudenosaunee belief that the life force of the earth gave life to humans. It also demonstrates the rationale behind the common name given to Skyholder (also the Creator) within our languages, Shonkwaya'tihson, which means "he completed our bodies."

Once his work was done with creating humans, the Creator informed them that it was time for him to return to the land of his grandmother—the Sky World. He showed them how they could communicate with him through the burning of tobacco, which pierces the sky, and he left them with directions about how he intended life on this earth to exist—the Original Instructions. The following excerpt describes part of what he told First Man and First Woman:

"I have planted human beings on the earth for the purpose that they shall beautify the earth by cultivating it, and dwell therein." Now he saw that he the Elder Brother came up over it and caused it to be daylight on the earth here present and that the daylight was beautiful and the light rays were beautiful, and it was agreeably warm.

Now at that time De 'haen 'hiyawa'khon' [the Creator] said, "Do thou look at that orb of light coming up over it, and that is beautiful in causing daylight to be on the earth and also it shall be an ever-present object of thought, and also it shall continue to give pleasure to they mind in that it will continue to warm the days to come and next to them the nights that shall come. That, too, thereby also all those things that grow, also all the game animals, shall continue to live thereby on the earth present here; all you who dwell here below on the earth present here shall continue to live thereby."[31]

Of great importance in the Creator's words are the instructions to plant and the explanation of the relationship between humans and the sun—who was the brother of Mature Flowers and who came to this world to assist Skyholder in the development of life on earth. This passage reflects the importance

Figure 1. Haudenosaunee Sky Dome Design.

of agriculture within Haudenosaunee society and the recognition within Haudenosaunee culture of the sun's vital role with respect to all life.

As mentioned earlier, the Creation Story remains a vital part of Haudenosaunee life. It is taught and related in many forms, ranging from the spoken to the written to the drawn, using several mediums. While many of these forms are ancient (such as the oral record and visual symbols), others are the product of contemporary society (such as the *Great Peace CD-ROM*, which gives a short version of the Creation Story).[32] The Sky Dome pattern combines old and new to represent the Haudenosaunee knowledge of creation, depicting the relationship between this world and the Sky World (see Figure 1). The bottom lattice pattern represents the water under Turtle Island. The designs drawn under the half-circles represent the life and vegetation of the earth. And the scrolls on top of the dome mark the tree of the Sky World and the connection between the two worlds. In other words, this depiction of the Sky Dome, like all other depictions of the Creation Story, demonstrates the relationship between the land of this world and the land of the Sky World. In that manner, it can be seen as a cosmological map illustrating the connection between the two worlds. It delineates the relationship between the earth and the other world that caused life as we know it on earth to exist.

KAYERI NIYORIHWA:KE – The Four Ceremonies

The second epic of the Haudenosaunee lies in the story of the founding of the Four Ceremonies, also known as the Four Dances. The following discussion of this story is not about the actual ceremonies. Rather, it explains how the ceremonies were brought to the Onkwehonwe and outlines the teachings of these ceremonies in regard to land. The Four Ceremonies—Ostowa'ko:wa (the Great Feather Dance), Kane:hon (Drum or Skin Dance), Aton:wah (the Men's

Chant), and Kayentowa:nen (the Peach Stone and Bowl Game)—are observed throughout the year as parts of the Haudenosaunee ceremonial calendar. The following retelling of this story is informed by my understanding of the oral record as well as Hewitt's recording of the story as part of the Creation Story.

It is said that some time after the Creator returned to the land of his Grandmother that the Onkwehonwe forgot those first lessons of the Original Instructions. At that time the Creator sent a messenger to remind the Onkwehonwe of the covenant they had made at the time of Creation. This messenger was a fatherless boy who was one of twelve boys born in a village all around the same time. The boys played together regularly and did so away from their parents. One day some of the parents followed them to see what the boys did together. They watched as the Twelfth Boy gave out directions to the others, telling one he would be responsible for singing the Great Feather Dance and instructing another that he would be the speaker for the Drum Dance and so on. Each was given a job. Shortly after, the Twelfth Boy told the others that it was time for him to leave but that they had to maintain their responsibilities and in doing so they would remind the people to be thankful for the life the Creator had provided for them in this world.

Often the story of the Four Ceremonies is combined either with the Creation Story or the story of the Peacemaker and the Great Law. Despite the fact that the Twelfth Boy was sent to this world after the Creator returned to the Sky World, the Four Ceremonies are seen as part of the Original Instructions of the Haudenosaunee.[33] In the version recorded by Gibson and Hewitt, the Creator gives these directions about the observance of the Four Ceremonies: "So then now every one of you must give strict attention. And, indeed, all you who live upon the earth share it equally; in the next place, the matter will continue thus in the future; and then they shall regard it as important; so then I, myself, too will regard it as an important matter, what I will leave here on the earth, the Four Ceremonies, or Rituals. You shall continue to keep those customs, and the ceremony shall continue to be observed."[34] The Creator's decree of all beings' equal right to share the earth is central to Haudenosaunee land philosophy, an idea that is explained further in the context of the Great Law of Peace (discussed later in this chapter).

In addition to the Creator's instructions to maintain the Four Ceremonies, the lessons of the ceremonies also provide key information regarding Haudenosaunee land philosophy. Collectively, they serve as a reminder of that original pact between humans and the Creator. So long as the Onkwehonwe remembered to be thankful for all of creation, the Creator's will—that life would continue to exist on this earth—would prevail over the powers of his brother, Flint. Individually, each ceremony plays a different role in the Onkwehonwe celebration and thanksgiving of life. For example, the Great Feather Dance is said to honour those first steps taken by Mature Flowers over the muskrat's dirt that had been placed upon the back of the giant sea turtle. The songs and dances recall and give thanks for creation. The Drum Dance depicts the Thanksgiving Address, and in so doing honours the gifts of Creation—all of the beings that exist in this world and the gifts they provide to humans. The Men's Chant is part of the process for naming babies, and it is also said to be the death song—birth and death, probably the two ultimate reminders of life. Finally, the Peach Stone Game recalls that great contest between the Creator and Flint (or Mature Flowers) for control of the land, the struggle over whether life would exist on earth or not. Cayuga Clan Mother Carol Jacobs relates the relevance of this teaching:

> We are told that when this land was being created, our Creator was challenged to a bet by his brother. The subject of their game was: would there be life? And in one throw, supported by all the living forces of the natural world, our Creator won this bet. He won it all for us. He won it for all of us. We commemorate this each year in part of our Midwinter ceremonies.
>
> This is not just a quaint legend. It is a reminder that, as scientists now agree, life on earth is the result of chance, as well as of intent. Life on earth is a fragile matter. That magnificent gamble could have gone the other way: life could just as easily not have been at all.
>
> That is a reason for constantly giving thanks. We know very well how close life still is to not being. The reminders are all around us.[35]

Jacobs reminds us that by winning control of the land, the Creator made it possible for life to continue on earth.

The Creator informed humans that it was their duty to maintain these ceremonies and that as long as they fulfilled that duty, life would continue. The Four Ceremonies recall the connection between humans and the rest of creation and serve as a reminder to be thankful for life and to protect it always. These stories remind us that land exists because of the sacrifices of many, and that as long as we are thankful life will continue.

KAYANEREN'KOWA – The Great Law of Peace

The Onkwehonwe maintained the teachings of the Twelfth Boy for many generations. His teachings served as the basis for a harmonious life on earth, but eventually a great darkness overcame many of the people and they lost sight of the harmony and balance provided for in the Original Instructions. Greed and violence became the governing powers over the territories of the Haudenosaunee. Some of the descriptions of the time include depictions of cannibalism and lakes and rivers that flowed with human blood. This contradicted the intentions of the Creator—in fact, it was the exact opposite of his directions to humans—but rather than allowing the Onkwehonwe to continue killing each other, he sent a messenger to return them to their original path. This messenger, known in English as the Peacemaker,[36] brought the Great Law of Peace and, in so doing, established the Haudenosaunee Confederacy.[37]

The Great Law is the most widely studied aspect of Haudenosaunee cultural history within both Haudenosaunee society and academia. Since the days of its formation, the Haudenosaunee have selected individuals to be students of different aspects of the Great Law, with duties ranging from the making of wampum belts to serving as a leader of a clan family. Such studies from within the Confederacy continue to this day and serve as an example of the Haudenosaunee intellectual tradition.

As the title denotes, Morgan's *League of the Hodenosaunee* focussed upon many of the traditions that are based within the Great Law. As a lawyer he was fascinated with the implications of a law created by a people whom he saw as "primitive." Again, Morgan—as a founder of American anthropology and "Iroquoian studies"—was followed by many other ethnologists who attempted to support his ideas and demonstrate a few of their own theories that either built upon his work or occasionally deviated from his initial findings. The ethnographic literature on the Haudenosaunee is written by such followers of Morgan as Horatio Hale, J.N.B. Hewitt, Alexander Goldenweiser, Arthur C. Parker, William Fenton, and Elisabeth Tooker. All of these academics endeavoured to understand the League of the Haudenosaunee and expended considerable effort in examining the Great Law from different angles. A constant theme that emerges from this literature, however, is the imposition of the authors' own ideas about Haudenosaunee society and government as "primitive" and less sophisticated than those of Western society. These anthropologists and ethnologists were followed by subsequent generations of academics, including Michael Foster, Floyd Lounsbury, and Marianne Mithun, who often utilized the fieldwork of their predecessors as a basis for their own studies of the Haudenosaunee. Like their predecessors, many of these scholars have called upon individual Haudenosaunee people to provide further information to assist in their reworkings of the earlier studies. Typically, they represent their Haudenosaunee "sources" with a greater level of respect than did many of their predecessors, often listing them as "collaborators" and occasionally giving them co-authorship. I have used some of these sources in my subsequent discussion of the Great Law.

In addition to the internal Haudenosaunee studies and external ethnographic studies, a third area of Great Law scholarship exists—one that is a combination of internal and external study, with origins specific to the Grand River Territory.[38] As will be discussed at length in later chapters, the Canadian government began pressuring the Grand River Haudenosaunee in the mid-1800s to replace the hereditary Grand Council of chiefs with an elected system (as provided for in the Indian Act). The Grand Council was not interested in this change and articulated to Canada its opposition in a multitude of ways: verbally to the Indian agent, via letters to the governor general, and occasionally through delegations of chiefs sent to Ottawa, London, and eventually the League of Nations.[39] Despite their clearly articulated objections, the Department of Indian Affairs continued pressuring the chiefs. As a result, on several occasions the chiefs also delegated to committees of individual chiefs the task of recording the laws of the Confederacy in written English to demonstrate to Canada that the Haudenosaunee government was legitimate and representative of the people. The work of these committees resulted in two different texts that exist today: the first by Seth Newhouse (1897),[40] which did not receive the full sanction of the council; and the second, produced by a collaboration of several chiefs, that was eventually accepted by the council and later published by Duncan Campbell Scott through the Department of Indian Affairs and the Royal Society of Canada in 1912.[41] One of the major contributors of the second text was John Arthur Gibson, who had also worked with ethnologists Hewitt and Goldenweiser. His work with Hewitt included a short study of the Great Law and the detailed study of the Creation Story, as discussed earlier. Goldenweiser focussed on Gibson's knowledge of the Great Law, and the resulting manuscript served as the basis for the Hanni Woodbury translation of the text in collaboration with Reg Henry (Haudenosaunee linguist from the Cayuga Nation) and Harry Webster (from the Onondaga Nation), entitled *Concerning the League*. This text is considered to be the most extensive of any written versions of the Great Law because of its original detail as well as the skilled translating collaboration of Woodbury, Henry, and Webster. It opens with a brief English summary of the text and then focuses upon a word-for-word translation of Gibson's words to Goldenweiser; Woodbury's translation process is very similar to the system used by Hewitt nearly a century earlier. These three texts have served as the basis for several contemporary English versions of the Great Law that have been produced primarily for internal study within Haudenosaunee communities.

The three above-mentioned texts (Newhouse, the 1912 Chiefs' version, and Woodbury's retranslated Gibson-Goldenweiser text), along with Hale's work on the Condolence Ceremony, are key sources for understanding the relationship between the Great Law and Haudenosaunee philosophy regarding land relationships. They are the most accessible and extensive sources of the available versions and, despite being contradictory on certain aspects of the Great Law, are quite consistent in the depiction of the thoughts about land. There are two major parts to the Great Law: first, the story of the Peacemaker and his work to unify the Five Nations; and, second, the actual aspects of law that they established. I will begin by offering a short summary of the Peacemaker's story.

The Peacemaker was born to a virgin mother who lived in the bush with her mother near the northern shore of Lake Ontario.[42] The women had left their village because of violence and made a life for themselves away from other humans. During the pregnancy the grandmother was informed that her grandson was being sent to this world to help rectify the violent state that people had slipped into. After birth, the boy grew quickly and his special gifts were apparent to his mother and grandmother. Eventually he informed them that it was necessary to travel back to their old village so that he could share the message of peace he had been born to teach. After this task was completed he prepared himself to visit the people to the south, who were consumed with blood feuds and other forms of violence. He embarked for the south in a white stone canoe and instructed his mother and grandmother to return to their village and remind the people there of his message of Skennen (Peace), Kasehstenhsera (Power), and Kanikonhri:yo (the Good Mind).[43] After he landed on the southern shore he encountered key people who assisted him in the formation of the Great Law, including Tekarihoken and Ayenwahtha, who become the first and second Mohawk Royaner as established under the law; Tsikonhsaseh,[44] who, as the first person to accept the law, secured the right for women to hold the selection rights of the Grand Council members; and Atatarho, a powerful sorcerer whose twisted mind and body were straightened out by the transformative power of the Great Law. With the support of other leaders, these people assisted the Peacemaker in the formation of the Haudenosaunee and the creation of the original Grand Council, consisting of representatives of forty-nine clan families[45] of the united Five Nations. The Great Law sanctioned a set of leaders for each of these clan families including a Royaner, Yakoyaner (Clan Mother), a Runner or assistant (sometimes referred to as a sub-chief or deputy), and a male and female "Faithkeeper." Each was given specific responsibilities to their families, to each other, and to the Great Peace. The Peacemaker also established that the names of the original fifty Rotiyanehson (plural form to reference all of the royaner) were to be titles that would be carried on in their matrilineal families for perpetuity.

The Great Law is a highly structured and ordered legal system. Rather than attempt to summarize it, I have chosen to retell key areas in order to illuminate how they contribute to Haudenosaunee land philosophy. There are several themes that relate to the discussion of land, including ideas about territory and boundaries, land as identity, interdependence and kinship, and collective responsibilities and rights.

Territories and Boundaries

Before the establishment of the Great Law, travelling was dangerous. There was a recognition that no one was safe outside of their own village. The story of the journey of the Peacemaker demonstrates those dangers. One of the first people he encountered was a cannibal, cooking his latest victim. The Peacemaker was able to transform the mind of the cannibal by initially tricking him and then demonstrating to him that it was not intended for humans to eat other humans. He taught him how to kill and dress a deer and reminded him of the teachings of the Creator. The power of the Peacemaker's message was able to clear the mind of the cannibal and bring him back to the lifestyle that the Creator had intended for humans. The transformation of the cannibal also demonstrates an important Haudenosaunee belief—that people have the ability to change. That theme is shown several times in the story of the founding of the Great Peace. Another danger in the Peacemaker's path occurred when a few of the Mohawks challenged his message by requesting that he climb a tree beside the river to prove his "power." When he reached the top, the young men chopped the tree down, sending the Peacemaker and the tree into the river. When the Peacemaker reappeared outside of the village the next day, the doubters were convinced of the sincerity and power of his message.

The greatest danger faced by the Peacemaker, Ayenwahtha, and the others who had accepted the Great Peace was the negative power of Atatarho.

Atatarho was responsible for the deaths of many, and he ruled the territory of the Onondagas through vengeance and threats. His power was described as such: "This man was possessed with great power as a wizard and no man could come to him without endangering his life and even the fowls of the air whenever they flew directly over his place of abode would die and fall down on his premises, and if he saw a man approaching him he was sure to destroy him or kill him."[46] It was at great personal risk that the Peacemaker and those who accepted the Great Law approached Atatarho in the attempt to convince him to join in their efforts of peace. Again, the power of the Great Peace combined with the united support of the leaders and their people eventually overcame the wickedness of Atatarho, and his mind and body were transformed. Upon the approach of Atatarho the people sang a song taught to them by a bird. The power of the song, along with the tidings of peace, aided in the transformation of Atatarho's twisted mind and body: "Then the twisting and contortionate movements of the fingers, and the snake-like movements of the hair of Tha-do-dah-ho ceased. Then he spoke and said, I will now answer the object of your mission. I now confirm and accept your message."[47] One of the stipulations for Atatarho's acceptance of the Great Law was that he would have a special role in the Grand Council. He would preside over the meetings of the Rotiyanehson (used in reference to the full council) and was given the responsibility of guarding the Great White Mat (a belt that symbolizes the meeting of the Grand Council). He was the first of the Royaner to have his title officially confirmed by having a woman—in his case, Tsikonhsaseh—place antlers on his head.[48]

Henry, Webster, and Woodbury translate Gibson's words on this matter:

> Thereupon Thatotaho' said, "This is what I will tell you about: while we recessed, we met, the whole crowd, and I told about what happened when it changed from its former manner of functioning. Indeed, one used to slaughter and scalp one another and shed one another's blood, and this has stopped; now it is changed, and something new has arrived, the Good Message and the Power and the Peace and the Great Law. Now the task is getting completed, and unity is emerging; thus they are standing up and placing antlers on the chiefs, whose work it will be to see to it that everything will become peaceful for men born here on earth. Moreover, now they are forming the League. Moreover, I am supporting it and I am abandoning all of the kind of work I used to do."[49]

Atatarho became the ultimate symbol of the Great Law's ability to over-come the greatest obstacles through peace rather than war. Through the Great Law, Atatarho went from being the very worst example of man to the very best. As a result of all of these transformations, the territories of the Five Nations once again become a safe place to travel: "now we have completed the task of forming the League; we now are all related to one another, so that now all of us shall treat one another kindly, and everyone will be at peace where one travels about."[50] In essence, the Great Peace transformed the territories of the Five Nations from places of great danger to a single place of peace and safety for the Haudenosaunee people.

The Great Law also established the relationship between the national territories of the five united nations. Prior to the establishment of the Great Peace the Five Nations warred with each other incessantly. The Onkwehonwe had forgotten the Original Instructions, and people from other villages were not to be trusted. The Peacemaker's message reminded people that it was the Creator's wish that people be kind to one another and that they live to-gether in peace; the Creator wanted the people to be united under the Three Principles. The Peacemaker determined that the only way to unite the people was to unite their territories. In his journeys, Ayenwahtha had made wampum strings[51] that he intended to use as mnemonic devices to carry messages of condolence and to serve as symbols of "official business."[52] Upon hearing the Peacemaker's discussion of a unified Haudenosaunee territory—marked by a single longhouse that stretched from the east to the west, with a fire for each of the Five Nations—Ayenwahtha strung the wampum into a belt that recorded the agreement of a united territory and marked the relationship between the nations that would flow from that agreement. Fittingly, the belt is named for the Mohawk Royaner who created it.

Cayuga Chief Jacob Thomas describes the Ayenwahtha belt as follows (see Figure 2):

> This is the emblematic Union of the Great Peace, of the Five Nations of the Mohawks, Oneidas, Onondagas, Cayugas and Senecas. The first left white square mark represents the Mohawks and their territory, second represents the Oneidas and their terri-tory, the heart represents the Onondagas and their territory, and this is the complete compact of the Five Nations Union having only one Union heart and this heart is the Great Peace and Charity, "Ka'nikonri:io," amongst themselves, and to abolish hostility of the

Figure 2. The Ayenwahtha Belt.

savage Nations. And the same heart represents where the Council
Fire, "Ronatetsistaien," of the Great Peace and Charity is kindled,
and it is the Council Fire of the Five Confederate Nations. And
the next white square mark to the right from the heart represents
the Cayugas and their territory and the next last white square mark
represents the Senecas and their territory.[53]

Building upon Thomas's description of the belt's record, it is also important
to note that the relationship between nations is associated through this belt.
The Ayenwahtha Belt is often described as the map of the Haudenosaunee
homelands. It frames the individual nations, how they are connected to each
other—both literally and figuratively—and their duties to each other and to
the collective Confederacy. Appropriately, the nations are denoted in white,
a symbol of peace, on a background of purple, which is sometimes a symbol
of war. Out of war, the peace was established between nations. Additionally,
the belt also reminds us that danger still exists outside of the domain of the
Haudenosaunee longhouse.

The Peacemaker organized the council into three groups seated at the council fire: the Onondagas would sit in the middle and serve as the Firekeepers;
the Mohawks and Senecas were placed to their right and took the role of
"Elder Brothers" or "Uncles"; the Oneidas and Cayugas were seated across from
them and to the Onondagas' left, taking the position of "Younger Brothers" or
"Nephews" (see Figure 3).[54]

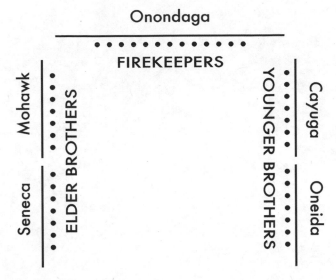

Figure 3. Grand Council Seating Pattern.

This seating pattern reflected the physical relationship between their territories and established the process of deliberation for the council.[55] Issues
would first be discussed and decided upon by the Elder Brothers. Once they had
reached consensus, their decision would be passed across the fire to the Younger
Brothers. Once they had reached consensus they would announce their decision to the Firekeepers, who would then confirm the matter.[56] The Peacemaker
also established that the easternmost and westernmost nations would have the
additional responsibility of serving as Doorkeepers, guarding the Confederacy
against outside hostilities. The Doorkeepers were also given the responsibility
of escorting those who sought to council with the Confederacy to the place of
the Firekeepers, following the paths of peace depicted in the Ayenwahtha Belt
(the white lines that extend beyond the outer nations' symbols). These processes
continue today, with the addition of dependent nations to the Grand Council
who have been integrated into the Younger Brothers' side of the house.[57]

The Ayenwahtha Belt also portrays the unification of the Five Nations'
territories. Many Haudenosaunee today use the belt as an analogy for a unified land, stating that those territories outside of the villages and gardens of
the ancient communities became shared territory under this belt.[58] This builds
upon the principle of the "Dish with One Spoon," an agreement for nations
to treat each other with care and caution, as instituted by the Great Law, and
has implications for contemporary land claims. For example, presently each of

the Six Nations (as well as each territory) is engaged in land claims processes. Most of these claims are articulated as belonging to one nation only, which could be seen as contradictory to the belief that the Great Law created one common territory for all of the Haudenosaunee. In Woodbury's translation, the Great Law provides this advice regarding internal national matters: "Now we decide that the law which shall guide them in each of our settlements, is that prevailing where they dwell, the chiefs of each single nation."[59] This statement, in combination with the principles of the Ayenwahtha Belt, reflects the confederate nature of the Haudenosaunee people and land. Internal issues within one nation are addressed by the leaders of that nation, and issues affecting two or more of the nations are addressed by the Grand Council.

Another area of the Great Law that concerns territory and boundaries is the separation between the "forest" and the "clearing." Clearings were associated with the village and the outlying gardens—and were typically considered the domain of women. Physically, the clearing was the collection of longhouses (the number of which varied depending upon the location and the timeframe; see Chapter 3), which were organized through the matrilineal clan families, and the fields that encircled the village centre. With women as the main cultivators of the gardens and the primary adults responsible for child care and rearing, the clearings were the spatial realm of women. Correspondingly, with the male responsibility for harvesting fish and animals and protecting the "clearings," the "forest" served as their domain. Accordingly, men also were given the duty of diplomacy and warfare. This relationship is evident in the formation of the Great Law. While it was the male leaders who were called together to form the Grand Council, the union was not complete without the corresponding female participation of their Clan Mothers—the joining of the men's forests with the women's clearings allowed for the completion of the Great Law.

Land as Identity

While the Great Law provides an explanation of the conceptualization of Haudenosaunee territories and boundaries, it also evidences the connection between land and identity. Among the Haudenosaunee, the names that the nations call themselves (and each other) denote key geographical features of their home territories (see Table 1). At the time of the establishment of the Great Peace, the major villages of each nation were known by these same names (e.g., the main Mohawk village was called "Kanyenke").[60] It appears that the nations were also known by these names, but not formally. When the Peacemaker went through the process of confirming the first Rotiyanehson, he also confirmed the names of the nations. In the Chiefs' version of the Great Law, it is cited as such:

> as the good tidings of Peace and Power first originated at Kan-yen-geh, you shall be called Ka-nyen-geh-ha-kah (Mohawk)....
>
> These being the second Nation who accepted the message of Peace and Power and as their settlement (from whence they came) was where the historic stone was situated (O-neh-yoht) it was named O-neh-yo-deh-ha-ka (Oneidas)....
>
> Your settlement is at the big Mountain, you shall therefore be called O-nen-do-wah-ka (people of the big Mountain) Senecas....
>
> you shall therefore be called (Queh-you-gwe-hah-ka) Cayuga, from your custom of portaging your canoe at a certain point in your settlement.[61]

The recognition of geographic identity demonstrates the relationship to the land the people came from, the land they belonged to. Through this naming, the Peacemaker intended that the land—the territory—would define the Haudenosaunee and how they would relate to the rest of the world. The Peacemaker also confirmed "council names" for each nation (see Table 2).

Table 2. Haudenosaunee Nation Council Names.

"Council" Names	English	Translation	Definition
Tehadirihoken[1]	Mohawk	between two matters	Plural form of Tekarihoken
Nihatirontakowa	Oneida	those of the great log	Refers to a log bridge the Peacemaker crossed to get to the main Oneida town
Hotisennakehte	Onondaga	the Name Carriers	From the Royaner Shakosennakehte
Sotinonnawentona	Cayuga	the Great-Pipe People	the Cayuga chief who represented them at the first council smoked a large pipe
Ronaninhohonti	Seneca	the Doorkeepers	Refers to one of the Senecas' official duties within the Grand Council

Source: Horatio Hale, *The Iroquois Book of Rights* (Philadelphia: DG Brinton, 1883; rpt. in Iroquois reprints series, Wm. Guy Spittal, ed., Ohsweken, ON: Iroqrafts, 1989), 78–79.

1 Spelling in this chart is taken directly from the Hale text and does not reflect standard contemporary Kanyen'keha spelling.

Most of these names are not used outside of the council, with the exception of the reference to the Cayugas as the "People of the Pipe." Today at Grand River this reference is regularly used to refer to the Cayuga Nation. These council names demonstrate that, like people, nations may also have multiple identities—often based upon their specific responsibilities as well as key aspects of their home territories. For example, in their role as Doorkeepers, the Senecas are referred to as guarding "the great dark door" in reference to the dangers that faced the Confederacy from the West.

The two sets of nation names reflect the connection between land and identity. Under the Great Law, individuals have been defined by the land to which they belong. That connection to land is based upon their family identification. Central to Haudenosaunee identity are the maternal bloodlines that determine one's nation. The Five Nations and the identification of their lands are the reflection of those original forty-nine matrilineal clan families. The mother's line determines the family (including the names children will hold), the clan, and the nation. As such, maternal identity becomes the basis of Haudenosaunee territoriality.

The connection to land also reflects the connection between the Great Law and the Creation Story. On several occasions, the Great Law refers to death and discusses the return of the body to the ground, echoing the first burial on the earth of Flint and Sapling's mother, Zephyr: "death is taking him back into the earth . . . they will lower his body into the opening. Thereupon they will refill it with soil, and when they finish, then, at that place, the two will mingle again, the body becoming soil again."[62] The Great Law also speaks of the comfort offered to the dead: "Oh, my grandsires! Even now that has become old which you established,—the Great League. You have it as a pillow under your heads in the ground where you are lying,—this Great League which you established; although you said that far away in the future the Great League would endure."[63] Additionally, the Great Law reminds the Haudenosaunee that the future generations come from the earth. People are instructed to walk carefully on the ground as the "coming faces"—the children yet unborn—are just below the ground's surface.

The relationship between land and identity is also demonstrated in the reintegration of Haudenosaunee people who have left the territory. Chief Jake Thomas asserted that when the Peacemaker, his mother, and grandmother travelled back to the village the two women originally came from to convey the Great Law, they were seated as visitors despite the fact that they came from that village.[64] After the Peacemaker left for his journey southward, the women returned to their old village. This alludes to a trial period of reintegration. This is also shown in a part of the law that discusses the manner in which people should be brought back into the community: "It is provided thus: That if any of the Iroquois People emigrate, 'ienshonwatinonke,' and reside in a distant country, the Iroquois Lords shall send a messenger and take a very broad belt of wampum and go and see them personally and address them by the wampum belt, they then shall re-immigrate home with them again."[65] Examples of the enactment of this section of the Great Law exist in the contemporary historical record, as evidenced in several cases of adoption by the Confederacy Council at Grand River in the nineteenth century.[66] Furthermore, the adoption of "alien" nations into the Haudenosaunee follows a similar process of integration.

Interdependence and Kinship

Along with the lessons on territory and identity, the Great Law also organized a kinship system based upon principles of interdependence. The Peacemaker formalized the kinship responsibilities across the Confederacy, in most cases building upon existing family systems.[67] Nations were to fit together internally and across the council. The Peacemaker, instructing the Rotiyanehson in the manner they were intended to view each other, said, "[we] shall have only one body, and only one head, and only one life . . ."[68] and "a single family we shall become, our various nations . . . now it is at one house, from now on you shall all sit together there, you of the five nations."[69] The Circle Wampum of the Haudenosaunee symbolizes the amalgamation of the fifty members of the Confederacy's Grand Council and the families they represent (see Figure 4). The fifty strings of wampum are of equal length, indicating the equality of the chiefs—the single, longer string indicates the special responsibility of one of the Onondaga Royaner as Firekeeper.[70] Paul Kayanasenh Williams and Curtis Arihote Nelson describe it further: "The two strings of white wampum that form the outer circumference of the Circle are symbols of the Great Law and the Great Peace. They are intertwined, since the one cannot be achieved or maintained without the other. The Chiefs are said to have linked their arms together so strongly that even if the Tree falls it will not break the union they have created with the Peace and the Law. This same expression finds itself repeated in later centuries in describing the way the Haudenosaunee and the British have linked their arms in the Covenant Chain."[71] The Circle Wampum has also been described as symbolizing family and duty to each other. If one string breaks or loses a bead, the entire belt is at risk. Similarly, if even one of the Haudenosaunee clan families is hurt, damaged, or in disarray, danger exists for all. Gibson and Goldenweiser attribute these words to the Peacemaker,

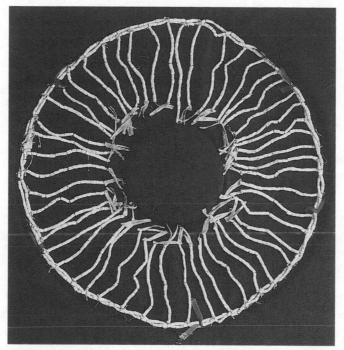

Figure 4. Circle Wampum.

which further explain these interdependent relationships: "Now you are all standing up on the land and you shall be tall tree trunks, rooted tree trunks; and as to that, everyone shall be on the same level among all of you tall tree trunks, and this is what it means, for you to be tall trees: you are the ones who will stand in front—at your backs they stand, your people—but as to you, you chiefs, it is on the same level that you stand which means that your various nations are all equal with respect to your power."[72] The Circle Wampum exists as a testament of equality and interdependence for the clans and nations of the Haudenosaunee.

The Condolence Ceremony

The Peacemaker also defined another set of relationships that are central to the Haudenosaunee practice of condolence. A basic premise of the Great Law lies in the understanding that a person in grief is not in their right mind; grief makes it impossible for someone to make the best decisions and to treat others with the kindness and respect necessary for peace. Ayenwahtha realized this when he was faced with the death of his daughters,[73] and he developed a process for consoling someone in grief that became known as the Condolence Ceremony. Since that time, condolence has been used to lift people from the grief caused by death so that they may direct their minds toward the future as one people. In that vein, the Condolence Ceremony is most directly related to the raising of new leadership within the Grand Council of the Confederacy. However, within the historical record (both oral and written) one can also find elements of condolence in events ranging from treaty negotiations to the exchange of prisoners.

When the Condolence Ceremony was established for the use of replacing a Royaner who had died, the Peacemaker divided the Haudenosaunee into two sides, with the Elder Brothers sitting across the fire from the Younger Brothers.[74] The Onondagas were included on the elder side and the remaining four nations kept their same positions, as explained previously. Within the Condolence Ceremony, the side that has suffered a loss is consoled by the other side, those who are "clear-minded." It is the duty of the "clear-minded" to wipe the tears, unblock the ears, and soothe the throats of those who are in grief. There are Fifteen Matters[75] that must be addressed in the ceremony, all of which come about as a result of the death. These matters are addressed through a series of songs and speeches, which culminate in the replacement of the deceased Royaner with another man of his maternal family who has been selected by his Clan Mother and confirmed by his clan, nation, and "brotherhood." The final stages of the ceremony come with the confirmation of the candidate by the "clear-minded" side of the fire and completed with a feast that seals the ceremony. This ceremony ties together the two "brotherhoods" and establishes the requirement of agreement across the fire in order to maintain the representation of the Grand Council. The following excerpt from *Concerning the League* exemplifies the importance of the Condolence Ceremony to the perpetuation of the Haudenosaunee:

> If, in some particular place one will come to be a mourner, thereupon it will be the clearminded ones who will take down the pouch. Thereupon a man will bend down near the wall where he will pick it up, the object made of [spotted fawn skin (a bag for holding mourning wampum strings)], and, throwing it on his back, take the road, walk to the place where one is in mourning, and at the edge of the ashes[76] he will stop, kneel down, and then he will speak up, this one, using gentle words, for it would not be fitting if he were to use strong language when one is, actually, grieving. Moreover,

he will use the thirteen matters for clearing the mind, indeed, the thirteen strands of wampum. Moreover, when he completes the rite in which he will raise the spirits of the mourners again, these, as soon as they recover, will follow again the path of the Great Law.[77]

There are aspects of the ceremony that directly impact the Haudenosaunee relationship with land and territory. The ceremony begins with the gathering of the clear-minded nations within their own territories. They prepare themselves to travel to the village (today, longhouse) of the grief-stricken nation where their "brother" nations have joined them to await the clear-minded condolers. A fire is built at the edge of the settlement where the aggrieved wait for their relatives from across the fire. As the condolers travel to the village of the one who has died, they recall the names of the Rotiyanehson as stated in the Great Law.[78] Greetings are exchanged when they finally reach the clearing of those in grief. These words are spoken when they meet "at the edge of the woods": [79] "Now to-day I have been greatly startled by your voice coming through the forest to this opening. You have come with troubled mind through all obstacles. You kept seeing the places where they met on whom we depended, my off-spring. How then can your mind be at ease? You kept seeing the footmarks of our forefathers; and all but perceptible is the smoke where they used to smoke the pipe together. Can then your mind be at ease when you are weeping on your way?"[80] This statement expresses the sentiments held by the Haudenosaunee for their old villages. Despite the need to "move on" and establish new clearings (in order to provide firewood and more fertile soil), they maintain a connection to their previous homes. This serves as a reminder to the Haudenosaunee that the places where their ancestors walked in the past continue to have an effect on their lives in the present. It is also a statement regarding the Haudenosaunee concept of history as a cycle that continues through time.[81]

Within the Fourteen Matters, there are additional concerns articulated relating to land and place. For example, the First Matter addresses tears of grief: "'We are removing your tears.' Moreover, a handkerchief is what they use, and 'when we wipe your tears, you will look around again, and you will notice them near you, moving about, your nephews and nieces, and then you will once more see the land, and you will hear again what is going on in the settlement; you will be happy in the future and you will think peacefully for at least one day.'"[82]

The Fifth Matter addresses konaktate, or "where one has one's space."[83] It is said that blood has stained their "place," which has various meanings, including home, bed, or designated seat. The words must be spoken in order to "wipe off" the stains, allowing their minds to again be at peace. All of the matters address the need to overcome grief so that the "good mind" may return, allowing for peace to exist "in one's place" and across the collective territory of the Confederacy. The kinship ties established through the Great Law allow for the condolence process to achieve this restoration of peace.

Collective Responsibilities and Rights

In addition to kinship ties and parameters of interdependence, the instructions of the Great Law also establish responsibilities laid out for the various groups of people of the Haudenosaunee—such as the women, the men, or the Rotiyanehson. Others also attribute the Great Law with creating "rights"— both individual and collective. The Haudenosaunee concept of "rights" is different from the typical use of the term in mainstream North American society. In this sense, rights are what one can expect if one upholds his or her duties to family, clan, nation, and Confederacy—and to the rest of creation. Essentially, Haudenosaunee rights exist in the sense that one has a right to enjoy life and the gifts of creation so long as one fulfills the responsibilities to the other beings of this world and the Sky World. The emphasis of "rights" is on the collective rather than the individual.

In its establishment of collective responsibilities and rights, the Great Law outlines several responsibilities regarding land and relationships with it. One of the most critical responsibilities exists within the principle of the "Dish with One Spoon." The stipulations of this agreement are described in *Concerning the League*:

> "It will turn out well for us to do this: we will say, 'We promise to have only one dish among us; in it will be beaver tail and no knife will be there.'" Thereupon the chiefs confirmed that so it should happen. Thereupon [the Peacemaker] said, "Now we have completed the matter, we will have one dish, which means that we will all have equal shares of the game roaming about in the hunting grounds *hutowaestahkwahek* and fields *kahetayetu'*, and then everything will become peaceful among all of the people; and there will be no knife near our dish, which means that if a knife were there, someone might presently get cut, causing bloodshed, and this is troublesome, should it happen thus, and for this reason there should be no knife near our dish."[84]

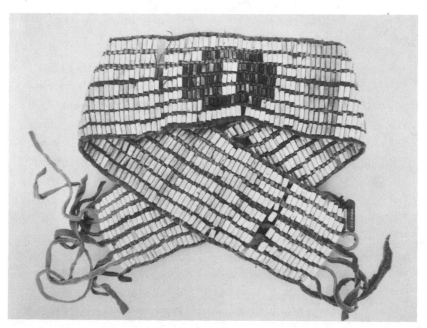

Figure 5. Dish with One Spoon Wampum Belt.

In addition to treating each other with care and caution, the founders of the Confederacy promised to share collectively in the harvests of the clearing and the forest. It is important to consider the economic implications of the "Dish with One Spoon" for the Confederacy. Under this law, the bounty of the shared hunting grounds is meant to be enjoyed by all; land and the benefits of land belong to everyone. The concepts behind the "Dish with One Spoon" were extended into treaty relations with other nations, both Native and European. The wampum belt in Figure 5 represents these concepts. The Condolence Ceremony recalls this agreement with the communal sharing of a beaver tail[85] by the Rotiyanehson when a new Royaner is raised into his position. The collective feasting on the beaver tail by the chiefs—with nothing sharp nearby—symbolizes the acceptance by all of the people to uphold this ancient agreement. This concept was later shared with non-Haudenosaunee nations as part of treaty agreements, including the Anishinabe and the British. In fact, it was a guiding factor integrated in the Covenant Chain relationship and the 1701 Nanfan Treaty (both between the Confederacy and the British Crown).

Under the Great Law, the responsibility of guarding the peace is not left only to the leaders. The Rotiyanehson are charged with the duty to guard the law and protect the Great Peace. But individuals must also be watchful and protect the Great Law:

> This, also I [Peacemaker] decree: if ever someone causes their affairs to decline in our grandchildren's generations, if thus it happens, then you chiefs, it is you who are to be responsible for all things concerning the welfare of the ongoing families while they live here on earth, and in addition for those yet to come from behind, our grandchildren, for this is what one will live by, the Good Message and the Power. Moreover, when it dies down, the Council fire, then someone should be able to climb our planted tree, Skaehetsi'kona, and if he is able to reach the top of the tree, then he should look around all over the earth. Then this one, if he observes an entrance opening up, a space for them to emerge, our grandchildren of the ongoing families, then, perhaps, their day is yet to come. Moreover, this will be according to rule, if thus it happens in the future. Moreover, all of this one will retain, which means that someone, specifically a chief, will be able to conceive the idea that it will be their day when everybody will reach consensus, the whole group. Moreover, now we have completed that task. So now situated families [lineages], certain ones, shall have them in perpetuity, the chief's titles.[86]

Responsibilities related to these include the duties of the Doorkeepers to serve as guardians of the territories. Their presence serves as a reminder not only of the fact that danger still exists, but also of the opportunities to extend the rafters and bring others under the protection of the "tree of the long leaves": "it is they who shall hold the power, the Great Warriors [the warriors were made into the Doorkeepers], for some particular kind of people may discover our house, and with these they shall discuss whether they have some message along, whereupon, indeed, we will extend the rafters of the League. Moreover, the two shall guard the doors where we have our house which is the place of the burning fire where smoke rises, piercing the sky, the place of the Good Message and the Power and the Peace and the Great Law."[87] The Doorkeepers were entrusted to guard the doors, protecting the Confederacy from harm, and to also serve as the first connection for friendly visitors who sought either to council with the Confederacy or to take shelter under the Great Law.

In order to bring about the Great Peace, the people had to agree to cease warring with each other. As a final marker of this agreement, the Peacemaker uprooted a tree and had the warriors cast their weapons of war into the ground below. The Woodbury text describes this as follows:

> Thereupon [the Peacemaker] said, "There is only one way for it to get done, for us to be able to hide the weapons from them: we will pull up our tree, Great Tall Tree, Great Long Leaf, and it will pass right through, making a hole through the earth. Thereupon we will pick up everything and throw it down where the earth is opened up, all of the war clubs, and the strong current in the earth will carry these away. Thereupon we will replant the tree, and they will never see the warclubs again, our grandchildren. Thereupon all will continue to think peacefully by day and by night as the families continue on."[88]

The Peacemaker gave the Haudenosaunee a system that guaranteed them a peaceful life, but he reminded them that peace only exists as long as they uphold their responsibility to leave the weapons buried in the earth and to use their minds—rather than their physical strength—to negotiate problems.

The greatest duty established under the Great Law is the obligation for the current generation to always consider those who will be born in the future in all of their actions. All decisions are to be made in their consideration: "in all their deliberations, legislations or official acts, self shall entirely be cast to oblivion and the general good only of the whole Confederacy sought after, having always in view not only the present and rising but also the coming generations for all time to come, whose faces are yet below the surface of the ground, 'Onhwentsakon:shon Taienkonsohtonnion:tie'—the unborn Progeny, 'Wahsenhnensewenrate,' of the Nation."[89] This statement recalls the Haudenosaunee belief that the future generations come from the land—the same place the body is returned to upon the conclusion of its time on this earth. It also supports the view that the land does not belong to the current generation but rather to those yet unborn.

The teachings of the Great Law describe the connections between politics and culture, especially in the responsibilities for the leaders to guide the people. Within the directions to the Confederacy leadership lies the road map showing how both the leaders and the people are to conduct themselves. It also links back to the earlier instructions found in the Creation Story and the Four Ceremonies. The directions to the chiefs, recorded in the Woodbury text, demonstrate the relationship between the Great Law and the Thanksgiving Address, as well as the affirmation of the relationship between this world and the Sky World, as taught in the Creation Story:

> (directions to the Chiefs) "do not ever disagree, thus there shall always be unanimity! It will be like a single person; you will have one body, and one head, and one heart, which means that as it became one family, when we unified, creating relatedness and kindness, each person will now be kind to one and all. Moreover, we have completed all matters that follow in the family through the generations, and these shall last as long as the earth exists, and as long as they are going to grow, the grasses and also the various weeds, and as long as the shrubs keep growing wild, the various shrubs, and as long as they [keep growing wild], the trees, all kinds of trees; and as long as springs emerge the water of rivers will keep flowing, also the large rivers and the various lakes; and as long as the sun keeps rising and setting and the moon keeps up its phases, and in the sky the stars do the same, and the wind is stirring on the land, and heavenly bodies continue to provide light by day and by night; thus, it shall last, the task we are completing, the Great Law, and these two will cooperate, the earthly land *uhwetsya'kekha'* and the other one, the heavenly land *tyuhwetsyate ne keahya'kekha'*."[90]

Through the directions of the Great Law, the Haudenosaunee were given a set of parameters within which they could use their collective strength to work toward the peace and health of their people within their collective territory. The Peacemaker also reminded them how the lessons of creation and the teachings of the Twelfth Boy connected this world to the Sky World. These connections between the earth and the sky are also reaffirmed later in the visions of Handsome Lake, known as the Karihwiyo.

KARIHWIYO—The Good Message of Handsome Lake

The Karihwiyo—the "Good Message of Handsome Lake," or "Gaiwiyo" in Seneca and Cayuga—is the fourth major epic of Haudenosaunee cultural history. It is also the only element that emerged after European contact. The Karihwiyo is the product of a set of visions experienced by Handsome Lake between 1799 and 1804. His visions have been the study of many anthropologists in the twentieth century, including Arthur C. Parker, William Fenton, and Anthony Wallace. They dubbed his visions the "Code of Handsome Lake" and have spent a great deal of time discussing the Karihwiyo within their defined themes of acculturation.[91] While one can find themes of accommodation (as a result of the realities of reservation life) within Handsome Lake's message, I find significantly more emphasis on cultural continuity and reinforcement of the Original Instructions than many anthropologists have chosen to focus upon.

Handsome Lake was visited by Four Messengers who were sent by the Creator to show him many things, including problems with the way in which some people were living at that time; the wishes of the Creator as to how people should live; and prophetic vignettes of things to come. He was shown these visions so that he could convince his people to mend their ways and return to the path the Creator intended for the Haudenosaunee. He was also shown signs that would signal the coming of the end of the world. Handsome Lake spent his remaining years travelling to various Haudenosaunee communities spreading the message of his visions. After his death in 1815, people from the Tonawanda Seneca community requested a retelling of Handsome Lake's message. Since then, the visions of Handsome Lake are retold every fall (as well as on select ceremonial occasions at other times of the year), as delegates from each of the Haudenosaunee longhouses travel throughout the territories reminding people of these critical teachings. Parts of the Karihwiyo are also emphasized in the Thanksgiving Address, such as in the recognition of the Four Beings.

Many of the themes of the Karihwiyo address relationships to land. These include statements about tilling land for crops, replacing the harvesting of game animals with domesticated stock, and home building. On the surface, these statements may be seen as a deviation from the original philosophy about land, but when considered further, they actually demonstrate both a reaction to a new reality and an affirmation of fundamental values that spring from the Original Instructions.

The words of Handsome Lake carry forward the wishes of the Creator to the Haudenosaunee on many issues. These messages served as instructions to the Haudenosaunee for maintaining their distinct identity in the face of extreme land loss and European attempts at acculturation. In Handsome Lake's vision, the Four Messengers demonstrated that men could till the land: "We feel that there would not be any harm if your people want to cultivate the land. Whenever a man works the land, his work should be neat and well done. His work should be right so it will produce things for his family to enjoy for much time to come. It is important never to be too proud and for people never to boast about what they can do. Avoiding this is a good practice and will bring unity among all people."[92] This signalled a change from older forms of agriculture, in the physical process of planting and harvesting as well as a shift from women as cultivators to the inclusion of men on a larger scale. While cultivation was historically the domain of women—under their control in the clearings—it was never strictly a female activity. Men always served as the primary clearers of the land and assisted with other aspects of the planting and harvesting tasks. For example, in the story of the Great Law, Ho'tatshehte', the first Oneida Royaner, originally had the job of guarding the cornfields near his village.

Some have misinterpreted early Haudenosaunee agriculture as women-only and criticize this aspect of the Karihwiyo as usurping the power of women, shifting it to the hands of men.[93] While the sanctioning of male-dominated agricultural forms was new, it did not usurp the place of women in agricultural activities. Women continued to garden and provide for their families' nutrition through the older agricultural forms, including the planting of the "Three Sisters"—corn, beans, and squash—as well as other supplementary plants. Deborah Doxtator characterizes the male-centred plowing agriculture as a component of the "external/forest economy"; in other words, the male-cultivated crops were typically harvested for trading purposes or fed to stock animals.[94] Women still gardened to meet the household and internal sustenance needs; men farmed to replace the external hunting and trading economy that was greatly diminished through the loss of land.

This additional agriculture, however, did signify a new way to interact with the land. Here, we see a shift from land supporting the forest, which supported the external economy, to the land more directly supporting external economic needs. In the end, land continued to provide for the needs of the Haudenosaunee—both through the female-cultivated gardens and through the male-cultivated "cash" crops. Related to this, also, was the rise in forestry—again part of the external economy—that occurred in many Haudenosaunee communities in the nineteenth century. In this connection, Doxtator observes that the Karihwiyo "was a religion of the clearing and although men's agriculture played a role, religious belief was focused on the continuation of the cycle of women's agriculture."[95] In other words, the message of the Karihwiyo—with its internal focus—concentrated on the continuity of Haudenosaunee society, with an emphasis on social structures that would ensure the survival of the people and the perpetuation of their Original Instructions.

A second thing that Handsome Lake was told regarding "appropriations" of European technology was in the area of home construction: "It is the way a white man builds a house. He builds one warm and fine appearing so if he dies the family has the house for help. Whoso among you does this does right, always providing there is no pride. If there is pride it is evil but if there is none, it is well."[96] Again, there are those among the Haudenosaunee who criticize Handsome Lake for what they believe is a shift from multi-family longhouses to single-family homes. What many of these critics do not realize is that the shift from large longhouses had started over a century before Handsome Lake's visions.[97]

A third change that the Four Messengers shared with Handsome Lake related to the keeping of stock animals: "The white man keeps horses and cattle. Now there is no evil in this for they are a help to his family. So if he dies his family has the stock for help. Now all this is right if there is no pride. No evil will follow this practice if the animals are well fed, treated kindly and not overworked. Tell this to your people."[98] This marked a major shift in the relationship with animals, but came about for two reasons. The reduction of land meant a reduction in hunting territory—despite the retention of hunting rights in surrendered lands, the reality was that the hunting grounds were greatly diminished. Furthermore, game animals were becoming scarce. Related to this, Handsome Lake was shown that some game animals would disappear altogether. Therefore, the Creator decreed that the Haudenosaunee could replace the harvesting of wild game with the raising and harvesting of domesticated animals—always with the provision that they treat the animals well and that they not be boastful of their accomplishments in this area.

Handsome Lake was also shown four visions relating to land dealings with Europeans. One concerned the future of the Buffalo Creek Territory:

> The messengers said, "Look downward upon the Buffalo Creek reservation."
>
> Se [*sic*] he looked and the place seemed honeycombed and covered with a net.
>
> Then the messengers asked him what he saw.
>
> He answered, "I saw the Buffalo Creek reservation and it seemed honeycombed like ice and covered with a net." So he replied.
>
> Then the messengers said, "Truly! We think that this reservation will fall." Now they said moreover that it was the duty of the chiefs to preserve it but it should be hard for some should take an upper hand.[99]

This prophetic vision came true in 1838 when some Seneca leaders and others signed away all of their national lands. This treaty was not confirmed, but a follow-up treaty in 1842 returned only the Cattaraugus and Allegany territories, forfeiting the lands of Buffalo Creek and Tonawanda Creek. The people of Tonawanda spent the next two decades working toward the return of their lands (securing title in 1857), but the Four Messengers proved to be right regarding Buffalo Creek. Today that land is part of the City of Buffalo.

A second vision dealt with the Haudenosaunee participation in foreign wars:

> Then said the messengers, "Look toward the setting sun.'
>
> . . . He answered, "I saw what seemed to be a man pacing to and fro. He seemed to be a white man and in his hand he seemed to have a bayonet with which he prodded the ground, and moreover, it seemed that he was angry." So he said when he answered.
>
> Then the messengers said, "It is true. He is a white man and in a temper. It is true. Indians must not help him and the headmen must honestly strive to prevent their followers from helping him."[100]

The general message here is quite clear: do not involve yourself in the white man's wars. Haudenosaunee participation in the American Revolution cost them dearly—both in terms of land and life. Parker suggests that this vision specifically dealt with the 1811 U.S. campaign against Tecumseh.[101] Others claim it foretold of troubles that would come about from the War of 1812.[102] It also seems relevant for more recent wars that saw both the United States and Canada draft Haudenosaunee men—in direct violation of their treaty relationships.

A third vision dealt with the penalty for selling land:

> I beheld a man carrying dirt in a wheelbarrow and that man had a laborious task. His name was Sagoyewat'ha, a chief.
>
> Then answered the messengers, "You have spoken truly. Sagoyewat'ha is the name of the man who carried the dirt. It is true that his work is laborious and this is for a punishment for he was the one who first gave his consent to the sale of Indian reservations. It is said that there is hardship for those who part with their lands for money or trade.[103]

This vision shows an eternal penalty for selling land. While Red Jacket is the example, some people take this passage literally, assuming he is the only one who will face this hardship in the afterlife.[104]

A fourth area regarding European land dealings is reflected in the prophecies concerning environmental degradation. While the visions do not depict who will be responsible, they demonstrate what has since proven true about the physical state of much of the Haudenosaunee territories (including those presently occupied by non-Haudenosaunee). Handsome Lake was shown water that was not drinkable and a river on fire. Today, traditional Haudenosaunee understand that many of Handsome Lake's visions have come true—all serving as signs that the end of this world is coming closer. In other words, the actions of human beings today harmful to the rest of creation have demonstrated a lack of thankfulness, and, as set out in the Creation Story, when the people become ungrateful and disrespectful, the Creator's control over this world will slip away.

While the Karihwiyo brought about new ideas in certain respects, its main focus lay upon reinforcing and maintaining the Original Instructions. It includes stories that remind people of the importance of sharing food with others as part of a community. There are several examples that recall the importance of the annual ceremonies and the special role of the Four Ceremonies in Haudenosaunee life. The Four Messengers refer to the Four Ceremonies as "the Great Amusements of the Sky World," reiterating the duty of the Haudenosaunee to maintain those teachings. There is also a connection between this world and the Sky World in those visions—Handsome Lake is told that beings of the Sky World participate in the longhouse ceremonies of this world and that the Creator is pleased to see his people carrying out his wishes. Handsome Lake was shown his own path to the Sky World, and on this journey he saw the things he had "bet" as part of the Peach Stone Game. This reminds people that the sacrifices of this world are rewarded in the Sky World. Ultimately, Handsome Lake's message reminded the Haudenosaunee of their duty to the rest of creation and gave them the tools necessary to survive as a distinct people in the face of full-scale colonization. Many of the principles of the Karihwiyo are recalled daily in the Thanksgiving Address, including words of recognition and thanks for the Four Messengers and Handsome Lake.

ooooo

The four epics discussed herein identify defining beliefs about land and the relationship intended to exist between the earth and the Onkwehonwe by the

Creator. The earth, as "our mother," meets the needs of the people in exchange for the people's thanks and protection. Land becomes a symbol of identity and serves as a basis for relationships between people (males to females; family to family; nation to nation; the Confederacy to external nations; etc.). The uniting of the Five Nations' lands allowed for the establishment of the Great Law and the elimination of internal warfare. Land is also a metaphor for life—the faces of the future generations "are below the ground" and the dead are returned to the earth, just as the Creator's mother had been at the beginning of the world. Handsome Lake's visions reinforced the earlier messages sent to the Haudenosaunee and also prophesied future problems with land—many of which have already come to be. The collective messages of Haudenosaunee cultural history remind us that land is the basis for life as we know it. It is a precious thing to be appreciated and protected.

CHAPTER 2

Kontinonhsyonni—The Women Who Make the House

Through the lessons of Haudenosaunee epics, women are taught to respect the earth and recognize the kindred spirit they share with her as the bearers of new life. Under the Great Law, women are recognized as leaders of the Confederacy in partnership with their male relatives. As leaders within the law, women are taught to consider the future generations in all their decisions. This duty played an important role in Haudenosaunee history after the arrival of Europeans, as the Confederacy leadership guided the people through often difficult times, including epidemics, warfare, and the introduction of conflicting religious ideologies. Following the American Revolution, the Haudenosaunee land base shrank considerably. In the nineteenth century, the visions of Handsome Lake provided a mechanism within which the Haudenosaunee were able to maintain their identity in the midst of accommodative change. Key aspects of the continued identity revolved around women's relationship to land—especially in terms of planting and the need to support and respect the Confederacy leadership. The Good Message of Handsome Lake also reaffirmed the earlier teachings about the responsibilities of women, and the followers of these visions continued to respect the roles and duties of women within the society.

The non-Haudenosaunee perception of the roles and responsibilities of Haudenosaunee women has been shrouded in a cloud of mysticism and misunderstandings from the time the first Europeans entered Haudenosaunee territory in the seventeenth century. Many of the early chroniclers attempted to portray a society based upon female superiority, probably due to their lack of experience with a culture based upon equality between the sexes. They appear to have been incapable of comprehending a people who govern themselves with the goal of equality and respect rather than superiority and dominance. Coming out of those early misperceptions were the later ethnographic representations of Haudenosaunee women "falling from grace," so to speak. For example, Hewitt, writing in 1933, claimed that "there is no connection between the women of today and the women of the past."[1] Because he did not witness an all-powerful gynocracy, he was left to assume that Haudenosaunee women had lost their status somewhere along the way since the days of Jesuit historians Pierre-François-Xavier de Charlevoix and Joseph-François Lafitau. It apparently never occurred to Hewitt to question those early sources. Clearly, he also missed the continued presence of Haudenosaunee women in the political structures of the Grand River Territory where he had conducted extensive ethnographic research.

The representations of Haudenosaunee women in the literature have portrayed them either as supreme ruling matriarchs or as little more than beasts of burden.[2] These depictions fail to represent the complexities of Haudenosaunee gender relationships. Furthermore, these depictions are almost always portrayed in comparison to Western society and its views of gender. For example, Horatio Hale wrote that

> the common notion that women among the Indians were treated as inferiors, and made "beasts of burden," is unfounded so far as the Iroquois are concerned, and among all other tribes of which I have any knowledge. With them, as with civilized nations, the work of the community and the cares of the family are fairly divided. Among the Iroquois the hunting and fishing, the house-building and canoe-making, fell to the men. The women cooked, made the dresses, scratched the ground with their light hoes, planted and gathered crops, and took care of the children. The household goods belonged to the woman. On her death, her relatives, and not her husband, claimed them. The children were also hers; they belonged to her clan, and in case of a separation they went with her. She was really the head of the household; and in this capacity her right, when she chanced to be the oldest matron of a noble family, to select the successor of a deceased chief of that family, was recognized by the highest law of the confederacy.[3]

While, in general, this description is accurate—especially regarding agriculture and child rearing—Hale felt the need to compare the Haudenosaunee with Europeans as his primary reference point. In this comparison, he skews the representation of Haudenosaunee women when he implies they belonged to an "uncivilized" people. One could argue that he is writing to his audience, which is true, but this type of representation perpetuates the stereotype of "Native as other," rather than simply "Native as Native." Like other ethnographers, Hale helped to perpetuate the representation of Haudenosaunee women first and foremost in comparison to European and American women in the written literature.

The first published and widely disseminated writings regarding Haudenosaunee women appear in the *Jesuit Relations*. Given the cultural biases and the blinders of their religious fervour, the Jesuits failed to recognize the complexities of social relationships within Haudenosaunee society. The same assertion can safely be made regarding their contact with most Indigenous peoples in North America. In contrast, however, are the writings of Lafitau, a member of the Jesuit Order who had been sent to the mission at Caughnawaga in 1696. His reflections on Haudenosaunee customs and beliefs differ strongly from those of his peers. He documented his observations of Haudenosaunee culture, and while he spent a great deal of time comparing them to ancient Greek society, his attention to culture demonstrated a greater interest and respect for Haudenosaunee beliefs than that exhibited by other Jesuits. Recognizing the failings of his peers, he attempted to portray a more accurate account of social structures, but swung the depiction too far in the other direction: "This will, doubtless, appear extraordinary to those who have noted, on reading the Relations, that it is said that only the men among the Indians are really free and that the women are only their slaves. Nothing is more real, however, than the women's superiority. . . . The men, on the contrary, are entirely isolated and limited to themselves . . . although the chiefs are chosen among them, they are purely honorary."[4] In his depiction of women, Lafitau portrayed men as mere pawns in a female-dominated Haudenosaunee world. He failed to recognize the balance represented in the various aspects of the society, despite the fact that he discussed the roles of Chiefs and Clan Mothers later in his text.[5] This statement has greatly influenced the canon of Iroquois gender studies, as it has been quoted, paraphrased, and otherwise borrowed by many scholars since its first publication.[6] It is an extremely influential—and inaccurate—statement about Haudenosaunee gender relationships that continues to have impact nearly 300 years after it was first made.[7]

Women and Creation

In order to understand the misrepresentation within the scholarly canon, we must examine Haudenosaunee values regarding women's relationship to land. As we have seen, the Haudenosaunee Creation Story serves as the basis for contemporary Haudenosaunee thought and philosophy. The relationships intended to exist between men and women have their roots in the Sky World and the early days of earth. Many examples flow from the story in regard to the relationship between humans and land, and, specifically, interpretations can be drawn that explain the relationship between women and land.

In the Creation Story, when Mature Flowers (who becomes Skywoman) travels to the village of her soon-to-be husband, she introduces herself as coming from "the place where my uncle has a standing tree."[8] From this we can infer that her village followed a matrilineal pattern for holding land, as her uncle was her mother's brother. This is similar to the later events at the establishment of the Great Peace, when the Peacemaker refers to people through their Royaner titles (i.e., the reference for the clan relatives—and in this case the entire Mohawk Nation—of Tekarihoken being called "Tehatirihoken"). The Royaner are often referred to as "uncles" by their clan relatives. This example also demonstrates the connection between a village and a clearing: one would not describe a place in reference to a standing tree unless it was in a clearing. This is another example that supports the Haudenosaunee belief that the Sky World is very much like the world below.

Similar to the society in the Sky World, the pattern of matrilineal identity appears to have already been in existence when the Peacemaker encountered the Five Nations. Likewise, there are several stories within the cultural history that discuss the formation of matrilineal clans. Some versions include this process at the time of Creation,[9] some place it with the establishment of the Four Ceremonies,[10] and others include it in the establishment of the Great Law.[11] Considering the matrilineal connection of the Creation Story, it is likely that the idea of matrilineal identity came with the Original Instructions but probably had to be restored at certain times in history—much like the restoration of clans to the Oneidas by the Peacemaker at the founding of the Great Law.[12]

Also based in the Creation Story is the name for the earth, Yethi'nihstenha Onhwentsya—our mother, the earth.[13] The earth literally is mother, as she holds the physical remains of the Creator's mother; and she becomes mother in a figurative sense, through the support she provides to all life. The plants that grow from her soil provide food and shelter for the animal beings (including humans), who also walk about on her surface. Another connection between women and land found in the Creation Story is the identification of important food plants—corn, beans, and squash—as female. This is recalled in the Thanksgiving Address and throughout many of the ceremonies of the Haudenosaunee. A strong connection exists between women and these plants that plays a critical role in the cultivation process and ceremonial activities related to planting and harvesting.

The Creation Story also explains the relationship between women and the bringing forth of new life. The Creator deemed that the moon—his grandmother—would be in charge of determining when new life would come to the world. Hewitt reports the words of the Creator to the first man and first woman of the earth in this regard:

> Verily you two understand all the matter that has come to pass. So that will come to pass that at the end of three days ye two shall watch to see what will take place. If it so be that thou, Awenhaniyonda (Attached Flower or Flower in Bloom) [the first woman], will notice that a change will come over thy life, that thou shalt see the Moon, the Grandmother of you two will commence to grow again, to grow anew, and that shall be a sign for knowing it if thus it shall come to pass that thou shalt see it thou shalt become aware that thy life has become new (that is, the dawn of a new life in her conception), so that will continue to be a sign that there will begin to start the formation of new human beings, who will overflow the earth as dwellers.[14]

Modern Western science confirms what the Onkwehonwe were told at the beginning of time: that the moon regulates the female human reproductive cycle and plays a critical role in women's fertility.[15] This relationship between the metaphorical grandmother, the moon, and the literal mother marks an essential aspect of the relationship between Haudenosaunee women and their children. Beyond the physical aspects of pregnancy and birth, female "power"—through the moon—determines new human life and as a result accords many responsibilities to women not only for the physical creation of new life but for the nurturing and protecting of new life, both present and future.[16] One of these duties is to ensure that life will continue for the future generations. One of the ways to do that is through the protection of land, which nurtures all life. In other words, as land is essential to life, women have the obligation to protect it in order to support the children yet unborn. Men share in this responsibility.

Women and the Great Law

While the Great Law established a new system of governance for the Five Nations, it also served to support older social systems that were given to the people by the Creator in the Original Instructions and the Four Ceremonies. This included the reinforcement of the roles of women as cultivators of the soil, as leaders of their families (in partnership with the men), and as the holders of the future generations. The Great Law recognized their "clearing" roles, including the primary care giving and educating of young children, the relationship with the soil as cultivators and sisters to the food plants, and the matrilineal descent of their families. Connected with the maternal descent were the national territorial boundaries. With identity determined through the female line, the national territories were also determined matrilineally.

The Great Law built upon the matrilineal system with the establishment of Clan Mothers as leaders of their families.[17] Lafitau appears to be the first written source to elaborate on his observations of the roles of Clan Mothers. He writes,

> Lest the chiefs usurp too great authority and make themselves too absolute, they are checked, as it were, by being given deputies[18] who share with them the sovereignty of the territory and are called also the *Agoianders*. . . . In each clan, each individual and distinct matrilineage has one person who acts as representative for it. The women choose them and are often in this position themselves. Their duty is to watch more immediately over the nation's interest; to keep an eye on the funds or public treasury; to provide for its conservation and watch over the use which should be made of it. When they have been chosen, they are recognized in councils but they are not shown before the allied nations as is the custom and practice for the chiefs.[19]

Of note are the economic duties Lafitau ascribes to the Clan Mothers. It is logical to assume this is connected to the agricultural base of the historic Haudenosaunee society.[20] Furthermore, Lafitau also observes the existence of male leaders' responsibilities toward the external realm, which complement the female internal duties. This has also been described as the men being in charge of forest activities and the women being responsible for clearing activities.[21]

As told in the Great Law, the Peacemaker confirmed women in the Clan Mother positions to honour Tsikonhsaseh. A woman who had lived along the warpath and had once benefited greatly from the wartime state, Tsikonhsaseh was the first person to be transformed by the words of peace and accept the Great Law. In honour of her personal sacrifices, the Peacemaker deemed that women would have prominent leadership positions under the government of the Haudenosaunee. The following excerpt from the Gibson-Goldenweiser text outlines additional rationale for the duties bestowed upon female leadership under the Great Law: "These are to be the principal ones (eyeya'takweniyoks), the women controlling the title names, because it is by means of all their suffering that people are born here on earth; and it is they who raise them. Moreover, their blood, this is what we have, we the people, for these are our mothers, the women, and this is why the families follow according to their blood lines."[22] Before the coming of the Great Peace, men gained their positions of leadership through physical strength and warfare. Through the Great Law, the Peacemaker established a means that created and recognized leaders of peace—men and women who had strength of mind—through the authority of the women as the voice of their families, who in turn chose their male representatives in council.

As he had outlined for the Chiefs and Clan Mothers, the Peacemaker also established the role of male and female Faithkeepers to assist with the ceremonial functions of the Royaner titles. Chief Jake Thomas echoes the words of Seth Newhouse regarding the duties of the female Faithkeepers: "It is provided thus: Ye, the women shall select and install two women for each Lord, as his cooks, to do cooking when people congregate at the Lord's residence when on some business with the Lord; for it is not good nor honourable for the Lord to send his people away hungry."[23] The Gibson-Goldenweiser text offers a more detailed explanation of the role of the female Faithkeeper: "Each chief has a female cook (godihont), an official, who is appointed in her own maternal family, at the same time that the chief is raised; she serves for life and is replaced at death by another. She is not the same as goyanegonah [plural of Yakoyaner or Clan Mother]. Her duties are to cook . . . in making a new chief.... At a special council, if special meals are needed, the chief may call on [her]."[24] These statements allude to the importance of these women, who included among their duties the cooking for ceremonies, underlying key values of hospitality as well as the power of food within a cultural context. This is illuminated further when one considers the importance of the food to the Condolence Ceremony, including the beaver tail shared by the Rotiyanehson as well as the concluding feast that seals the confirmation of the new leaders. If these foods are not cooked, shared, and eaten, the condolence is not complete and is therefore void. Furthermore, there is an understanding that food has a direct connection to the function of the mind. With the mind at the centre of Haudenosaunee governing practices, food's influence and role—and those responsible for its preparation—are respected as critical to the workings of the Grand Council. In other words, the female Faithkeepers are absolutely essential for the perpetuation of the Confederacy system and critical to a properly functioning Haudenosaunee government.

In addition to specific duties for female leaders, women are also discussed in the Great Law as holders of the land. Several of the written sources on the Great Law discuss women as landholders, especially those of Thomas and Newhouse. For example, Thomas reiterates the writings of Newhouse in a section entitled the "40th Wampum": "It is provided thus: That the lineal descent of the Five Iroquois Nations shall run on the female side and the women shall be considered as the progenitors of the Nation, and the title of ownership of the land or soil of the Nation's country shall be vested in the said women, and the descendants of these women shall follow the status of their mothers 'Ka'nihsten:sera Kahwatsirakwe'ni:io',' with respect to clans, 'kataratenion,' which are the distinguishing marks of families."[25] Thomas also makes this statement: "We do now give and assign these honourable, noble and Sacred Lordship Titles, and the soil of our land to all our Mothers, 'Kwa'nistenhokon:'a,' the women of the Five Nations, and they shall be the proprietors, 'Enkontakwenia:ien Onakara,' of the same."[26]

It is important to note that these statements about women "owning" the land refer to the matrilineal aspect of Haudenosaunee society and do not exclude the male members of a matrilineage. Identity and land are intimately connected, so it is only logical that since identity follows the female line so does land. Women hold their land in a manner similar to the way they hold their families. Women do not *own* their families, but rather they are the carriers of the family lines. Furthermore, in Kanyen'keha, in order to speak about "ownership," one actually talks about something being "attached" to the person. For example, wakenonhsayen—"I have a house"—literally means "it to me, a house is set down." In order to talk about duties and responsibilities the same term—ayen—is used. The idea of English-language ownership does not completely match with the Kanyen'keha equivalent. In English, ownership is usually used to convey ideas of "possession" and "rights" to something, but in Onkwehonwe'neha ownership denotes a connection with something and a responsibility to it. Similarly, it is often said that as Haudenosaunee, we do not have "rights" but rather we have "duties"—or things that are "set down" to us. For example, when someone is made a leader in the longhouse, duties have been "attached" to him or her, it has been "set down" for that person to take care of those tasks. To summarize, in English we might say "it belongs to me," but in Onkwehonwe'neha we are really saying "I have a relationship with it." That distinction becomes important in the discussion of Haudenosaunee women (and men) as landholders.

At present, there is a lot of discussion about the relationship between the Clan Mothers and the Grand Council within Haudenosaunee communities. Many cite an old tradition of women's meetings that have not been maintained by all of the clan families. Newhouse and Thomas refer to women's councils as established under the Great Law:

> 73rd Wampum: 74th Wampum: 75th Wampum:
>
> It is provided thus: That the women of every clan, "ka'tara," in the Five Nations shall have a Council Fire, "Iohnatetsistaien," which shall ever be burning for the purpose of holding a council of the women of the clan when in their opinion it is necessary for the interest and advantage of the people and their commonwealth. The decision, conclusion or recommendation of such a council shall be to introduce for consideration into the Council of the Confederate Lords by the "War-chief," "Rarontaron,"[27] of that clan.[28]

A great deal of confusion exists about these women's meetings. Many families have not maintained their duties to their clans, resulting in several non-functioning or poorly functioning families within the governance structure. Often members of these families complain that their women are not "given a voice" in the affairs of the Grand Council and will cite the fact that the "women are not meeting." They do not realize it is their responsibility—through *their* families—to maintain all of those processes. They cannot expect the Rotiyanehson to do that—it is not in their realm as men. Furthermore, often people are confused about these "women's meetings," not realizing that, as Newhouse and Thomas point out, there are equivalent "men's meetings" to discuss family business, when necessary:

> 76th Wampum:
>
> It is provided thus: That the "warriors" of every clan, "ka'tara," of the Five Nations shall have a Council Fire, "Ronatetsistaien," which

shall ever be burning for the purpose of holding a council of the "warriors" of the clan when in their opinion it seems necessary to hold such a council to transact such business as may be needful for the welfare of the clan, or the people. It shall have the same rights as the Council Fire of the Women, "Iotiiane:shon Iohnatetsistaien."[29]

These men's and women's councils are not mentioned in the Gibson-Goldenweiser text. While it may have been an omission, it is possible that Newhouse added this characteristic to refer to an informal practice of the clan families that was not necessarily part of the Great Law. In other words, it may have become a common policy but not official law. Either way, it is logical that all the people should have a voice in the matters that affect them, and these meetings refer to an orderly way to ensure just that. Haudenosaunee culture stresses balance, and this is another example of how that balance is achieved. In many clan families from across the Confederacy, there are "clan meetings" held wherein issues such as the replacement of a Royaner or a Clan Mother are discussed and decided. As Doxtator writes, "the Rotinonhsyonni [Haudenosaunee] political ideal was based on the idea of balance of responsibilities and in ensuring that no one group could act alone."[30]

The Great Law confirmed the matrilineal structuring of Haudenosaunee society through the clan families. While these forty-nine families comprise the base relationship within the Confederacy—as demonstrated in the Circle Wampum—the Peacemaker provided additional groupings of these families that created other relationships. The most recognizable of these are the national identities, but there exists another level of inter-clan organization within the nations. Among the Royaner, these groupings are often referred to as "brother" chiefs, but when addressing the families, they are referred to as Kontenhnoteronh, the sister clans.[31] In council the male leaders of these clans consult with each other first within their "brotherhood" and then consult with their "cousin" chiefs of the same nation.[32] Within the female aspect of this relationship, Thomas asserts that if a clan has no suitable candidates for a vacant position they borrow someone from their sister clans to fill the position until a suitable replacement arises from within the original clan. He also states that if the female line of a clan goes extinct the title is to be transferred to a family from one of the sister clans.[33]

Another key aspect of Haudenosaunee society found in the Great Law is the practice of adoption. The Peacemaker provided that individuals, families, and nations who sought the peace would be protected under the Tree of Peace. He also instructed the leaders to provide for integration of these refugee people through their adoption into Haudenosaunee society via the matrilineal clan system. Under this process, it is the responsibility of the women—specifically the Clan Mother—to select people to join their family. The actual process involves the whole clan, both men and women, as they are expected to accept the new member (or members) into their family and accord them the same sense of obligation as they do to their existing blood relatives. In times of war, the women were also given the opportunity to adopt prisoners to replace deceased family members. During colonial times, the women's adoption of both refugees and prisoners often provided for the expansion of Haudenosaunee territory.[34] Therefore, adoption became a tool for building and rebuilding the Haudenosaunee populace, acquiring new lands, and expanding the Haudenosaunee domain.

Women and Land in the Historical Record

The greater part of the early historical record regarding the Haudenosaunee is preoccupied with stories about men. On the one hand, it is logical, since men are typically those charged with the responsibility of diplomacy within Haudenosaunee society. Accordingly, they were usually the first to meet a group of travellers entering Haudenosaunee territory. On the other hand, it is also indicative of the paternal society from which these writers came. Women in European societies did not often hold positions of power and typically garnered little respect from their male counterparts. As products of that society, it was difficult for these travellers to comprehend a society based upon mutual respect between the sexes, and, since they could not comprehend it, they often failed to see what was right in front of them. Despite this common omission, the written historic record does hold many statements made by and about Haudenosaunee women. Read chronologically from the seventeenth to the nineteenth century, the writings follow a pattern wherein the first commentaries share "observations" (made often without direct contact between the author and actual Haudenosaunee women), and later writings often quote statements made by Haudenosaunee women or on their behalf.

Seventeenth Century

In the seventeenth century, the Jesuits wrote extensively about the Haudenosaunee, usually in an extremely critical fashion. There are numerous passages that mention women, but usually the comments are in reference to converts (numbers, disease, deaths, etc.) and rarely offer much information about village life or other issues specifically regarding women. In addition, the only favourable depictions of the Haudenosaunee—women included—were accorded to those who accepted Christian teachings, as in the following 1657 entry from the *Jesuit Relations*: "The women having much authority among these people, their virtue produces as much fruit as anything else, and their example finds as many more imitators."[35] Women who chose not to accept their message were often characterized as "whores" or "sneaks" who attempted to sway their converts.[36] Aside from missionary records, one of the earliest references to Haudenosaunee women is found in the travel journal of Dutch trader Harmen Meyndertsz van den Bogaert, recorded in December 1634 at the Mohawk village of Canagere:[37] "Three women came here from the Sinnekens [Oneidas] with some dried and fresh salmon. . . . They sold each salmon for one guilder or two hands of sewant (wampum). They also brought much green tobacco to sell, and had been six days underway. They could not sell all their salmon here, but went with it to the first castle. Then we were supposed to travel with them when they returned."[38] This passage is well known among the Haudenosaunee, and discussion of the passage often centres on the fact that these women appear to have been travelling alone. This alludes to the relative safety experienced by women in the Haudenosaunee territories as accorded under the provisions of the Great Law.[39] Also noteworthy in van den Bogaert's journal is the fact that rather than waiting for the women to return, his party hired a man to lead them to the Oneida[40] territory, demonstrating apparent discomfort with the role of guide being held by a female.[41]

As we have seen, the forest fell within the domain of men and, accordingly, it was men who typically travelled for the purposes of hunting, fishing, and gathering, and for diplomacy. Because of their knowledge of the land, fur traders often employed Native guides to assist them as they travelled from village to village in search of pelts and other items of trade. On rare occasions, however, there is mention of women who also joined in these trading expeditions. William Beauchamp relates a story from 1656: "The women carried the burdens, but not in all cases. When Chaumonot and Menard went from Onondaga to Oneida in 1656, at nightfall in the forest the chief addressed his band as usual. 'He also made a speech complimentary to the women, who were carrying the provisions of the journey, praising their courage and constancy.' On many occasions the men carried quite as much. This depended on circumstances."[42] As noted by van den Bogaert, women did travel from village to village, although probably less frequently than men.[43] In this example, we see that the women assisted with carrying the supplies. Also of note is the mention of the encouragement speech given by a man to the women in recognition of their hard work. This type of acknowledgement is still common within Haudenosaunee society and serves to represent the types of reciprocation accorded within the culture.

Several seventeenth-century recorders comment on the role of the Clan Mother, without realizing the full significance of this position. Many of these references reflect an elementary understanding of the position and yet do provide evidence of the importance these women had in their communities. Hale relates a story from the *Jesuit Relations* about a Clan Mother who left her Mohawk homelands to live among the French Catholics in the North:

> That this rank and position were greatly prized is shown by a remarkable passage in the *Jesuit Relations*. A Canienga [Mohawk] matron, becoming a Christian, left her country, with two of her children, to enjoy greater freedom in her devotions among the French. The act, writes the missionary, so offended her family that, in a public meeting of the town, "they degraded her from the rank of the nobility, and took from her the title of Oyander, that is honorable (*considerable*)—a title which they esteem highly, and which she had inherited from her ancestors, and deserved by her good judgment, her prudence, and her excellent conduct; and at the same time they installed another in her place."[44]

The implications of this action bring to mind questions: Was the woman removed because she became Christian, because she left the community, or both? It also serves as a small window into the divisions created within communities and families when the missionaries induced some to follow, while others chose not to. It is important to consider this with the knowledge that the Mohawk Nation had suffered a 75 percent population loss less than forty years prior to this event.[45] Many also recognized a connection between the diseases and the missionaries. These facts help to illuminate the decision of this family to remove the duties of Clan Mother from their sister who had deserted them. It also demonstrates that the missionaries were disrupting not only the spiritual practices of the Haudenosaunee but the political ones as well. An important note, however, is that while this one woman was lost to her family and community, the other women of that clan seemed to come together to reclaim what was actually the domain of all of them, not solely hers. The priests did not appear to realize that the title she held was an aspect of joint ownership. Since the woman had removed herself from her family and community, her female relatives did exactly what they had to do to protect themselves and the future generations of their clan. In this, the women of that clan family took the necessary action to protect their common rights—and those of their future generations—under the Great Law.

While men had the primary responsibility of diplomacy, women often travelled along and participated in peace and treaty talks. One of the earliest records of this practice is found in the *Jesuit Relations* of 1671, as related by Beauchamp: "Teotonharason was an Onondaga woman who went with the ambassadors to Quebec, and was highly esteemed for her nobleness and wealth. She may have been the one mentioned in the Relation of 1671. 'It was one of these principal persons who formerly first brought the Iroquois of Onondaga, and then the other nations, to make peace with the French. She descended to Quebec for this purpose.'"[46] It has long been noted—both within Haudenosaunee records as well as in Euro-American written records—that Haudenosaunee women were responsible for declarations of war. Within the culture, it is said that since women are the ones who bring life forward, they are the only ones who have a right to determine the risk of losing life in battle.[47] Charlevoix commented, very disparagingly, in regard to this aspect of Haudenosaunee culture: "Here if anywhere, it is fair to presume, that the man ought to have been master of his own acts, and yet we find that he could not go upon the warpath unless the women were willing."[48] Later, some writers challenged the extent to which women held this power within Haudenosaunee society,[49] but whether they formally declared war or not, women clearly would have held sway over war parties, as they were in charge of the food storage and warriors would have to be outfitted for travel and battle by the women. As demonstrated above, women were essential to the warring process, but they also held great influence over decisions of peace. Often when the Haudenosaunee made peace with another people—and especially during the seventeenth and eighteenth centuries—the other nations sought the protection of the Great Law.[50] Through the power of adoption—a clan right maintained through the Clan Mothers—women determined the integration of peoples from other nations. Along with human numbers (which were greatly needed following the epidemics) often came territory. Indeed, territorial gains were important factors in the Haudenosaunee adoption of Mahicans, Hurons, Eries, Tobacco, and Neutrals, to name but a few.

The seventeenth century was a very tumultuous time for the Haudenosaunee—probably the period that brought the greatest amount of change in our history. The impact of disease cannot be underestimated in considering the actions of the Confederacy during this century. Haudenosaunee borders were constantly being threatened by voyageurs attempting to control the fur trade. Warfare again became a major part of their lives. Refugees from neighbouring nations had to be integrated into Haudenosaunee society and served to replace the many lives lost to disease and battle. There was also the intrusion of colonizing missionaries who gained a foothold (albeit much smaller than what they achieved amongst other Native nations in the Northeast) in several Haudenosaunee communities. Through these difficult times, Haudenosaunee women maintained their responsibilities as they reacted to the tumultuous world around them. Alongside the men, the women struggled to maintain the values of Haudenosaunee society in those changing times.

Eighteenth Century

The historical record of the eighteenth century contains statements *about* Haudenosaunee women as well as those made *by* Haudenosaunee women. Often the women's statements were officially made through men they chose to be their voice in council. Understanding the role of "speaker for the women" is critical to understanding the history of the Haudenosaunee, especially in this time period.[51] While it may not have been a regular aspect of the Grand Council,[52] hearing the voice of the women was never uncommon and played a critical role in the treaty-making era of the eighteenth and nineteenth centuries. Since most of the treaty councils dealt with land transfers and territorial boundaries, many of the recorded statements of this era allude to "women as landowners" and attest to the importance of their opinion in these matters. As discussed above, this relates to the aspect of Haudenosaunee society that addresses women as the proprietors of the land (as attributed in the Great Law), since they bring future generations into the world. Typically, these speakers for the women were sent with messages regarding land. Some have misconstrued the actions of the women as superseding the voice of the chiefs,[53] but it actually is another example of the balance required within Haudenosaunee society. Doxtator helps explain this relationship between women and their spokesmen: "These women did not address councils directly but employed specialized male speakers and orators to present their wishes and opinions to the civil chief or Royaner councils. Even in presenting their ideas these prominent women and men needed to cooperate with one another in order to gain credibility among the community's various constituents. To speak by and for oneself alone meant that one was attempting to act alone which had less credibility than speaking in concert with other groups within the community."[54] This example alludes to the Three Principles of the Kayaneren'kowa: by utilizing a good mind (kanikonhri:yo), strength is gathered through unity (kasehstenhsera), resulting in peace (skennen). By bringing their voices together, women build upon the strength of their men in council, all with the vision of peace in mind.

One of the most detailed sources regarding Haudenosaunee opinion of the treaty era is found in the records of Sir William Johnson. Many historians have relied upon these records as a basis for discussing eighteenth-century Haudenosaunee history. As the imperial superintendent general of Indian Affairs, Johnson collected a great deal of evidence about the relationship between the Crown and the Confederacy during the mid-1700s. His knowledge of Haudenosaunee culture and languages, as well as his family connections[55] within the Mohawk Nation, accorded him access to many important internal Haudenosaunee discussions in his lifetime. As a result, many contemporary Haudenosaunee scholars also recognize Johnson's papers as important documents of the colonial era. Within his papers, Johnson made occasional references to the political participation of women within the Confederacy. He writes,

> About noon all the women of the chief men of this castle met at Sir William's lodging, and brought with them several of the sachems, who acquainted Sir William that they had something to say to him in the name of their chief women.
>
> Old Nickus (Brant) being appointed speaker, opened his discourse with condoling with Sir William for the losses his people had sustained, and then proceeded:—
>
> ... Brother, by this belt of wampum, we, the women, surround and hang about you like little children, who are crying at their parents' going from them, for fear of their never returning again to give them suck; and we earnestly beg you will give ear to our request and desist from your journey. We flatter ourselves you will look upon this our speech, and take the same notice of it as all our men do, who when they are addressed by the women, and desired to desist from any rash enterprise they immediately give way, when, before, everybody else tried to pursuade them from it and could not prevail.[56]

As Doxtator explains, this passage demonstrates that words carried more weight when they were representative of the whole rather than of individuals. The Clan Mothers at Canajohare, a village on the banks of the Mohawk River, knew this and brought along with them many of their chiefs, whose presence affirmed their support of the women's words. The men's presence did not detract from the fact that the words spoken by Nickus were those of the women—it simply demonstrated to Johnson that the men supported the women in their concern. William Stone[57] noted that Johnson met with the Clan Mothers in the days that followed, offering condolences for relatives killed in an ambush at German Flats by settlers of the area.[58] On 10 May 1758 he answered their request, "I shall comply with your request to return, and heartily thank you for the great tenderness and love expressed for me in your speech."[59] Johnson regularly referenced the power and influence of the Clan Mothers and attempted to stay in the good graces of the women. He also recognized the need to make amends for the lives taken by the squatters and appropriately addressed the Clan Mothers in order to do so.

At the outset of the American Revolution, both sides in the war courted the assistance of the Haudenosaunee. While the internal deliberations regarding their options were not written, there are comments found that allude to the complex discussions that were taking place within the Confederacy. For example, in 1776, General Schuyler (of the colonist forces) met with representatives of the Haudenosaunee at Schenectady, a town of the New York colony built within traditional Mohawk Territory. On the eve of that meeting, the women presented his messenger with a belt at a meeting in one of the Mohawk villages. Stone relates the record of the matter:

> Brothers, the Commissioners of the United Colonies and the people of Albany: This belt we present you, and hereby renew the covenant that was made last summer; and we bet that no disturbance shall be made up here, and that the said covenant may not thereby be broken: that in case the troops were to come up, it might create great uneasiness, as they and Sir John were of one blood; and that in case Sir John was disturbed, it might touch their blood, and we beg some other mode may be pointed out whereby this uneasiness may be settled.[60]

Schuyler responded to the women's belt the next day in Schenectady: "Brothers: Your women have sent us a belt. We beg you to assure them of our regard, and to entreat them to prevent your warriors from doing any thing that would have the least tendency to incur our resentment, or interrupt that harmony which we wish may subsist to the end of time."[61] To this, the Mohawk speaker replied, "Brother: You may depend on it that we will use our utmost influence with our warriors to calm their minds. You may depend on it, likewise, that our sisters will use their utmost influence for the same purpose."[62] These passages demonstrate the influence of Haudenosaunee women regarding the alliances built and maintained with other nations and the fact that the Americans were as aware of this as the British.[63]

Following the Revolutionary War, male and female leaders continued to guide the Haudenosaunee as they worked to rebuild their villages and nations. The years immediately following the war were filled with councils between the Haudenosaunee and the British and between the Haudenosaunee and the Americans, and regularly concentrated on negotiating land cessions and boundaries. The record of a treaty council held in Albany in 1788 includes a speech made by the women regarding land. Beauchamp's description of it follows:

> At a council in Albany in 1788, Good Peter, an Oneida chief, after speaking for the men, delivered the women's message. "You have heard our voice; we now entreat you to open your ears and hear a speech from our sisters, the governesses.
>
> "Brother, our ancestors considered it a great offence to reject the counsels of their women, particularly of the female governesses. They were esteemed the mistresses of the soil. Who, said our fore-fathers, bring us into being? Who cultivate our lands, kindle our fires and boil our pots, but the women? . . . They entreat that the veneration of their ancestors, in favor of women, be not disregarded, and that they may not be despised; the Great Spirit is their Maker. The female governesses beg leave to speak with the freedom al-lowed to women, and agreeably to the spirit of our ancestors. They entreat the great chief to put forth his strength and preserve them in peace, for they are the life of the nation."[64]

The women who sent this message were reminding the Americans that, from their perspective, women had to be considered in land deliberations. They were aware that American men were not used to dealing with women politically, but they were informing them that they would have to get used to it.

Through their roles as cultivators of the soil and the bearers of new life, women claimed a place in land negotiations. This place was shared with the men—as all important matters in Haudenosaunee society require gender balance. Haudenosaunee women at Buffalo Creek echoed these assertions at a council held in 1791. Beauchamp cites the treaty record: "The elders of the Indian women at Buffalo, May 14, 1791, came to Colonel Proctor, and said through their speaker, 'You ought to hear and listen to what we women shall speak, as well as to the sachems, for we are the owners of this land, and it is ours. It is we that plant it for our and their use. Hear us, therefore, for we speak of things that concern us and our children, and you must not think hard of us while our men shall say more to you, for we have told them.'"[65] When the council reopened, the Seneca leader Red Jacket[66] was selected to further identify the wishes of the women. Lucien Carr notes that the spokesman had previously been opposed to what the women advocated but apparently was swayed by their opinions in the matter.[67] Red Jacket carried the women's message:

> Now, listen, Brother; you know what we have been doing so long, and what trouble we have been at; and you know that it has been the request of our head warrior (Cornplanter) that we are left to answer for our women, who are to conclude what ought to be done by both sachems and warriors. So hear what is their conclusion.
>
> Brother: the business you have come on is very troublesome, and we have been a long time considering on it, ever since you came here, and now the elders of our women considering the greatness of your business, have said that our sachems and warriors must help you over your difficulties for the good of them and their children.[68]

A similar situation was documented in 1797 at a Seneca treaty council.[69] The negotiations had not gone well and, as a result, the chiefs closed the council. The women were then approached by Mr. Morris, who persuaded them to reconsider the land sale. They, in turn, appointed a speaker to address their opinion regarding the treaty, as related by John N. Hubbard:

> Cornplanter being the principal war-chief, appeared on this occasion in their behalf.
>
> He said, —"They had seen with regret the mis-conduct of the sachems; that they thought also the action of Mr. Morris was

too hasty; but still they were willing the negotiations should be
renewed; and hoped they would be conducted with better tempers
on both sides."

Mr. Morris offered a few conciliatory remarks in reply; and
Farmer's Brother, on the part of the sachems, represented these
proceedings of the women and warriors, as in accordance with the
customs of their nation.[70]

This passage recognizes the role of the women as mediators. The sale included
most of what is now western New York State. Some might question the wisdom
of this sale on the part of the Senecas, but, nonetheless, the record demonstrates
that the men and women worked together to receive the best deal they thought
they could get in that situation.

Overall, the historical record is sparse in terms of documenting the
experiences of Haudenosaunee women. In fact, women were rarely even
mentioned by name unless they were partnered with a prominent white man,
as was, for example, Molly Brant (Mohawk wife of Sir William Johnson).
Another exception lies in the historic references to Mary Jemison, a woman
born of Scottish heritage who came to live amongst the Seneca at the age of
nine. She was formally adopted by a Seneca family and lived the remainder of
her life as a Seneca. The American government offered on several occasions to
"free" her from her captivity, but Jemison let it be known that she chose to live
with the Haudenosaunee and as a Haudenosaunee woman.[71] The Americans
recognized her choice but accorded her separate treatment from the rest of
the Seneca people. Following the Big Tree Treaty in 1797, Jemison's home
along the Genessee River was secured as a separate reservation. She laid out
her territory to the American commissioners, and her knowledge of the land
accorded her a large tract, as William L. Stone notes: "thanks to her knowledge
of certain boundaries and the general lay of the land, she was granted some
thirty thousand acres instead of a hundred and fifty which the commissioners
thought they had allowed."[72] In this allocation of land, it has been noted that
Jemison received special treatment because of her European background, but
she lived as a Seneca and provided for her Seneca children and grandchildren
the best that she could—as would be expected of any Haudenosaunee woman.
She knew that the Americans saw her as one of them, but she used that
"privilege" in order to secure additional support for her Seneca descendants.

Nineteenth Century

The reservation era began in the 1780s and 1790s as a result of treaty negotiations, but the difficult realities of a greatly decreased land base became full-blown in the early 1800s. The Haudenosaunee were faced with rebuilding their villages and homes (in formerly unoccupied areas in several cases), re-establishing their nation councils and accommodating new adoptees—all while adjusting to a decreased territory that negatively affected the harvests from both farming and hunting. Coinciding with this major change in settlements were the visions of Handsome Lake.

As recorded in the Good Message, Handsome Lake was spoken to by messengers of the Sky World and was shown the destruction occurring amongst the Haudenosaunee. He was also shown ways in which future destruction could be held at bay. While the Good Message of Handsome Lake accepted the new role of men cultivating crops as their neighbouring white farmers did, it also reinforced the traditional roles of women as cultivators.[73] Handsome Lake was also told that it was acceptable for the Haudenosaunee to build frame houses—a shift from the ancient longhouse structures that had begun in some communities a century prior to his visions. While this marked a shift away from the matrilineal extended-family homes, the Good Message provided for the reinforcement of both the clans and the matrilineal government structure of the Great Law. Several scholars have failed to recognize these provisions of the Good Message as supporting the esteemed position of women in Haudenosaunee society. They criticize the above-mentioned changes as "usurping power from the women," but as outsiders to the traditional longhouse community they fail to recognize the continuity of women's roles and status amongst the followers of the Good Message.[74]

The shift to reservation life was stressful for all involved. At Grand River, not only were the people struggling with a smaller territory, they were also dealing with a territory new to almost all of them. Additionally, they were faced with changes brought about by having different nations—and different languages—in such close proximity to each other. The leaders, both men and women, had to learn how to deal with the consolidated reality of the Grand River tract while also assisting their families in making the adjustment. Stone's biography of Joseph Brant provides an example of the adjustments occurring at that time. Stone describes a meeting that occurred on 22 May 1802, wherein the women addressed the chiefs:

> Uncles: Some time ago the women of this place spoke to you, but
> you did not answer them, as you considered their meeting not suf-
> ficient. Now a considerable number of those from below having
> met and consulted together, join in sentiment, and lament as it
> were the tears in our eyes, the many misfortunes caused by the use
> of spirituous liquors. We therefore mutually request that you will
> use your endeavors to have it removed from our neighborhood,
> that there may be none sold nigher to us than the mountain. We
> flatter ourselves that this is in your power, and that you will have
> compassion on our uneasiness, and exert yourselves to have it done.
> *Strings of Wampum.*[75]

Apparently the chiefs had not answered the women's previous request because
they had addressed the council without having representation from "below"—
referring to those nations settled along the lower parts of the river.[76] Again,
we see the importance among the Haudenosaunee of gathering the minds
of the people to determine the best course of action in a given situation. The
women continued their requests to the Council:

> Uncles: The division and separation of the warriors from the chiefs
> gives us much uneasiness; we therefore entreat you, both chiefs
> and warriors, that you will bury all dispute, that our affairs may go
> on with the usual friendship and tranquility. As for our part, we
> have been in a great measure a principal cause in influencing our
> male relations; but we now drop it, and promise to observe a quite
> different conduct, and we hope in future that no reports shall be
> able to rekindle the fire of contention.
> *Strings of Wampum.*[77]

This passage demonstrates two critical details: first, the women were fulfilling
their responsibilities toward mediation and peacekeeping; and, second, they
were recognizing the errors in their own actions that had contributed to the
divisions in the community. They were taking responsibility for their actions
and calling upon all parties to do the same in this call for unity. Joseph Brant
gave the reply:

> Nieces: We are fully convinced of the justice of your request; drink-
> ing has caused the many misfortunes in this place, and has been,

besides, a great cause of the divisions, but the effect it has upon the people's speech. We assure you, therefore, that we will use our endeavors to effect what you desire....

Strings.

Nieces: With respect to your request to bury all differences, we heartily comply with it, and thank you for the wisdom you showed in here interfering. It was the custom of our ancestors for the women, by their moderation, to heal up all animosities. Be assured, therefore, that we bury every thing disagreeable that may have happened hitherto, and in future we shall be upon our guard against tales, and also saying any thing thoughtlessly ourselves....

Strings.[78]

The words and wampum that passed between the women and the chiefs on that day appear to have achieved the intended goal of clearing their minds and reuniting the people. These passages demonstrate the manner in which respectful exchange was intended to occur, as outlined by the Peacemaker

The 1802 council also demonstrates the continuity of female involvement at the political level following the settlement of the Grand River Territory. First, Beauchamp discussed the following at a Grand River Council on 30 June 1804: "'The sachems and principal war chiefs, warriors and principal women of the Six Nations,' carefully considered some matters, and signed a report. Four of the signers were women, out of twenty-four in all. Names of the governesses and principal women appear in some New York land sales, but not in all alike."[79] As noted, there was a precedent for women to sign documents such as these, but it was not overly common. It does signify, however, that the women remained active in the governmental affairs of the Confederacy at Grand River. In that same vein, women were recognized as landholders from the early days of settlement in the territory, and women holding land was commonplace. In 1834, the council was forced into negotiations with Crown representatives, who promised to protect remaining Haudenosaunee lands in exchange for the surrender of lands already settled heavily by non-Native squatters. Recognizing their inability to remove the squatters themselves—and the reluctance of the Crown to intervene—the Confederacy Council expressed their desire to have a minimum of 200 acres of land allotted to every man, woman, and child.[80] Despite the cessions of the 1830s, the practice of individual land allotments did not occur amongst the Six Nations until the surrenders of the 1840s, which created the consolidated territory of the Grand River often referred to as the "Six Nations Reserve." Those surrenders resulted in just 100-acre allotments to families, which were registered under the head of household. As both men and women received these initial allotments, the position of women as landholders continued.

ooooo

While the written historical record is sparse in its mention of Haudenosaunee women, there are important glimpses into women's relationship to the land. These often brief notations demonstrate that women continued to uphold their duties to their families, clans, nations, and territories. The female leadership used the provisions of the law regarding adoption as a means to rebuild their communities after epidemic disease and warfare had diminished their numbers. Through these adoptions, the territorial jurisdiction of the Haudenosaunee also often expanded. When necessary in certain treaty councils, women also exercised the right to have their views heard through an appointed speaker. On several occasions, the written record documents these women's statements regarding the sale of land. These records also typically note a lesson imparted upon the Confederacy's treaty partners wherein the women instruct the Euro-Americans that under Haudenosaunee law they have a right to participate in the decision-making process. This was an important lesson for those on the other side of the discussion, as they were not accustomed to the political participation of women in their governments.

As outlined at the time of creation and through the establishment of the Great Peace, Haudenosaunee women would continue to maintain their duties, long after their people migrated from homeland territories to the east and settled along the banks of the Grand River.

PART II
Haudenosaunee Land Tenure: From Iroquoia to the Grand River Territory

CHAPTER 3

Teyohahá:ke—Two Roads

The coming of the Europeans to North America certainly caused extreme changes in a very short time, but they were not the first changes experienced by the people of Turtle Island. Like all societies, a continuum of change exists from the beginning of time to today for the Haudenosaunee. That must be acknowledged in order to ascertain who and what the Haudenosaunee are today. For that reason, it is dangerous to overemphasize any particular moment or period over others. However, because this study endeavours to understand the impact of European contact upon the Haudenosaunee relationship to land, a thorough discussion of the contact period is necessary. To discuss change, the state of affairs before Europeans came to Iroquoia—the territories of the Haudenosaunee— must first be explored. That quest presents many challenges: there are no written records from the time; the oral record was scattered by the events that followed contact; and the archeological evidence is incomplete. This forces contemporary scholars to piece together the evidentiary fragments that do exist to get a glimpse into the Haudenosaunee world of the sixteenth century. Adding urgency to this work, the historical study of Indigenous so- cieties at "first contact" has become a legal requirement for Aboriginal rights cases. The Supreme Court of Canada has determined that the moment of "first contact" between a Native people and Europeans and the fifty years that follow "contact" are the starting points in assessing whether or not an activity will be recognized as an Aboriginal right as referred to in Section 35 of the Canadian Constitution. This chapter will build upon the Haudenosaunee

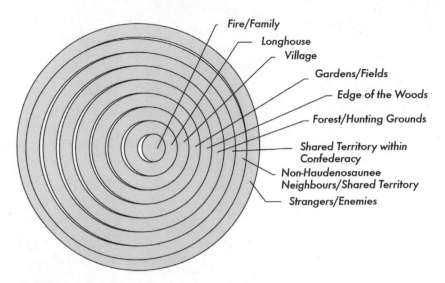

Fire/Family
Longhouse
Village
Gardens/Fields
Edge of the Woods
Forest/Hunting Grounds
Shared Territory within Confederacy
Non-Haudenosaunee Neighbours/Shared Territory
Strangers/Enemies

Figure 6. Haudenosaunee Societal Spheres.

records regarding peace agreements and relationships both internally and with other Native peoples, written documentation that alludes to events prior to European contact, and archeological evidence pertaining primarily to Haudenosaunee village sites.

Circles of Influence

The Haudenosaunee explain their world by using various spheres of existence and temporal boundaries (see Figure 6).[1] These realms build upon each other in terms of identity and understanding of one's place in the world. They also represent a Haudenosaunee view of spatial relationships and the connotation of shared spaces—which become more prevalent as one moves out from the centre. These circles of influence have not remained static and were impacted significantly by "contact" and colonization.[2]

The primary realm of Haudenosaunee life on the eve of the arrival of Europeans was the village. On an individual level, the family hearth served as the hub of daily life as well as the primary unit of identity. Each longhouse consisted of several family units that comprised the larger longhouse family, typically all members of an extended matrilineal family or clan (and men of other clans who had married into the family). Two of these small family units would share a fire pit and undoubtedly would have shared in the work and benefits of that primary fire. The relationship that existed between those two families is a basic unit of Haudenosaunee society—the balance and interdependence between two sides "across the fire" from each other. Considering this, it is little wonder that the Haudenosaunee languages utilize the same linguistic root to discuss family and fire. As discussed in Chapter 1, the concept of two sides who sit across the fire from each other is used to explain the relationship that exists between different clans, between men and women, and between Younger Brother nations and Elder Brother nations. Moving out from that initial fire, the seventeenth-century Haudenosaunee would next identify themselves with the collection of family fires that made up a single longhouse, and often a single clan family or part of one. This secondary realm of identity played a critical role in village life. The longhouses would have been represented in council through their clan family identities, with male and female leaders of each "house" or clan.[3] Garden plots were divided up among the longhouses, and the people of each longhouse would first have the duty of maintaining their crops and would then have been expected to assist others as time and resources allowed. The village was a collection of these homes and, as a result, was a collection of families. The people of a village worked together to support the overall needs of their community through the collective work of farming and harvesting.[4] The ordering of the longhouses and their physical relationship to each other appears to have been primarily dictated by geographical features. Palisades and other security measures were used in times of external threats. This trend continued into the colonial period.

The village was surrounded by the gardens and fields, which were worked by the clan families of the village. The primary crops for the Haudenosaunee of this time were the "Three Sisters"—corn, beans, and squash—but these were supplemented with many other food plants as well. Vegetable gardens were closer to the village to accommodate regular harvesting, while fields with corn and winter squashes and beans were farther out. While women were in charge of the agricultural activities, they were joined in the work when necessary by the men and children.

Surrounding the gardens and fields were open clearings that stretched to the woods: this space is referred to as "the wood's edge" and is important socially, militarily, and diplomatically. On an internal societal level it marked the connection between the forest, primarily the domain of men, and the clearing, primarily the domain of women. Men and women both participated in the activities of the clearing as well as the forest, but these spatial domains were divided based on the gender balances of duties in each area. The main activities of the forest—hunting, warfare, and diplomacy—were the responsibility of the men, while the women had the primary responsibilities for the clearing activities of farming, food preparation, and child rearing. These two domains were not gender-exclusive, however, and men and women shared in the work of each area in certain regards. For example, men assisted with planting and harvesting tasks and women often accompanied men on the hunt and on diplomatic endeavours. Doxtator writes, "The balanced relationship between the two sides and between the two kinds of land usage (the clearing and the forest) was essential to the workings of Rotinonhsyonni [Haudenosaunee] interaction with their land."[5] As she notes, the primary existence of balance in Haudenosaunee society is reflected in the balanced interactions between these two types of land.

The wood's edge served as a critical boundary for determining whether outsiders were approaching a village with intentions of harm or diplomacy. Runners would lead a diplomatic mission, carrying the message that friendly visitors were approaching the village. They would come to the edge of the woods and wait for village representatives to meet them and receive their message. This procedure was followed by people of other Haudenosaunee villages and nations, as well as non-Haudenosaunee.[6] If people entered the clearing without following these protocols, they were assumed to be enemies and the military protection of the village would be called upon. Because the actions taken at the wood's edge boundary determined whether outsiders were friends or enemies, this space became a critical aspect of Haudenosaunee government. The first part of the Condolence Ceremony is referred to as "At the Wood's Edge" and recalls the greetings of friends and relatives at this boundary.

While the wood's edge was the determining line for diplomacy, oftentimes visitors would be met in the forest by villagers before they approached the clearing. Certainly, the determination of whether an outsider was a friend or foe would have been made at that place whenever possible. The forest provided many resources to the Haudenosaunee. Most hunting took place in the forest, as did the gathering of nuts, berries, and medicinal plants. The forest provided necessary firewood as well as the resources for building and repairing longhouses, palisades, and canoes. It could also be seen as a buffer between villages, and the farther one went into the forest away from the village, the less it was seen as connected to a particular village. As outlined in the Great Law, the forest was shared territory amongst the villages of a nation. It also became shared territory between nations in terms of resources (as determined under the principles of the Dish with One Spoon), but there was recognition of the territories having national identities (see Figure 2 and

Table 1). Doxtator describes the interactions between national territories of the Confederacy:

> Diversity among the nations was a great benefit in this system. If crops or hunting failed in one region, other brother, allied nations could prevent hardship by sharing their bordering resources. Since resources bordered one another and potentially overlapped, the Confederacy was necessary to regulate any disputes. Each nation had a slightly different ecology which gave the Confederated nations strength in accessing a diverse resource base. The land along the Mohawk River occupied by the Mohawks, was a silty loam that continued to have very high fertility into the nineteenth century. Mohawk forest hinterlands in the seventeenth century were 'mostly full of fir trees' in a landscape that supported diverse game resources, while the rich fertile valley lands were flat 'abundant', and easily cultivated. The seventeenth century Oneida forest territories were heavily forested by hardwoods, such as sugar maple, walnut, oak and chestnut trees, and by fruit trees such as apple and plum. Clearings for agricultural use co-existed with the surrounding wood cover which supported wild life resources. Available animal species used as food were bear, deer, rabbit, ducks, geese, pigeons, turkeys, as well as eels, and fish. During the seventeenth century a tree-less grass plain supporting herds of elk and buffalo existed within the agriculturally fertile Onondaga territories. The Seneca and Cayugas cultivated numerous varieties of corn beans and squashes on the extensive flats of the Genesee valley surrounded by patches of open grasslands and forests.[7]

The diversity of the Haudenosaunee national landscapes provided for collective economic security, as they shared the bounty of the individual territories across the Confederacy.

Besides the internal agreement to share the wealth of the forest among all the nations of the Confederacy, the Haudenosaunee created similar treaties with many of their neighbouring nations. These agreements established shared hunting grounds with allied nations, and, accordingly, those shared spaces were generally safe places for the Haudenosaunee and their allies. In the case of neighbouring nations who were hostile to the Confederacy, the forest separating the nations was deemed to be dangerous territory but was often still used for harvesting. In cases of agitation, that forest space often became the site of military actions. As with allied nations, once peace was attempted, the provisions of their agreements would outline a sharing of that part of the forest between the Confederacy and their former enemies. Often the subsequent peace agreements were built upon the principles of the Dish with One Spoon and the extension of it from the Haudenosaunee to their former enemies.

Coming of the O'seronni[8]

The French first visited northeastern North America in 1534. While they did not enter the home territories of the Haudenosaunee, Jacques Cartier's expedition visited neighbouring nations, including the St. Lawrence Iroquoians, who are considered to be relatives of the Haudenosaunee.[9] The legacy of that expedition affected the Haudenosaunee in various indirect ways, primarily through the infiltration of European diseases and trade goods. The first documented interaction between Haudenosaunee individuals and Europeans was a confrontation on 30 July 1609 at Crown Point along Lake Champlain between French and their allied Native[10] forces and Mohawk warriors. The entire event lasted only moments as the French and their allies shot at the Mohawks with harquebuses; Champlain claimed to have killed three of their targets and asserted they were "chiefs."[11] There does not appear to be an oral record of the event to corroborate Champlain's claims.

The most important aspect of this event was probably the introduction of the Haudenosaunee to firearms, a new technology that would change the way warfare was conducted.[12] While the battle apparently resulted in several deaths, the impact on Haudenosaunee communities was otherwise minimal, with the actual number of Haudenosaunee people having "contact" being extremely small. Despite those facts, however, in *Mitchell v. Canada (Minister of National Revenue)* (2001), the Supreme Court of Canada deems this event to be the one from which the interpretation of Mohawk rights would stem.[13] This brief moment in time—which involved a small number of Mohawk men—has been chosen as the cornerstone for Mohawk (and, by association, all Haudenosaunee) "Aboriginal rights" as recognized by the Canadian government. Two later dates may be more logical choices for the date of "first contact"—1613 and 1634. The Kaswentha Treaty was made in 1613 and was the first Haudenosaunee treaty with a European nation. The first recorded visit of a European to a Haudenosaunee village came in 1634, under the expedition of Dutch trader Harmen Meyndertsz van den Bogaert.[14] Both events

Figure 7. Kaswentha.

represent contacts more consistent with real interaction and exchange rather than the volleying of cannonballs and arrows. They are also more consistent with Haudenosaunee principles of exchange in their predication of peace as well as the participation of official Haudenosaunee leadership. Had Canada chosen either of these subsequent dates as the beginning of "contact," it would have marked a shift back toward a level of respect originally agreed to in the early treaty relationships. Instead their choice seems to reflect the more contemporary relationship of contention between the Haudenosaunee and the Canadian government.

Weaving the Kaswentha

The first amicable Haudenosaunee-European interactions occurred with Dutch traders east of the Mohawk Nation. The Dutch first entered the eastern neighbouring territory of the Haudenosaunee in 1609, via Henry Hudson's expedition up the Hudson River. They established a trading relationship with the Mahicans, eventually building a small fort near present-day Albany. Initially the fort was known as Fort Nassau, but it was rebuilt later and renamed Fort Orange. It was there, in 1613, that Mohawk representatives negotiated a Dutch trading agreement known as the Kaswentha, or Two Row Wampum to the Haudenosaunee, believed to be the first treaty between Europeans and Native Americans. While the trading specifics are not well known today,[15] the relationship that was built from this first treaty served as a cornerstone for all subsequent Haudenosaunee-European treaties and other government-to-government relationships.

On the surface, the Kaswentha represented a trading relationship, but on a deeper level it laid the foundation for interactions between the Dutch and the Haudenosaunee. The two sides agreed to trade with each other under the premise of a relationship founded on essential principles. In the wampum record of the treaty (see Figure 7), the two parallel purple lines depict the Dutch on one side and the Haudenosaunee on the other. The entire belt represents an ever-flowing river in which the vessels of the two nations travel side by side. The parallel aspect of the two lines represents the idea that the two will never cross paths but will remain connected (by the three white rows of wampum that separate them) through the principles of peace, friendship, and mutual respect.[16] In essence they agree to live as peaceful neighbours in a relationship of friendship predicated under an agreement to not interfere in each other's internal business. The contemporary oral record of the treaty also notes that individuals could choose which boat to travel in, with the understanding that one must be clear in one's choice and avoid "having a foot in both."[17] The premise of non-interference demonstrates the desire to be allies rather than make one side subjects of the other.

The ideals of the Kaswentha demonstrate diplomatic sophistication, and the philosophies it was built upon not only were central to later Haudenosaunee treaties but were even borrowed by the Europeans in their dealings with other Native nations.[18] The diplomatic process of the treaty as well as the provisions of it evidence the connection between this treaty and aspects of the Great Law. The Dutch time in North America was cut short by the British, but the legacy of this Dutch trading agreement with the Haudenosaunee guided British policy for over 200 years following Holland's retreat from the New Netherlands colony. It continues to guide Haudenosaunee foreign policy to the present day.

Diseases of Trade

The first documented visit of a European to a Haudenosaunee village came in 1634 as the Dutch trader Herman Meyndertsz van den Bogaert made his way to several Mohawk villages on a trading expedition. Van den Bogaert's impact on those Mohawk villages was minimal, not only because his delegation was small and not well equipped for full-scale trade but also because European influence had reached those villages many years before his visits. By this time, most Haudenosaunee villages had been touched by indirect European contact, primarily in two powerful arenas: trade goods and disease. European trade goods had been quickly integrated into Native trading networks that predated European arrival in North America. Due to the efficiency and scale of these networks, it was not necessary for anyone from a particular village to have ever met a European in order for the village to use iron pots, metal knives, and trade beads, nor for that village to feel the impact of European diseases.

It is difficult to assess the full impact of the trade goods upon Haudenosaunee society, but it is clear that the goods were integrated very

quickly and certainly changed many daily activities inside Haudenosaunee villages. "The changes were often swift, frequently divisive," write Williams and
Nelson: "It was not so much the firearms that transformed Haudenosaunee
society. Other technology had a far more important impact. The steel axe and
hatchet meant that clearing forest was no longer done by girdling trees. Metal
hoes and plows transformed gardening. By the latter half of the seventeenth
century, the coming of draft farm animals and the plow meant that the men
took over parts of the women's role in the fields and also that single-family
farms became viable."[19] The social and economic changes brought about by
European technology were among the issues addressed by Handsome Lake
at the end of the eighteenth century. While Williams and Nelson are correct
in their commentary about the transformations brought about by European
technology, it is important to note that critical aspects of Haudenosaunee life
persisted: they maintained a primarily agricultural economy, they continued
making their traditional implements (although on a smaller scale with certain
types of objects, such as pottery), and they sustained their communal clan-
based government and society in the face of European colonization.

Travelling along the same paths as the trade goods—and often with the
actual goods—European diseases entered many Haudenosaunee communities, despite the lack of presence of their original European carriers in those
villages. At the time of van den Bogaert's travels, Haudenosaunee villages were
already experiencing outbreaks of smallpox, influenza, and other diseases in
epidemic proportions. It is estimated that in the decade between 1630 and
1640, over 75 percent of the Mohawk Nation died from these sicknesses.[20]
During this period all the nations of the Confederacy suffered a similar fate,
with an overall estimated population decrease of 50 percent. As both Matthew
Dennis and Daniel K. Richter point out, these "childhood diseases" had the
greatest impact on the adult Haudenosaunee population.[21] Those most likely
to survive the epidemics were children and people over the age of forty.[22] This
left the worker population of the Confederacy villages greatly diminished.
As a result, the survivors quickly grew dependent upon trade goods, which
replaced the more labour-intensive traditional implements (such as pottery).
In order to meet their needs for trade goods, the Haudenosaunee increased
their beaver-hunting activities. They moved farther into northern and western
hunting grounds to meet the demands of the fur trade, resulting in direct
competition with many of their neighbouring nations who had also grown
dependent upon the fur trade and its trade goods. The competition caused
diplomatic and physical struggles over control of hunting territories and trade

regulation with the various European nations. Beyond the economic factors involved in the trade competition, the Haudenosaunee and their neighbours were also reeling from the massive population losses due to disease. The various Native nations of the Northeast were looking to rebuild their internal structures; many attempted to do so through the adoption of refugees[23] and the integration of captives[24] from competitors' villages.

This period (roughly from 1640 to 1680) is often referred to as the "Beaver Wars." Several theories have been developed about why the Haudenosaunee took part in this often bloody competition. One theory, put forward by Aquila[25] and Richter and Merrell,[26] suggests that imperialistic desires and a dependence on trade goods were the primary factors for Haudenosaunee strikes against their neighbouring nations. Haudenosaunee dependence upon trade goods is well established, but their imperial motivations are more questionable.[27] The Haudenosaunee had experienced death at a scale not previously faced, except possibly during the times immediately prior to the establishment of the Great Law. The grief of these losses must have crippled the survivors both emotionally and economically. When death is experienced on such a scale there is not time to grieve properly. In the Great Law, the impact of this extreme grief is demonstrated when Ayenwahtha became a hermit after the loss of his wife and daughters. As noted in Chapter 1, the Haudenosaunee condolence process is critical to the health and well-being of the people following the death of a relative, leader, or other community member. Without the time and ceremonies associated with proper mourning, the Haudenosaunee were surely crippled by grief. As a result, they entered the fur trade era with injured economic and social structures. What some see as "imperialism" might be better described as aggressive efforts to rebuild their communities in the wake of massive loss.

Clearly, the impact of grief is essential to gaining an understanding of the collective mind of the Haudenosaunee people at this critical juncture in their history. With a grief-stricken and depleted population, the Haudenosaunee set out to repair both the human and economic impacts of the epidemics through their campaigns against their neighbours to the north, west, and south in the mid-seventeenth century. Beyond the motivations for warfare, the impacts of the epidemics also help to explain the inroads of Christianity into some Haudenosaunee communities.

Missionaries Among the Haudenosaunee

Missionaries appear to be most successful in conversions when working with people facing extreme situations. Today, that is often the case in either war-torn or poverty-stricken societies.[28] In other words, societies that are unstable (or recently destabilized) and economically poor are often more willing to accept a new way of looking at the world than those that are stable and prosperous. That was also the case four centuries ago when the Jesuits and other Catholic orders[29] began their mission work among the Indigenous peoples of North America. Most missionaries sent to the Northeast were of the Jesuit Order. Their papers and reports (later published as the *Jesuit Relations*) document the great difficulties they faced in their efforts to convert the Haudenosaunee to Catholicism. They found greater success among the Algonquins and Hurons, competitors to the Haudenosaunee in the fur trade. They did, however, achieve some success among the Mohawks and Onondagas in the mid-1600s, establishing missions in communities of both nations.[30] These missions had a great impact on both nations, leading to the migration of many people northward in the late 1600s.

Along the Mohawk River, the Jesuits set up missionary work in the village of Caughnawaga in 1655. Here they documented a number of converts, including a young woman who committed to becoming a nun, Kateri Tekakwitha. She was heralded as the "Lily of the Mohawks" by the priests and put forward by them as a role model of what other young Mohawk women could aspire to.[31] Kateri is an interesting case in a completely different way than how the priests viewed her, however. She was the daughter of a Mohawk man and an Algonquin woman. Her mother had come to the Mohawk Valley as a refugee, probably because of epidemics that had decimated her own community. She married a Mohawk man, but in retaining her identity as an Algonquin she clearly did not fully assimilate into Mohawk citizenry, as many other refugees had. In 1666, the Catholic Mohawks of Caughnawaga moved their entire village to a spot on the St. Lawrence River near Montreal,[32] claiming religious persecution from their non-Christian Mohawk relatives.[33] Kateri was among the converts who made the journey to the northern territory, which at that time was primarily used by the Haudenosaunee for hunting purposes. Given the large number of refugees who had been taken in by the Mohawks, it is quite likely that Kateri was among many Algonquins and other adoptees who had found refuge among the Mohawks but who, in fact, were returning to their homelands on the St. Lawrence along with the Jesuits.[34] In other words, their desire to follow the priests northward may have been at least partially motivated by their desire to return to their original homelands. In these situations, what was reported as "religious persecution" by the Jesuits may have actually been attempts by the Mohawks to convince their new family members (adoptees/refugees) to acclimate themselves to Haudenosaunee ways. Given the connection between missionaries and diseases, they may also have been attempting to protect their communities from epidemics.

Clearly, some of the Catholic converts at Caughnawaga were either non-Mohawk or had recently become Mohawk.[35] But there must have been converts among other Mohawks as well. It seems likely that the Jesuits found success with this population as a result of the grief and agony caused by the epidemics. Historian Ronald Wright says that, for the Indigenous peoples of the Americas, "the sheer loss of people was devastating enough (Europe reeled for a century after the Black Death, which was less severe), but disease was also a political assassination squad, removing kings, generals, and seasoned advisers at the very time they were needed most . . . to conquered and conqueror alike, it seemed as though God really was on the white man's side."[36] Most families would have been nearly wiped out by the diseases, and the mourning survivors must have questioned their own existence. Their traditional medicines appeared useless against these new diseases, which must have created a great deal of confusion about their traditional faith.[37] At this weak point, the Jesuits grasped an opportunity to infiltrate the Mohawk villages and achieved success among many. While they could not stop the dying, they offered an afterlife depicted as much better than the suffering the Mohawk experienced in this world. They also provided food and shelter to people who had nothing left upon the deaths of their loved ones. Their neighbours—the families across the fire from them—were facing similar fates, so the traditional societal structures created to care for those in mourning would not have been able to successfully function at that time.[38] The conversion of many Mohawks (and later Onondagas) is often depicted as a triumph of Christian over Haudenosaunee philosophies, but it would not have been nearly as successful without the germ "partners" of the priests that decimated Haudenosaunee (and other Native) villages. In regard to land, the success of the Catholic missions among the Mohawks and Onondagas resulted in the removal of hundreds of Haudenosaunee people from their original homelands into the hunting territories along the St. Lawrence River. It also resulted in a philosophical divide that played a key role in later disputes between the French and British—which typically placed the Haudenosaunee in the middle.

Territorial Expansion

In the seventeenth century, the Haudenosaunee territorial domain expanded often as they took in refugees from other nations. Typically, these refugees came from neighbouring nations—Mahican, Huron, Algonquin, Erie, Neutral, and others—who already shared hunting grounds with the Haudenosaunee. The movement of these groups to join the Confederacy brought their families and their lands within the domain and protection of the Great Law. In most cases, the refugees and adoptees moved to the Haudenosaunee homelands, often setting up villages near the established national villages of the original Five Nations. Their presence contributed to the national and Confederacy economies as well as toward rebuilding the decimated populations of the Haudenosaunee. Their lands contributed further territorial jurisdiction to the Haudenosaunee and added to the collective hunting territories.[39] In accordance with the Great Law, the adopted peoples were allowed to maintain their internal political and cultural structures and were accorded representation through their host nations. For example, the Erie people were taken in by the Seneca Nation and allowed to maintain their distinct identity as Erie as long as they chose. Their concerns were carried to the Grand Council via the Seneca Rotiyanehson. After many generations, most of the Erie families had intermarried with the Senecas to the extent that their distinct Erie identity was replaced by a Seneca one. While these types of interactions between refugee villages and original villages contributed to an increased population, the impact on traditional village structures and daily activities was probably minimal in most cases.

In a travel narrative from 1677, English traveller Wentworth Greenhalgh recorded observations from a trip into the homeland territories of the Oneidas, Onondagas, Cayugas, and Senecas. He made this journey on official business for the British government, laying much of the groundwork for the Covenant Chain treaty negotiated later that year. His records emphasize basic village descriptions, an estimate of fighting men, and a description of where their corn was grown (see Table 3).

Table 3. 1677 Observations of Haudenosaunee Villages from
Wentworth Greenhalgh.

NATION	Town Name	Houses	Stockade	fighting men	Corn Fields
Maques[1]	Cahaniaga	24	Yes	300 total	Bordering river bank
	Canagora	16	Yes		
	Canajorha	16	Yes		
	Tionondogue	30	Yes		
	Village	10	No		
Onyades	(one town)	100	Yes	200	Around the village
Onondagos	(town)	140	No	350	Two-mile clearing around the perimeter of the town
	village	24	No		
Caiougos	Three towns	100 total	No[2]	300	Reported "an abundance of corn" but no mention of fields
Senecques	Canagaroh	150	No	1000 total	Describes all villages as being well stocked with corn
	Tiotohatton	120[3]	No		
	Canoenada	30	No		
	Keint:he	24	No		

Source: Wentworth Greenhalgh, "Observations of Wentworth Greenhalgh in a Journey from Albany to the Indians Westward, 1677," in Snow, Gehring, and Starna, *In Mohawk Country*, 189–91. This report has been published many times over, including in the New York Colonial Documents series.

1   Greenhalgh's spellings are shown to provide examples of the diversity of spellings utilized in the colonial records.

2   Greenhalgh noted that the Cayugas intended to build a centralized village the next year with plans for a stockade.

3   Greenhalgh noted that the houses in this Seneca village were the largest they saw on their journey.

Greenhalgh's report is not overly detailed but provides a glimpse into the Haudenosaunee homelands of 1677. Of note, he observed the use of stockades by the eastern nations and the lack of use among the western nations. This almost certainly reflects the fact that the Mohawks and Oneidas experienced more frequent interactions with British colonists who bordered their territories, as compared to the Onondagas, Cayugas, and Senecas, who were more distant from the colonial settlements. Doxtator provides a detailed description of the Haudenosaunee villages of this era:

> The structures of settlement patterns used by Rotinonhsyonni peoples were spatial expressions of the pulsating nature of time and space in that longhouses, villages, reserve homesteads and clans are forms that are designed to react to expansion and contraction of population, land and resources. The central village contained within it the flexibility to expand or contract according to seasonal necessity. In seventeenth century Iroquoian culture, the village as a form represented the idea of the collective activity primarily of winter sharing of food and shelter. The annual main village population fluctuated expanding at some seasons and nearly empty at others. Eventually after 15–30 seasons of occupation, the village itself was abandoned for a new settlement or settlements. The construction of the seventeenth century village reflects this periodic, semi-permanent function with the capacity to accommodate varying numbers of people. Wooden post and bark sheeting structures were easily dismantled moved and remodeled expanding or contracting (getting longer or shorter) depending upon the need to accommodate people. Village sites show repeated building, dismantling and rebuilding of structures. At the Draper site, a late Ontario Iroquoian village near Toronto, the village itself expands outward from a central core. The form of the palisaded village provides for this type of expansion or contraction in circles of increasing size.[40]

These types of village structures accommodated population shifts both for the seasonal fluctuations and for the influx of refugees.[41]

The greatest impact of the refugee population to Iroquoia occurred within the societal sphere of the forest. The competition for furs decreased as the populations of their neighbours decreased, allowing the Haudenosaunee to expand their hunting territories without major military conflicts. This also contributed to the establishment of satellite villages in several key areas of the hunting grounds. Richard Hill has noted that between 1665 and 1675, a number of Seneca, Cayuga, and Oneida families moved into the northern hunting grounds once occupied by the Hurons along the north shore of Lake Ontario. According to Hill, "by 1670 they occupied six villages and welcomed French traders and missionaries. In 1673 Count Frontenac and 400 men visited these *Iroquois du nord* of Cataraqui (Kingston, Ontario) and built Fort Frontenac."[42] The establishment of these northern satellite villages demonstrates the utilization of the hunting grounds for settlement as well as harvesting purposes. Certainly these northern villages were also an assertion of Haudenosaunee jurisdiction in an area that had once been primarily used by the Hurons, many of whom had been adopted into various villages of the Confederacy.

Forging and Maintaining the Covenant Chain

Shortly after the British took control of Fort Orange (renaming it Fort Albany), they sought a formal trade relationship with their Haudenosaunee neighbours. A treaty council was held in September 1664, resulting in the first recorded agreement between Great Britain and the Five Nations. In this treaty, the British hoped to place themselves in the same position their Dutch predecessors had created between themselves and the Confederacy under the terms of the Two Row Wampum. The relationship was further expanded thirteen years later in a treaty known as the Covenant Chain of Friendship, also made at Fort Albany.

The 1664 Fort Albany Treaty written record names the Haudenosaunee as the "Maques" and the "Synicks"[43] and includes the following agreements:

1. Imprimis. It is agreed that the Indian Princes above named and their subjects, shall have all such wares and commodities from the English for the future, as heretofore they had from the Dutch.

2. That if any English, Dutch, or Indian (under the protection of the English) do any wrong, injury or violence to any of ye said Princes, or their Subjects, in any sort whatsoever, if they complained to the Governor at New York or to the Officer in Chief at Albany, if the person so offending can be discovered, then that person shall suffer punishment and all due satisfaction shall be given, and the like shall be done for all other English Plantations.

3. That if any Indian belonging to any of the Sachims aforesaid, do any wrong, injury or damage to the English, Dutch, or Indians

under the protection of the English, if complaint be made to ye Sachims, and the person be discovered who did the injury, then the person so offending shall be punished and all just satisfaction shall be given to any of His Majesties subjects in any Colony or other English plantation in America.

. . .

These Articles following were likewise proposed by the same Indian Princes & consented to by Colonell Cartwright in behalfe of Colonell Nicolls the 25ᵗʰ day of September 1664.

1. That the English do not assist the three Nations of the Ondiakes Pinnekooks and Pacamtekookes, who murdered one of the Princes of the Maques, when he brought ransomes & presents to them upon a treaty of peace.

2. That the English do make peace for the Indian Princes, with the Nations down the River.

3. That they may have free trade, as formerly.

. . .

5. That if they be beaten by the three Nations above menconed, they may receive accommodacon from ye English.[44]

The 1664 treaty stipulated that the British would provide the same goods to the Haudenosaunee as the Dutch had before them. The British also promised to provide refuge to the Five Nations if they were defeated in their war with the "River Indians" (the Mahicans). Additionally, the treaty included stipulations for separate criminal jurisdictions, with both sides accepting responsibility for prosecution of their own citizens should they commit a crime against either Natives or colonists.[45] Of great importance in the text of this treaty is the recognition of the distinct status of both parties from each other, similar to the aspect of the Kaswentha that recognized that the two sides would not interfere in the internal governmental issues of the other. The 1664 Treaty recognized both the British and the Haudenosaunee as sovereigns with their own "subjects" and laid out the principles upon which these two governments would work together but remain distinct as allies, neither becoming subject to the other. Like its predecessor, the Kaswentha, the 1664 Treaty foreshadowed the later Covenant Chain of Friendship that was developed in the 1670s and nurtured over the decades that followed its inception.

As with the 1664 Treaty, the council held at Fort Albany in 1677 articulated a British desire to assume the Dutch responsibilities agreed to over sixty years prior. The peace conference was held between the colonies of New York, Maryland, and Virginia, and four of the five nations of the Haudenosaunee.[46] The negotiations involved provisions of trade, but in accordance with Haudenosaunee diplomatic principles the heart of the treaty involved the formation of the relationship that would flow from the formal agreement. While the colonies were probably focussed upon the economic relationship the treaty guaranteed, the Haudenosaunee were intent upon developing the foundation for a relationship that would govern the interactions between themselves and the British for the rest of time.[47] In order to do this, they employed deeply metaphorical concepts in their discussion to define the relationship they were building together with the British. For example, the treaty record documented the following statement from Garakondie, speaking on behalf of the Haudenosaunee: "[We] do thank the gentleman there that they do exhort us to peace, for we are so minded ... we desire now that all that is past may be buried in oblivion, and do make now an absolut covenant of peace, which we shall bind with a chain. For ye sealing of ye same do give a belt of 13 deepe."[48] In his reference to "burying the past," the speaker was using symbols from the Great Law. In the years between this treaty and its 1664 predecessor, there had been disagreements between colonists and individual Haudenosaunee resulting in losses on both sides. In this peace treaty, the two sides offered condolences for those losses they had inflicted upon each other. This treaty did not negate the previous relationship; it actually used the original treaty as a basis for further development while acknowledging how both sides had been responsible for damaging their agreement and relationship. Like a marriage, the treaty relationship did not end because of violations by either party; instead, the subsequent treaty addressed the wrongdoings and created a means to rectify the wrongs.

While the ideas contained in it were familiar, the metaphor of the Covenant Chain as representing the treaty relationship was new to the Haudenosaunee. From that point forward, the concept of the Covenant Chain continued to develop and was eventually described as a silver chain holding both the British sailing ship and the Iroquois canoe to the "Great Mountain" (Onondaga). It was described as a three-link silver chain representing "peace and friendship forever." These metaphors became central to the ensuing relationship of the Haudenosaunee and the Crown. Furthermore, the Crown borrowed the ideology and the terminology in their treaty making with other Indigenous nations in North America. British and Indigenous treaty records document the Crown's application of the Covenant Chain relationship to many other nations throughout the Northeast, including the Ojibwa, the Mississaugas, and the Delaware, to name but a few.[49]

As the British applied the Covenant Chain to their other treaty relationships, the Haudenosaunee later sought to include other British colonies in the agreement as well. Williams and Nelson note that, in June 1691, a council was held in Albany with the governor of New York.[50] There, the Haudenosaunee encouraged him, on behalf of the Crown, to strengthen the relationship of the other British colonies to the Covenant Chain. An excerpt of the record explains their desires:

> Brother Corlaer[51]
>
> We have not much to give or say but return our hearty thanks for the good you do us, as we have always been in the Covenant Chaine, but of late New England, Virginia, Maryland and adjacent Colonys did not put in their arms into the chain; pray animate them to make us strong, and assist us according to the covenant made between us, and altho' an angry Dog should come and endeavour to Bitt the chaine in pieces with his teeth, yet we will keep it firme both in peace and warr and do renew the Old Covenant, that so the Tree of Wellfare may flourish and that his roots may spread thro' all the Country.[52]

This passage demonstrates the metaphors of the Covenant Chain as well as the White Roots of Peace referred to in the Great Law.[53] The Haudenosaunee were seeking to have their treaty relationship extended to all representatives of the British Empire in North America. Thus the Covenant Chain would "grow" and adapt to other parties on the British side of the agreement. Similarly, as refugees from other nations joined the Confederacy, they would accept the responsibilities through the treaty as allies of the Crown from the Haudenosaunee end of the chain. Also of great importance in this example is the reference to the New York governor as "Brother." The Great Law established a framework within which peoples of different blood could become family. Building upon that ideology, familial relations were extended to Haudenosaunee allies in the same way. The idea that the British had become brethren to the Haudenosaunee through their treaty relationships was taken very seriously by the Haudenosaunee. It was seen as an extension of the Great Law, which directed that family members take care of each other and assume

responsibilities for each other. The British may not have felt as strongly about
the newly formed kinship bonds, but they used the terminology extensively
in their relations with the Haudenosaunee and other Indigenous peoples
throughout the treaty period.

Peace councils were held in Albany almost annually[54] for a century
following the forging of the Covenant Chain. At each meeting, delegates from
both the British and the Haudenosaunee would recall the original meetings
where their relationship had been formalized.[55] The Haudenosaunee would
remind the British that they inherited the position of friendship from their
Dutch predecessors, and the British would reaffirm their promises of peace
and friendship forever. Presents and wampum belts were often exchanged as
symbols of the ever-flowing mutual friendship between the Crown and the
Confederacy. This process of reaffirmation gained the metaphorical description
of "polishing the chain." When the Covenant Chain was first created, the
British had important reasons for representing this pact of friendship through
the metaphor of silver. On 23 June 1755, William Johnson recalled the
explanation of the day in response to a Haudenosaunee request to see the
written records of all their treaty negotiations with the British:

> Behold Brethren these great books, 4 folio volumes of the records
> of Indian Affairs which lie upon the table before the Colonel.
> They are records of the many Solemn Treaties and the various
> Transactions which have passed between your Forefathers and your
> Brethren the English, also between many of you here present & us
> your Brethren now living.
>
> You well know and these Books testify that it is now almost 100
> years since your Forefathers and ours became known to each
> other. That upon our first acquaintance we shook hands & finding
> we should be useful to one another entered into a Covenant of
> Brotherly Love & mutual Friendship. And *tho' we were at first only
> tied together by a Rope, yet lest this Rope should grow rotten & break we
> tied ourselves together by an Iron Chain. Lest time or accidents might
> rust & destroy this Chain of Iron, we afterwards made one of Silver, the
> strength & brightness of which would subject it to no decay. The ends of
> this Silver Chain we fix't to the Immoveable Mountains, and this in so
> firm a manner that no mortal enemy might be able to remove it.*[56] All
> this my Brethren you know to be Truth. You know also that this
> Covenant Chain of Love & Friendship was the Dread & Envy

of all your Enemies & ours, that by keeping it bright & unbroken we have never spilt in anger one drop of each other's blood to this day. You well know also that from the beginning to this time we have almost every year, strengthened & brightened this Covenant Chain in the most public & solemn manner.

You know that we became as one body, one blood & one people. The same King our common Father, that your enemies were ours that whom you took into your alliance & allowed to put their hands into this Covenant Chain as Brethren, we have always considered and treated as such.[57]

Johnson's words were presented as the official Crown position on their relationship with the Confederacy, as he had been appointed the imperial superintendent general of Indian Affairs, replacing the New York colonial superintendent in 1755. Johnson was "polishing the chain" by recalling the philosophy behind their alliance, drawing from the familial metaphors that were central to the Haudenosaunee understanding of their mutual obligations with the British. On that same day, Johnson also demonstrated the connection between the chain and key metaphors of the Great Law: "[it was hoped that the Tree would] be nourished by refreshing Streams, that it may grow up as high as the Heaven and be proof against every envious Wind; that its branches may be large & numerous enough to afford sufficient shelter for us & all our Brethren to come & consult under it; and that our Children's Children may bless the hand that planted it."[58] Here, Johnson asserts the British desire that the Haudenosaunee—symbolized by the Tree of Peace—would remain strong and forever allied with the Crown. Time has demonstrated that the British memory of these words, spoken on their behalf, was not long-lasting, but that does not negate their existence and their importance to both sides.

While the relationship of the Covenant Chain has faced times of difficulty both in its early years and in the last two centuries, the initial treaty between the Haudenosaunee and the British, and its subsequent treaties, continue to bind the two nations for all time. The uniqueness of this relationship is demonstrated in a document approved by the Haudenosaunee External Relations Committee for presentation to the Canadian Royal Commission on Aboriginal Peoples:

> In contrast to the treaties between Canada and indigenous nations whose lands are within its boundaries, relations between the Haudenosaunee and the Crown are not based on any single treaty

council or transaction. They are a continuum based on principles or concepts that themselves are drawn from the Great Law of Peace. The principles of respect, friendship, unity of mind, and peace are embodied in the Two Row Wampum and the Silver Covenant Chain. The idea that nations can be of one mind without becoming subsumed one by one or the other is constant in those relations and is drawn from the Great Law of Peace. This historical record shows:

- that the Haudenosaunee conducted international relations not only with the British, but also with other nations of the world,
- that the British and others willingly adopted the treaty and council procedures of the Haudenosaunee and understood not only what they were doing, but also the purposes of those procedures and processes,
- that the Haudenosaunee have adhered consistently to the concepts of the Two Row Wampum and the Covenant Chain,
- that the concepts represent a continuum in relations, dynamic and flexible in dealing with often turbulent changes in politics, war and peace and evolving technologies, while constant and consistent in fundamental principles.[59]

As laid out in this summary of the relationship, the Covenant Chain was a critical relationship for both the Haudenosaunee and the British. It demonstrates both the interdependence and the independence central to the relationship. Without this alliance, the British surely would not have succeeded in eliminating their European competition for colonial control over much of North America. Unfortunately, the Haudenosaunee memory of that relationship has proven to be much longer than that of their brethren, the British. The colonists' weak memory proved problematic in colonial times, as it does today.

The Treaties of 1701: A Call to New Order

The years immediately following the forging of the Covenant Chain were tumultuous for the Haudenosaunee. They were dealing with hostilities between themselves and many of their western neighbours—Native nations allied with the French—over hunting grounds and control of the fur trade. Eventually the French were drawn directly into the fighting, with French military leaders invading several Haudenosaunee villages. The English reluctantly joined the hostilities to assist the Haudenosaunee, in accordance with the provisions of the Covenant Chain. The disputes that occurred during this period were complicated. There were times when the Haudenosaunee and some of the western nations entertained peace, sometimes with success. Additionally, the French regularly sent messengers to Onondaga requesting peace. And the British were often reluctant participants in supporting their Five Nations allies. The result of all of these hostilities and alliances was that Haudenosaunee territorial control of the western and northern hunting grounds shifted continually. Internally, many Haudenosaunee villages came under French and French-allied Native attacks. With battles in the homelands and the hunting grounds, the pressures of this "war"[60] affected Confederacy territories both internally and externally.

The most famous French-led attack within the Haudenosaunee homelands was the 1687 Denonville campaign against the Seneca village of Ganondagan (also known as Ganagaro) and three surrounding satellite villages. The Senecas had received warning of the impending attack and had vacated their villages. Denonville, the governor general of New France, reported that they destroyed nearly one million bushels of corn as they burned all the food storages and longhouses along their path.[61] The French disturbed some of the graves at Ganondagan, in search of metal that was scarce at that time. They also took wampum and glass trade beads from the Seneca dead. The economic losses suffered by the Senecas in terms of their corn storage was coupled with the disrespect inflicted upon the Seneca dead. This combination may well account for the continued recognition of this campaign as especially brutal among contemporary Haudenosaunee people.[62] The French also attacked several Onondaga and Mohawk villages around this time, having similar impacts upon those nations.

Under the provisions of the Covenant Chain, the Five Nations held council with the English regularly. Often during this period, the meetings would include the request for English assistance in their struggles against the French and the western nations. The Haudenosaunee were clear, however, to explain that it was in their hands to make peace with the French if they so chose. At one such meeting in Albany in 1685, the Confederacy spokesman explained to the New York governor: "Where shall I seek the Chain of Peace? Where shall I find it, but upon Our Path? and whither doth Our Path lead us, but unto this house? this is a House of Peace ... neither Onontio[63] or Corlear is our master, and that no man has the right to command us."[64]

Sovereignty was central to the Haudenosaunee standing at this time, even while under attack by the French and their allies. They clearly understood the need to demonstrate their autonomy and the fact that they were not subjects of the Crown. Under the Covenant Chain, however, they recognized their mutual responsibilities with the English when either was under attack. This was noted by the Confederacy speaker at a March 1689 council held in Schenectady between the Mohawks and New York representatives, following a French attack upon the English. In the words of the Confederacy speaker: "The Governor of Canada sends to Onondaga, and talks to us of Peace with our whole house, but War was in his Heart, as you can see by woeful Experience.... He has broken open our House at both Ends, formerly in the Senekas Country, and now here.... Our Forefathers taught us to go with all Speed to bemoan and lament with our Brethren, when any Disaster or Misfortune happens to any in our Chain.... Our Chain is a strong Chain, it is a silver Chain, it can neither rust nor be broken."[65]

The Haudenosaunee were weakened by the warfare and attacks on their villages. Around 1693 they began to consider the French offers for a peace meeting. This started with their talks of peace between themselves and the "Dionaondades," allies of the French who included the Wyondot, Huron, Wendat, and others. When the Confederacy spokesmen informed New York governor Fletcher about this potential peace, the governor tried to convince the Confederacy to cease their informal discussions with New France governor general Frontenac.[66] Despite the promises of respect, trust, and peace made in the Covenant Chain, the English failed to see that their recognition of the Haudenosaunee as allies rather than subjects meant that they were free to ally themselves with any other nations they chose, including the French.

The French and English reached a peace agreement in 1697, but the hostilities continued between the Haudenosaunee and the western nations, as they were not included in the treaty negotiations. A year later, a series of peace conferences were held between the Haudenosaunee and the French and several of their Native allies. Again, the British began to rebuff the Haudenosaunee-French discussions. It appears that the British felt they could council with the French but were not willing to recognize the Haudenosaunee right to do the same. In September 1700, the French sponsored a peace conference between themselves, several of their allies, and the Haudenosaunee. A preliminary peace was agreed to between the Five Nations, the Hurons, the Odawas,[67] the Abenakis, the Montagnais, the Sault, and the French.[68] This peace was finalized in August 1701, after several weeks of meetings in Montreal. It became known as the Great Peace of Montreal and, as Williams and Nelson write, accorded the Haudenosaunee over twenty years of relative peace following its signing:

"during that generation [of peace], the population of the Confederacy more than doubled, both through natural growth and through adoption of other nations."[69] The peace created through the treaty allowed the Haudenosaunee the opportunity to rebuild their economic and political strength, and, as noted, their longhouses continued to be places of refuge for many other Native peoples. In many ways, this peace allowed the Confederacy time to regroup after the devastation of the epidemics and related warfare of the seventeenth century.

The Haudenosaunee-French alliance was completed just two months after the Albany signing of the 1701 Nanfan Treaty between the Confederacy and the British. At the Albany treaty council, the Haudenosaunee were careful not to disclose their simultaneous treaty discussions with the French.[70] The Haudenosaunee were always clear about their right to ally with whomever they chose; however, they also knew the talks with Nanfan, the new governor of New York, would go much more smoothly if they kept their French connections under wraps (as England had again declared war against France in May of that year). In this treaty, the Five Nations were seeking the protection of their northern and western hunting grounds, which had come under major attack in recent years. They called upon the provisions of the Covenant Chain, wherein the English promised to protect Haudenosaunee interests. The final agreement of this treaty was reached on 19 July 1701, after ten days of council. The terms of the treaty are highly debated because on the surface the agreement appears to be a surrender, from the Haudenosaunee to the Crown, of their entire northern and western hunting grounds. However, British interpretation at the time (and throughout the next six decades, at least) was that the Haudenosaunee understood the treaty to place these territories under the protection of the King—following under the provisions of the Covenant Chain wherein the Crown promised to protect Haudenosaunee interests. In the Nanfan Treaty, also known as the Beaver Hunting Grounds Treaty, the Five Nations were specifically referencing their hunting territories and saw the agreement as an undertaking by the Crown to ensure Haudenosaunee use of those lands for perpetuity. The main text of the treaty follows:

> Wee say upon these and many other good motives us hereunto moveing have freely and voluntarily surrendered, delivered up and forever quit claimed, and by these present doe for our heires and successors absolutely surrender, deliver up and for ever quit claime unto our great Lord and Master the King of England

called by us Corachkoo and by the Christians William the third
and to his heires and successors Kings and Queens of England for
ever all the right title and interest and all the claime and demand
whatsoever which wee the said five nations of Indians called the
Maquase, Oneydes, Onnondages, Cayouges and Sinnekes now
have or which wee ever had or that our heires or successors at any
time hereafter may or ought to have of in or to all that vast tract of
land or Colony called Canagariarchio beginning on the northwest
side of Cadarachqui Lake and includes all that vast tract of land
lyeing between the great lake of Ottawawa and the lake called by
the natives Cahiquage and by the Christians the lake of Swege and
runns till it butts upon the Twichtwichs and is bounded on the
westward by the Twichtwichs by a place called Quadoge containing
in length about eight hundred miles and in breadth four hundred
miles including the Country where Beavers and all sorts of wild
game keeps and the place called Tjeughsaghrondie alias Fort de
Tret or wawyachtenock and so runns round the lake of Swege till
you come to a place called Oniadarundaquat which is about twenty
miles from the Sinnekes castles including likewise the great falls
oakinagaro, all which was formerly posest by seaven nations of
Indians called the Aragaritka whom by a fair warr we subdued and
drove from thence four score years agoe bringing many of them
captives to our country and soe became to bee the true owners of
the same by conquest.

Which said land is scituate lyeing and being as is above expressed
with the whole soyle the lakes the rivers and all things pertaining
to the said tract of land or colony with power to erect Forts and
castles there, soe that wee the said Five Nations nor our heires nor
any other person or persons for us by any ways or meanes hereafter
may claime challenge and demand of in or to the premises or any
parte thereof alwayes provided and it is hereby expected that wee
are to have free hunting for us and the heires and descendants
from us the Five Nations for ever and that free of all disturbances
expecting to be protected therein by the Crown of England but
from all the action right title interest and demand of in or to the
premises or every of them shall and will be utterly excluded and
debarred for ever by these presents.[71]

In the years that followed this treaty, different British officials made reference to this as a surrender to the Crown, but they were usually corrected—by their own leadership—with an explanation of the Confederacy's understanding of what the treaty meant. The explanation was that the Haudenosaunee saw this as a promise of protection by the British against the French, their allies, and any other people who might encroach upon those lands against the wishes of the Haudenosaunee. In this promise of protection, the British were echoing the words of their predecessors who had offered similar protection to the Haudenosaunee in the 1664 Fort Albany Treaty (section 5).

When considering the Nanfan Treaty, one must also recognize the dependence of the English upon the Haudenosaunee at that time. The English had just declared war on the French again, and they knew that they were dependent upon the Haudenosaunee to assist them should that war spill over from Europe to North America. The Covenant Chain alliance had also accorded the English prominence in the Northeastern fur trade, an economic reality that provided invaluable assets to the Crown in order to help finance their worldwide imperial endeavours. The leadership of the New York colony was well aware of the English dependence upon the Five Nations, as evidenced by the 13 May 1701 letter of Robert Livingston, New York secretary of Indian Affairs (1675–1721): "of the Five Nations, I need not enumerate the advantages arising from their firmness to this Government [New York], they having fought our battles for us and been a constant barrier of the defence between Virginia and Maryland and the French, and by their constant vigilance have prevented the French from making any descent that way."[72] It would be simple to view the Nanfan Treaty as a surrender of territory by a "weak Indian Nation" to a "strong European power," but that was not at all the case. The Haudenosaunee and the English had truly become intertwined through the Covenant Chain and, while they remained separate peoples, they were dependent on each other like family.

In 1701, the Confederacy assessed the situation they were in: caught between England and France and France's Native allies. They determined what outcome they desired: a recognition by both European powers that the Five Nations were autonomous and had the option of allying with both or neither. Finally, they took the steps to achieve that outcome by treating with both, as well as the other involved Native nations. In this they were extremely practical and pragmatic, making agreements with the English and French (and their Native allies) that were not ideal but that served the primary goal—peace and protection for the Haudenosaunee people.[73]

Eighteenth-Century Territorial Changes

In the seventeenth century, Haudenosaunee territorial control grew as the Confederacy expanded their hunting grounds and adopted refugees from many of the neighbouring nations. These refugees often brought territory with them that became recognized as Haudenosaunee hunting grounds (most of the refugees moved into the Haudenosaunee homelands). As had always been the case, the Haudenosaunee continued to establish satellite villages in the hunting ground territories, including the newly annexed lands. Starting in the late 1600s, the Haudenosaunee experienced challenges to their jurisdiction over much of the northern and western hunting grounds. They attempted to address these issues through a series of military actions and eventually secured peace with many of the Indigenous nations involved, as well as with the French. They also attained British promises to protect the Haudenosaunee interests in those hunting grounds. The Five Nations continued to provide refuge to dislocated peoples in the eighteenth century, but often those refugees did not add to the Haudenosaunee territories as had their adoptee predecessors. The result was an expanding Haudenosaunee population without an equivalent territorial expansion. In fact, the Five Nations were experiencing a reduction in territory and resources. This reduction started in the hunting grounds but eventually made its way into the homelands, thereby affecting the internal aspects of many Haudenosaunee communities.

The largest internal territorial pressures were experienced by the Mohawks, as British colonists pushed their way into the fertile Mohawk Valley.[74] As the easternmost Haudenosaunee nation, the Mohawks had the greatest amount of interaction with Europeans, especially the British. Some of the colonists were invited in by the Mohawks through alliances of friendship. Others bought their way in, often securing fraudulent titles to vast tracts of land. These land swindles became epidemic in the Mohawk Valley and were cause for growing tensions between the Mohawks and the colonists. Starting in the late 1600s, Mohawk leaders called upon the English to address this problem. For example, sworn depositions were made by "Henry & Joseph two of the Maquase nation" on 31 May 1698, whereby they filed sworn complaints to New York colonial officials regarding fraudulent land sales registered by Col. Peter Schuyler, Dr. Godfry Dellius, Maj. Dirk Wessells, and Capt. Evart Bancker.[75] The two Mohawk men charged that the four named colonists had convinced them to sign the papers of sale under the guise of providing protection over the lands in the war against the French. They were told that their signatures named the four as their "Guardians or Trustees," with a promise that "as long as any of the Maquase nation lived, the land should be theirs and their Posteritys for ever."[76] In addition to this complaint, they reiterated a complaint against an earlier illegal sale:

> The said Henry and Joseph doe further Complain to his Excellency that about three years agoe when they were out a fighting against the French Six Idle drunken People of their nation took upon them to sell a vast Tract of Land belonging to his Excellency's Complainants called Ikohere, (Skohere) of so large an Extent that a Young man has enough to doe to runn over it in a day's time, and that for the value of thirty Beavor-skins in Rum and other goods; which Land Arent to ye Magistrates of Albany who gave them no Releife but on the contrary the said Col. Bayard obtained a patent of Col. Fletcher ye last Governour for the said unlawfull purchase of their Land which caused the said Complainants upon Col. Fletchers arrivall at Albany to apply unto him for Justice and Complained in the presence of Col. Peter Schuyler and Jar. Dirik Wessells and the Interpretess: that there was a Patent granted to Col. Bayard of their Land which they never sold; nor had those who pretended to sell, any right to doe the same. did [*sic*] therefore pray the said Col. Fletcher to destroy the said Patent and make it voide who promised in the presence of the aforesaid Persons to do the same but hitherto it is not done to the great disquiet and dissatisfaction of the Complainants; which causes them to renew their prayers to your Lordship for Justice in that matter.[77]

The written record does not reveal what actions, if any, were taken by the colonial officials in this case. This began another legacy of the Confederacy, the tradition of calling upon the Crown to govern its own people and prohibit their violation of Haudenosaunee rights through land encroachments. Many of the treaty councils and peace meetings of the eighteenth century included lengthy discussions of this problem.

Often the British responded to Haudenosaunee land claims by offering to build a fort in the neighbouring area so as to monitor the actions of British subjects in the area. One of these British settlements was Fort Hunter, established around 1700. While such forts were built by the British to protect Haudenosaunee land interests, they often had the opposite effect, as they introduced more Europeans to the Haudenosaunee interior. This proved true as white settlement around Fort Hunter expanded greatly after it was established—sometimes legally and sometimes not. In 1712, for example, 2,500 Palatine Germans purchased the right to occupy land in the Mohawk Valley at Schoharie.[78] While the Mohawks of the area had consented to this sharing of land with the Palatines, it still led to increased competition for land and resources.

On another front, the Six Nations leadership also let it be known that they were well aware of the value of the lands they had agreed to share with the British colonists. In a famous speech made at the Treaty of Lancaster in 1744, Canasatego, an Onondaga Royaner, declared the following: "We know our lands have now become more valuable. The white people think we do not know their value; but we know that the land is everlasting, and the few goods we receive for it are soon worn out and gone."[79] Canasatego put the British on notice that they were not dealing with a people ignorant of Western economics. At the Albany Conference ten years later, Hendrick Tekarihoken, a Mohawk Royaner, echoed similar sentiments:

> What we are now going to say is a matter of great moment, which we desire you to remember as long as the Sun and Moon lasts. We are willing to sell you this large tract of land for your people to live upon, but we desire that this may be considered as part of our Agreement that when we are all dead and gone your Grandchildren may not say to our Grandchildren, that your Forefathers sold the land to our Forefathers, and therefore be gone off them. This is wrong. Let us all be as Brethren as well after as before giving you Deeds for Land. After we have sold our land we in a little time have nothing to show for it; but it is not so with you, your Grandchildren will get something from it as long as the world stands; our Grandchildren will have no advantage from it; they will say we were fools for selling so much land for so small a matter and curse us; therefore let it be a part of the present agreement that we shall treat each other as Brethren to the latest Generation, even after we shall not have left a foot of land.[80]

This "sale" was prefaced by a promise by the British that their future generations would respect their Haudenosaunee peers. In other words, the treaty was only binding so long as the British descendants treated the Haudenosaunee descendants as brethren. Hendrick's words about Haudenosaunee land loss were prophetic, but his reminder to the British about their vows of brotherhood was soon forgotten by the Crown.

Also at the Lancaster Treaty Council, Canasatego attested to the belief that a people's right to territory stems from their origins and extensive interactions with that place. In particular, he alludes to the Haudenosaunee Creation Story (in reference to "coming out of the ground"), wherein the Creator formed human beings from clay and brought them to life with his breath:

> When you mentioned the Affair of the Land Yesterday, you went back to Old Times, and told us that you had been in Possession of the Province of Maryland for above one hundred Years; but what is one hundred Years in comparison to the length of Time since our Claim began? Since we came out of this ground? For we must tell you that long before one hundred years our Ancestors came out of this very ground, and their children have remained here ever since.... You came out of the ground in a country that lies beyond the Seas; there you may have a just Claim, but here you must allow us to be your elder Brethren, and the lands to belong to us before you knew anything of them.
>
> It is true, that above one hundred years ago the Dutch came here in a ship.... During all this time the newcomers, the Dutch, acknowledged our right to the lands....
>
> After this the English came into the country, and, as we were told, became one people with the Dutch. About two years after the arrival of the English, an English governor came to Albany, and finding what great friendship subsisted between us and the Dutch, he approved it mightily, and desired to make as strong a league, and to be upon as good terms with us as the Dutch were....
>
> Indeed we have had some small differences with the English, and, during these misunderstandings, some of their young men would, by way of reproach, be every now and then telling us that we should have perished if they had not come into the country and furnished us with strouds [blankets] and hatchets and guns, and other things necessary for the support of life. But we always gave them to understand that they were mistaken, that we lived before they came amongst us, and as well, or better, if we may believe what

our forefathers have told us. We then had room enough, and plenty of deer, which was easily caught; and though we had not knives, hatchets, or guns, such as we have now, yet we had knives of stone, and hatchets of stone, and bows and arrows, and those served our uses as well as the English ones do now.

We are now straitened, and sometimes in want of deer, and liable to many other inconveniences since the English came among us, and particularly from that pen-and-ink work that is going on at that table.[81]

Canasatego's words demonstrate continuity in the recollection of the history of his people with the British. In addition, his message summarizes many of the ecological changes resulting from European colonization. In this, he asserts that treaties and other agreements have had a direct impact in causing the "poor" times the Haudenosaunee were then faced with.

Town Settlements, Refugees, and Housing Patterns

Most of the written record of this period focuses upon external Haudenosaunee land dealings, especially treaty councils. Less evidence exists regarding the internal impacts of those land deals on the villages and nations of the Haudenosaunee. Information reflected in the written record documents town settlements, the impact of refugees within villages, and shifts in housing patterns.

The Mohawks, as the easternmost nation, faced the largest onslaught of British people and culture. As they made room in their territory for the colonists, they shifted into a more sedentary village pattern. In the previous centuries, they occupied a village from fifteen to fifty years and moved once the neighbouring fields lost fertility and nearby resources became scarce. In the eighteenth century, the Mohawks established permanent villages, often referred to in the records as "towns," but continued to inhabit satellite villages.[82] The length of village site occupation extended, but the types of interaction remained fairly constant in this period. The satellite villages demonstrate the continuity of hunting and other harvesting activities. They also had taken to living in "small cabins" (as noted in 1705 by Reverend Moore, regarding Fort Hunter), but not exclusively, as is often assumed.[83] In 1750, Conrad Weiser and Daniel Claus documented a journey through Mohawk country to Onondaga. In this journal they describe Fort Hunter: "This castle had a garrison of [*left blank*] soldiers, otherwise most of the inhabitants were Indians [who lived] in houses built of tree bark. We had to take up quarters at one of the Indian chiefs, by the name of Brant,[84] in German, Brand, and we really could not find fault with it; for he lived in a well built, 2 story house, provided with furniture like that of a middle class family; there was nothing wanting in our food or drink or in our beds."[85] This passage demonstrates a diversity of housing structures in use in the Lower Mohawk town. While it is quite clear, based upon archaeological and written evidence, that the Mohawks had ceased building longhouses by this time, they did continue to construct a variety of houses, some of logs, some of poles and bark, and some in combination of both.[86] Often the shift from longhouses and other bark structures to log cabins is presented as a sign of acculturation; however, as evidenced in the Claus and Weiser account, the Mohawks had adapted log structure technology and combined it with available resources. In other words, this became an adaptation rather than an acculturation.

Like all the Five Nations, the Oneidas experienced an influx of refugees in the eighteenth century, including the most well-known of all the refugee nations to the Confederacy, the Tuscaroras. The Tuscaroras originated in the Carolinas and spoke a language similar to those of the Haudenosaunee.[87] When the Five Nations reported the addition of the Tuscaroras to the Confederacy, they were described as follows: "they were of us and went from us long ago, and now are returned and promise to live peaceably among us."[88] British colonists had moved into their homelands, and the Tuscarora efforts to remove them became known as the Tuscarora War. They were defeated by the colonial forces and sought refuge with their northern relatives of the Confederacy.[89] In 1713, an Onondaga speaker reported to the governor of New York about their standing as a protected nation under the Haudenosaunee: "They have abandoned their Castles and are scattered hither and thither; let that suffice; and we request our Brother Corlear to act as mediator between the English of Carrelyna and the Tuskaroras that they may no longer be hunted down, and we assume that we will oblige them not to do the English any more harm, for they are no longer a nation with a name, being once dispersed."[90] The record states the Tuscaroras were officially accepted as the sixth nation of the Confederacy in 1722, and the name "Six Nations" appears in a treaty with the British in the following year.[91] In the 1730s, members of the Meherrin and Nottaway nations sought Haudenosaunee protection and settled among the Tuscaroras.[92] As was the case with many refugees in the 1700s, these adoptees added to the Haudenosaunee population but not to the territorial base of the Confederacy.

Similar to the Oneidas, the Onondagas also established satellite villages near the main Onondaga town to accommodate their refugee population. Doxtator writes that "by the mid-eighteenth century, Onondaga was in fact, made up of five smaller towns, each in the form of a scattered clustering of houses. This dispersed town settlement pattern ... reflected the composite nature of many landless national fragments coming together under Rotinonhsyonni protection. While previous village patterns had incorporated different clans within a shared area, eighteenth century villages incorporated different refugee groups who lost their own lands and so brought no new territories with them. As a result they had to connect to existing Rotinonhsyonni lands and social organizations."[93] In the Haudenosaunee oral record, it is explained that these refugee satellite villages allowed the adopted Haudenosaunee to acclimate to their new surroundings and relatives. In accordance with the Great Law, these villages also provided a means by which refugees could maintain their distinct social, political, and religious structures, if they so chose.

The Cayugas experienced a population influx as members of the Conoy, Nanticoke, and Tutelo nations sought refuge in their territory. The Conoy Nation, originally from the Potomac River area, approached the Haudenosaunee and were allowed to settle in Confederacy territory in Pennsylvania in the 1740s. They joined the Nanticoke Nation at Otsiningo and by 1758 the two peoples were considered to be one nation. The Nanticokes (relatives of the Delaware Nation), who originally lived in the Maryland-Delaware area, had sought Haudenosaunee protection in 1743. By 1753, then living on the Chemung River, the Nanticoke were admitted into the Confederacy, under the wing of the Cayugas, who referred to them as Ganawagohono ("people of the rapids"). The Tutelo Nation fled from their southern homelands in the Virginia area in 1753, being allowed refuge among the Cayuga Nation as well.[94] They maintained a distinct identity under the Cayugas for over a century, with most of them following their new relatives to the Grand River Territory in 1784.[95]

In the eighteenth century, Seneca political jurisdiction covered their homelands region in the Genesee River Valley and spread into the Confederacy's western hunting grounds of the Ohio River Valley and present-day southern Ontario. In these lands, the Senecas took in peoples from scores of different nations, most of whom adapted to a Seneca identity over time. Like their eastern neighbours in the Confederacy, the Senecas had altered their residential patterns from the centralized large villages of the previous century to smaller, more dispersed settlements.[96] While some longhouses remained in the older settlements,[97] new Seneca villages were comprised mainly of cabin-like structures that accommodated two families who shared a single hearth. While this was a major shift from the longhouses of previous generations—where several families belonging to a larger matrilineal clan shared one housing structure—the shared hearth of the cabins allowed for the primary unit of interdependence—the relationship "across the fire"—to continue. This also allowed for a continuity in relationships within a clan, wherein the two families could continue to assist each other as their ancestors had within the longhouses (and as many of their contemporaries continued to do at that time). The dispersed pattern of the newer villages was another adaptation; with the houses further apart, it would require more work for attackers to have a significant impact in terms of destroying a village, and with fewer people living in smaller quarters, the spread of infectious disease was lessened. The Senecas had an extensive network of satellite villages throughout the Ohio River Valley, where they remained active in the fur trade throughout the mid-1700s. Members of the eastern Haudenosaunee nations also hunted in this area as commercial game became exhausted in areas closer to their homes. In many ways, the Seneca territory became a melting pot of various peoples who were blending into Haudenosaunee society.

Like the century before it, the 1700s witnessed major demographic changes for the Haudenosaunee. They continued to accept new peoples into the Confederacy, including the Tuscarora, who became known as the sixth nation. Population shifts, epidemic disease, and threats of warfare affected the housing needs of the nations. In many ways, the shifts in population match the shifts in housing types. The newer, smaller cabins also contributed to a more defendable village structure. Doxtator summarizes these shifts:

> Rotinonhsyonni ecological, demographic and settlement patterns
> of the seventeenth and eighteenth centuries helped to direct the
> different responses of each community to changes in the nineteenth
> century. The Mohawk response came from a tradition of nearly a
> century of successfully integrating European ideas of land tenure,
> and aspects of their agricultural complex into the Rotinonhsyonni
> pattern of the two sides. The Seneca lived more removed from the
> dense European settlement than the Mohawks. They experienced
> far less ecological change and did not adapt their settlement or
> economies to incorporate so closely European ideas. The overall
> demographic decline of the Rotinonhsyonni population during the

eighteenth century led to re-combinations of groups and involved incorporating refugee nations…. Eighteenth century settlement innovations such as the Mohawk permanent village and the shift among all Rotinonhsyonni to smaller cabin-sized dwellings helped to direct nineteenth century responses to decreases in land bases.[98]

Even though villages, houses, and land holdings had changed, the Haudenosaunee persisted in their view of the land as central to their being. In 1732, in the midst of filing a land claim against Philip Livingston, the Mohawk speaker summed it up best: "then Mr. Livingston has murdered us asleep, for our land is our life."[99] Clearly, the Haudenosaunee not only continued to see the earth as Mother, but still understood their dependence upon her for their survival and the continuation of all life.

Tarnishing the Chain

As evidenced in the various land disputes between the Confederacy and the British, strained relations were commonplace in the eighteenth century. While British officials often tried to make amends to the Haudenosaunee for colonists' encroachments and land thefts, the reality inflicted a toll upon the Covenant Chain. British colonists also warred against some First Nations in the South who were related to the Haudenosaunee, in particular, the Tuscarora Nation. Similarly, the French continued to court the Haudenosaunee and made many successful inroads among the Senecas and Onondagas, in addition to the French-friendly settlements along the St. Lawrence. In fact, by 1750 it appeared that the Confederacy might back the French in the brewing war between French and British colonial interests. If it were not for Sir William Johnson—and the close bonds he held with many Haudenosaunee leaders—the British might have lost their most important North American ally. Had that occurred, the Crown would certainly have lost much of its territorial interests as well.

Johnson had become a skilled diplomat in his dealings with the Haudenosaunee. By learning the Mohawk language, Johnson gained an important edge in his work with the Confederacy. He was able to better understand the Haudenosaunee perspective in council meetings and, as a result, developed a much deeper understanding of Haudenosaunee society than any other British official working with the Six Nations. His ability to articulate key aspects of Haudenosaunee philosophy gained him a great deal of trust among the Confederacy leadership of the day. He even participated in a condolence ceremony to raise a new Royaner at Onondaga in 1756.[100] Examples of his knowledge appear in passionate speeches that demonstrated a strong memory, such as his address to the Grand Council at Onondaga on 25 April 1748:

> Brethren of the Five Nations,
>
> I will begin upon a thing of long standing, our first Brothership. My Reason for it is, I think there are several among you who seem to forget it; It may seem strange to you how I a Foreigner should know this, But I tell you I found out some of the old Writings of our Forefathers which was thought to have been lost, and in this old valuable record I find, that our first Friendship Commenced at the Arrival of the first great Canoe or Vessel at Albany, at which time you were much surprized but finding what it contained pleased you much, being Things for your Purpose, . . . you all resolved to take the greatest care of that Vessel that nothing should hurt her; Whereupon it was agreed to tie her fast with a great Rope to one of the largest Nut trees on the Bank of the River. But on further consideration in a fuller Meeting it was thought safest, Fearing the Wind should blow down that Tree, to make a long Rope and tye her fast at Onondaga which was accordingly done and the Rope put under your Feet That if anything hurt or touched said Vessel by the shaking of the Rope you might know it, and then agreed to rise all as one and see what the Matter was and whoever hurt the Vessel was to suffer.
>
> After this was agreed on and done you made an offer to the Governor to enter into a Bond of Friendship with him and his People which he was so pleased at that he told you he would find a strong Silver Chain which would never break, slip or Rust, to bind you and him in Brothership together, and that your Warriors and ours should be as one Heart, one Blood, &ca. and that what happened to the one happened to the other. After this firm agreement was made our Forefathers finding it was good and foreseeing the many Advantages both sides would reap of it, Ordered that if ever that Silver Chain should turn the least Rusty, offer to slip or break, that it should be immediately brightened up again, and not let it slip or break on any account for then you and we were both dead.[101]

While he did not achieve unanimous trust and support from the Haudenosaunee, Johnson's influence allowed the British to maintain a grasp on the Covenant Chain and the continued alliance of the Haudenosaunee. His ability to "polish the chain" after the actions of British subjects had tarnished it proved absolutely essential to the continuity of the Haudenosaunee-British alliance.

However, in June 1753, the relationship became so strained that the Confederacy declared the Covenant Chain broken. Haudenosaunee speakers, such as Hendrick Tekarihoken, addressed New York governor Clinton, raising issues of French raids and land frauds. "We are come here to remind you of the ancient alliance agreed on between our respective forefathers," said Hendrick. He continued:

> We are united together by a covenant chain and it now seems likely to be broken not from our fault but yours. . . .
>
> My heart aches because we Mohawks have always been faithful to you… especially in this last war [when] there was no assistance given you but by our Nations, and had the war lasted some time longer we would have torn the Frenchmen's hearts out. . . .
>
> You sit in peace and quietness here whilst we are exposed to the enemy. . . . It is by your means that we stand every hour in danger. . . .
>
> When our brethren the English first came among us we gave and sold them lands, and have continued to do so ever since, but it seems now as if we had no lands left for ourselves. . . .
>
> We desire our brother [Governor Clinton] to let us see the patents [title deeds] . . . by this we shall know who have cheated us.
>
> I am going to tell you how many persons we design to drive away from our lands. Viz. Barclay, Pritchett's wife who lives just by us and who does us a great deal of damage by selling us liquors and by that means making us destroy one another. . . . We let her have a little spot of land and she takes in more and more every year.[102]
>
> [Clinton's response was not favorable; Hendrick left after making the following statement:]
>
> When we came here to relate our grievances about our lands, we expected to have something done . . . and Brother you tell us that we shall be redressed at Albany. But we know them so well, we will not trust to them, for they are no people but Devils. . . .

The covenant chain is broken. . . . You are not to expect to hear of
me any more, and Brother we desire to hear no more of you.[103]

In September, Johnson met with the Confederacy at Onondaga in an attempt
to mend the Covenant Chain. An Onondaga speaker declared that the Chain
was renewed and explained the Confederacy's concern about the French
hostilities in the Ohio River Valley.[104]

The various Haudenosaunee concerns and their problems with Governor
Clinton inspired the Board of Trade to organize the Albany Conference in
June 1754.[105] The British used this conference to reaffirm the Covenant Chain
and also to plant subtle reminders that through the Chain, the Haudenosaunee
had an obligation to support any military efforts of the British against the
French. In addition to the comments about the French, New York governor
James DeLancey addressed Haudenosaunee settlement patterns: "We are
informed that you now live dispersed from each other contrary to the ancient
and prudent custom of your Forefathers; and as you are by this means,
exposed to the attempts of your enemies, we therefore in the most earnest
manner recommend to, and expect it from you, for your own safety, to collect
yourselves together, and dwell in your National Castles."[106] Part of DeLancey's
concern centred on the Onondaga settlement of Oswegatchie, known to be
French-friendly. To DeLancey, the presence of French support among some
of the Six Nations could have led the others of the Confederacy to shift
away from the Covenant Chain and support the French in the upcoming
war. Responding to DeLancey, the Haudenosaunee explained that some
of the more distant villages appreciated the treatment they received from
the French but promised that they would remind those villages about the
Covenant Chain and encourage them to act accordingly. They also continued
to call attention to their land claims. Finally, they requested that Johnson
be reinstated in his former position of managing Indian affairs for the New
York colonial government. DeLancey requested, and was granted, a one-year
trial period in which the colony would investigate the land claims under the
newly established Albany Commissioners of Indian Affairs. The Albany
Commissioners proved themselves unsuccessful, and in 1755 Johnson was
named imperial superintendent general of Indian Affairs, reporting to the
British government rather than the colonial one. He attempted to address
the issue of fraudulent patents in instructions to New York governor Charles
Hardy on 20 May 1755:

> You are therefore in His Majesty's name, to give the most explicit
> Assurances to the said [Five] Nations or Cantons of Indians of His
> Royal Resolution inviolably to Observe the said Treaty [the 1726
> confirmation of the 1701 deed] on his part, and to defend and sup-
> port them in the quiet Possession of their said Hunting Grounds;
>
> And you are not upon any Pretence whatsoever to grant lands to
> any Person whatever within the Limits described in the said Deed,
> but to use Your utmost Endeavours to prevent any Settlements
> being made within the same. . . .
>
> And whereas purchasing Lands from the Indians, without a
> Licence from His Majesty or from any Person acting under
> his Authority, is inconsistent with his rights and may indanger
> the Peace and Security of his said Province, It is, therefore, His
> Majesty's Will and Pleasure, that you do not upon any Pretence
> whatsoever make a Grant or Grants to any Person or Persons of any
> Lands within the said Province purchased of the Indians, without
> a Licence and obtained from you for that Purpose.[107]

While Johnson's position is clear, the record demonstrates that the colonial
government did not heed his instructions (as a representative of the imperial
government), and full-scale encroachment persisted in the Mohawk Valley
without intervention on New York's part.

In 1755, full-scale war had broken out again between the British and the
French, and the Crown sought the assistance of their old allies through the
Covenant Chain. Often in their attempts to garner Haudenosaunee support
in the war, British officials appealed under both the Covenant Chain and the
1701 Nanfan Treaty. On 16 April 1755, Governor Shirley of Massachusetts
provided the following instructions to Johnson:

> You are to produce to the Indians of the Six Nations a Deed which
> will be delivered to you by Col. Shirley and in my Name to recite
> to them the following instructions . . .
>
> Whereas it appears by a Treaty of the Five Nations made at
> Albany on ye 19 day of July 1701 between John Nanfan Lt. Govr.
> of the Province of New York that the saied Five Nations did
> putt all their Beaver Hunting which they won with the sword
> 80 years ago, under the Protection of the King of England, to

be Garrantyed by him to them & their use & it also appearing
by a Deed executed in the year 1726 between the three Nations
Cayugae Senekae & Onondaga & the then Govr. of New York
that the saied three Nations did surrender all the land lyeing and
being sixty miles Distance taken directly from the Waters into
the Country beginning from a Creek call'd Canahoge to the Lake
Okswego extending along the saied Lake to ye Falls of Okniagara
& along the Lake Caderaquis to Sodons Creek & from Sodons
Creek to ye Hill called Tegurhunksaroda & from thence to the
Creek called Cayuga-aga as is now particularly describ'd in the
saied Deed including all the Castles of the aforesaid Three Nations
with all the Rivers Creeks & Lakes within the saied Limits to be
protected & defended by his saied Majesty His Heirs & Successors
for ever to & for the life of them the saied three nations their Heirs
& Successors for ever. And it appearing that the French have
from time to time by Fraud & violence built strong Forts within
ye Limits of the saied Land, contrary to the purport of the [saied]
Covenant Chain & ye saied Deed & Treaty, you are in my name to
assure the Saied Nations that I am come by His Majesty's Order to
destroy all ye saied Forts & to build such others as shall protect &
secure the saied Lands to them their Heirs & successors for ever
according to ye intent & spirit of the Saied Treaty & therefore call
upon them to take up the Hatchet & come & take Possession of
their own Lands.[108]

Later that year, General Braddock asserted similar sentiments to the
Haudenosaunee through Johnson:

as it appears that the French from time to time by fraud and by
violence have constructed strong forts within the limits of the
aforesaid lands in contravention of the agreements expressed in
the said contract and treaty, you will assure the said nations in my
name that I have come on the part and in the name of His Majesty
to destroy all the said forts and to build some which will suffice to
protect the said lands and *to insure them to them and their successors
for ever agreeably to the object and the spirit of the treaty. And, for
this purpose, summon them to take up the hatchet and to come and take
possession of their own lands.*[109]

These passages not only note the desire of the British to gain Haudenosaunee assistance in the war but also demonstrate that the British recognized these lands as being Haudenosaunee territory. Further evidence regarding the British use of the Nanfan Treaty was recorded in a letter Thomas Pownall wrote to Johnson from New York on 16 August 1755:

> Mentioning the Deed by which the English became guaranty to the Indians for the use of their lands &c., & put the expedition upon the footing of coming not to possess their lands & take the Dominion of them, but to drive the French off who by fraud & violence had encroached upon them, to destroy their forts & build such others as should protect their lands to their own use according to the true spirit & Tenor of our alliance & Covenant Chain. *I showed them the Deed, explained the state of the Case, as it arose from the Indians own idea of it,*[110] and dictated every word of the Instruction. Upon which the General said this by God is giving some reason for what we are going to do, & I added not only a reason, Sir, but a right. I should be glad to hear from you what effect the giving the Treaty this turn, had upon the Indian Affairs.[111]

The British references to the 1701 Nanfan Treaty, and their oath to protect Six Nations interests as articulated in that treaty, proved successful as the Haudenosaunee joined their war efforts—although reluctantly in many cases—against the French.

It is also important to note that the British were not only aware of the Haudenosaunee affinity for the Nanfan Treaty, but they were also well acquainted with the Haudenosaunee understanding of that treaty. In 1755, Johnson described the Six Nations' viewpoint in this way:

> That memorable and important act by which the Indians put their Patrimonial and conquered lands under the Protection of the King of Great Britain their Father is not understood by them as a cession or surrender as it seems to have been ignorantly or wilfuly supposed by some, they intended and look upon it as reserving the Property and Possession of the soil to themselves and their heirs. This property the Six Nations are by no means willing to part with and are equally averse and jealous that any Forts or Settlements should be made thereon either by us or the French.[112]

Johnson's words are especially important when considering the Crown's later representation of the treaty and its impact upon the Grand River Haudenosaunee following their move there in 1784.

"Great Frauds and Abuses"

Like many of their predecessors, the British colonists of the 1760s pushed farther and farther into Haudenosaunee territory, often without the proper consent from the Confederacy. The colonists' land encroachments continued to spread in the years following the Seven Years' War. British disregard of their promises to protect Haudenosaunee land interests also grew. Once the French were out of the way, the British appeared less concerned about maintaining the Covenant Chain. Williams and Nelson assert that British policy makers desired to protect the Haudenosaunee interests.[113] Unfortunately, in order to maintain some balance within the colony, those charged with enforcing policies often failed to do so.

Tensions grew between the Haudenosaunee and the British over several key issues. First, the Mohawks were extremely frustrated over the Crown's failure to reverse New York's upholding of the Canajohare and Kayadohsera patents.[114] This came despite the fact that Johnson himself had attested to the illegality of these patents. He noted that the signatories to the deed had been approached one by one instead of in open council and that they included people who had no right to the land, children, and people who had been so drunk when they signed that they later had no knowledge of their actions.[115] On 26 June 1763, he noted the obvious imbalance between British and Indigenous concepts of land rights: "The lawsuit concerning the upper Mohawks property having yesterday ended in a Manner verry dissatisfactory to the—because as it is alleged matters in equity cannot be considered a Common Law, and a Pattent however fraudulently obtained in a Claim superior to all Justice and Reason."[116] The fact that colonial officials would use any avenue available to them to usurp Haudenosaunee land was well proven in this case. The British provided further disappointment through their occupation of French-built forts in the Ohio Territory. They had promised to destroy them when the French were removed from the Haudenosaunee hunting grounds but instead had begun improvements upon them. Finally, a Connecticut-based land speculating group, the Susquehanna Company, declared its intentions to settle 300 families along the Susquehanna River—an important area within Haudenosaunee, and specifically Seneca, hunting grounds. This land had never been ceded. This fuelled Seneca discontent and pushed them to consider the urgings of war from their southern and western allies.

In response to the many issues raised to the Crown by various Native nations, including the Haudenosaunee, the King issued a Royal Proclamation on 7 October 1763. Excerpts of the decree follow:

> And whereas, it is just and reasonable, and essential to our Interest, and the Security of our Colonies, that the several Nations or Tribes of Indians with whom we are connected, or who live under our Protection, should not be molested or disturbed in the Possession of such Parts of our Dominions and Territories as, not having been ceded to or purchased by us, are reserved to them, or any of them, as their Hunting Grounds.
>
> And whereas great Frauds and abuses have been committed in purchasing Lands of the Indians, to the great Prejudice of our Interests, and to the great Dissatisfaction of the said Indians. In order, therefore, to prevent such Irregularities for the future, and to the end that the Indians may be convinced of our Justice and determined Resolution to remove all Reasonable Cause of Discontent, We do, with the Advice of our Privy Council strictly enjoin and require, that no Private person do presume to make any purchase from the said Indians of any lands, reserved to the said Indians, within those parts of our Colonies where We have thought proper to allow Settlement; but that, If at any time any of the said Indians should be inclined to dispose of the said Lands, the same shall be Purchased only for Us, in our Name, at some public Meeting or Assembly of the said Indians, to be held for that purpose by the Governor or Commander in Chief of our Colony respectively within which they shall lie.[117]

There are several key phrases within the Royal Proclamation that are directly relevant to Haudenosaunee issues with the Crown. First, the Proclamation specifies two different types of Crown-Native relations: those with whom they "are connected" and those who "live under [their] Protection." While the British had promised to protect Haudenosaunee interests in their territories, the Haudenosaunee fell under the first category as "connected" nations, meaning that they remained sovereign. This is evidenced directly in many references to the Covenant Chain, with the analogy of "linking arms" metaphorically connecting the two peoples. Second, the idea of "great frauds and abuses" spoke directly to the fraudulent patents in the Mohawk Valley.

While there were certainly other Native claims made against British colonists, the Mohawk patents were very fresh in the Crown's memory and they were under extreme pressure from the Haudenosaunee and Johnson to address the wrongful patents and New York's upholding of them. Finally, in the King's stated desire "to remove all Reasonable Cause of Discontent," he was referencing (among other situations) Pontiac's Rebellion of 1763–64, which had received support from many of the Senecas as well as several allied nations of the Confederacy. It was clear to the Crown that if they did not address the many issues of the Haudenosaunee and their Native neighbours, they were likely to band together against the British and their colonists. It was hoped that the Royal Proclamation would put an end to that possibility. In many ways, it probably did assist in reducing the support for Pontiac's War (both from the Haudenosaunee as well as other nations) against the British, but it actually did nothing to address the past abuses nor did it create a forum that could address them. It was simply crafted as a preventative tool for future situations. Hindsight demonstrates, especially regarding Haudenosaunee interests, that it was very limited in that regard as well.

As the Crown's representative to the Six Nations, Johnson had the responsibility of disseminating information on the Royal Proclamation to the Confederacy. On 24 December 1763, he declared the proclamation in effect throughout the territories of the Haudenosaunee.[118] Next, he set out to visit the different nations, but his travels were hindered by winter weather. He wrote about the proclamation on 23 December, noting its failure to address past wrongs:

> I am hopefull that . . . there Lordships will be able still farther to contribute towards the salutary Points in view relative to the Indians. This Proclamation does not relieve their present Grievances which are many, being calculated only to prevent the like hereafter, altho' there are numberless instances of Tracts which have indeed been purchased, but in the most illegal & fraudulent manner, all which demands redress. I have at this Meeting made the best use in my power of His Majesty's Proclamation for convincing the Indians here of his gracious & favourable disposition to do them Justice, & shall communicate the same to all the rest.[119]

Despite his misgivings about the proclamation, Johnson set out to inform the Haudenosaunee of its declaration and intent. Before the end of January 1764, Johnson had met with each of the Six Nations.[120]

But, as Williams and Nelson have noted, the Royal Proclamation was being used as a tool for both peace and war. They write, "Johnson wanted to reassure the eastern nations of the Confederacy that they 'need be under no apprehension' concerning their lands, to prevent them from joining the war against the British, while at the same time encouraging them to join the British army that would punish the Shawnees and Delawares and others who had fought the British. The situation was delicate: the Senecas had also attacked the British, and the other nations of the Confederacy were reluctant to fight their own people."[121] The above describes the situation prior to the 1764 Niagara Strip Treaty. In many ways, that treaty became a means for both the Haudenosaunee and the Crown to repair part of their very strained relationship. The Senecas offered important parts of their territory to be placed under the protection of the King. Surely, part of their motivation must have been appeasement for the participation of some of their people in Pontiac's efforts. Coupled with the transfer of land to the protection of the King, the Senecas also made a personal gift of the islands in the Niagara River to Johnson.[122] Notably, this "gift" directly violated the Royal Proclamation. The islands were given directly to Johnson and were not first surrendered to the Crown—as required under the proclamation. However, in recent court cases, the "gift" has been upheld and the land remains firmly in the hands of non-Haudenosaunee.[123] The placement of the lands under the King's protection has also been misinterpreted. The Seneca cession was very specific and limited it to be used "only for the King's purposes," disallowing patents to private individuals.[124] Johnson described the conditions in a letter to Cadwallader Colden on 23 August 1764:

> The Senecas have likewise given up to His Majesty all the land from Lake Ontario to Lake Erie 4 Miles in Depth on each Side of the Strait for the use of the Several Garrisons which is more than Double the Quantity their Deputys agreed to last Spring, the Isleands (one of which is verry large) they insisted on my acceptance of, to show their esteem, & make my mind easy (as they called it) after the Delays I had met with.

> The behaviour of the Senecas cannot fail, operateing Strongly on the Shawanese & Delawares, as well as all the Nations for they are a people of much power, & Influence over the rest.[125]

Seneca influence with the western First Nations was considered critical for the British in order to gain stability in the Ohio region. For their part, the Senecas trusted in the limitations of the treaty, especially in the fact that they had placed their lands under the King's protection but had not made an actual cession. They believed this would protect their various interests, and they trusted that the British had finally addressed some of their most pressing concerns. Yet, in its limitations, the Niagara Strip Treaty closely resembled the 1701 Nanfan Treaty.

While the 1764 Niagara Strip Treaty brought the Senecas firmly back into the Covenant Chain, issues around the eastern border between the Haudenosaunee and the British still needed to be formally addressed. The line described in the Royal Proclamation was intended to be temporary only, and the responsibility of securing a permanent line with the Haudenosaunee fell upon Johnson. A treaty council was held at Fort Stanwix in October 1768 to achieve this goal. Given past transgressions, the Haudenosaunee were reluctant to relinquish any more territory. During a private Haudenosaunee council at Fort Stanwix, a speaker reminded Johnson of these concerns:

> Brother
>
> We have been some time deliberating on what you said concerning a boundary line between the English & us, and we are sensible that it could be for our mutual advantage, if it was not transgressed, but daily experience teaches us that we cannot have any great dependence on the white people and that they will forget their agreements for the sake of our lands, however, you have said so much upon it, that we are willing to believe more favourably in their cases.[126]

Johnson's participation in the council and his personal promises carried a great deal of influence toward convincing the Haudenosaunee to consent to the treaty. They did so with an understanding that the Covenant Chain would never again be allowed to tarnish. This they clearly stipulated in their agreement to the treaty: "We now tell the King that we have given him a great and valuable country, and we know that what we shall now get for it must be far short of its value. We make it a condition of this our agreement concerning the line, that His Majesty will not forget or neglect to show us his favour, or suffer the chain to contract rust, but that he will direct those who have the management of our affairs to be punctual in renewing our ancient agreement."[127] The Haudenosaunee well understood the value of the land they ceded; they did so not for the financial compensation but because of the bonds

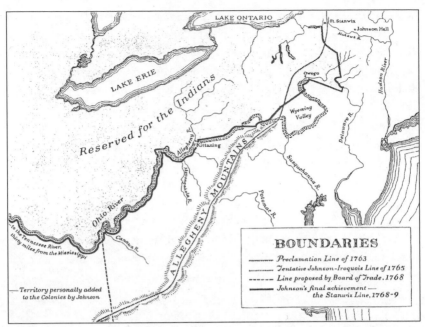

Map 1. Map of 1763 Royal Proclamation and 1768 Fort Stanwix Boundaries.
Source: From the Collection of the Haudenosaunee Standing Committee on Burials and Repatriation.

of family they shared with the British. While the Haudenosaunee ceded "a great territory" they were careful to retain hunting rights within the ceded lands and limited the British from hunting on "our side of the line." This marked a shift in Haudenosaunee-British relations. Previously, in an extension of the principle of the Dish with One Spoon, the Haudenosaunee and the British had agreed to share hunting grounds. This was an obvious attempt on the part of the Confederacy to protect their remaining lands from future encroachment, which often began with colonists hunting on Haudenosaunee lands. This attempt, and the entire treaty, failed to do what it had set out to accomplish. Just five years later, in 1773, British trader George Croghan estimated that 60,000 whites had violated the Fort Stanwix Treaty line and had settled in Haudenosaunee territory (see Map 1).[128]

The failure of the 1768 Fort Stanwix Treaty—and the obvious violation of it by the colonists—greatly saddened the Haudenosaunee. It became another reminder of the Crown's inability, or unwillingness, to protect their interests, even when promised under the most solemn of agreements. On 21 May 1783, Joseph Brant reiterated the disappointment with that treaty:

Wherefore, we on our side have maintained an uninterrupted attachment towards you, in confidence and expectation of a Reciprocity, and to establish a Perpetual Friendship and Alliance between us, of which we can give you several instances, to wit, a few years after the Conquest of Canada, your people in this country thought themselves confined on account of their numbers with regard to a Scarcity of Land, we were applied to for giving up some of ours, and fix a Line or Mark between them & us. We considered upon it, and relinquished a great Territory to the King for the use of his Subjects, for a trifling Consideration, merely as a Confirmation of said Act, and as a proof of our sincere regard towards them. This happened so late as the year 1768 at Fort Stanwix, and was gratefully accepted and ratified by the different Governors and great men of the respective Colonies of the Sea Side, in presence of our late Worthy Friend and Superintendent, Sir William Johnson, when we expected a Permanent, Brotherly Love and Amity, would be the Consequence, but in vain.[129]

Again—as Canasatego had articulated nearly forty years earlier—Brant reminded the British that the Six Nations had not ceded the land for the financial compensation, but rather had done so under the belief that family members have an obligation to provide for each other. The idea of brotherhood was articulated in the Kaswentha and the Covenant Chain. Following the principles of the Dish with One Spoon, the Haudenosaunee again demonstrated the need for family to take care of each other. In these agreements, the Haudenosaunee had extended their land—which had provided for them—to their new brethren, the British. In the actions of the British colonists, and the Crown's unwillingness to enforce their own laws, it had become painfully clear that the Crown was not nearly as good a brother as the Confederacy.

A Call to War

Beyond its inability to address Haudenosaunee and other Indigenous land grievances, the Royal Proclamation fuelled growing discontent among many of the people of the Thirteen Colonies. Many historians deem it to be a primary impetus of the War of American Independence that started twelve years later. As tempers flared, leaders of both the British and the colonists courted the Haudenosaunee, seeking assistance in the impending struggle. Initially, the Grand Council favoured neutrality in the war, but eventually determined that

each nation would make its own decisions about its individual national participation.[130] Collectively, the Confederacy was deeply affected by the violations of
the Fort Stanwix line. They knew it was the colonists[131] actually perpetrating
the violations, but they also believed that the Crown had a responsibility to
protect Haudenosaunee territory, regardless of who was violating the agreements. Many also felt that the conflict was between "a father and child" and it
was not their place to interfere. Others remarked on their esteem for both the
British and the colonists and wished not to take sides between two peoples
for whom they cared.

At the onset of war, the individual nations attempted to remain neutral.
Very quickly, however, many of the Mohawk warriors were enticed to support
the British. Shortly after that, several Oneidas (along with some Tuscaroras)
joined colonial forces. The Onondagas, Cayugas, and Senecas maintained
neutrality until 1779, when the Americans marched into their territories
on a rampage ordered by General George Washington. Troops with the
Clinton-Sullivan Campaign tore through the western Haudenosaunee
villages, destroying all of the major towns with a massive military action.[132] The
Haudenosaunee of these villages fled to Fort Niagara, where they took refuge
with the British. Facing similar attacks, many of the Mohawk people had fled
their homelands, making their way to British protection at Fort Niagara or
Lachine. Many Oneidas who did not support the Americans also made their
way to Niagara. As might be expected, many of the once-neutral Onondagas,
Cayugas, and Senecas joined British forces against the Americans following
the Clinton-Sullivan Campaign.

Both before and during the war, British military leaders promised the
Haudenosaunee that, in the event of a British surrender (which they never
believed would happen), the Crown would compensate any territorial losses
(including homes, crops, and land) experienced by their allies. In 1779, General
Haldimand (commander-in-chief of British forces in Quebec) echoed an
earlier promise made by Carleton:

> Some of the Mohawks of the Villages of Conajoharie, Tujondarago,
> and Aughwago, whose settlements there, had been upon account of
> their steady attachment to the King's Service and the Interests of
> Government Ruined by the Rebels; having informed me, that my
> Predecessor Sir Guy Carleton, was pleased to promise, as soon as
> the present Troubles were at an end, the same should be restored
> at the Expence of Government, and the said Promise appearing

to me Just, I do hereby ratify the same, and assure them the said
Promise, as far as in me lies, shall be faithfully executed, as soon as
that happy Time come.[133]

These promises, along with the refuge provided at Niagara and Lachine,
were not products of recent negotiations between the Haudenosaunee and
the British but came as the result of the Covenant Chain relationship. The
first British-Haudenosaunee treaty, established in 1664, provided that the
British would shelter the Five Nations if they were to lose their war against
the "River Indians." The 1701 Nanfan Treaty carried similar provisions as the
Haudenosaunee placed their hunting grounds under the protection of the
King. These promises were echoed in subsequent treaty agreements, demonstrating the continuity of the relationship between the two allies, whereby
the Crown guaranteed the protection of Haudenosaunee interests and, in
the event of a war loss, promised to provide adequate financial and territorial
compensation for any losses.

However, in 1783, when the British negotiated the Paris Peace Treaty
with the Thirteen Colonies, they failed to include provisions for their
Haudenosaunee allies in the treaty. In order to make amends for the oversight,
General Haldimand set about finding a territory suitable to compensate the
Haudenosaunee land losses in the war. Eventually the Haudenosaunee at Fort
Niagara selected the lands along the banks of the Grand River as their new
homeland; their selection was formalized under an agreement with Haldimand
in October 1784.

Ironically, the Americans were even less successful in addressing the needs
of their Oneida and Tuscarora war allies than the British had been. Under a
series of treaties (several of which were later deemed to be fraudulent) that
followed the war, the American colonists eventually claimed practically all
Oneida lands in what became New York State. The majority of the Oneida
people left their homelands, settling in a number of different places: Onondaga,
Grand River (with relatives who had supported the British during the war),
Thames River (on land they purchased from their treaty funds), and Wisconsin
(territory offered to them in exchange for some of their original lands). Today,
their recognized reservation land in New York State consists of just thirty-two
acres.[134] The Tuscarora fared better, as the Senecas offered them land along
the Niagara Escarpment not far from Fort Niagara. Many of the Tuscaroras,
like their previous host Oneidas, also chose to settle along the Grand River.

Beyond the different territorial impacts felt by the individual nations of the Confederacy, the Haudenosaunee remain affected to this day by the choices of some to enter the war. In the end, those who supported the British and the Americans drew all of their people into the conflict despite the desires of many to remain neutral. Both the British and the Americans failed to adequately provide for their allies after the war was over. The end result was an extremely limited territory within the original Haudenosaunee homelands, a resettlement of many Haudenosaunee into the western and northern hunting grounds, and internal strife that greatly weakened the familial bonds created by the Great Law. In many ways, the Confederacy has spent the last two centuries attempting to rectify the internal problems caused by the decisions to participate in the American Revolutionary War.

ooooo

The Haudenosaunee-British treaties of this period stand in a continuum under the umbrella of the Covenant Chain and treaties preceding it. British promises of refuge and protection in the event of war losses were made repeatedly but were never necessary until the British defeat in the American Revolutionary War. Under their treaties and other agreements, the British had promised to protect Haudenosaunee interests in their hunting grounds along the Grand River—territory that had been placed under the King's protection eight decades earlier in the Nanfan Treaty. This land was selected by many of the Haudenosaunee to become their new homeland. On 21 May 1783, Joseph Brant, as speaker for the Six Nations, addressed General Haldimand at Quebec in regard to the Crown's responsibilities to the Haudenosaunee:

> Brother,
> We, the Mohawks, were the first Indian Nation that took you by the hand like friends and brothers, and invited you to live amongst us, treating you with kindness upon your debarkation in small parties. The Oneidas, our neighbours, were equally well disposed towards you we fastened your ship to a great mountain at Onondaga, the Center of our Confederacy, the rest of the Five Nations approving of it. We were then a great people, conquering all Indian nations round about us, and you in a manner but a handfull, after which you increased by degrees and we continued your friends and allies, joining you from time to time against your enemies, sacrificing

numbers of our people and leaving their bones scattered in your enemies country. At last we assisted you in conquering all Canada, and then again, for joining you so firmly and faithfully, you renewed your assurances of protecting and defending ourselves, lands and possessions against any encroachment whatsoever, procuring for us the enjoyment of fair and plentiful trade of your people, and sat contented under the shade of the Tree of Peace, tasting the favour and friendship of a great Nation bound to us by Treaty, and able to protect us against all the world.[135]

In traditional Haudenosaunee fashion, Brant endeavoured to remind the British of the provisions of the Covenant Chain and demonstrated how the Six Nations had maintained their end of the relationship. Brant was also putting the Crown on notice as to their obligation to compensate the Haudenosaunee for their wartime losses. For many of the Haudenosaunee, that compensation meant land, as much of their territory had been lost, first, to settlers who violated the Fort Stanwix Treaty and earlier treaties and, second, to the Americans when the British signed it over to the United States through the Treaty of Paris.

   With their understanding of land as life, the Haudenosaunee were making clear the obligation of the British to secure them in a new homeland where they could once again live alongside the British as stipulated in the Kaswentha and the Covenant Chain. While this new homeland could not replace their old villages, fields, and surrounding forests—the lands that held the bones of their ancestors—they looked with hope toward moving to the hunting grounds and rebuilding their villages there. They knew that their new village sites would continue to provide for them as had the land of their original homes. After all, they had not been failed by creation, they had been failed by their relationships with other peoples. The hope was that the new homeland—carved out of their hunting grounds—and their rights to it would prove to be more respected by the British than their original homelands had been.

CHAPTER 4

Shotinonhsyonnih—They Built the Longhouse Again

Between 1784—the removal to and settlement on the Grand River—and 1847, the date of the last formal reduction of Haudenosaunee lands along the Grand River tract,[1] the Six Nations (along with the dependent nations)[2] endured great hardships. As they re-established their lives, they carved a homeland out of part of their western hunting grounds.[3] In this context, the speeches of several key Royaner from this era capture the sentiments of the Six Nations people regarding their dependence upon and respect for the land. In speech after speech, they call upon the King's representatives to recall the alliance between the Haudenosaunee and the Crown and, in so doing, preserve and protect the interests of the Six Nations along the Grand River, especially in regard to land. Yet, this eight-decade period, much like the eight decades preceding it, is marked by the inadequacy of Crown policies and laws—and their applications and interpretations—in upholding and implementing the promises the King and his representatives made to the Six Nations people. Time and time again, the Crown demonstrated that its promises to protect Haudenosaunee interests would be set aside in favour of the interests of white "settlers" along the Grand River tract.

Near the end of this era, and as a direct result of the Crown's unwillingness to protect Haudenosaunee lands from white squatters, the Six Nations found themselves in a situation similar to that experienced in the 1780s: moving again and having to start over, clearing land, building homes, and re-establishing their families. It was as if time had dealt them an eerie déjà vu: many of the

Grand River Haudenosaunee were again forced to relocate—the third move in as many generations for most of these families.

Return to the Homelands

Most Haudenosaunee villages had to be abandoned during the Revolutionary War. As refugees at Niagara and Lachine, many Haudenosaunee were faced with difficult choices of where to resettle their families at the close of the war. Conditions were difficult at both refugee locations, with widespread sickness, hunger, and despair. The Haudenosaunee needed to re-establish themselves in their own villages, where they could again provide for themselves and have greater control over their destiny. The British promised compensatory lands in Canada,[4] but the decision to leave their homelands in the east was not easy for any of the Haudenosaunee, with each nation having different concerns to consider and options to weigh.

Most of the Mohawks did not have the option of returning to their homelands in the Mohawk River Valley. As active allies of the Crown in the war—and due to the failure of the Crown to make provisions for any of its Haudenosaunee allies in the Treaty of Paris—the Mohawks *had* to find a new home. Toward the end of the war, many of the Mohawks took refuge at Lachine as well as with their eastern relatives in the Mohawk territories of Kahnawake, Akwesasne, and Kanehsatake. The majority of Mohawks,[5] however, made their way to Fort Niagara, where most of the other Haudenosaunee nations (primarily Onondaga, Cayuga, Seneca, and Tuscarora) took refuge after their villages and crops had been burned to the ground by the Clinton-Sullivan Campaign.[6] The Haudenosaunee protested to the British over having been omitted from the provisions of the peace treaty, and the Crown realized that it needed to make amends for this omission as soon as possible.[7]

As with the lands of the other Haudenosaunee nations, the Oneida territory had been ravaged during the war. While several of their villages were destroyed, the Oneidas had greater damage to try to repair: their nation had been divided in terms of what role they should have taken in the war. Many of the young men chose to support the Americans and became military leaders of the pro-American Oneida forces during the war, even fighting against Mohawk and other Haudenosaunee warriors who were supporting the British. But not all Oneida people had agreed to join in the war, and certainly most never would have chosen to have their young men fight against their Haudenosaunee relatives in battles such as the Battle of Oriskany and the

Clinton-Sullivan Campaign.[8] At the close of the war, the Oneidas not only had to rebuild their homes, they had to rebuild their nation and repair their relationship within the Confederacy. As with the divisions that split them at the onset of the war, the Oneidas could not come to one mind about where they would settle after the fighting concluded. While most chose to stay in their homelands, several Oneida families[9] chose to move to the western hunting grounds with the pro-British supporters of the Confederacy. Many of the Tuscaroras (who had settled among the Oneida in the 1720s) left the Oneida territory during the war and took refuge at Fort Niagara.

After the Clinton-Sullivan Campaign, there was practically nothing to return to in terms of physical houses, yet the burned-out villages were still home to the Onondagas, Cayugas, and Senecas. For them, it was the land of their birth and the place where their ancestors were laid to rest. For many, there was no real choice but to go back and rebuild their lives on their homeland territories. Others, however, decided that the best place to provide for the future generations of their nations would be on their hunting grounds to the west. These choices left families physically divided, but in many cases they managed to remain connected across the miles.[10]

As noted previously, the Mohawks were forced to select a new homeland, as their valley had been forfeited by the British to the Americans in the Treaty of Paris. The British sought the assistance of Joseph Brant in selecting an acceptable territory to replace the lands lost in the war, as they had promised their Haudenosaunee allies they would do at the start of the conflict. While Brant was not a Royaner, the Confederacy leadership knew that the Crown recognized Brant as one of their leaders and allowed him to speak on their behalf in the belief that his standing in the British military, his English language skills, and his personal connections to colonial British leadership[11] would secure them a more just compensation than any other negotiator would be able to achieve. Despite many historical representations to that effect, Brant was never given complete authority to act on behalf of the Six Nations. Instead, the Rotiyanehson met with him regularly, giving him instructions based upon the needs of their clan families and nations. Under this direction, Brant served as the spokesman in the selection of the Grand River tract as a new Haudenosaunee homeland.

A New Homeland

The terms of the 1783 Treaty of Paris failed to address the needs of the Haudenosaunee and actually surrendered the remaining Mohawk lands to the United States. Crown representatives in North America quickly realized the implications of this omission and subsequent land cessions, as articulated in the following excerpt of a letter from Allan Maclean (commander of the British post at Niagara) to Sir Frederick Haldimand, dated 18 May 1783:

> The Indians from the surmises they have heard of the Boundaries, look upon our Conduct to them as treacherous and Cruel; they told me they never could believe that our King could pretend to cede to America what was not his own to give, or that the Americans would accept from him, What he had no right to grant. That upon a representation from the Six Nations, in the year 1768, The King had appointed Sir William Johnson as Commissioner to Settle the Boundaries between the Indians & the Colonies, That a line had been drawn from the head of Canada Creek (near Fort Stanwix) to the Ohio, that the Boundaries then settled were agreable to the Indians & the Colonies, & never had been doubted or disputed since—That the Indians were a free People Subject to no Power upon Earth, that they were the faithful Allies of the King of England, but not his subjects—that he had no right Whatever to grant away to the United States of America, their Rights or Properties without a manifest breach of all justice and Equity, and they would not Submit to it. . . .
>
> I should wish that Captain Brant Might be detained in Canada for some time, he is much better informed & instructed than any other Indians, he is Strongly attached to the Interest of his Country men, for which I do honour him, but he would be so much more sensible of the Miserable Situation in which we have left these unfortunate People, that I do believe he would do a great deal of Mischief here at this time, I do from my Soull Pity these People.[12]

Clearly, Maclean and Haldimand were well aware of the previous promises made by the Crown in favour of the Haudenosaunee as well as the Haudenosaunee understanding and expectations of those promises. Maclean's suggestion to deter Brant from taking action over the treaty came too late.

Brant's message to Haldimand at Quebec two days later, on 21 May 1783, addressed the issue:

> Brother Asharekowa[13] and Representatives of the King,
>
> The sachems and War Chieftains of the Six United Nations of Indians and their Allies have heard that the King, their Father, has made peace with his children the Bostonians[14] . . . wherefore they have now sent me to inform themselves before you of the real truth, whether it is so or not, that they are not partakers of that Peace with the King and the Bostonians . . .
>
> Wherefore Brother, I am now sent in behalf of all the King's Indian Allies to receive a decisive answer from you, and to know whether they are included in the Treaty with the Americans, as faithful Allies should be, or not, and whether those Lands which the Great Being above has pointed out for our Ancestors, and their descendants, and Placed them there from the beginning, and where the bones of our forefathers are laid, is secure to them, or whether the Blood of their Grand Children is to be mingled with their Bones, thro' the means of our Allies for whom we have often so freely Bled.[15]

The Haudenosaunee learned of the omissions and cessions of the Treaty of Paris and called upon the Crown to explain itself and to uphold the promises it had made prior to the war, promises consistent with the established relationship formalized in the Covenant Chain and other subsequent Haudenosaunee–British treaties. Haldimand and other Crown representatives sought authority from Britain to compensate the Haudenosaunee as promised and to assuage the growing discord amongst the Haudenosaunee upon learning of the King's neglect of their interests at the treaty table in Paris. In August 1783, Lord North replied to Haldimand's requests for direction: "These People are justly entitled to Our peculiar Attention, and it would be far from either generous or just in us, after Our Cession of their Territories and Hunting Grounds, to forsake them. I am, therefore, authorized to Acquaint you, that the King allows you to make those Offers to them, or to any other Nations of the friendly Indians, who may be desirous of withdrawing themselves from the United States, and occupying any lands which you may allot to them within the Province of Quebec."[16] The British were aware of their failure to protect Haudenosaunee interests as well as their error in ceding lands that were not theirs to cede. Lord North's words confirm that the ensuing Haldimand "grant" was not a gift but rather an attempt at compensation—an important distinction to be made when compared to later statements made by imperial representatives.

In meetings with Brant and other Haudenosaunee leaders, Crown representatives laid out several options as relocation sites for those of the Six Nations who wished to move to lands still under British protection. The options all lay within lands that were within the parameters of the Beaver Hunting Tract, lands the Crown had already acknowledged as belonging to the Haudenosaunee.[17] Finally, two sites received serious consideration: one on the Bay of Quinte, not far from the British military base of Kingston;[18] the second along the Grand River, not far from Niagara and the homeland territories of the Seneca Nation. Records seem to indicate that Brant initially favoured the Quinte option, primarily because of its distance from the Americans.[19] Haldimand agreed to make the necessary provisions of transfer in order to initiate the Six Nations' move to the Bay of Quinte. However, upon returning to Fort Niagara and meeting with the Rotiyanehson, Brant was instructed that the Confederacy leadership preferred the Grand River site and instructed him to make the necessary arrangements with Haldimand to secure those lands instead.[20]

John Deseronto, another Mohawk military leader, decided that he preferred the Quinte location and suggested those who wished could follow him there. The British were not in favour of splitting the Haudenosaunee into two settlements, but because of the initial offer made for the Bay of Quinte and the subsequent selection of the Grand River by the Six Nations Rotiyanehson, they decided to offer both tracts of land to the Haudenosaunee.[21] Deseronto's people came primarily from the Fort Hunter village sites of the Mohawk Valley, and many of them were amongst the Lachine refugees. The site they chose was actually the former territory of some Cayuga and Seneca people who had made their way around Lake Ontario in the early 1600s. At the Bay of Quinte, they re-established a Mohawk community. On the other site along the Grand River, the Haudenosaunee settlers represented an amalgam of all of the Six Nations, as well as people from other nations who sought the protection and fellowship of the Confederacy as they, too, attempted to re-establish their lives following the war. Connections between these two communities remained strong throughout the resettlement period, with many people moving back and forth between them throughout the nineteenth century.

The following excerpt from Rev. John Stuart's May 1784 report to the Society for the Propagation of the Gospel (SPG) outlines some of the factors involved between the two resettlement options:

> A part of the Mohawks having removed, last Summer, from LaChine to Niagara, the remainder of them set out, the beginning of May, for a place called the Bay of Kenty, 40 miles above Cataraqui, to take possession of lands assigned them by Genl Haldimand. It is not yet determined, whether the whole Tribe, together with their Brethren at Canajohare, will unite in this new Settlement.—as Captain Brant, with a number of the Mohawk and Canajohare Chiefs have in contemplation to form a grand Settlement on a River, 40 miles above Niagara, on the Canada side of the Lake; being encouraged to do this, partly, by the mildness of the climate, the fertility of the soil, and the convenience of hunting. But those of the Mohawks, who are actually gone to the Bay of Kenty, are determined to remain there, that they may enjoy the advantages of having a Missionary, Schoolmaster, and Church.[22]

Doxtator makes similar observations and also compares the geographical and geological differences that probably influenced the decisions as well:

> The Grand River Valley lands allowed for a diverse economic base. They were made up of heavy rich clay loams which were ideal for European crops, and other lighter and silty loams, which were best for traditional Rotinonhysonni [sic] women's agriculture. The land was forested by southern hardwoods and white pine. These lands were very much like those in the Mohawk Valley and the interior of New York State. In the Carolinian biotic zone the large tract supported a greater variety of species of birds animals and plants than at Tyendinaga, which perhaps made it more suitable for settlement by a larger more diverse population of 'six nations', particularly since some of the nations were less interested in incorporating European-style agriculture.[23]

As Doxtator points out, the terrain of the Grand River Valley was quite similar to the homeland territories of the Six Nations, allowing for the reestablishment of similar agricultural (traditional Haudenosaunee horticulture and European farming methods) and harvesting (hunting, fishing, and gathering) activities. For those of the Six Nations who were not familiar with this specific land, the similarities in climate, soils, trees, and animals would have made the transition easier—both physically and emotionally—than if they had selected to move farther west or farther north. The proximity to the Niagara area and the re-established Seneca, Cayuga, and Onondaga villages in the original homelands certainly provided another key incentive to the Grand River option. This proximity allowed for the kind of continued relationships between the Grand River Haudenosaunee and their relatives to the east that exist to the present day. The Neutral adoptees[24] who were then living with the Six Nations also would have recalled the Grand River Valley as their former homelands.[25] Despite the logical connections to the Grand River territory for the Six Nations, that land was not home to them. While they were accustomed to moving their villages (although the frequency of those moves had been reduced significantly during the eighteenth century), in this case the extreme move did not allow them years of planning, nor did they have sufficient time to prepare the new lands for settlement (clearing trees for villages and planting, preparing building materials for homes, etc.). The migrations to both the Grand River and Bay of Quinte were marked with hunger, sadness, and uncertainty—all multiplied by the impact of the grief caused by war, grief that time had not allowed to be properly handled through the traditional condolence processes. As the people set out for their new homelands, they surely had thoughts of the part of the Condolence Ceremony that recalls the old villages that had been abandoned, visible along the path that the Condolence must follow, and the grief that can rise up from that experience.

Rebuilding the "Longhouse" at Ohsweken

In Kanyen'keha, the term *Shotinonhsyonnih* explains the process of settlement on the Grand River by the Six Nations people. The word literally means "they have built the house again," referring to the metaphorical longhouse that brought the Five Nations together to live under the Great Law of Peace at the time of the Peacemaker. Similar to the "building" of that original metaphorical longhouse, the "house" referenced in this term is not referring to the rebuilding of physical structures (although much of that would have been happening); it refers, instead, to re-establishing the social structures of the Confederacy in the new Grand River homelands. Along the Grand River, the Haudenosaunee reconvened the Grand Council, began carrying out their spiritual responsibilities in terms of ceremonies and interactions with the natural world, and rebuilt their families within the same systems of balance and reciprocity originally organized within the ancient longhouse structures. In

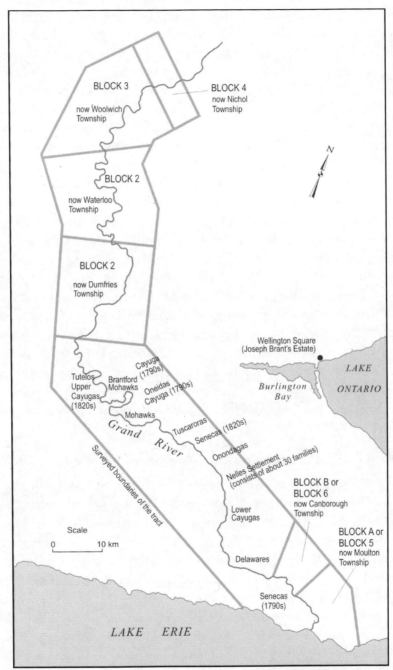

Map 2. The Settlement of the Six Nations along the Lower Grand River. Source: George Beaver, Mohawk Reporter *(Ohsweken: IPACS, 1996), 18.*

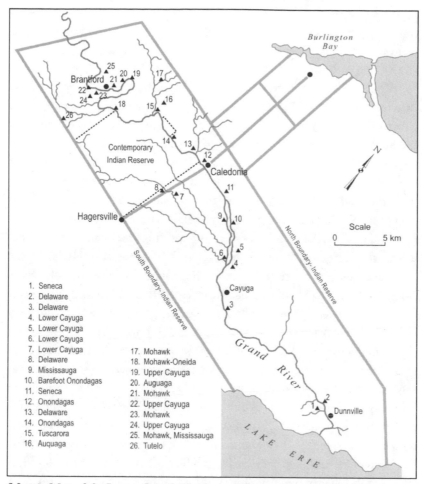

Map 3. Map of the Lower Grand, Haldimand Grant, Showing Indian Settlements, 1783–1849. Source: George Beaver, Mohawk Reporter *(Ohsweken: IPACS, 1996), 19.*

all of this, the Grand River Territory became a smaller version of the original amalgamated Haudenosaunee lands and societies documented and illustrated in the Ayenwahtha Wampum Belt.

The initial Haudenosaunee settlements in the Grand River Territory followed national patterns, although their grouping was not always a direct reflection of the original ordering of nations in the homelands. Instead, the Grand River villages were settled by nations under the guidance of specific leaders and dotted the banks of the lower Grand River—apparently chosen for such natural features as meadows, particular tree varieties, and ease of river access (see Maps 2 and 3). It is likely that the leaders whose names became connected to the specific villages were clan leaders of some variety and in many cases held Royaner titles—such as "Onondaga Clear Sky," named after an Onondaga Royaner.

While there is very little documentary evidence of the internal village structures, council records from the early 1800s indicate that many of the villages had council buildings or designated meeting places where different Indian Affairs superintendents recorded meetings with Confederacy leadership on different issues.[26] Haudenosaunee governance models would have been put in place to govern the internal affairs of these villages. When issues arose that had implications for all of the Six Nations, a Grand Council was held at the Onondaga Village. These villages—as denoted by their names— had a nation-specific designation, but as a result of intermarriage and other factors the villages were not nation-exclusive. This was also true in the old homeland villages but probably with even greater frequency given the much closer proximity of the different nations to each other within the Grand River Territory. Evidence of the impacts of intermarriage on internal land holdings is demonstrated in the words of Mohawk Royaner Isaac Locke in 1829: "With regard to dividing the land to the several tribes and then to families, we see great difficulties would arise in consequence of intermarriages."[27] Locke was responding to the suggestion of the Indian Department that the Grand River Territory be divided into six portions, one for each nation of the Confederacy.

Economically speaking, establishing the Grand River settlements was a difficult process for the Six Nations. Given the long time it took to clear land, the Haudenosaunee had previously stretched their village moves out over several years. The removal from Fort Niagara in the fall of 1784 did not allow enough time to clear the Grand River lands for village sites or for the building of adequate housing for the quickly approaching winter. Once again, little written evidence can be found recording the hardships of the resettlement era. However, it is assumed that many hardships were endured by those initial Grand River families. The lack of cleared fields and seed around Fort Niagara would have led to food shortages for both the journey to the Grand River and the first winter in their new homelands. It would have taken years before sufficient lands could be cleared for the village sites and surrounding fields.

The Haldimand Deed

As discussed previously, the Crown authorized Sir Frederick Haldimand to secure a tract of land as compensation for those of the Six Nations who had supported the British in the war and whose lands had been forfeited by the Treaty of Paris. Once the Six Nations articulated their desire to settle on the Grand River tract, Haldimand set out to secure title to the lands from the Mississaugas, who had taken up residence in the area during the eighteenth century. Under the 1701 Nanfan Treaty, Britain already recognized this territory as the domain of the Haudenosaunee, but apparently Haldimand felt that he should insure against any residual claims by the Mississaugas. This was formally addressed in the Mississauga Surrender of 22 May 1784. The council record states:

> After the usual Ceremonies and compliments was made Pokquan a Mississaga [*sic*] Chief rose & Spoke as follows
>
> Father
>
> Some days ago your message with this Belt were received, desiring us to assemble at the great Council Fire, kindled at this place by the King our Father, we accordingly collected our people as soon as possible, and are now ready to hear your business with us.
>
> Returned the Belt
>
> Lieut Colonel John Butler then Spoke
>
> Children
>
> I have received the Commander in Chief's Order thro' Sir John Johnson, to purchase some land, the property of you the Mississaugas laying between the Lakes Ontario, Huron & Erie for the use of such of your Brethren of the Six Nations, as may wish to plant and Hunt thereon, as well as for an intended Settlement of such of His Majesty's faithful Subjects who have assisted him during the late War, as wish to settle and improve the same; it would be needless for me to add more at present as I have already explained every circumstance as clear as light, to you the Chiefs, as in my power to do, Therefore expect your immediate answer.
>
> A Belt.

Pokquan Mississaga Speaker

Father & Brethren Six Nations: We have considered your request.

Father

We the Mississagas are not the owners of all that Land laying between the three Lakes, but we have agreed and are willing to transfer our right of soil & property to the King our Father, for the use of his people, and to our Brethren the Six Nations from the head of the Lake Ontario or the Creek Waghquata, to the River La Tranche [Thames River], then down that River until a south course will strike the Mouth of Catfish Creek on lake Erie, this tract of land we imagine will be quite sufficient both for the King's people, and our Brethren the Six Nations, who may wish to settle and Hunt thereon; Your request or proposal, does not give us that trouble or concern, that you might imagine from the answer you received from some of our people the other day, that difficulty is entirely removed, we are Indians, and consider ourselves and the Six Nations to be one and the same people, and agreeable to a former and mutual agreement, we are bound to help each other.

Brother Captain Brant, we are happy to hear that you intend to settle at the River Oswego with your people, we hope you will keep your young men in good Order, as we shall be in one Neighbourhood, and to live in friendship with each other as Brethren ought to do.[28]

Here, the Mississaugas notify the British that they "are not the owners of all that Land." In this, they are stating that there are others with interest in this territory—most certainly recalling the use of that area as Haudenosaunee hunting grounds. Records of other Mississauga land surrenders often contain similar statements, and it appears that they were implying one of two things: that no one actually owns the land; or that they were selling land they knew was not theirs, but if the Crown was willing to pay they would willingly "surrender." In this particular case, however, clearly the Mississaugas were expressing a willingness to share the territory they had been using for roughly a century, as well as recalling the mutual responsibilities between themselves and the Haudenosaunee based within older treaty relationships.[29] Finally, Pokquan, on behalf of the Mississaugas, was very clear about the extent of the territory that his nation was surrendering under this agreement. Later imperial interpretations of the territory, based upon survey information, deemed the Mississauga sale to have excluded the headwaters of the Grand River from this surrender—the basis of the Crown's refusal to recognize later Six Nations claims to those lands.[30]

Beyond the boundaries described by the 1701 Albany Treaty, other evidence exists demonstrating that the imperial representatives were well aware of the status of the territories Haldimand would offer to the Haudenosaunee as being within the hunting grounds of the Six Nations. In August 1783 Lord North wrote to Haldimand concerning this:

> The King ... much approves of your having sent Major Holland to ... survey the North Side of Lake Ontario, as well as of your intention of carrying into execution your endeavor to prevail upon the Mohawks to settle to the Northward of the Lake, provided the Country should be found well suited for their convenience. These People are justly entitled to Our peculiar Attention, and it would be far from either generous or just in Us, after our Cession of their Territories and Hunting Grounds, to forsake them. I am, therefore, authorized to acquaint you, that the King allows you to make those Offers to them, or to any other Nations of friendly Indians, who may be desirous of withdrawing themselves from the United States, and occupying any Lands which you may allot to them within the Province of Quebec. It is to be hoped, that from thence they will be able to carry on their Hunting on their former Grounds, and return with their Furs and Peltry, where the British Traders can meet them, with their Wives and Children, in Security, and being under our protection their Attachment to His Majesty may continue, and this Country may enjoy the advantages of their Trade. In the assortment of Presents to be sent out to you for these People you will find a supply of Tools and Implements for Cultivation, which, it is judged will be useful in the formation of their new Settlements, in case they avail themselves of the Offers which you may make to them.[31]

This statement also demonstrates the desires of the Crown to continue to benefit from the Native fur trade—another justification for recognizing the territorial claims of the Six Nations to the lands under the 1701 Albany Treaty.

If Haldimand had immediately proclaimed the Grand River lands to be the property of the Six Nations following the Mississauga surrender, the Haudenosaunee would have had time to plant crops that would have been harvested in time for the following winter. Understandably, the Haudenosaunee at Niagara were getting restless.[32] They continued to receive reports that the British might not follow through with their promises to compensate the land losses after the war.[33] In fact, some Delaware families actually moved to the Grand River Valley in 1783, before a formal confirmation of the land to the Six Nations was made. The Delawares had sought refuge with the Six Nations at Niagara upon the close of the war. Their move to the Grand River is mentioned by Allan Maclean in a letter to Haldimand: "this horrid report Spread by the Oneidas has Occasioned a Number of Delawares to quit Buffaloe Creek already and Cross at Fort Erie and go to the Grand River 50 Miles beyond fort Erie, Officers are sent up to endeavour to prevent any more from emigrating if possible."[34] Maclean's letter expresses the desire for the Crown to relieve the unhappiness of the Six Nations (and their dependent nations) as well as the possibility of their leaving Niagara without a formal agreement between themselves and the British.

It took over five months for Haldimand[35] to declare the lands as Six Nations property, which occurred on 25 October 1784, in the following proclamation:

> Whereas His Majesty having been pleased to direct that in Consideration of the early Attachment to his Cause manifested by the Mohawk Indians, & of the loss of their Settlement they thereby sustained that a convenient Tract of Land under His Protection should be chosen as a Safe & Comfortable Retreat for them & others of the Six Nations who have either lost their Settlements within the Territory of the American States, or wish to retire from them to the British—I have, at the earnest Desire of many of these His Majesty's Faithfull Allies purchased a Tract of Land, from the Indians situated between the Lakes Ontario, Erie and Huron, and I do hereby in His Majesty's name authorize and permit the said Mohawk Nation, and such other of the Six Nations Indians as wish to settle in that Quarter to take Possession of, & Settle upon the banks of the River commonly called Ours [Ouse] or Grand River, running into Lake Erie, allotting to them for that purpose Six Miles Deep from each Side of the River beginning at Lake Erie, & extending in that Proportion to the Head of the said River, which them & their Posterity are to enjoy for ever.[36]

When it came time for the Haudenosaunee to move to the Grand River lands, they were deeply in need of provisions and foodstuffs for the upcoming winter. The Haudenosaunee had been receiving food and other aid from the British military while living at Lachine and Fort Niagara; similar provisions were necessary for the move to the Grand River as well as for the first winter in their new homelands. Even after the first winter, life continued to be difficult on the Grand as it took years to clear land for fields, build adequate homes, and establish villages on their new homelands. While the Delawares who had moved to the Grand River in 1783 certainly would have assisted their Six Nations "uncles,"[37] the needs must have far outweighed the assistance they would have been able to provide.

The migration of Six Nations people to the Grand River was actually spread out over several years, probably due to the difficulties of resettlement. This situation is evidenced in a letter from David and Aaron Hill (Grand River Mohawks) to Sir John Johnson dated 15 April 1790:

> Having been informed by Colonel Butler of the receipt of a Letter from You, mentioning His Lordship's wish to know, when we would choose to have *our Deed for the Lands, granted us on the Grand River, it being the Wish of the Six Nations in general we have to request the Deed as soon as possible,*[38] being informed the Americans are Raising Troops and Ignorant of what their intentions may be, think the sooner our Boundaries are pointed out the greater will be our Satisfaction, and wish to know how much of the Land to the South of the Grand River we may Expect will be reserved for our Hunting, and further request His Lordship will order a Surveyor, to Survey the Tract granted us, that in future we may be certain as to our Boundaries.
>
> There being a number of the Six Nations who mean to move over to the Grand River and the season being considerably advanced a number of them nearly destitute of Provision, request His Lordship will allow them provision in order to Enable them to move, and until such time as they may be able to support themselves.[39]

These words attest to the difficult economic conditions experienced by the Six Nations. This letter also refers to the desire for a deed to the Grand River tract and clear boundaries. It alludes to the issue of title that arose shortly after Haldimand left his position as governor of Quebec—an issue that plagues the

Grand River Haudenosaunee to the present day and is at the centre of several land claims, most notable of which is the Headwaters Claim.[40]

An Unclear Title

As expressed by David and Aaron Hill, the Six Nations were eager to have the borders of their Grand River lands clearly defined. There was rumour to the effect that the Crown might lessen the acreage of the Grand River tract once the lands were surveyed.[41] This caused great concern among the Haudenosaunee. Beyond rumour, there was real reason for uneasiness: Haldimand's successors determined that he had not used the proper seal[42] on the 1784 Proclamation, a clerical error on his part that allowed other imperial representatives in Upper Canada to question the legitimacy of the land "grant."

In order to press the issue of title and boundaries, there were several requests for a formal survey. As Joseph Brant wrote to Lord Dorchester: "The Deed or Grant for the lands here which you are going to give us, we hope you will make the Deed or grant near the same sort which General Haldimand first promised to us, we hope the Council will not restrict us too much—otherways we shall look upon it not much better than a Yankee deed or grant to their Indian friends."[43] This passage indicates not only the concern for the security of the Haldimand Proclamation but also serves as an excellent example of Brant's political mind. While he was certainly justified in arguing against a significant reduction of lands from Haldimand's Proclamation, he also knew that the comparison to Britain's former colonies would cast a certain shame upon the imperial representatives in Canada. The Crown representatives had their own concerns about the extent of the Haldimand Proclamation; by January 1791, a committee of the executive council had noted that "His Lordship pointed out the expediency of ascertaining the nature & extent of these claims to give full effect to any promises, and to gratify any reasonable expectations in which the faith of the government might be concerned, in such a way as would best answer the end of making a permanent provision for the persons interested & their descendants."[44]

In May of that year, Henry Motz (Lord Dorchester's civil secretary) wrote to Sir John Johnson regarding the requests for confirmation of Haldimand's Proclamation:

> On the subject of Joseph Brandt's [sic] letter respecting the lands
> on the Grand River I am to observe, that *without doubt the Indians*
> *are entitled to the full accomplishment of Governor Haldimand's*

promise to them without any diminution, and it shall be carried into execution accordingly.[45] ... As to the nature of the deed it should be framed in every respect according to their own wishes, so as to secure the true interest of themselves and their posterity for ever in the most effectual manner. It will be very desirable that they should consider this matter fully among themselves, and bring forward the heads of the deed they wish to receive. You will be pleased to recommend this measure to Captain Brandt, and to acquaint him with His Lordship's sentiments ... in general.[46]

While this letter came from Motz, it clearly references the position of Lord Dorchester regarding the Six Nations' land issues. A government committee was struck to investigate the claims of the Six Nations, and its report, dated 24 December 1791, stated, "as the faith of Government is pledged to the Mohawk Chiefs ... every precaution ought to be taken to preserve them, in the quiet possession and property of them and the Committee submit, that an Act of the provincial Legislature, or a grant under the great seal of the province be made in favor of the principal Chiefs, on behalf of their Nation, or persons in trust for them, for ever."[47] Echoing Dorchester's sentiments, this committee recognized that if the honour of the Crown was to be upheld, Haldimand's Proclamation had to be confirmed.

The formal survey of the Grand River territory was finally completed in 1791, as described in a report of the Nassau District Land Board:

> Mr. Jones[48] having finished his Survey, laid a Plan of the Grand River before the Board, who having called in Capt Brant, Tekarihokea, Shascouanie, Agageghte [?], Gonehsaneyonte, Kayendadirhon ... and several of the Principal chiefs to aid the Land Board with their advice & Council—It was unanimously agreed upon and Determined that the Bend of the River easterly nearly two Miles from its Mouth or issue into Lake Erie, & the Mohawk Village shall be the two fixed Points & that a straight line drawn from one of these points to the other shall form the Center Line of the Indian Lands on the Grand River & that two Parallel lines to this Six Miles Distant on each Side of the Grand River Shall form the Bounds between them & the Settlement of Nassau—This arrangement is Signed on the Map of the Grand River by the Members of the Land Board & the Aforementioned Chief—[49]

This description only details the lower half of the Grand River. While the Crown had promised to deliver the full length of the river valley, that never happened. The upper part, not mentioned, became one of two major points of contention between the British authorities and the Six Nations under the Headwaters Land Claim; the other being the extent of Crown control over both the internal government of the territory and over the alienation of land.

The most documented Six Nations voice in regard to the unclear title for the Grand River lands was that of Joseph Brant. Brant had compared the lack of a clear deed with the types of "promises" made by the Americans to their Native allies. Brant, and other Haudenosaunee spokesmen, also compared the compensatory lands of the Grand River with those they had left behind in the homelands. In a letter to William Claus, deputy superintendent of the Indian Department, Brant wrote that "He [General Haldimand] knew well that we left a valuable and flourishing Country, and property far more valuable than the Lands of the Grand River. He also knew that our Attachment to the British Government was so strong that we would never think of returning to that Country (Mohawk River) that we had forsaken, and that we were determined to share the same fate with the British."[50] While in general the Grand River Haudenosaunee were satisfied to make the tract their new homeland, they did not forget their former homes, nor were they naive about the value of what had been forfeited as a result of the war. Their homelands consisted of millions of acres, held the bones of their ancestors, and contained significant clearings for villages and agriculture as well as bountiful forests. There were many reasons for their selection of the Grand River to replace those lands, but they were well aware of their sacrifice. In addition to that initial sacrifice, Lord John Graves Simcoe was attempting to reduce the Grand River lands by nearly one-third, down to 677,000 acres.[51]

Up to this point, all of the major stakeholders had agreed that the Six Nations should have a full confirmation of Haldimand's promises. First, the lands had been recognized by the Crown in the 1701 treaty as belonging to the Haudenosaunee.[52] Second, the Mississaugas were very clear in their 1784 surrender of their interests; both they and the Haudenosaunee were well aware of the extent of the lands described based upon their interactions with that territory for hunting, fishing, and other purposes. Third, a series of government representatives concurred that it was the duty of the Crown to confirm what Haldimand had promised, both as compensation for lost territory and as a point of honour for their positions as representatives of the King.[53] Despite the rumours and other concerns, it appeared, in 1791, that the Haldimand

Deed would be confirmed and the Six Nations would be secure in their new homeland. That turned out not to be the case.

Simcoe became lieutenant governor of Upper Canada in 1791 and was given the responsibility of clearing up the discrepancies between Haldimand's promises, subsequent land surveys, and non-Native claims within the Haldimand Tract.[54] Simcoe's major concerns were in the area of the Six Nations' direct land dealings with non-Natives. Shortly after moving to the Grand River, Brant and other leaders made land grants to some of their Loyalist neighbours from the Mohawk River Valley.[55] Brant also began leasing portions of the Grand River tract in order to provide income for the Haudenosaunee as they re-established their homes and villages. Simcoe's interpretation of the Haldimand Proclamation, coupled with his application of the Royal Proclamation to this situation, led him to believe that the Six Nations did not have the right to convey their lands without royal assent.[56] This became the major point of contention between Simcoe and Brant in defining both the boundaries of the Grand River tract and the nature of Haudenosaunee land title.[57] In January 1793, Simcoe issued his own deed to the Six Nations for the Grand River tract: in this he cut off one-third of the territory and declared that the Six Nations had no right to convey their lands through lease or sale to anyone but the Crown.[58] These actions were contradictory to his own statements about the nature of the relationship between the Crown and the Haudenosaunee, as evidenced in statements he made to the Six Nations in June 1793:

> Brothers,
>
> . . . the documents, records and treaties between the British Governors in former times, and your wise forefathers . . . all established the freedom of your nations. . . . These authentic papers[59] prove that no King of Great Britain ever claimed absolute power or sovereignty over any of your lands or territories that were not fairly purchased or bestowed by your ancestors at public treaties; they likewise prove that your natural independency has been preserved.[60]

Simcoe's actions caused the Haudenosaunee to question their relationship with the Crown. On the one hand Simcoe recognized Haudenosaunee independence, yet in his deed to the Grand River lands he clearly expressed that the Haudenosaunee were not free to administer their own business matters in regard to land, a principle that would become official British policy in regard to Indian lands in North America. With Brant as the spokesperson, the Six Nations denounced the Simcoe Deed[61]—a position that continues to be held by many Six Nations people today.

These discussions about the boundaries of the tract, the nature of the Six Nations' land title, and the Simcoe Deed fell quite short of the reasonable expectations of the Six Nations. The Haudenosaunee have continually refused to accept the Crown's excuses for not delivering the full extent of the Haldimand Deed. This became an important element of the political relationship between the Confederacy and the Crown that persists to this day. Records of various statements of claim can be found throughout the Government of Canada files, and several times these grievances were laid before the governor general. One example of these grievances came through Mohawk Royaner Tekarihoken at an 1819 Council:

> I remember very well before the Lands were purchased by Colonel Butler that the Mississagues said "We do not wish to sell the lands, we will give you all the lands from the Grand River to the River Thames down to Lake Erie." The Government lessened the gift to Six Miles on each Side of the Grand River, from its mouth to its Spring. Yet we replied to the Mississagues "Since you have been so kind to us, we will divide our Presents with you." We are Surprised to find the Government says, that we own the Lands to the Falls only as we have Writings to prove otherwise. We have them here and are ready to produce them.
>
> The Original Deed from General Haldimand Produced by John Brant.[62]

This statement also outlines the Haudenosaunee understanding of their relationship with the Mississaugas.[63]

The Haudenosaunee continued to press their claim to the Grand River headwaters despite the lack of support from British officials. Mohawk Pinetree Chief John Norton (Teyoninhokarawen)[64] even travelled to England in 1804 in an attempt to get support from imperial officials in conferring what Haldimand had promised. Norton was well received in England but failed to convince the Colonial Office to reverse Simcoe's decision. The major source of Norton's opposition came from the Indian Department and its deputy superintendent general, Col. William Claus.[65]

Evidence shows that at least some British officials were well aware of the fact that the headwaters had been promised to the Six Nations. Selkirk's principal agent in Upper Canada, Alexander McDonell, demonstrates as much in the following letter to Lord Selkirk: "I cannot avoid mentioning to your Lordship another Tract on the Grand River in the purchase of which money might be vested to great advantage—It is the remaining part of that granted to the Six Nations, from the N.W. Boundary Line of Mr Clark's Block, to the Sources of the River. This Tract has not as yet been purchased by the Crown, from the Chippawas, but it must be whenever the Six Nations require it. It has been surveyed by Mr Jones & contains 104,264 Acres of excellent Land."[66] Here, McDonell proposes a clear and logical solution to the headwaters dispute: make the purchase from the Mississaugas and then convey it to those whom it has been promised. Unfortunately, McDonell's suggestions were not followed by the government.

Despite the fact that the Crown had failed to uphold Haldimand's promises to the Haudenosaunee—promises made in compensation for losses in the American Revolution—the British did not hesitate to approach them when fighting broke out again in the War of 1812. The Grand River Haudenosaunee were extremely divided over what to do in response to the request. They would have been aware that some of their Haudenosaunee relatives might be supporting the Americans and would have wanted to avoid any possible military conflict with their Confederacy brothers. They were also still rebuilding their communities after the fallout from the last British war. Their population had not increased significantly (see Appendix 1), their economy had yet to stabilize, and they were still grieving the loss of hundreds of their people during the Revolutionary War. Finally, they were reminded regularly that the British had not kept their promises in terms of the Haldimand Proclamation.

The issue of the war caused a major split within the Mohawk Nation, between the Upper and Lower Mohawks.[67] The Lower Mohawks, led by Pinetree Chief John Smoke Johnson, favoured answering the British call for assistance. They viewed this as their treaty obligation. The Upper Mohawks, however, argued against joining the British efforts because of their dissatisfaction with the status of the Haldimand Deed.[68] Some of the Upper Mohawks even contemplated assisting the American forces along with their Seneca supporters in New York State. The Lower Mohawks, along with warriors from several of the nations, took up the British cause. The Upper Mohawks avoided the war until it came to them through American raids of Six Nations villages. The split between the two groups of Mohawks lasted long after the war concluded, however. Later, at the 1815 Burlington Bay Council, Claus condoled the Haudenosaunee and other British war allies. He also indicated that the previous treaty relationships between the British and the assembled allies remained intact. Through this, Claus reaffirmed the Covenant Chain, the 1701 Albany Treaty, and the Great Peace of Montreal.

The Six Nations appealed the Headwaters case to Lord Bathurst in 1821, but his response only stood to support the idea that the Six Nations had no legitimate claim to the headwaters, based upon several technicalities that presented themselves years after the Proclamation. Bathurst replied to the Six Nations' claim:

> The description therefore of the Land which is given in the close of the Proclamation must be taken with reference to the general inaccuracy and contradiction of all geographical descriptions of America at that time, when the country was unsurveyed and unknown, and when information became as to the course of Rivers was derived either from reports of individuals, or from other sources which afterwards proved altogether incorrect.—As the course of the Ouse, or Grand River become known, it was found that the head of the River was not within the purchase made from the Chippawas in 1784, and that that purchase therefore did not comprise the lands to which the five Nations now lay claim. I do not find indeed that any Claim of the Nature now advanced years afterwards, with a view to the Settlement of Emigrants, made a further purchase from these Indians which put His Majesty in possession of the Land lying between the head of the Grand River and that purchased in 1784, which is the Subject of Your present Application—
>
> Under these circumstances His Majesty cannot but consider the Colonial Government justified in allotting to Settlers, instead of reserving for Your use, such part of the land now claimed by you as was not purchased in 1784, for the Chippawas—[69]

Bathurst was referring to Simcoe's position that the Mississaugas did not own the land they surrendered to the Crown in 1784, which was later conferred upon the Six Nations. Ironically, when the Crown made a later purchase, seeming to clear up the errors of Haldimand's Proclamation, the provincial authorities then conferred the lands of the headwaters upon white squatters who had taken up residence in the disputed territory. Here, the Crown had the opportunity to rectify a wrong it had perpetrated against the Six Nations, but instead of living up to its responsibilities to the Haudenosaunee they chose to favour squatters who had no legal or moral claim to the territory. The contemporary Grand River Haudenosaunee continue to argue that the Crown failed to "give full effect" to Haldimand's promises—promises he was fully authorized to make.

The history and nature of the Haldimand Deed debates are critical to understanding the state of Haudenosaunee land tenure on the Grand River, both past and present. For their part, the Six Nations demonstrated a strong desire to secure and protect their territory for the prosperity of their people—in perpetuity. Emphasis was placed on the idea that Grand River was to be a territory for all of the Six Nations (and dependent nations) who chose to move there; that the territory was to provide for all who made it their home. They asserted that the land had to be held in common (as their previous lands had been), with an emphasis on common resources, such as hunting, fishing, communal gardens, timber, plaster beds, etc. Their sentiments continued to define land as a means of providing for the people—in this case through agriculture, hunting, fishing, and leasing annuities. These debates are also a telling example of the Crown's neglect of its responsibilities to the Six Nations.

The Complicated Joseph Brant

Beyond his fame, there is probably not a more complicated figure in contemporary Haudenosaunee history than Joseph Brant. From his youth he was influenced by British customs and society. Some portray him as having been consumed by a fascination with European ways, to the extent that his loyalties were divided when it came to fulfilling his obligations to the Six Nations.[70] Others portray him as *the* protector of his nation and the Confederacy during a most troubled time, and a hero to Natives and whites alike.[71] Through contemporary eyes, he was probably all of these things and more. He was referred to as a "chief"—an English title that has no single Kanyen'keha translation. While often a Royaner is referred to as a chief, others often are referenced with that title as well—including "unofficial" leaders such as Brant.[72] Sometimes he is also referred to as a "war chief,"[73] another term without a direct Kanyen'keha translation. He quite possibly might have been a Pine Tree Chief (also known as a Self-Made Chief)—a man who is recognized for exceptional leadership and commitment to his people and selected by the Rotiyanehson to serve the Grand Council—however, there is no proof of Brant being given this title in either the written or oral historical records.

Given that Brant was not a Royaner, it is unusual that he would have been allowed to serve as the speaker,[74] not only for the Mohawks but for the entire Six Nations. However, the Confederacy Council recognized the British affinity for Brant and saw that as an opportunity to maintain the interest of the Crown and continue to have their treaty alliances upheld. He was extremely well skilled in speaking and writing both Kanyen'keha and English—important tools for a spokesman of the Six Nations at that time. His familial ties to the Johnson family, with their military and government connections, also appealed to the Confederacy. Brant's military efforts on behalf of Britain brought him high esteem among the British leaders who were selected to govern Quebec and Upper Canada. Those same military efforts also accorded him a great deal of respect among many of the Haudenosaunee men who fought under him during the Revolutionary War and other battles. Considering all these factors, the Rotiyanehson allowed Brant to speak on behalf of the Confederacy in many instances but did not accord him full authority in negotiations. Rather, he met regularly with the council and took direction from them, especially during the negotiation of resettlement.

After the move to Grand River, Brant continued to serve as a Haudenosaunee spokesman in different situations. It was during this time that Brant began taking more authority than appears to have been accorded to him in several key areas. Primary among those areas were land issues arising from the disputed title under the Haldimand Proclamation. On 24 November 1796, Brant addressed William Claus regarding the intentions of Haldimand:

> Brother
>
> I understand from some of the Great Men here, that General Haldimand did not know the Value of these lands. What does this now signify? The lands he has granted to us. Admitting that he did not know, . . . do they suppose that he would have granted us the less? No, he was no stranger to our long and faithful Services and Loyalty.—He knew well that we left a valuable and flourishing Country, and property far more valuable than the Lands on the Grand River. He also knew that our Attachment to the British Government was so strong that we would never think of returning to that Country (Mohawk River) that we had forsaken, and that we were determined to share the same fate with the British.[75]

In his words of respect for Haldimand, Brant also takes the opportunity to remind Claus that the Six Nations had lost very valuable territory as a result of their alliance with Great Britain. While this statement certainly reflected the sentiments of the Six Nations, it also served to remind the future deputy superintendent general of Indian Affairs as to the obligations of the Crown toward the Haudenosaunee.

With Brant and Simcoe opposing each other's interpretation of Haldimand—and Simcoe's subsequent replacement "deed"—Brant became a bitter critic of provincial interpretations of Haudenosaunee land rights. Many of his arguments are presented in a letter he wrote to James Green (military secretary to various commanders in Canada from 1795 to 1807) in December 1797:

> here we have even been prohibited from taking tenants on them, it having been represented as inconsistent for us being but King's allies to have king's subjects as tenants; consequently I suppose their real meaning was, we should in a manner be but tenants ourselves, as for me I see no difference in it, any farther than we are yet not free,—they seemingly intended to forbid us any other use of the lands than that of sitting down or walking on them. It plainly appears by this that their motives can be no other than to tie us down in such a manner, as to have us entirely at their disposal for what services they may in future want from us, and in case we should be warned out & obliged to remove, the lands would then fall to them with our improvements & labour.
>
> ... many things that they omitted in the account of losses, for instance our hunting grounds that were very extensive besides several other tracts of land were never mentioned ...
>
> ... observe that this goes very little ways in clothing the poor and helpless, and the country is so much changed that hunting is of very little account to the young & robust ...
>
> ... caused us to make such a large sale at once that the matter might come to a point, and we might know whether the land was ours or not.[76]

Brant's arguments were extensive, covering several key areas of grievance with Simcoe's interpretations. First, Brant compared Simcoe's declaration (against the leasing of Six Nations lands) to effectually making the Haudenosaunee tenants on their own territory. In this, he used the Haudenosaunee status as allies, not subjects, as a justification for why they should be able to deal with their lands as they saw fit—a matter of sovereignty. Second, Brant clarified that the compensation for lands lost as a result of war and the Treaty of Paris were minimal in comparison to what was left behind in the homelands. In this he also remarked about the changed economic condition in the new homelands. This related directly to his third point: the Six Nations needed to sell some of their lands in order to boost their economy, and these sales also forced the issue of the nature of the title the Six Nations held to the Grand River lands. Because of letters such as these, Brant appears to be the spokesman for the Confederacy, but there is no evidence that he was given that authority. Rather, it seems that because of his writing skills (as well as oratory in other situations) he was charged with the responsibility of articulating concerns to officers of the colonial government by the Grand Council. It must also be noted that many of Brant's personal land and financial interests were impacted by the government interpretations of the land sales;[77] he had motivations that went beyond the good of his people.

A letter from Brant to Sir John Johnson,[78] also in December 1797, shows Brant's personal reflections on his role in the situation that the Grand River Haudenosaunee found themselves in regarding their territory. He wrote,

> our design was to be on the same footing with Respect to our Lands as we were before the War on the Mohawk River, that is to have the free and indisputable Right to them as we understood we should when we first took them, and remain a free people as formerly we were after we had obtained this I would have a Map drawn of the Grand River, and such parts as might really be useless to us I would have Cut off, and have the remainder, Entailed, as Sufficiency for the whole of the Five Nations. . . .

> What I most lament is that my sincere attachment has ruined the Interests of my Nation unless an alteration takes place—after we had got through the difficulty of the late War by which we lost our Country we had known that this would have been our treatment we had still an opening left to seek out an Independent situation which we might have maintained with Credit to ourselves now it is too late, for we are now become so attached to this place that it would be too hard for us to quit it, besides we would be ashamed for

the world to see our situation. Dear Sir I cannot avoid remarking that it is not only a Breach of faith but it is also cruel treatment I have wrote the feelings of my heart with the freedom of a Warrior as I know you to be a Warrior yourself I expect you will take it in a favourable light.[79]

Brant again echoed the Grand River Haudenosaunee's beliefs about their land: "the footing with respect to our lands as we were before the war." Echoes of this sentiment can be found scattered throughout much of the written historic record of the time, with almost verbatim statements from several Royaner to the same effect.[80] They based this position upon their previous standing in their homelands as allies of the Crown; they coupled this with the Crown's assurances that the relationship had not changed simply because the Haudenosaunee now made their homes on their former hunting grounds. Brant's acceptance of some responsibility for the situation is also very interesting. This indicates both an awareness of his "weakness" for the British and the possibility that some of the British might have used that against Brant and his people. Finally, he addressed the fact that while it might appear an option to relocate again, the Six Nations had already been through too much to even give it honest consideration. In short, Brant was admitting to Johnson that he was caught in a bad situation and called upon his friend to assist him. Brant made similar statements to Robert Liston[81] in a communication dated 29 December 1797: "I must conclude that the original intention was that the Nations should hold the Land as an absolute and indefeasible Estate or at least that every advantage & Emolument that might or could in any way arise from it should be absolutely theirs . . . we certainly should not have neglected and refused to accept a more independent retreat elsewhere and I cannot avoid adding, that without the benefits which might arise from this small Territory we cannot subsist, Our Spirits must fail, and it would be impossible for Us to remain the same People."[82] While this letter echoes many of the laments of the letter to Johnson, these statements carry less personal feeling and more declaratory indications; it reflects the more public persona of Joseph Brant.

It appears that Brant's public persona had a major impact on many people, even those belonging to other Indigenous nations. In fact, Brant was selected by the Mississaugas to negotiate on their behalf in May 1798. As William Dummer Powell wrote, "our wiseacres have given to Jo. Brant so decided a superiority in the late negocition, that the Missasgue's who own the Territory between York and the western population of the Province have adopted him in the place of their great Chief Wabkenine who was murdered it is supposed by some rangers. They say that Brant is fittest to be their Chief because he alone knows the value of Land."[83] Obviously other Indigenous nations viewed Brant as successful in protecting the Six Nations' land interests. They recognized his standing among the British and, in the case of the Mississaugas, sought that recognition in order to further their own negotiations with the Crown.

While the Mississaugas viewed Brant as an honourable man, fit to stand in the place of their deceased chief, the record demonstrates that Brant acted not only in the best interests of the people he was representing but also on behalf of himself.[84] In many of the large-scale leases executed along the Grand River in the 1790s, Brant reserved large tracts of land for himself and his family and also received financial compensation. The grant of the portion known as Block No. 1 to Philip Stedman in 1795 makes the following allowance for Brant as an individual: "Reserving, nevertheless, out of and from the said Tract of land, full one thousand acres, and no more, to be pitched and laid out for the use, and at the election and choice of Captain Joseph Brant of the said Grand River, five hundred acres of which to be a pinery."[85]

While Brant advocated leasing to boost the Six Nations' economy, he also benefited financially from many of the transactions. In fact, Brant had been advocating for his own interests from the beginning in regard to the Grand River tract. He negotiated for himself a personal land grant on Burlington Bay, where he built a large home and spent a significant portion of his time. After his death, members of the provincial government identified cases wherein Brant received personal compensation at the expense of the Six Nations, such as those referenced in a communication from Francis Gore, lieutenant governor of Upper Canada, to Lord Castlereagh in 1809:

> Brant who was the agent of the Five Nations, for the disposal of their Lands, selected such purchasers, as were found willing to defraud the Indians,—in order to enrich himself, a certain sum of money was in the first instance given to Brant, for making a bargain for the Block at an undervalue. The real value was, six shillings and three pence an acre, New York Currency, but the purchaser was to have it for four shillings, on condition also, that Brant was to have besides, a seventh share of the purchase, for which the purchaser was to pay him the difference between six shillings and three pence, and four shillings an acre. So that independently of the first sum reserved, which according to the quantity of Land in the Block,

varied from, one thousand to fifteen hundred dollars—It also received for his one seventh share, from nine hundred and sixty pounds, to fourteen hundred pounds New York Currency.[86]

Actions such as these contradict Haudenosaunee values of sharing and must have tainted his image among the conservative Confederacy leadership when they learned of this.

While Brant was often selected as the mouthpiece for the Confederacy in meetings with the British, his primary official duty to the Confederacy was to act with power of attorney for certain land cessions. This power was conferred upon him in a statement signed by thirty-five chiefs on 2 November 1796:

> Whereas His Excellency Frederick Haldimand Esquire late Governor of the Province of Quebec did by a certain Instrument under his hand and Seal give and Convey to the Six Nations a certain Tract or Parcel of Land Situate on the Grand River, of River Ouse, (then) within the Province aforesaid Extending Six Miles on each side said River from its Mouth to its Source to them and their posterity for ever—And whereas the said Nations are desirous to dispose of a part thereof to such person or persons as may be inclined to purchase the same, in order that the monies arising out of the Sales thereof may be laid out and Converted to the purchasing an Annuity or Stipend for the future support of themselves And their posterity.[87]

The statement goes on to authorize Brant to sell 310,391 acres,[88] documenting not only Brant's power of attorney but also its limitations. Under it, Brant actually surrendered 352,707 acres[89]—14 percent more than he had been authorized to sell. In 1830, the provincial government deemed that to be a negligible oversight: "It occurs to us to remark upon this schedule, that the lands specified in it *somewhat exceed in the whole the quantity which is mentioned in the power of Attorney to Capt. Brant*—a difference *probably* unimportant as the boundaries given in the last mentioned instrument were it is *presumed*, understood and intended to comprise all the tracts particularized in the schedule."[90] Ironically, when Haldimand had made a more innocent error in *granting* Six Nations lands—he used his military seal rather than his government seal on the proclamation—his error was deemed irreparable for the Six Nations.[91] In other words, errors in favour of the British were acceptable but errors in favour of the Haudenosaunee were not.

Also of importance in Brant's power of attorney is the rationale behind allowing these sales. At a Confederacy Council in 1834, Royaner Henry Brant recalled the Haudenosaunee oral record regarding some of Joseph Brant's land actions:

> In the investigation of those Documents as the Trustees have ascertained that the Late Captain Joseph Brant was their accepted agent to act as such for the Six Nations. And as we the present Chiefs of the Six Nations have in our investigations likewise discovered that the Late Joseph Brant was impowered by the Six Nations to act as their Agent. He was appointed as their Agent from his having a more perfect comprehension of the Manner in which business is transacted by the whites.
>
> The Chiefs did not intend when they appointed him their Agent that it should be in Captain Brant's power to act as he thought proper.[92]

Henry Brant's statements reflect the mixed feelings about Brant and his work on behalf of the Grand River Haudenosaunee.

This discussion of Brant only touches the surface of Brant's complicated position in Six Nations society.[93] Brant did work on behalf of the Haudenosaunee people, especially in helping to secure the Grand River tract through Haldimand.[94] But the fact that Brant also served his own interests in his many land dealings complicates his standing within the Six Nations community. Brant was an authorized spokesman and negotiator but was never given sole authority at any time. Several of his personal gains were obvious to the community—his large home in the Mohawk Village and a new home in Burlington—and that must have given pause to many. In fact, in 1801, the council released him from his spokesman duties and replaced him with a group of twelve Royaner who were to serve as the signing authority for the community.[95] He could still assist in dealing with the British but his authority had been taken away.[96] Brant helped secure Six Nations land interests on the Grand River Territory, but his side dealings and his poor relationship with Simcoe also inhibited those interests.[97]

Land Grants and Leases

Shortly after arriving on the Grand River, Brant and other Confederacy leaders made land grants to white Loyalist "friends" they knew from their former homelands (primarily the Mohawk Valley). While Brant was often the mouthpiece, many of these decisions were made by nation councils or the Confederacy Council. The words of these leaders are not nearly as well documented as those of Brant, but important references can be found.

Simcoe left Canada in 1796, being replaced by Peter Russell as administrator of Upper Canada. Russell is reported to have been much less adversarial to Brant and other Six Nations leaders.[98] Some of his writings even indicate that he understood the position of the Six Nations and sympathized with their situation, as demonstrated in the following excerpt of a July 1797 letter to the Duke of Portland:

> ... had the Five Nations conceived the lands on the Grand River were given to them upon any other footing than that on which they formerly possessed those on the Mohawk River, they would never have come to settle in this Province; That they were a free & independent Nation; —That their affection for their Father the King of Great Britain had induced them to leave a most fertile Country every way competent to their Support, in order to live under His Majesty's Protection, as they disliked the people who inhabited the Country they had forsaken;
>
> That Sir Frederick Haldimand had received them with open arms, and promised to buy for them the land they had made choice of on the Grand River; That he afterwards told them he had bought it from the original Proprietors, & given it to them and their posterity forever. That they then considered this Gift as a free unequivocal Grant of Country, with every Power over the disposal of it, which they had over their lands on the Mohawk River. These they could sell or give away at their pleasure, and they conceived that their power over the Grand River land was the same. When White Men had informed them that they were mistaken, they applied to Lord Dorchester and to Governor Simcoe for a new Grant. This was promised them; and a Grant had been offered to them by Governor Simcoe which they rejected, because it did not convey this Power. They were then promised that their Requests should be laid before their Father the King.[99]

In this letter Russell articulates two important points: 1) the Haudenosaunee believed they held title to their Grand River lands in the same manner as they had in their previous homelands; and 2) Haldimand had made promises on behalf of the Crown that Simcoe failed to uphold. Russell attempted to rectify this by agreeing that the Six Nations should have the right to lease their property so long as the Crown was involved in the final contract.[100] This set the stage for legalizing several leases already entered into between Brant and various white settlers and land speculators. It also allowed confirmation of the land grants made to friends of the Six Nations by Brant and other Confederacy leaders. In those confirmations, however, the government often went beyond the actual terms of the original grants, as with the additional acres included in the block grants.

While it has been argued by other scholars that Brant wished to encourage assimilation amongst the Grand River Haudenosaunee,[101] many of the grants were actually made under terms of friendship and familial connections with the Six Nations. Recalling those land grants, Royaner Henry Brant explained the reasoning used in deciding to share these lands with their Loyalist friends: "The Chiefs have in their recollection that some whites settled on the Grand River at the same time with the Six Nations. The Chiefs permitted those whites to settle there from the circumstances of those whites having endured the same difficulties which they themselves had experienced."[102] While the land grants were made as gestures of peace and friendship and out of pity for the condition the Loyalists found themselves in, the Six Nations were not naive. They realized that they had no authority over these white men who, despite being their friends, might later try to sell the lands for their own benefit rather than share the profits with the Six Nations, the actual owners of the lands. They attempted to curtail these potential problems in the official terms of the land grants.[103] For example, a 1787 Loyalist land grant included the following clause: "never to be transferred to any other whomsoever."[104] Standard provisions such as this indicated the Haudenosaunee intention to assist their friends in providing for their own families through the sharing of Six Nations land.

By the 1830s, however, many of these Loyalist friends had far exceeded the boundaries of their grants. As noted by Royaner Henry Brant: "the Chiefs allotted to those whites small portions of Land to settle on. But the Chiefs are now surprised to find that some of the Farms of those whites now reach as far back as three miles into the Forest."[105] Statements from council exemplified the nature and diversity of the grievances against these individuals who had been given land based upon their friendship with the Six Nations.[106] The abuses by many of these land grantees grew and became one of the arguments used by the provincial government in seeking to convince the Six Nations to surrender important tracts of land in the 1830s and 1840s.[107]

Beyond military alliances and old friendships from the Mohawk Valley, several grants were based on a much deeper connection to the Six Nations people: these grants were made to white men who had married into Haudenosaunee families. One such grant was made to John Dochsteder, who had married into the community. Problems with this grant were discussed at an 1806 council:

> Among these difficulties we may also include, that tract of land disposed of by the late Mr. Dochsteder, You know that the Chiefs, many of whom are now deceased, gave to him, as well as the others, who had served in the war with them an allotment of land, this was enlarged to him in regard to his children, who belonged to our tribes; and by us are considered, as being legitimate, according to our customs, he had first been married to a Cayuga woman by whom he had one daughter, and at her decease to a woman of the Onondagas, by whom he had another daughter: both children he brought up in the house with himself before and after the deaths of their mothers—The tract thus given him he extended without our knowledge, by a fraudulent survey, which when we first discovered, expecting it to be for the benefit of the Orphans in compassion to them we have made no remonstrance, thinking that as they had acquired the superfluous wants of Europeans, they might stand in need of it all.[108]

In essence, the council was allowing the Dochsteder children to choose how they would live their lives and, if they chose to live as whites, they were to be provided for through the inherited rights of their mothers. Ultimately, the desires of the council in this situation were not carried out because their father had sold the property to a land speculator named Canby, who claimed over 20,000 acres as a result of the transaction.[109]

The Dochsteder grant and a grant made to John Huff (another white man married to a Haudenosaunee woman) were discussed at an 1809 Confederacy Council meeting:

> Brothers,
>
> A piece of land that was given to a John Huff for the good of his family who are of a Delaware mother—we find he is selling

off—therefore as we have forbid these sales it is our request that all those who have attempted to purchase be expelled, and his family left in peaceable possession.

Brothers,

A tract of land that was granted to John Dochsteder, who had also a family of our nation; but who sold a great piece of land to a Mr Canby which exceeded what we intended to give but as we expected that the income or payment to be derived therefrom would fall to his family who were our people we did not oppose it; but that not having been the case—we desire that justice may be done them—The farm in possession of his daughter of the Onondagas and Grand son of the Cayugas we confirm to them.[110]

As evidenced in the Dochsteder[111] case, his failure to provide for his family with the land that had been granted to them (through him) resulted in a call for justice by the chiefs. In both cases, the land rights of the Haudenosaunee children were confirmed; as the original land grants had intended, those lands continued to be set aside for the support of those Six Nations families. In later council meetings, when land cessions were being discussed, the rights of children of mixed parentage continued to be upheld. It appears that because of their family's land grant these children were not fully integrated members of any of the Six Nations villages, but the Council continued to recognize their rights to land as Haudenosaunee citizens.[112]

Of course, granting property to the offspring of a white man and a Six Nations woman confirmed the matrilineal tradition of the Haudenosaunee. However, in some families their affinity for, and connection to, a Six Nations identity—as well as their respect for the authority of the Confederacy leadership—faded as a result of the influence of their non-Native relatives. This became a major point of contention among those who were connected to families holding Brant leases (as opposed to land grants). Many of those families attempted both to claim a liberal interpretation of their leases and to argue for land grants and annuity payments as Six Nations citizens. At an 1835 council, Lower Mohawk[113] Chief Johnson said that "our people connected with the Whites and who are to get Government deed favoured on Joseph Brant's Leases we exclude from any further share of either our Lands or money."[114] In essence, the council was asserting that their people could not have it both ways: an individual could not gain twice from Six Nations lands. This council decision had nothing to do with ethnicity but rather reinforced the relationships entrenched in Haudenosaunee treaties such as the Kaswentha and the Covenant Chain. They were simply informing those who fell into that category that they had to choose which way they were going to interact with the Grand River Territory. They could either be Haudenosaunee citizens holding communal land rights and receiving annuity payments, or they could be white leaseholders who were about to have those leases transferred to sales, making them landowners under the laws of the province. These sentiments were echoed later in 1835 regarding the Johnson family: "Issac Locke Mohawk Chief [said] ... we wish that the family of Johnston who are now running out the leases of the Land which they claim on our Lands should not be permitted to do so as we do not think that they have Joseph Brant Leases and we do not wish to lose any more of our Lands upon every pretense to a claim. That family are too far removed from Indian Blood to have any Indian Rights."[115] While it might appear that the Mohawks (Locke was speaking for his nation in this case) were referring to blood-quantum in this statement, they were actually talking about the Johnston family's connection to Haudenosaunee identity. In their minds, if an individual was asserting their rights as Brant leaseholders they had "chosen the other ship" (referring to the provisions of the Kaswentha). Again, members of this family were attempting to have the best of both worlds—at the expense of their Haudenosaunee relatives.

Russell's reinterpretation of the Simcoe "deed" allowed the confirmation of many leases made by Brant and other Confederacy leaders. Brant's rationale for the leases is often debated, but less discussed are the motivations of the Confederacy leadership in these decisions. At a Confederacy Council meeting in 1803, it was requested that a "permanent fund" be established from leasing proceeds.[116] This request matched one of Brant's arguments for leasing. The economics of the Grand River Territory demanded a certain amount of cash for the community to function. Hunting became more difficult every year due to the encroachments of white squatters, leaseholders, and land grantees who pushed beyond the boundaries of their acknowledged lands, as noted at the 1803 council meeting: "Our Tract of land is now surrounded by white people so that our hunting is done away. Many in our Nations [are] perfect Strangers to farming, and should we be deprived of making the most of our landed property, many must Starve."[117]

In many ways, the Haudenosaunee economy was still greatly impacted as a result of the Revolutionary War and removal. Many of the Six Nations villages in the original homelands had, before 1776, become permanent villages. Those villages had developed over decades, which accorded time to build log cabins, barns, and other buildings necessary for the more permanent-style villages that had become prominent in the eighteenth century. Twenty years in the Grand River Territory, even in the best conditions (which was not the case), would not have been enough time to replace all the structures lost in the war. These factors contributed to the dependence of the Six Nations upon their annuity funds from leased Grand River lands. And, as Williams and Nelson propose, the Six Nations leased their lands, rather than selling them, with the knowledge that the lands would revert to them as the Haudenosaunee population grew and more land would be needed for settlement.[118]

White squatters, who took up residence illegally on Six Nations land, presented another problem. In some cases these squatters negotiated permission with individual Haudenosaunee, but surely those involved must have known this violated both Haudenosaunee and British law. On the Six Nations side, this was a question of individual versus collective rights, which the Confederacy was very clear on, as evidenced in the words of Tekarihoken (John Brant) in 1831: "because individuals have no right to convey the common property of the Six Nations. Although it may be possible that partial renumeration [sic], who without legal right gave the possession, it cannot in justice and equity follow, that the Six Nations should be satisfied, or bound to comply with such sales, because if this principle be admitted a few individuals might soon dispose of the property of the whole Six Nations."[119] In regard to the white squatters, the Royal Proclamation was binding upon British subjects and anyone else who wished to settle in Upper Canada. Despite the fact that both legal systems involved in these transactions deemed such actions illegal, the provincial authorities rarely attempted to rectify these situations.[120] A significant number of the squatters (probably, in fact, most) never even bothered to secure a fraudulent purchase from any Haudenosaunee individual—they simply came upon a piece of land, looked around to see if any other white man was there and, if finding none, took possession of it.

The Haudenosaunee were persistent in laying their grievances against the squatters before the provincial and imperial governments. Government officials repeatedly promised to rectify these abuses but rarely kept those promises.[121] The Haudenosaunee knew their influence with the British government was not what it once had been, primarily because United States military threats were no longer a major concern. Therefore, Haudenosaunee leadership had to negotiate for the best settlement they could get from the provincial government in regard to the squatted-upon lands. While the Six Nations sought redress for the squatter problem, the province sought further land cessions from the

Haudenosaunee. The solution the Confederacy offered was to lease the lands that had been improperly squatted upon. Onondaga Chief Echo spoke to the issue at the Confederacy Council on 31 January 1833:

> Brother it is the same case with our lands by the lower parts of the Grand River we are willing that those lands occupied improperly by the Whites should be likewise leased for our benefit. All the Land below the Road leading from Camboro to Rainham we wish to be leased without reserve for our benefit. Brother what we have consented should be leased as expressed in the forgoing parts of my speech we conceive to be enough—we are convinced that Lands are the true wealth of both Indians and Whites. Brother I beg you will excuse my language yours and mine are entirely different. Brother we recollect times past we have sold a great part of our lands and we do not think that what remains is more than we require for the prosperity and comfort of our posterity.[122]

In addition to evidencing the Haudenosaunee attempts at compromise, Echo's words express important sentiments about Haudenosaunee land philosophy. They recognized that the whites placed great financial value upon land, but the value he expressed for the Haudenosaunee was beyond financial. The Kanyen'keha word for "valuable" is *kanó:ron'*, which is translated to mean: "it is expensive, precious, valuable, hard to come by."[123] For the Haudenosaunee of the 1830s—like their ancestors who deemed land as the one who "provides for our needs"—land was certainly all of these things. Economics were only one small piece of that relationship. When Echo stated that his language and English were completely different, he was clearly articulating this difference in land philosophy. He had not seen evidence of the whites having an affinity for land beyond its economic value. He also made it clear that the Haudenosaunee considered it necessary to hold on to their remaining lands. Later in the same council, he also recalled the Six Nations alliances with the Crown:

> The King promised us that we never should come to poverty we also have been faithful in performing our promises, also the additional Tribes, the Delewares, the Tutulies and the Nanticokes—Brother some of us the old Chiefs went through the two last wars and some of our young men went faithfully through the last war we have therefore to me reason for saying that this Land belongs to us. *Brother you have told us that if we lease our lands we should be*

the richest Indians in the province but we think that we had better keep
our Lands as the money might go away but the Lands will stand fast.[124]

The Six Nations knew the true value of the land was not financial. Land was still seen as "Yethi'nihstenha Onhwentsya," and Echo let the province know that the value of the land exceeded any price they might place upon it.

The Six Nations grew quite savvy in their land dealings with the province during the 1830s. They had surrendered land for the town plot of Brantford in 1829, but the province repeatedly asked for more land to accommodate the growing town. There were frequent negotiations regarding the money owed for certain parcels, such as those of churches. Several of these parsonage lots remain unpaid for and are part of ongoing Six Nations land claims (see Appendix 2). Royaner Isaac Locke, speaking on behalf of the Upper Mohawks, addressed the issue of these church lots at an 1834 council:

> with respect to the remainder of Brantford there was no men-
> tion made of Land to be granted gratuitously for the building of
> a Church or Churches but there were some lots designated for
> that purpose, with the understanding that they were to be paid
> for—Brother at the Council held at York the Lieut. Governor
> said that our Lands here were granted to us as a remuneration for
> the services of our forefathers and we wish to have the same hold
> of our property here that we held over our property there in the
> States—At the time of Sir Wm. Johnson and of Colonel Claus
> and of General Haldimand they each of them promised that we
> would be remunerated for all such losses as we sustained—Brother
> as you are now our Agent and under the same Government as the
> persons above named we expect you will fulfil those promises.[125]

Beyond demonstrating that the Six Nations expected to be paid for church lots, Locke also reiterated the fact that the Haudenosaunee believed that they held their lands in the same manner as they had in their previous homelands. They also began pressing for a written accounting of their monies, surrendered lands, and remaining territory (see Map 4).[126]

Life in the Villages

While most of the written record for this time period focuses on external land relations and council proceedings, some records document aspects of village life, demonstrating how the Haudenosaunee were actually interacting with

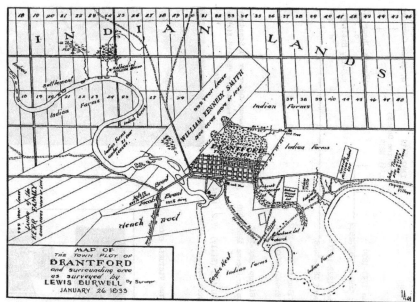

Map 4. Town Plot of Brantford and Surrounding Area, 1833. Source: Brant County Museum; as credited by Grand River Branch—United Empire Loyalists' Association of Canada. http://www.grandriveruel.ca/Newsletter_Reprints/93v5n1Loyalist_Land_Holdings_P1.htm. The map is a recreation of a map drawn by surveyor Lewis Burwell in 1833.

their land. The villages were the domain of families and, in structure, much like the villages of the old homelands. These settlements were governed by local leadership representing the families living there. Proceedings of village councils were not recorded in writing, probably because they were considered the business of that particular village and did not pertain to the external relationships with whites. Because of this lack of evidence regarding internal village workings, most of the written documentation in this area comes from white travellers who chronicled their journeys through the territory. This includes the journals of surveyors commissioned by the province to set boundary lines for the tract. Brief descriptions appear, based upon typically short visits to different Six Nations villages. Other depictions are found in the journals of missionaries. The travellers, surveyors, and missionaries were usually chronicling events and activities for which they had very little context, but, all things considered, their writings still provide insight into Six Nations life during this era.

Some of the earliest descriptions found come from the reports of the Society for the Propagation of the Bible and addressed their desire to increase the numbers of converted Haudenosaunee. Often these reports by missionaries include early censuses of the Grand River Haudenosaunee (see Appendix 1). For example, in a July 1788 report, the Mohawk Village (referred to by the missionary as "New Oswego") was reported to be comprised of: "Men 120, Women 154, Children 125, Total 399."[127] The missionaries were concerned with assessing their success in terms of converts. While some were optimistic in this regard, many wrote in dismay regarding their struggles to convince the Haudenosaunee to "be saved." The British supported these ideals not only for Christian purposes but also for political ones. They expected much less agitation from a Six Nations population that followed the same religious philosophy they did.[128]

While it has often been assumed that the Mohawks were almost completely Christian before arriving on the Grand River, these missionary records suggest otherwise. For example, Methodist missionary reports from 1834 and 1836 declared half of the Mohawk population to still be "pagan" in their beliefs.[129] The other nations remained much more steadfast in maintaining the ceremonies of the longhouse as the basis of their faith, including those of the Upper Nations of Cayugas, Oneidas, and Tuscaroras. The Lower Nations were often considered almost impenetrable by various missionaries; most reported only minimal success among some of the Delawares and none among the other Lower Nations.[130] It appeared that one of the largest challenges these missionaries faced was the lived contradictions of many of the Christians surrounding them (both Native and white). The Reverend Alvin Torry discussed these problems in 1823: "The Delawares . . . Some of this Nation attend pretty regularly at one of my appointments among the whites. Others possess their prejudices, which appear to have been formed upon the immoral conduct of the white people. . . . The Cayuga's and Onondaga's are the next nation above, and though they are far the most moral, and have the best regulated community, they are entirely unfriendly to the Gospel . . . 'the Mohawks have the Gospel,' say they, 'yet rum causes them to commit wickedness.'"[131] Longhouse believers often equated Christianity with lax morals, based upon the troubles they had seen among those of the Mohawks (and neighbouring whites) who had chosen the Church. While this indicates a split between longhouse followers and Christians, it does not support the reported divisions between entire nations based upon religion.

Most of the Haudenosaunee had made the transition from small bark long-houses to cabins while still living in their original homelands. However, their new cabins had a strong interior resemblance to their former houses. These similarities were often duplicated in houses on the Grand River, as noted by a visitor to the Cayugas in 1817: "the fire is still in the middle of their dwellings: the earth, or block of wood suffices for chair, and table; and planks, arranged round walls, like cabin births, form their beds."[132] While this particular visitor was quite dismayed at the "rude" accommodations of the Cayuga, these interiors demonstrated a strong connection to older structures and within that a physical manifestation of the family relationships they symbolized. The same traveller also visited the Mohawk Village and cited "Dr. Aaron" (Hill) regarding the impacts of the War of 1812 raids inflicted upon that settlement: "the village had been injured much during the war, which had put a stop to its improvements, and dispersed the inhabitants over the country."[133]

The Grand River visitors also made note of agricultural and hunting activities of the Six Nations. The survey diary of Augustus Jones refers to planting grounds shared by the Mohawks and Cayugas in 1797.[134] When the Crown in 1829 suggested that the Six Nations divide their remaining lands into six tracts, one for each nation, Mohawk Royaner Isaac Locke responded that it would be too difficult because of shared cornfields between the Mohawks, Cayugas, and Oneidas.[135] An 1808 provincial government report references Seneca cornfields along the lower part of the river on a tract that was to be ceded to the Crown.[136] Both of these references note the presence of nation-based and even inter-nation communal farming. Though the Haudenosaunee adapted some Western technologies in their agriculture, basic values and familial practices continued.

Another economic practice that continued on the Grand River lands was hunting and fishing. Despite the difficulties caused by land cessions, land disputes, and unauthorized flooding, Six Nations men continued to hunt and fish across the territory and beyond the tract's boundaries, in accordance with acknowledged parameters of their hunting territories recognized by the Crown in 1701. Mohawk Pinetree Chief John Norton noted that among the Haudenosaunee some of the best hunters were also excellent farmers: "The Mohawks are improving rapidly, there are several so much agriculturists as to raise three or four hundred bushels of Wheat in the Year, those who suppose that the being farmers will deliberate them from being Hunters are mistaken. the most industrious at the plough, generally shew themselves the most persevering at the chase, when in Winter they throw aside the hoe and take up the gun."[137] As with the continuity of growing corn and other crops, the persistence of hunting and fishing demonstrates the continued connection between the Haudenosaunee and the natural world.

Unfortunately, the harvest of both animals and plants did not always meet the needs of the Six Nations. Poverty and starvation were reported in different years when problems with the crops were experienced. These hard times were not reflective of the Haudenosaunee failure to plan for the future, but rather indicated the fragile economy of the territory, which had not had a chance to stabilize in the thirty years since migration. In terms of building up an adequate supply of food to sustain a poor harvest, the Six Nations simply had neither enough time nor enough surpluses to establish an adequate buffer.[138] While they are not identified in the records reviewed, it can be assumed that whatever stores of corn and other crops the Haudenosaunee had built up by that point would have been impacted by the War of 1812—either through sharing corn with British troops or by theft and destruction at the hands of the Americans.

While life in the Haudenosaunee villages along the Grand River was not without its problems—especially during the War of 1812 and other times of famine—the Six Nations had re-established themselves on their new homelands. They rebuilt their villages with the help of the family and nation structures that had given them the strength to endure hardships in the past. They continued to pursue similar economic practices: some old, like planting and hunting; some new, like leasing.[139] They continued to conduct their business within the Confederacy structure, and that structure remained mindful of the lessons of Haudenosaunee cultural history. The Rotiyanehson began and ended their councils with the Thanksgiving Address (usually referred to in the records as "opened with the usual ceremonies"), indicating their ongoing commitment to uphold their responsibilities to their people and to all of creation. Words of condolence continued to be used in the council to address the losses of Royaner, Clan Mothers, and even imperial officials. They also persisted in holding their lands in common, despite pressures from the province to alter this practice. When it became clear that changes had to be made in order to protect their territory, the Confederacy Council developed systems of allocation based upon Haudenosaunee values. In this, everyone was to receive land, not just heads of families. The council also called for the continuation of communal "national" lands surrounding the council house as a testament to the fact that no one owns the Council Fire: it belongs to all. They also made a provision to maintain access to communal resources such as timber, sand, gravel, and plaster beds. Subsequent dubious land cessions inhibited the enactment of some of these provisions (primarily, the amount of land accorded to each person was reduced to 100 acres per family), but the spirit of holding the land in common and benefiting equally from the bounty of the territory persisted.

Land Cessions in the 1830s:
External Pressures, Internal Reactions

From the time of settlement on the Grand River, the Haudenosaunee continued to hold property communally, although in a slightly different manner than in their original homelands. The primary difference was found more often in the mixed-nation villages, which often saw property being passed from a father of one nation to children of a different nation. Furthermore, those villages that were built close to each other often shared cornfields, with two or more communities planting and harvesting in a communal manner. The external pressures upon Six Nations lands during the 1820s and 1830s were extreme, yet the values of communal landholding persisted, as evidenced in the historic record.

In October 1829, at a Six Nations Council held at the Mohawk Village, the lieutenant governor first suggested that the Six Nations divide their lands in order to protect them:

> [Isaac Locke, a Mohawk Chief] With regard to dividing the land to the several tribes and then to families, we see great difficulties would arise in consequence of intermarriages and the Mohawks, Oneidas and Cayugas being located so near each other, we cannot expect the Oneidas and Cayugas to abandon their houses and improvements and remove to such allotments of land as may be selected for them without renumeration [*sic*], which we the Mohawks have not to give them, nor do we wish to see our cornfields divided, because it may lead to misunderstandings amongst our tribes.

> [VanEvery, Cayuga] Our Chiefs who are dead and gone had the firmest confidence in the King for he had always assured them that their lands should be secured to them and their children without encroachment for which we are thankful.

> With respect to dividing our lands among the several tribes of the Confederacy, we leave to our Elder Brothers the Onondagas—we remember that our forefathers had their respective territories and villages, but our situation is now different.

> We are much grieved to see that our lands are likely to be overflowed by the dam of the Welland Canal Company—we entreat the assistance of the Governour. We are willing to lease

> our unoccupied lands, that is above Brantford and at the mouth of
> the River, but such as we at present occupy to remain as they are.
>
> Whatever plans the Government may adopt we understand is to
> be for the benefit of our several tribes forever. . . .
>
> We wish the interest money to be paid every year at the same time
> we receive our presents.[140] We also wish a correct statement of our
> money now at interest.[141]

Locke's statements regarding the difficulties in dividing the lands of the
Mohawks, Oneidas, and Cayugas demonstrate that while there was a crossing
of "national" boundaries within the villages (meaning that the villages were
becoming inter-tribal), the communal aspect of the land continued. In fact,
the close proximity of the villages seems to have created a more collective
attitude toward the larger tract—sentiments that were in complete opposition to the lieutenant governor's suggestions. VanEvery, speaking on behalf
of the Cayugas, recalls the belief of his predecessors in their friendship with
the Crown, another reminder to the government of its responsibilities to the
Six Nations. He also reminds the council that in their original homelands the
lands were held by individual nations, but he notes that the Grand River situation was "now different." Next, he leaves the final decision to the Onondagas
in accordance with Confederacy Council protocols. In his final statement, he
requests a proper accounting of the Six Nations annuity funds; he mentions
the trust in the King but does not hesitate to ask for reassurance.[142]

The squatter problem continued to worsen in the late 1820s, and the only
recommendations provincial and imperial officials made were that the Six
Nations surrender more land. With each request for more land, the Indian
superintendent and the governor (as representatives of the Crown) promised
to protect the reduced Six Nations tract from further interference by white
settlers. For example, at a meeting with the Confederacy Council on 22
March 1830, the superintendent (John Brant),[143] speaking on behalf of the
governor, promised that the legislature would address the squatter issue.[144]
At the same meeting, the governor's message requested allowance for a road
from Long Point to Canby Town, as well as discussing the surrender of the
Brantford Town Plot.[145] The government was as consistent in making those
promises as the settlers were in breaking them.[146] As evidenced earlier, the
Haudenosaunee continued to remind the Crown of its responsibilities to the
Confederacy as allies and toward protecting their lands in accordance with

the Covenant Chain, the Beaver Hunting Tract Treaty, and the Haldimand Proclamation. While the Crown continued to be delinquent in its promises, the Haudenosaunee persisted in its reminders.

Besides the squatter issues, other land pressures came about as a result of the dam building on, and subsequent flooding of, parts of the Grand River. Meanwhile, populations were growing in previously ceded town plots such as Brantford, Dunn, and Cayuga. Some of these pressures appear in the written records of several Confederacy Council meetings. For example, several important statements were made at the 19 April 1830 council held at the Onondaga Council Fire:

> [John Jacobs, Cayuga Chief] . . . The Government is able to get our lands out of the water.
>
> Onondaga Chief [not named],—we reserve to ourselves the right of fixing the price of the lots in Brantford, both occupied and unoccupied. The votes of the Six Nations on these subjects are unanimous—let no one hereafter say that they were not present nor did not concur in the present vote.[147]

Chief Jacobs referred to the flooding of lower parts of the Grand River as part of the diversion of Grand River waters from Dunnville for the Welland Canal. The council never consented to those dams, but once they were constructed the government promised that the Six Nations would be compensated both for lost crops and lost lands.[148] The Onondaga chief made two important statements in regard to the land issues of the day. First, he made it clear that the council, rather than the Indian Department, would set the prices for the Brantford lots. Second, he asserted that these decisions were made in accordance with Confederacy protocols—an important persistence of tradition in the face of change. The Six Nations grudgingly accepted that they could not stop these changes[149]—and that the Crown was unwilling to stop them—but they asserted that they would make changes on their own terms and in accordance with their own values. In these actions, the Confederacy Council was guided by the unity created under the Great Law in order to provide for their people through their remaining, united lands.

The decision to keep the lands united rather than subdivide them by individual nations was based within many provisions of the Great Law. Lower Mohawk Royaner John Johnston articulated one of those provisions in an 1833 Council meeting: "we have reason for saying that [we] wish to keep the remaining Lands united, for union is through Six Arrows, together are not to be broken, one by one they are easily."[150] In this statement, Johnston recalls the metaphor used by the Peacemaker at the time of the founding of the Great Law: "a single arrow is easily broken, but five arrows tied together are strong." His words help to explain the importance of the council's repeated decisions to keep the lands united as the common property of all.

The Grand River Navigation Company: A Symbol of Negligence and Fraud

While the Crown failed to protect the Grand River Haudenosaunee repeatedly against various land grabs, quite possibly its greatest negligence came through the investment of Six Nations trust funds in the Grand River Navigation Company. This project cost the Haudenosaunee hundreds of thousands of dollars on ill-advised stock purchases, and the company claimed and flooded hundreds of acres of prime Six Nations property. The initial investment was made by the superintendent general of Indian Affairs, Samuel P. Jarvis, without the consent of either the Six Nations Trustees (a three-man body formed in 1797 to protect the financial interests of the Haudenosaunee) or the Confederacy Council. When the Six Nations learned of this purchase from their funds, they demanded clarification from their trustees, who covered for Jarvis and ensured them that their investment was sound and would eventually accord them great profits.[151] The chiefs were not convinced and became exceedingly concerned when the company began claiming various tracts of Six Nations lands and other natural resources. Cayuga Royaner Fish Carrier addressed this issue on 23 July 1834:

> Brother we are now more at our case with respect to the Grand River improvement and we are acquainted with the laws respecting that improvement and think the Agent has not been guided by that Law in his operations. At your last council you told us that you had great pleasure in informing us that our Lands would be safe from injury from the overflowing of the River. We are sorry that the law is not the guide by which the operations of the Company have been directed. Mr. Thomson the agent of the Grand River Company claimed for the Company a piece of Land from John Nelles six miles up the River and 50 chains wide. We think it proper to report the proceedings of the Agent to our Superintendent as he is taking our Stone and Timber and has not paid for any of it.

... Brother we wish the Governor to send down a civil Engineer
to the Grand River to view the plans of the Engineer of the Grand
River Navigation Company. So that it may be ascertained that
that company shall not claim more of our Lands than is absolutely
required for the purpose of the improvements contemplated. After
the Engineer has made the necessary Examination it is desired by
the Chiefs that he may be instructed to make a written report of
what Lands the Company claimed and what Lands he conceived
necessary for the performance of the Works.[152]

Despite not being consulted on the initial investment, the council made it
clear that they expected to be informed of all future developments, both of
the company and its use of Six Nations natural resources.

Still, the situation between the Haudenosaunee and the Grand River
Navigation Company did not improve. The flooding had more than financial
ramifications, as noted in an 1838 report of the New England Company:[153]

The Number of Indian Inhabitants on the lower Part of the
Grand River has lately considerably decreased, owing to the
Dams across the Grand River, for the Purpose of improving the
Navigation, having flooded to a considerable Extent the bordering
Lands, and introduced Agues and Fevers into Situations formerly
healthy. Other Parts which the Indians used to frequent have
been disturbed and intruded on by White Settlers improperly
and illegally introduced, but whom no Prosecutions in the Court
of Upper Canada have yet been able to dislodge. Among the
numerous Complaints and Petitions which Sir George Arthur
states he has received from the Indians, there is certainly none
entitled to more immediate and serious Attention than this
Grievance, nor any Cause that militates so much against the
Operations of every one who sincerely desires effectually to benefit
the Indian Population.[154]

The earlier flooding had also had similar negative health impacts,[155] but this
time the Six Nations were actually paying for their lands to be flooded, their
health to be compromised, and their natural resources to be taken.

Councils between the Six Nations and representatives of the Crown in
the 1830s and 1840s continued to be consumed with the issues of squatters,

poor business investments (made by the trustees), and other grievances of the Confederacy against the provincial and imperial governments. The Six Nations feared that the navigation scheme would fail and they would lose not only the lands that had been taken but also a significant portion of their annuity. Johnston discusses one of their attempts to remove themselves from the company: "So anxious were the Six Nations to extricate themselves from the arrangement that they were prepared in 1839, with the government's approval, to sell as many as 40,000 acres—fully one-sixth of their remaining lands—to a settlement enterprise if in return it undertook to purchase their stock in the navigation company. Satisfactory terms could not be arrived at, however and the proposed deal fell through."[156] Through all of this, the trustees were unable to keep Indian Affairs officials from investing more and more of the Six Nations funds into the company.[157] As the Six Nations had feared, it soon became clear that the company would fail. Samuel Peters Jarvis, superintendent general of Indian Affairs, had made the decision to invest in the navigation venture upon the suggestion of the lieutenant governor of Upper Canada, Sir John Colborne. When the company's failings began to appear, Colborne convinced Jarvis to invest further in order to buy out white investors who were personal friends of Colborne. The City of Brantford held the mortgage on the company and foreclosed on it in 1861. Despite the fact that Jarvis could not account for funds taken from the Six Nations' accounts and had actually combined his own personal accounts with Indian funds, he was never prosecuted.[158] The Six Nations have grieved their financial and property losses at the hands the Grand River Navigation Company (and its influential friends) before many levels of government, all unsuccessfully to date. Canada maintained that the responsibility in this situation is imperial and not local, despite the transfer of liabilities under the 1867 British North America Act. The inability of the council to get proper redress from the Crown—from the post-1840 Province of Canada to the Dominion in 1867—in this situation had long-term effects on the confidence of some of the Six Nations people in their own government, leading to political destabilization in the decades that followed.

Land Consolidations and the 1841 "Surrender"[159]

While initially resisting the government proposal for internal land divisions, the Confederacy Council did eventually concede. However, rather than effecting the terms articulated by the council, Jarvis (on behalf of the imperial government) came up with a new proposal—known as the 1841

"Surrender"—which he convinced seven chiefs to sign on 18 January 1841. The chiefs did so without the authority of the full council.

The government had created this scheme as a means of covering their own errors regarding Six Nations lands. As Johnston explains, "over the years whites had frequently been encouraged not only by Indians but by officials too to move on to Indian lands with the assurance that they would enjoy a pre-emptive right to it once it was surrendered and put up for sale."[160] This was confirmed on 7 September 1840 by John Gwynne, a barrister appointed by Jarvis to scrutinize the Six Nations' land affairs. Jarvis had pressure from all sides to settle the land questions once and for all. He framed the 1841 "Surrender" in order to calm the fears and agitations of the white settlers who had been led to believe that their title concerns would be quickly addressed. It is less clear what motivated the seven chiefs to participate in this scheme.

A month after the "Surrender" was signed in Kingston, a petition was forwarded to the governor general claiming that the authority of the signatories was an incomplete representation of the Confederacy. The sentiments of the seven chiefs[161] who signed the document were described in a meeting held with Charles Bain (deputy warden of forests at Grand River) held on 16 February 1841:

> The chiefs stated further that while willing to surrender a portion of their lands they still wanted the government to reconsider what had been done on the grounds that the chiefs who signed the surrender acted only as individuals and not as representatives of the whole of the Six Nations. Moreover, they claimed that two of the signatories, one of whom was Skanawate (John Buck), were prevailed upon to sign by Jacob Martin, the Mohawk interpreter for the occasion. Bain also reported, however, that if even if [*sic*] the Six Nations were willing to surrender all or part of their lands they wanted more time to deliberate on details and particularly on the reserve to be allotted them, a subject not covered in the 18th January document. Bain's report was enclosed in a letter Winniett sent to Jarvis on 18 February 1841.[162]

Despite the fact that the signatures were questionable at best, Jarvis moved forward with the scheme.

A series of petitions followed over the next two years, until 1843, when the governor general established the Rawson Commission to investigate the matter. By this time, most of the signatories had recanted their support of the

1841 "Surrender."[163] One, Peter Green, claimed he had not signed at all.[164] There were also allegations that John Smoke Johnson had been promised land for his support, but when that promise was not carried out he withdrew his support.[165] In the summer of 1843, the Six Nations responded to the commission, requesting "the larger tract that the Rawson Commission had recommended ... many of the lands sought after on the south side of the Grand River ... 55,000 acres ... certain tracts, including the Johnson Settlement, the Eagles Nest, the Oxbow, and the Martin Tract, should be retained and leased on a short term basis so that younger Indians more acculturated to white ways could ultimately be placed on them."[166] In addition, the Six Nations stated their opposition to, as Charles Johnston writes, "any proposal to reserve portions of the Six Nations' lands for such 'visionary' schemes as town plots on the grounds that they did not sell off quickly enough to satisfy the Indians' financial needs."[167] The commission considered the points of the petition, and their final ruling, dated 4 October 1843, made provisions for all of the above except the one regarding town plots. This is likely the primary reason that the Six Nations today still own small tracts of land in several towns within the original tract. The "reserved" lands under this ruling would total 55,000 acres—representing only about 5 percent of the territory originally promised by Haldimand. The so-called "surplus" lands were to be sold for the benefit of the Six Nations' annuity (which was in need of replenishing after the navigation fiasco). The final boundaries of the newly created "reserve" were agreed upon by the council and the government in 1847.[168]

To add insult to injury, the Crown again failed to fulfill its promises in regard to protecting the significantly reduced Six Nations lands from white squatters. Once everything was settled and the final boundaries set, the Six Nations were forced to compensate those squatters who had to be removed from the newly reserved lands for their "improvements." The monies came from the Six Nations annuity funds. The 1841 "surrender" demonstrates continuity in the unwillingness of the government to protect Six Nations lands from squatters, speculators, and the government itself. While the Royal Proclamation was used as a justification for not recognizing full title of the Grand River tract belonging to the Six Nations, the government failed to enforce the Royal Proclamation when it came time to apply it to white settlers.

1847 Mississauga Settlement

In the spring of 1847, the Credit River Band of Mississaugas approached the Six Nations, looking for a place to retire to after the surrender of nearly all of their remaining lands near Lake Ontario. Recalling their bonds of friendship and brotherhood, the Confederacy allowed the Mississaugas to settle upon the southeast portion of their recently reduced lands.[169] The Mississaugas and the Six Nations came to an agreement at that time regarding the provisions of the Mississauga settlement upon the Haudenosaunee lands. However, the Indian Department failed to carry out the financial aspects of the agreement, which led to later renegotiations between the two nations, first in 1865 and then again in the 1890s and 1900s. In 1896, the Confederacy Council charged a committee with the responsibility of determining the provisions of the 1847 and 1865 agreements. Their report, dated 3 February 1896, is excerpted below:

> We have carefully gone into the matter and after reviewing minutes of Council we find as a fact that the Mississaugas, after several days Councils by the Six Nations Chiefs, when the Mississaugas Chiefs were present, it was decided on the 7th day of May 1847, that the Mississaugas were granted permission to make their future home on a block of land on the South East corner of Tuscarora and composed of from Lots 1 to 12 in the 1st and 2nd concessions of the said Township of Tuscarora, containing 4800 on the following conditions Viz:
>
> 1st Mississaugas nor any member or family of them, shall not exchange, sell or convey any part or portion of the said parcel or block of land to any tribe or member or family of any tribe or to any people save and except to members or families of the Six Nations without the knowledge and consent of the General Council of the Six Nations and sanction and approval of by the Governer [*sic*] General.
>
> 2nd The door to the timber and for making from the maple trees sugar, be open in Common and family on whose lot may be a deficiency of timber, may if convenient have it from lots without the block assigned and set apart for the tribe and in like manner any family of the Six Nations will be privileged to have timber from off the said block if found necessary, or either of the parties that of making sugar from maple trees under the general regulations.
>
> 3rd The Mississaugas to repay to the Six Nations the amounts paid by them for the improvements on the block or respective lots within and composing the tract.

We also find at a Council meeting held in May 1865: the said Mississauga tribe was granted permission to occupy 1200 acres in Oneida on same conditions as those in Tuscarora.[170]

Neither the 1847 settlement nor any subsequent agreement ever surrendered the Six Nations interest in these lands. They all, however, do provide for the primary use of that part of the territory by the Mississaugas. In effect, this sharing of territory with the Mississaugas meant another reduction in Six Nations lands, bringing the total area under sole Six Nations jurisdiction down to about 49,000 acres. The Indian Department's failure to pay the Six Nations for the improvements of the tract became one of many grievances addressed by the Rotiyanehson in the latter part of the nineteenth century.

ooooo

Many threads of continuity wove together through this difficult era in Six Nations history: threads of displacement, resettlement, broken promises, and fraud. These threads appeared over and over, continually reducing the Grand River Territory—much like the great abuses of the Mohawk Valley land grab of the 1690s and 1770s. But through all of that, the Six Nations managed to weave together their lives with the Grand River lands. The record shows that despite the heartache of removal from their homelands and in spite of the Crown's failed promises, the Haudenosaunee did rebuild "their house" on the Grand River. In this house, they left a legacy for the generations that followed them to persevere through losses, to use their words and their minds to protect their people and their land, and to always maintain their relationships with that land and all of creation.

　　This era also saw a shift in the relationship between the Haudenosaunee and the British. While the Confederacy held tight to the Covenant Chain— and continually reminded the British to do the same—the Crown began to move away from its commitment of "peace and friendship forever." While they did not wish to go to war with the Haudenosaunee, their dependence upon them as military allies waned following the War of 1812. As a direct result, British Indian policy began to shift from relationships based on treaty obligations to one of paternalistic oversight, heralding "civilization" to "children" who had once been "brethren." This change in British policy was expedited as the imperial government sought to transfer its responsibilities for Indian affairs to the colonial government.[171]

As a direct result of the failures of the Crown to protect Haudenosaunee lands on the Grand River, this era was plagued with a series of Six Nations territorial reductions. On most occasions, illegal land transactions—violating both Haudenosaunee and British laws—were eventually sanctioned by the imperial government. These land transactions not only left a legacy of Haudenosaunee distrust for the settlers and their governments but also serve as the origins of several contemporary Six Nations land claims, such as the Grand River Headwaters, Brantford town plots, Nelles' Tract, Young's Tract, and the Grand River Navigation Company.[172]

Through this loss of land, the Haudenosaunee found themselves in a very similar position to that faced by their families at the close of the Revolutionary War—forced to abandon their homes and villages and the bones of their ancestors in order to relocate and build their lives in a new place. The migration was shorter in this case but certainly not without grief and hardships. At least with this move, their families—and representative governing structures of the Grand Council—remained intact, unlike the situations faced by many in the 1780s. But the "house" of the Confederacy was damaged by the events of this era. The 1841 "Surrender," coupled with the inability of the Chiefs to stop the navigation ventures, created concern among some of the people regarding their Confederacy leadership. The 1841 "Surrender" demonstrated that the Crown was more than willing to deal with an unrepresentative body if it was to its benefit. As the middle of the nineteenth century approached, the Six Nations turned their minds toward rebuilding their homes and protecting their lands for future generations.

CHAPTER 5

Skanata Yoyonnih—One Village Has Been Made

Following the 1847 agreement to consolidate their lands, the Haudenosaunee were faced with moving once again, as their ancestors had been forced to do during and after the American Revolution. Fortunately, this time their new homes were not far from the old, but the move still required considerable effort and sacrifices in terms of homes and villages that were built on land surrendered under the agreement. But rather than allowing their losses to consume them, the Haudenosaunee set their minds toward building a new consolidated community, in effect making one "village"[1] comprised of all of the nations. In the consolidated territory, land allotments of 100 acres were made to all Six Nations families as a means of subdividing the land. The consolidated settlement patterns followed along the lines of the older dispersed settlements along the river. Despite the individual allotments, the land continued to be held in common, and the Confederacy Council created policies that governed the communal responsibilities to both individual allotments and the entire tract.

While the Six Nations were dealing with the changes in their territory, the imperial government was also experiencing change. The Crown continued to devolve its responsibilities in Indian Affairs to the colonial government. They, in turn, continued to explore assimilationist methods and policies for dealing with what they saw as the "Indian problem." Despite this push for assimilation, the Confederacy Council was willing to work with the devolved Indian Department as long as the policies they attempted to enforce did not conflict with the Haudenosaunee vision for their own community. Under the British North America Act, the newly formed federal government assumed responsibility for the administration of Indian Affairs. Six Nations issues were addressed under this new system by a visiting superintendent locally and by the superintendent of Indian Affairs at the federal level. Toward the end of the nineteenth century both the local and federal administrations began to impose their policies more and more upon the Six Nations Council— actions the council did not accept. As a result, the relationship between the Confederacy and the Dominion (in right of the Crown) weakened. The Six Nations, furthermore, did not accept the authority of the Indian Department over their affairs and regularly laid their issues before the governor general as the Crown's representative in Canada, as provided for in the treaties between the Haudenosaunee and Great Britain.

Indian Affairs and the visiting superintendent often encouraged any po-litical dissension they saw forming within the Six Nations community. They then used the dissension they helped to create as justification to criticize the Rotiyanehson and call for their replacement. In this, the government had ulterior motives regarding Six Nations land. The Confederacy Council had forwarded a series of land claims, which the government knew had legal basis. Later, the government also attempted to claim Six Nations land through the Soldier Settlement Act (as they had done in other Native communities), an action adamantly opposed by the council. Through all of these attacks, the Confederacy Council continued to govern the territory guided by values and principles of the Great Law. As the community grew, they developed policies and procedures to address land issues in key areas including inheritance, mar-riage disputes, annuity payments, adoption, enfranchisement, band transfers, leases and sales, "national parks," and communal property. These policies could be deemed a "code of land rights" for the Grand River Haudenosaunee, but in actuality they represent policies of responsibility. Through all of these, the council laid out key parameters around the use of land, including the belief that land was intended to support children and the duty of all landholders to respect their property and not plunder the natural resources it contained.

The Consolidated Community

As the council worked out the final boundaries of the consolidated territory, many of the Six Nations people began their moves onto the reserved tract. For the first time ever, people of all of the Six Nations (and the dependent nations) were living in one connected "clearing," with no significant "forest" between nation- and family-based settlements. In essence this large "clearing," in Doxtator's words, became a single Six Nations "village."[2] While plenty of forested lands remained, the new tract was divided into 100-acre allotments, placed in the names of family heads. In most cases, extended families (those related by clans, blood, and/or nation affiliations) were located near each other. The result of these locations was the creation of neighbourhood-type settlements across the consolidated territory—many of which still exist in the community. As such, the reserved lands became like a single "village," with the surrounding clearing (although in literal physical arrangement, the community became a mosaic of small individual "clearings") providing the internal economy of the community. The "forest" (or exterior) became off-reserve lands where Six Nations people often went to work in order to supplement the farming/gardening and other economic activities[3] of the "clearing." Six Nations people also continued to use this "forest"—land outside of the consolidated settlement—for harvesting purposes (hunting, fishing, plant gathering).

The idea of subdividing the territory into family-based units first arose in the 1820s. At that time, the council was opposed to the allotment suggestions of the lieutenant governor, citing reasons such as the difficulty of relocating villages that were close together and the complication of dividing shared cornfields.[4] The Rotiyanehson eventually consented to the allotments, hoping the concessions would provide the necessary structure to protect the remaining Haudenosaunee lands from squatters and land speculators.[5] Unfortunately, the 1841 "Surrender" caused a great deal of turmoil within the council and among the people. The ensuing consolidated territory consisted of just 55,000 acres, allowing for only 100-acre family allotments—representing at least a 50 percent reduction (increasing by the number of family members)[6] from the decision of the council during the 1830s discussions with the province, when they determined there would be 200-acre allotments to every man, woman, and child.[7] At the time, 100 acres probably seemed like a large tract of land, but the many generations that sprang from those 1840s families often consisted of hundreds of descendants—amounting to less than one acre per person if the tract had been divided among all of the heirs across those generations.

While most of the families were dealing with their third (or more) removal in less than seventy years, they did not allow their grief and sense of loss to consume them. Instead, they set their minds toward clearing land, building homes, and re-establishing their farms. Much of the reserved tract was wooded, especially that of the lower part of the Grand River, which became known as the "Lower End" (also referred to as "Down Below"). While forested land still existed in the "Upper End," much of it had already been cleared for farming as people had moved from the Upper villages (Mohawks, Oneidas, and Cayugas) during the 1830s. The settlement patterns on the reserved territory followed very closely the village dispersal patterns along the Grand River during the initial settlement. Those original villages were built primarily on the northeast side of the river, but the consolidated tract was located almost exclusively on the southwest side, with the exception of limited parcels retained by Tuscaroras and Onondagas along the northeast side of the river.[8] The Upper End was also superior in terms of soil type; the lands upstream consisted of clay and clay loam, while the Lower End was primarily only clay.[9]

With the cleared lands and better soil types (more suited to farming), the Upper End was extremely advantaged in the early days of settlement on the consolidated territory. It also appears that the families were more willing to adopt European-style farming methods, giving them even greater advantages. While the willingness to alter their planting and harvesting techniques may have been an indication of changes in philosophy,[10] most of the advantages accorded to the Upper End were probably coincidental. The result, however, was a growing economic disparity between the two ends of the territory. This disparity is often referred to as a "conservative v. progressive dichotomy,"[11] a theory that can be discounted by evidence of both Christians and longhouse followers in both areas. In the 1830s, missionaries reported that longhouse followers had a significant presence in *all* of the major villages.[12] It is unlikely that significant demographic changes in faith occurred in only ten years. In reality, there were great diversities across the newly consolidated territory that were far more complicated than a two-way split. Depending on the issue or the topic, lines would probably have been drawn in many different directions, not simply geographically or religiously.

I have referred to the consolidated Grand River tract as "one village," using the analogy of traditional Haudenosaunee village patterns. However, a village in the Western sense of the word also developed shortly after the consolidation. Bearing the same Kanyen'keha name as the entire community, the Village of Ohsweken grew at the intersection of two major crossroads through the reserved lands, near the centre of the territory among primarily Tuscarora[13] families. The visiting superintendent, David Thorburn, suggested that the council relocate their meetings from the Onondaga Village (near Middleport, Ontario) to the growing village of Ohsweken in the 1860s. Eventually the council consented in order to reduce overall travelling time for the chiefs, although dissension was expressed by several of the Onondaga Royaner. Construction began in 1863 and the grand opening took place in January 1865, commemorated with a recitation of the Great Law.

This time period also saw the continuation of older community social structures and the rise of many new organizations. Longhouse followers gathered at three different longhouses spread out across the territory. In the 1890s the Seneca Longhouse branched off from the Onondaga Longhouse, and established themselves "Down Below" near both the Onondaga and Lower Cayuga Longhouses. The Upper Cayuga Longhouse served as the ceremonial gathering place for the people of the "Upper End," gaining the name of Sour Springs Longhouse, based on its close proximity to the Sour Springs, a sulphur spring located in that part of the territory. Several social organizations were developed as well, including the Six Nations Agricultural Society, an Orange Lodge, and several brass bands. Churches such as Kanyenkeh (St. Paul's Anglican Church) and the Tuscarora (later Ohsweken) Baptist Church continued to serve the religious needs of the Christian element of the community. Education was also a key area of concern and development for the consolidated community. Many of the old villages had schools already established, but those schools had to shift as the people moved onto the consolidated lands as well. By the 1860s, the Six Nations people had six schools to choose from, including the Mohawk Institute, a residential school operated by the New England Company on Six Nations lands in the City of Brantford, and the Thomas School, which was operated by the council.

Government Attempts at Assimilation

As the need for military assistance from the Six Nations waned so did the official recognition of their status as allies to the Crown. Government policies shifted from protecting (at least in name) the sovereign rights of the Six Nations toward attempts to "civilize" and integrate them and their lands into the fabric of Upper Canada. Of course, these policies affected other Indigenous nations in similar ways, but it is important to note that each Indigenous nation had a unique relationship to the Crown based on their individual treaty agreements. Starting in the 1830s, the Crown became preoccupied with addressing the "complications" of their relationships with the different Native peoples in Upper Canada, most notably the expense of administering the Indian Department and upholding their financial promises to their Native allies, including the annual presents. As many governments do, the government of Upper Canada (and, after 1841, the Province of Canada) established commissions to investigate and report on the matters, including six in total between 1828 and 1858. Each report built upon the findings of those previous to it, and all contributed to the growing attempt to "protect, civilize, and assimilate" the Indian population.

The 1828 report focussed its central recommendations on the development of a reserve system; Indian Affairs officials spent the next eighteen years attempting to implement that suggestion on the Grand River. The Bagot Commission, the fifth to study the "Indian problem," made several recommendations regarding claims and disputes of the Grand River Haudenosaunee. This report was released in January 1844, three years after the 1841 "Surrender," and recommended a compromise that would reserve enough land to provide 100-acre allotments for each Six Nations family. This recommendation was carried out in the 1847 settlement that established the consolidated territory. The commission also recommended that the government purchase the Six Nations' interest in the Grand River Navigation Company, since the investment had been made without the consent of the Confederacy Council. The government did not accept this recommendation.[14]

The Pennefather Commission of 1858 suggested extreme spending reductions in an attempt to streamline Indian Affairs.[15] Part of the implementation of the recommendations included the end of the annual presents. Like the Bagot Commission, the Pennefather Report included summaries of evidence from each Native community in the Province of Canada. Specific recommendations were made for many of these communities as well, but nothing of note was mentioned regarding changes in government relations with the Six Nations. The report did note, however, that $32,000 had been spent from Six Nations funds to reimburse squatters for their "improvements" on the consolidated tract.[16] Despite recommendations for major reductions in spending and other policies, the overall direction of the Pennefather Commission was to increase the pursuit of assimilation policies.[17] Partnered with this commission report, Pennefather also championed the Civilization Act of 1857, which allowed for land division through enfranchisement. Native governments, including the Six Nations, protested the provisions of this act as a violation of the Royal Proclamation and treaty agreements.[18]

Under the 1867 British North America Act, the Dominion government was created and accorded the responsibility of administering the Indian Department under the new federal structure. The Dominion exercised its power over "Indians, and Lands reserved for the Indians" through its first Indian Act in 1869. News of the act spread quickly, and in June 1870 the Grand Indian Council called a meeting.[19] At this council, leaders of various Native communities from southern Ontario and Quebec met at Six Nations to address concerns about the new government policies established in the act, including a provision that would replace the hereditary Confederacy Council of Grand River with an elected band council. The assembled leadership rejected the new act—section by section and on the whole—in their deliberations. They rejected the government's threats to eject Natives from their territories for not possessing a location ticket from the Indian Department and took exception to the provision that stripped a "Status Indian" woman of her band membership and land rights if she married a non-Indian. While many of the leaders agreed that provisions needed to be taken to protect Native lands from non-Indian husbands/fathers who might attempt to squander their family's property, they disagreed with the Dominion attempts to claim authority over lands and membership in this manner.

Despite wholesale denouncement of the 1869 Indian Act by various Indian communities, the Dominion continued to develop assimilation policies that attempted to "eliminate the Indian problem." The Indian Advancement Act was passed in 1884 with the sole purpose of instituting elected band councils to replace traditional governments—like the Haudenosaunee Confederacy Council at Grand River—that continued to exist in many communities. These elected band councils were to be structured like municipalities and, in the words of Williams and Nelson, were intended to be "brown imitations of the federal elective system."[20] The creation of band councils was an important step toward achieving the departmental goals of assimilation and civilization. The Confederacy Council was quick to react and denounce the provisions of the act.[21] The relationship between Six Nations and Indian Affairs deteriorated from this point forward.

The Six Nations (and their Haudenosaunee relatives in other communities) had a growing list of grievances regarding aspects of the Indian Act and other government programs and initiatives. Williams and Nelson summarize some of the key concerns:

> Residential schools and missionary schools and institutions were used to diminish Haudenosaunee languages and religious observances. The Indian Act made ceremonies associated with Midwinter and Green Corn thanksgiving illegal.[22] By the early 1900s, anyone raising money to make claims against Canada without the permission of the superintendent general faced imprisonment. Any Indian who became a doctor, lawyer or university graduate automatically lost his right to live in his community or be considered one of its people.[23]

Many of these issues served as the basis of grievances made by the Confederacy to the governor general and other government officials. For example, in March 1898, the Six Nations sent a delegation "in accordance with the long established custom" to address the governor general on issues of amendments to the Indian Act, fishing rights along the Grand River, and other treaty concerns.[24] Despite the colonial impositions on the part of the Dominion, the Rotiyanehson never failed to remind the Crown's representatives of the Six Nations' status as allies and never failed to act in accordance with their understanding of their responsibilities under their treaty agreements.

Development of Council Land Policies

While the Dominion and Indian Affairs personnel attempted to legislate the internal workings of First Nations communities from the outside, the Confederacy Council created its own provisions for governing the community internally. The council developed policies and procedures for dealing with a variety of issues, including property. Prior to the 1847 territorial consolidation, property disputes were addressed by village councils and other family leaders. Written records were not known to have been taken at these village councils so the nature of those decisions is unknown. However, it is logical that the policies developed later by the Grand Council to govern the consolidated lands mirrored procedures practised in the smaller villages of earlier generations. Most of the issues arising from land disputes related to membership and land rights.

The council was faced with the responsibility of governing the consolidated community within the constraints of a greatly reduced territory—with essentially no "surplus" lands—as well as an annuity that had been significantly reduced due to the ill-fated and unsanctioned investments of Six Nations funds into the Grand River Navigation Company. Dealing with these realities, the Rotiyanehson created patterns and policies to guide their decisions in the cases that came before the council regarding property. Several categories of property were addressed by the Confederacy Council. As outlined below, these categories demonstrate the council's major areas of concern and patterns of land policies.

Inheritance

Most of the property-related cases heard by the council involved inheritance issues. These ranged from estates with confirmed wills to arguments between potential heirs in cases without approved wills. In estate cases without a will, the council regularly relied upon the Indian Act as a framework for property distribution. Some would consider this a symbol of acculturation on the part of the council, but the chiefs adapted the provisions of the act to fit with their own view of fairness and propriety. Depending on the particular situation, the council would apply the provisions of the act where they deemed them appropriate and in accordance with community values.

The distribution most common using the provisions of the Indian Act was a division of property wherein the widow(er) would receive one-third of the entire estate (usually the part of the property with the house and other improvements), with the remaining two-thirds distributed between the children.[25] An example of this division was in the disposition of the estate of Jacob General in 1882: the council distributed one-third of the property to his widow, "as the law dictates," and the remaining two-thirds was divided between their seven children.[26] It is important to note that the only cases that came to the council were those that needed dispute resolution. There certainly would have been many estate cases without a will where the family and other interested parties reached an agreement without the intervention of the chiefs. The actual number is unknown but, based upon conservative estimates, it is approximated that 20 percent of cases came to the Council for adjudication.[27] Similarly, cases with a will would also only have been addressed to the council in situations of dispute.

Certain moral offences could void the typical distribution, however, as found in the case of the will of William Murdock in 1890. The council record provides the following synopsis of the case:

> Last will of Wm Murdock:
>
> Two wills were read; neither accepted; the first (made in 1885) left his estate to his wife but she was not living with him at the time of his death, was living with another man and had a family with him.
>
> The second will was made in Oct 1890 and left the estate to his father; but his father was a white man and cannot hold property; applied the Indian Act to the decision; found that the wife was not of 'good moral character' and therefore was eliminated from inheritance; determined his two brothers (Joseph Murdock and Thomas Dixon) would inherit the estate in two equal shares.[28]

It must be noted that the Indian Act provided that a woman of "poor moral character" could be excluded from property rights; however, the council applied this rule to both men and women in the cases of abandonment and adultery.[29] Their interpretation of moral character was consistent with the traditional Haudenosaunee views of marriage. These included the expectations of monogamy, non-violence, and providing for the family (the duty of both spouses). Another provision prohibited divorce but did allow separation; however, the first spouse was always considered the "lawful" spouse. The provisions also upheld that all children were to be provided for, regardless of their parents' marital status.[30]

In other situations, the council made decisions contrary to the Indian Act. In the case of the estate of John Gibson, the council actually divided the property into six equal shares with the widow receiving only a one-sixth share instead of the one-third directed by the Indian Act.[31] The remaining shares were divided between their three sons and two daughters. While no explanation was given, no grievances were filed against the division of the property,[32] leading one to assume that all of the parties involved accepted the division as fair.[33]

In inheritance cases where the deceased left only children as heirs, if everything was equal in their relationship with the deceased parent, the property was divided equally between all children, or the heirs of any deceased children. Many of the cases heard by council, however, included claims by children or others who had cared for the deceased property owner. In these cases, the council gave caregivers priority in property division. In *James Johnson v. Festus Johnson* (March 1886), the council awarded the entire estate of Festus Johnson, not to his heirs but to those who took care of him before his death; the council found that James Johnson and his sisters did nothing to assist with their father's care and therefore forfeited any inheritance.[34] Often, the council would make property allocations dependent upon the commitment to care for surviving spouses or dependent children, as demonstrated in the settlement of the estate of Elijah Turkey in July 1915: "With reference to the property of the late Elijah Turkey situated on Lot No. 27 RR the Council decided to locate his daughter Mary Turkey on Twenty acres together with granary at once. The eight acres not being occupied by the widow of the late Elijah Turkey to go to Mary Turkey at her step-mother's death. But in return she must take good care of her step-mother through all her sicknesses and at time of death bury her."[35] The emphasis on caring for the deceased or their dependants is indicative of Haudenosaunee values. It reinforces the belief that land was meant to provide for people, and that people have a responsibility to care for the land and each other.

Confirmation and Interpretation of Wills

In developing its land policies, the council assumed the responsibility for confirming wills.[36] Certainly, this decision was most likely inspired by a desire to make estate cases easier to manage, although most community members did not opt to make a will declaring their desires for property dispersal upon their death. In the early 1900s, the Department of Indian Affairs asserted that they were the only authority in confirming wills.[37] This was met with a grievance from the Confederacy Council, as the department had upheld council's right to confirm wills for several years prior.

The council also had to determine whether or not a will was binding in the case of wills it had not confirmed. In at least one case, the council accepted the provisions of a verbal will, where the wishes of the deceased had been articulated to several individuals who provided testimony to the council when the estate case was heard.[38] Several of the cases also drew the attention of the Department of Indian Affairs when it deemed the council's interpretations of wills to conflict with the Indian Act. An example is found in the estate of James Johnson (1907): "With reference to the request of the Department of Indian Affairs for explanation as to the relationship of the late James Johnson and Matilda Winney (Johnson). The Council will explain as follows:—That the late James Johnson and Matilda Winney, were immorally living together as man and wife for 28 years. The legal widow of the said Jas Johnson is Annie Fish. The property in question however was acumulated [sic] during Matilda Winney's time therefore the Council decided that the property should go to her, and her family according to the wish of the late James Johnson by Will."[39] This case demonstrates the commitment of the council to base its decisions within principles of Haudenosaunee propriety and fairness, regardless of the Indian Act.

Marriage Disputes

The cases of marital disputes that came to council often dealt with property concerns. Typical situations centred on couples who had decided they could no longer live together and were looking for redress in terms of property divisions and custody of children.[40] In their interpretations of these cases, the council again often looked to moral standards as a basis for their decisions. A committee of chiefs was charged with investigating the relationship to determine who was at fault and to provide their suggestions for the council's actions. In most cases, the council would accept the report of the committee and enforce their suggestions for property disposal and custodial placements for minor children.[41] In the cases of marriage disputes,[42] the committees and the council were extremely concerned with determining fault for the relationship problems, usually stemming from charges of adultery and abandonment. In those situations, an individual might lose what had been his or her property prior to the marriage, as in the case of Lucius Henry (1916): "The Council decided to instruct the Secretary to issue summons for Lucius Henry for next Gen'l Council to explain his action in deserting his family. In the meantime Emmie Isaac and their child is to remain on his property until further notified by the Council."[43] This particular case did not appear again in the council records, so it is unknown whether or not Mr. Henry returned to his family or left his property to his child and the child's mother. However, the message of the preliminary decision is clear: if a person abandoned his or her responsibilities, his or her property could be transferred in order to meet the needs of an abandoned spouse and children.

In situations where one spouse was deemed to be at fault and where the other was willing to forgive the indiscretion, the errant spouse was given the opportunity to make amends.[44] A spouse deemed to be at fault who refused to return forfeited any joint property as well as the custody of and annuity monies for any minor children, as demonstrated in *Joseph Hill v. Mary Hill* (1924): "The Council appointed a Committee as follows: Chiefs Fred Martin, Isaac Kick, Robt. Froman, Ed. Doxtater, D. McNaughton and Robt. Henhawk to arrange a settlement if possible. The Committee reported that they were unable to arrange a settlement between them as the wife refused to go back to her husband although he is prepared to take her back. Therefore the husband Jos. Hill is to have the full control of his property and have the care of the children. The Council decided to approve of the findings of the committee."[45] This case and others similar to it demonstrate two key aspects of the confederacy structure. First, each Royaner had the responsibility to counsel his people and provide advice and encouragement in troubled situations; and, second, compassion was shown to individuals who made mistakes, but if that person was unwilling to make amends then he or she was no longer eligible to receive the financial "benefits" of the family (property and annuity monies). This also reflects the importance of children in Haudenosaunee culture—the interests of the husband and wife in marriage disputes always took a secondary role to the needs of any children from the marriage. That is why the council would transfer the personal annuities of the errant parent to the custodial parent as a means of providing additional support for the children.

Other Disputes

Land disputes often arose between neighbours, usually concerning boundary lines or natural resources such as timber. Boundary lines became a reality in the community with the 100-acre allotments that followed the territorial consolidation. Tensions around these lines often grew as the original parcels became subdivided through inheritance and sales. The Locating Line Committee—a standing committee of the council consisting of Royaner trained as surveyors—was charged with the duty of addressing such issues. Other cases in this category often included disputes over property sales. In those instances, the council would hear the evidence of all parties involved and make a decision based upon their interpretation of the evidence. In all cases, however, the council had a general policy that issues should first be addressed to the respective chief or chiefs of the parties to the complaint.[46] Here, the council was reminding chiefs of their responsibility to work within their extended families and nations as mediators when necessary. Many of these cases were, in fact, family matters fully capable of being addressed within the extended family structures of the Haudenosaunee. The rationale, also, was to reduce the number of complaints coming to the full council, reserving that time for cases that did, in fact, have implications for the broader community.

Paylists and Annuity Accounts

The Six Nations annuity accounts were created from the financial proceeds of land leases and sales across the larger Grand River tract, starting in the 1780s. While financially based, the creation of the annuities did serve as another example of the use of land to provide for the needs of the Six Nations people. This represents an important continuity of Haudenosaunee values and relationships with land; land continued to provide for the needs of the people, as a mother provides for her children.

The proceeds of the annuity were dispersed semi-annually to all Six Nations people appearing on the paylist, the official membership of the community. Tensions arose over the paylist when the Indian Department attempted to impose its membership regulations upon the Six Nations,[47] despite contradictions with Haudenosaunee definitions of membership. For example, the Indian Act of 1869 defined Native women married to white men as having forfeited their Indian status via marriage; any children from these marriages were also deemed ineligible for Indian status. Under Haudenosaunee law, one might lose the rights of citizenship only through acts deemed to be in violation of the Great Law (such as murder or treason). Furthermore, under the matrilineal kinship system, Haudenosaunee paternity is unnecessary for citizenship.

As the Indian Department increased its interference with local governance, the council did modify their criteria for appearing on the paylist because the department refused to send annuities for persons they deemed to be non-members.[48] Furthermore, it was determined by the council that marriage outside of the community greatly affected the families. For example, in 1915 the council raised concerns about the departures from the community of young people who had married non-Indians as well as the impact of those marriages on the annuities.[49] The council raised similar concerns for Six Nations citizens who married Natives from other communities.[50] In both situations, there was a general impression that non–Six Nations spouses had less attachment to the community and often were found to have abused the property or resources of their spouse.[51] These concerns originated with the problems of land grants among mixed-marriage families such as the Dockstetters in the late 1700s.

Official Six Nations policy eventually conformed to the Indian Act, wherein Six Nations women who married non-Indian men were struck from the paylist. This decision contradicted the traditional law of the Confederacy. It appears to have been based on two rationales. First, the Indian Department was refusing to pay the annuities for women in these marriages, so if the council maintained their membership the overall annuity to the entire community would have been reduced. Second, the historic experiences of the community had demonstrated that white men who married into the community often plundered the resources of their wives and children. It is not known how many women were struck from the paylist due to out-marriage because Indian Affairs personnel—not council—removed their names. In the marriages between Six Nations women and men belonging to another Indian band in Canada, the woman's name was transferred to the band list of her husband. If the marriage dissolved or if the woman was widowed, she was allowed to return to Six Nations and after a short readjustment period (usually a year), wherein the woman demonstrated her commitment to returning to the community, her name was restored to the paylist. Such was the case for Lucy Brant and her child in 1881:

> In regard of Mrs. Lucy Brant who was erased from our list when she married a young man named Brant from Bay of Quinte and two or three years after they moved down to the Bay and soon after he died and about three or four months after she and her daughter

returned to their reserve with the full intention of residing here. The
Council then placed her name and her daughter on the pay list but
the Indian Department disallowed [it] . . . we think we shall have
better chance to place her on our list and ask the Supt Gilkison to
use his influence with the Supt General to confirm our decision.[52]

Lucy Brant's case also reflects the interference of the Indian Department in
what was an internal community matter.[53]

Beyond the issue of out-marriage, the council also defined other ways in
which a member might forfeit annuities. These included immoral activities
such as adultery or abuse of timber privileges. Later, the criteria for removal
also included leaving the community for a period of more than five years, but
the council made provisions that allowed former members to be re-recognized
upon their return to the community.

Adoption

As we have seen, the Great Law provides a structure for naturalizing people
of other nations into the Haudenosaunee through adoption. The processes of
adoption remained consistent with the principles of the Great Law for the
Grand River Haudenosaunee. However, as a result of Indian Affairs' policy
interference regarding membership, the Six Nations were forced to utilize
adoption to officially reintegrate people who by Haudenosaunee law were
already citizens. The case of Lucy Brant and her daughter stands as a classic
example of one of the types of adoptions practised by the Six Nations Council
to counteract Indian Affairs legislation.[54] The council regularly "adopted" the
children of Six Nations members who had married into other Haudenosaunee
communities but eventually returned to the Grand River Territory.[55] Again,
under Haudenosaunee law, these people were already citizens, but the for-
mality of adoption allowed these individuals to be placed on the Six Nations
annuity paylist. They did not similarly accommodate those children of Six
Nations–white marriages.

The Council also adapted policy in regard to adoption eligibility. Most
important was an ancestral link to the community on either the maternal or
paternal side. This was not part of the criteria for adoption as provided for
under the Great Law, but was developed to accommodate conflicts with the
Indian Department. It was probably also due to the shrinking annuity and
the need to ensure that those people living in the community were provided
for. Most of the adoption cases heard by the council involved the enrolment

of "illegitimate" children born to unmarried Six Nations mothers or fathers.[56] At different points during the period examined, the council policies varied regarding the requirements in these areas. Originally—and in accordance with Haudenosaunee values—any child born to a Six Nations mother was eligible for enrolment. Children of Six Nations men were also accorded the same consideration.[57] Eventually that policy shifted to one requiring both parents to be Six Nations members.[58] There existed in all cases a great deal of contention with the Indian Department, as the Indian Act declared "illegitimate" children to be ineligible for band membership. In many cases, the department took years before confirming adoptions, depriving families of the children's annuity funds during that time. For example, the council had adopted several illegitimate children in November 1894, but Indian Affairs did not confirm those adoptions until September 1897.[59]

Moral character and family or community contributions were also considered in adoption applications. A classic example of these considerations is evident in the adoption of Jonas Smith in 1902, as noted in council minutes:

> Council decided to add Jonas Smith to the paylist; his mother (a direct descendant of Capt Joseph Brant) was on the Six Nations paylist until she married a man from the Oneida Reserve; she was restored to the Six Nations paylist when she returned.
>
> The young applicant has resided on this reserve for the past 17 years, and is very industrious, and he has always borne an exemplary character. He has no interests in the Oneida reserve.[60] The Council in view of the good character of the young man decided to follow precedent cases wherein Indians have been adopted and placed on the paylist of the band, after years of probation and after a record for good conduct and industry had been established by the applicant. They therefore decided to place his name on the paylist.[61]

Obviously, the council was placing this case within the context of the policies they had developed over several years in dealing with the membership situation created by Indian Affairs. They looked to the overall character of the applicant and his record of positive contributions to the community. He exemplified the expectations of a Haudenosaunee citizen and demonstrated a confirmed commitment to contribute to the overall welfare of his family at Grand River and to the community as a whole. Furthermore, he was the son of a Six Nations mother, and in this action the council acted not only in accordance with their adapted adoption policies but also within the parameters of citizenship as established under the Great Law.

Pension List

For individuals without a source of income beyond the annuities, the council developed a process whereby members could apply for temporary relief or for permanent assistance through a pension list. The pension list also authorized assistance for retired council employees.[62] Members who held land were usually deemed ineligible for the pension list but were often offered short-term relief, as seen in the application of Elizabeth Johnson in 1901: "Council refused to place Elizabeth Johnson on the pension list because she has land. They did issue her a relief order for $2."[63] This policy reflected the idea that land holdings accorded a person (or family) the ability to provide for him- or herself. In 1906, the council passed a bylaw requiring "near relatives" to meet the needs of aged and disadvantaged family members beyond their pension and annuity monies.[64] In other words, they formalized the extended-family responsibilities of Haudenosaunee social structures within council policies. This came in response to a growing number of relief applications from sick and elderly members of the community. Under this provision, family members could apply for a loan to assist needy family members, as demonstrated in the 1917 case of Jim White and Eliza White: "The Council decided to allow Mr. Jim White the sum of $2.00 per week relief for Eliza White (mother) in the form of a loan and if he should die his property will go to the nation, the Council will then take action."[65] Through the use of his land as a guarantee for the loan to assist his mother, White's case also demonstrates that land belonging to "close relatives" was also expected to assist those in need.

In times of great need across the community, the council would increase the annuity payments in an attempt to offset hardships such as crop losses or epidemics.[66] In the later years of this era, the Department of Indian Affairs became increasingly less co-operative in processing such orders from the council.[67]

Enfranchisement

The 1857 Enfranchisement Act offered aspiring Natives the opportunity to relinquish their Indian rights in exchange for becoming subjects of the Crown. Three young Mohawk men from Grand River were among the first Indians to apply for enfranchisement. Elias Hill was the only successful applicant, not only from Six Nations but from all of the First Nations communities to which the act applied.[68] The chiefs opposed the decision of the local commit-tee in this case, primarily because the act allowed for the allotment of twenty hectares of reserve lands to successful applicants. They feared the long-term implications for the consolidated Grand River lands through the application of this legislation.[69] The "opportunity" for enfranchisement continued to appear in subsequent legislation, including the Indian Acts of 1869, 1876, and 1884.

In a review of Six Nations Council records from 1880 to 1924, only four cases of enfranchisement applications arose; however, a preliminary review of the files of the Indian Department during those same years produced 197 cases.[70] Obviously, most people interested in enfranchisement did not bother to address the council; they were on the fast track to leaving the authority of the Six Nations Council behind them as they became full-fledged Canadians. The council minutes regarding the application of Frederick Loft address the many concerns of the Confederacy regarding the application of the Act:

> The Council refused to endorse the application of Mr. F.O. Loft who is applying to the superintendent General of Indian Affairs for enfranchisement, upon the following reasons. 1st we claim that our land is not Crown land, but that it is granted to us by Deed by King George the III through Sir Frederick Haldimand in 1784. 2nd we do not approve of cutting up our land as we have no land to spare for that purpose. 3rd Therefore we hope that the Superintendent General of Indian Affairs and the Governor in Council will not enforce the sections with reference to enfranchisement upon us, and further we would ask the Governor in Council to continue to exempt us from the operation of those sections that is from 82 to 93 of the Indian Act.[71]

The Act also called for the payment of annuity shares to any successful ap-plicant—another provision that reduced the land-supplemented economy of the community. Ironically, Frederick Loft later championed the causes of Indians across Canada, including the fight against enfranchisement. In reac-tion to his political activism, the Indian Department attempted to have Loft involuntarily enfranchised because of his educated status. Peter Kulchyski, in a paper focussed on Loft's activism, asserts that the department was at-tempting to use the enfranchisement provisions of the Indian Act as a tool "to remove troublemakers and educated Indians as a whole."[72] Loft was successful in maintaining his status despite the attempts of the Indian Department to involuntarily enfranchise him. Of the four cases cited in the council minutes, only one was supported by the chiefs: Wm. Eugene Martin's application in December 1915.[73] No explanation is offered for the council's support of his application.

Band Transfers

The Indian Act provided that Indians could transfer their enrolment from one community to another through an application process. Most cases of band transfers occurred through marriage (the wife was almost always transferred to her husband's band).[74] Other cases[75] often involved entire families who had relocated to other communities and desired to transfer their interests to those bands; such was the case with the Joseph Lewis family in 1906: "Chief Tobias of the Moraviantown Reserve addressed the council regarding the transfer of Joseph Lewis from Six Nations to his band; council approved the transfer of Joseph Lewis and his family but would not allow him to take his and his family's shares of interest money."[76] As in the cases of enfranchisement, the council deemed band transfers—and the accompanying annuity transfers—to be detrimental to the larger community because of the resulting depletion of the community's annuity funds.

The Indian Department created a major stir within the Six Nations Council when they supported the application of Robert Brant to transfer himself and his family to the membership list of the New Credit reserve in 1912. The Brant family took with them seven shares of the capital monies amounting to $1,321.95, or $188.85 per person.[77] Beyond the financial losses, the council was especially opposed to this application because of the provisions of the Mississauga Settlements (1847 and 1865) that declared the New Credit lands still belonged to Six Nations—and provided that changes to the New Credit membership had to be confirmed by the Six Nations Council.

Leases and Sales

Some Six Nations landholders desired to either sell or lease their property as a means of providing or supplementing income. Council allowed land sales only to other Six Nations members, or in some cases to council.[78] One exception to this rule was found in 1884. John and Catherine Hill sold their property to "St. Regis Indians Mitchell Muskatoe and Angus Garo ... they then sold the land to Alex R. Jamieson (a member of Six Nations Indians); sales upheld."[79] It appears that this exception was allowed since the final sale resulted in the property belonging to a Six Nations member.

Leases were allowed both internally and externally. Lessees, whether Native or white, only had a right to use the land but not to harvest any resources from it (for example, timber or sand). In 1916, the council declared it unnecessary to approve leases between Six Nations members but suggested that people continue to do so in order that the registry remain updated.[80] The council allowed Six Nations property owners to lease their lands to white tenants conditionally. Criteria to determine worthy lessees included a positive assessment of both character and farming ability. In 1914 the council refused the lease application of George W. Hill to Harry Ireland "on the grounds that it is reported that Mr. Ireland's character is such that the Reserve will get no credit to have him here as a tenant."[81] As in other situations, the Indian Department began declaring authority over leasing in the 1880s, which was met with strong declarations of dissatisfaction by the council.[82]

Character

The council assessed moral character as a factor in residency rights not only for guests (lessees) but also for Six Nations members. Within marriage disputes, immoral character would often result in either the loss of property use or actual loss of ownership. Morality sometimes became a factor in Six Nations members being removed from the community, as found in a 1914 council warning to a member: "The Council decided that one David Williams of Oneida whose character is such that he is an undesirable be removed from the Reserve, as also that of Mrs. Sims, if she chooses to live with him in adultery."[83] Mrs. Sims was a Six Nations member.

Moral assessment was also applied in cases of intermarriage. In 1898, the council noted that "white women who marry an Indian man but leave him unjustly shall be removed from the reserve; if a white woman is widowed she can remain as if she were an Indian woman but if she marries a white man or an Indian man from another band then she will be removed."[84] This policy reflects both a judgement of morality as well as the application of other developed membership policies within the community.

In 1881 a man who murdered his wife was deemed to have "forfeited their property." It is unclear whether or not there were heirs in this case. In 1888, property rights were upheld in a land transfer where a daughter sold property to her mother before being sent to prison for an unspecified offence.[85]

Land Prices

It appears that there has never been an established assessment of property value at Six Nations. Instead, landowners electing to sell or lease have negotiated with their buyer or lessee based upon what both parties deem to be fair. At different times in the record, however, the council would establish set values for properties they were dealing with (see Table 4). In 1882, the council planned to build a dam on McKenzie Creek and established compensation for flooded lands at eight dollars per acre.[86] That is the same price that council paid when they purchased four acres from Mary Bomberry "for quarrying purposes" in 1887.[87]

Table 4. Documented Land Prices/Assessments, 1902–1917.

DATE	# ACRES	ASSESSMENT/PRICE
1902 Estate purchase	50	$375 total ($7.50/acre)
1908 Council purchase	2	$100 total ($50/acre)
1911 Estate settlement	10	$90 total ($9/acre)
1912 Council purchase	1.5	$50 total ($33.34/acre)
1913 Council purchase (Ohsweken)	6.25	$50 per acre
1913 Gravel pit purchases (policy)	n/a	$25 per acre
1917 Estate assessment	16.25	$15 per acre

Sources: SNCM, January 1902; February 1906; October 1908; December 1912; February 1913; and May 1917.

The increased values of the 1908 and 1913 purchases, as shown in Table 4, represent parcels of land in the Village of Ohsweken (located next to the Council House). It appears that this property was deemed to be of greater value because of its location. Similarly, the 1912 purchase was for the relocation of a school. The three estate assessments (1902, 1911, and 1917) increase in value, presumably due to inflation. Hundreds of quit claim deeds—for member-to-member land sales—were confirmed by the council at this time, but purchase amounts were not recorded with the land transfers. Most of the cases referenced by council were either council purchases (usually for the expansion of the Village of Ohsweken) or cases of estate settlements.

Lands were also assessed for purposes of collateral in loan applications. The standard rate between 1880 and 1910 was five dollars per acre for "improved lands"—defined by the Indian Department as having "a good bush and the same is fenced."[88] The council increased the collateral value to ten dollars per acre in 1913 to offset increased building costs.[89] In cases where a member failed to repay a loan, the council might either repossess the land or reclaim it only for a time when they would lease it to recover the amount of the loan and return the property to the owner upon repayment.[90] The Loan Fund was administered by the council, but the overall amount in the fund was set by the Indian Department (out of the Six Nations Capital Funds). Tensions rose in the 1910s over the refusal of the department to increase the Loan Fund from $20,000 to $50,000 as the council wished in order to better meet the needs of the community. The department eventually increased the fund to $50,000 in 1914, "with certain conditions."[91]

National Parks and Communal Property

The allotments of the consolidated territory left essentially no surplus lands to accommodate future development needs or population growth. When the council decided to build the new Council House in the Village of Ohsweken, they had to purchase land from individuals in order to do so. The resulting property, complete with the Council House, was deemed to be national property, belonging to all of the Six Nations people. The council also recognized other designations of national and communal property, including the Sour Springs,[92] sand and gravel pits[93] and the "National Park," Kanyegheh.[94]

Property belonging to deceased individuals without heirs was declared national property upon the closing of the estate file. In some cases, the council would maintain the property, but usually it was auctioned to the highest bidder with the proceeds being forwarded to the trust accounts, as in the estate of Isaac Duncan in 1894.[95] Similarly, when the estate of Joshua Williams (1909) failed to produce any heirs, the council declared that "the land property shall devolve upon the people of the Six Nations."[96]

The council did reserve certain tracts from allotment in order to accommodate special needs in the community. For example, the property surrounding longhouses and churches had to be registered, but the council created a trustee system for properties such as these, with the property being listed in the names of the trustees but not as "owners." The council originally reserved the Sour Springs from allotment, but in March 1923 the council offered the six-acre Sour Springs lot for sale to the highest bidder. This also coincided with a financial crisis caused by the Indian Department's withholding of funds needed to pay for council and other community expenses.[97]

Resources deemed to be public property also fell into the category of national property or communal resource, including sand, gravel, and plaster beds. Individuals wishing to harvest from the reserves of these resources had to pay a set fee based on the amount they took. For example, in 1914 individuals taking sand from Six Nations lands had to pay fifteen cents per yard.[98] In 1881, the plaster beds were offered for lease, the proceeds to be paid to the council for the benefit of the community; the council reserved "lime stones and stones for building purposes" for use by "any person or persons [of the community]."[99] A stone quarry was opened to the public in 1883, "each person to pay $1 per cord plus labour."[100]

In many cases, timber was also considered a communal resource, but people were allowed to cut wood on their own property as long as it was deemed necessary. The general philosophy around timber, as expressed by the council, was one of respect for and conservation of the forests of the community. The general criteria for use of timber included the following:

- Dead or downed wood could be used by the property owner; if the larger economic picture was bleak, individuals were allowed to sell this wood outside of the community as an income supplement.
- Green wood could be cut in order to provide for a house or other structure; even on personal property the expectation was that a person would only cut what was absolutely necessary.
- Individuals could apply to harvest wood from national lands, but only in times of great need would they be allowed to do so for re-sale purposes.[101]

Timber issues arose on the Grand River lands as early as the 1780s. On the consolidated lands, the council established forest wardens charged with the responsibility of curbing timber exploitation (by both whites and Natives). The job regularly proved quite dangerous, and even life-shortening in the case of Mohawk Royaner George Henry Martin Johnson.[102]

Hunting and Fishing

The Six Nations have always viewed hunting and fishing within the context of their relationships within their territory and to all of creation. On the consolidated Grand River lands, these relationships continued. As recognized in the many treaties between the Confederacy and the Crown, the Six Nations continued to hunt and fish within their traditional harvesting territories.[103] While Western governments have defined hunting and fishing within the context of "rights," the Haudenosaunee (and other Indigenous peoples) view these activities in the context of responsibilities. The gifts of the waters and forests were intended for human consumption as long as humans maintained their duties of thankfulness and conservation (as demonstrated in the regulation of timber). But the ability of the Haudenosaunee to control natural resource conservation was greatly inhibited through the various land reductions of the Grand River Territory, especially in regard to off-reserve lands.

Similarly, fishing was greatly affected by the dams and other "improvements" on the Grand River. The council addressed the negative impacts on the fishery in several land claims against the Grand River Navigation Company and other river improvement projects.[104] In March 1898, the council notified the Canadian government of Haudenosaunee fishing rights along the river: "owing to the fact that that was one of the conditions of the original Treaty between the Six Nations and the British Government, and was one of the conditions of the agreement entered into by the Six Nations Council and the Grand River Navigation Company when the Dunnville and other Dams were built that they shall have all the privileges to fish along the River and at these dams without any restrictions whatsoever."[105] This indicates not only the persistence of fishing activities but also the continuity through which the Six Nations articulated their treaty rights.

Land Responsibilities

Along with the "rights" of Six Nations membership and land ownership came several responsibilities. The community expected that individual family allotments would be used to provide for the family. They also expected that the land and natural resources found on it would be taken care of by the landowner, as evidenced again in the discussion of timber. Starting in the 1860s, the council also adapted the provincial system of statute labour in order to get roads built and maintained within the territory. The *Consolidated Regulations of the Six Nations Indians of the Grand River* (1910) provided "two days statute labor for each male 21 years and upward, and for each owner of real estate, in addition, one day for 25 acres owned."[106] While the concept officially came from the Canadian government, the idea of having a duty to contribute to the needs of the larger community was certainly not a new concept for the Haudenosaunee.

While much of the discussion around council land policies could be deemed an examination of land "rights," these were actually policies of responsibility, principles that included:

- Parents have a responsibility to provide for their children;
- Adult children have the responsibility to care for sick parents and provide for their needs—your "birth right" becomes your "birth responsibility";
- Spouses who maintain their marriage vows should be provided for upon death of the other spouse; and
- Landowners must respect their property and not plunder its resources.

People who maintained their responsibilities to family and their land were allowed to hold and use land as a means of providing for their needs.

Through these policies the council upheld the values of collective land ownership. Even though individuals held allotments within the consolidated territory, they really only held the right to use that land and pass it on in their family (or to whomever they chose) as long as they fulfilled their responsibilities. In essence, the longhouse "rights" of older times transferred themselves to individual property "rights" in more modern times. In the longhouses of old, individual families had their own bunk and storage areas, sharing the larger space with many other families. This was transformed as the longhouse structures changed, first through smaller longhouses, then "short houses," and then cabins and other smaller family structures. The final product (and all of the transformations between longhouse and individual family house) resulted in individual "bunks" within the Six Nations territory, but the land was still held in common, just as it had been in the former homelands. The overall Grand River Territory was a single metaphorical longhouse, and while the "bunks" had become separated by fields and bush, this "longhouse" comprised the same "rights" and responsibilities as the older house structures. In their land policies, the council continued to hold individuals responsible to the whole community: past, present, and future. And in these policy developments, the council upheld their responsibilities as Rotiyanehson to always have their minds on the future and to make decisions accordingly.

In order to implement policies and assist with other bureaucratic procedures, the council eventually created staff positions. Some of these directly involved land policies and were addressed through a series of paid committees and positions filled mostly by chiefs (both Royaner and sub-chiefs). These included the Locating Line Committee, charged with surveying and making recommendations in boundary disputes; Forest Wardens, who enforced timber regulations and ejected trespassers from the territory; "Pathmasters," who enforced statute labour duties; "Poundkeepers," who enforced animal regulations; the Disputes Committee, a judicial review "board" that would investigate and hear evidence in disputes; and Estate Committees, which had duties similar to the Disputes Committee. The council accorded levels of responsibilities to these various committees and positions but always retained ultimate authority and responsibility in all of these areas. The council also became an employer, hiring (usually from the ranks of chiefs) a secretary, an interpreter, and a speaker of the council. By far the most time-consuming of these positions was that of secretary, with the duties increasing many times over from its origins in the 1870s.[107] As we will see in the next chapter, the position of secretary would become another contentious issue between the council and the Indian Department on several occasions, most notably upon the 1915 death of Josiah Hill, who served as council secretary for more than forty years.

Te Yonkhi'nikònhare Tsi Niyonkwarihotenhs— *They Are Interfering in Our Matters*

While the Six Nations Council governed the internal workings of the community and developed polices for dealing with land and other issues, they also had to navigate a rocky relationship with the Dominion and the external pressures it placed upon the Confederacy leadership. The assimilationist policies of the Dominion government greatly agitated the Six Nations Council in the latter part of the nineteenth century. The Department of Indian Affairs was the primary agent of Canadian policy implementation for Indian communities, Six Nations being no exception. In that role, the department became the sparring partner of the Confederacy Council as the council objected to many aspects of the "civilizing" policies of the Dominion and the enforcement of those policies through Indian Affairs. Council minutes recall scores of issues that arose between Six Nations and the federal government, and an examination of these records reveals four major areas of concern: departmental interference with council decisions, the imposition of Indian Act provisions that violated council autonomy and Confederacy sovereignty, negligence in the Caledonia Dam grievance, and council control over lands and accounts. These four issues stand out with respect to their impact on the community and the relationship between the Confederacy and the Crown.

Six Nations and the Dominion of Canada:
A Tumultuous Relationship

The Confederacy Council was caught off-guard in the 1880s when the Department of Indian Affairs (formally established as a separate department in 1880) started to interfere in council decisions the department had previously deemed to be the domain of the Confederacy.[1] The department began claiming authority in areas such as the conferral of wills,[2] estate distribution,[3] and council hiring decisions.[4] Other branches of government often participated in these Indian Department actions of interference with internal Six Nations affairs. There was also an attempt on the part of several Canadian governments (federal, provincial, county) to supersede Haudenosaunee laws and policies with their own. All of these impositions were met with solid rebuttals from the Six Nations Council, which asserted its own authority over Six Nations affairs.

In some cases of interference, the council and the department were able to reach an understanding after the issue had been raised.[5] In other cases, the two sides remained adamant in their respective positions, causing the relationship to deteriorate. Most of these situations resulted from shifting policy interpretations by the department. For example, in 1914 the department attempted to supersede the decisions of the council-appointed Locating Line Committee and declared the committee to have no authority. The council quickly reminded them that the department had approved of the committee appointments and had never had a problem in the past with the work of the committee.[6] The same type of departmental interference occurred in several estate cases where the department overrode council decisions.[7] Prior to these cases, the council had had ultimate authority over estates, with the department simply serving as an appellate body in cases of dispute.[8] Another situation arose around the cancelled plans to build a permanent hospital at Six Nations. While the council had initially approved of the idea, in 1912 they reversed their decision, citing the fact that nearly one-third of the Six Nations people were gone from the community at different points of the year (so if they required medical attention, they would be seeking it elsewhere) and that the hospitals in the neighbouring community were sufficient to meet the needs of the community.[9] The council also chastised the department for purchasing the land for the permanent hospital without consulting the council.[10] The department disagreed with the council's decision. One of the first developments undertaken by the 1924 Elected Band Council, with the full support of the Indian Department, was the building of the Lady Wellington Hospital in the Village of Ohsweken.

One of the larger controversies that plagued the council-department relationship surrounded the appointment of a replacement, in 1915, for the position of council secretary following the death of Chief Josiah Hill. The council took applications, interviewed potential candidates, and selected Asa R. Hill as the new secretary. The department refused to confirm this decision,[11] stating that the council was giving too much power to a single family and that there had been "several complaints."[12] They told the council to repost the position, which they did—apparently to clear up any concerns of nepotism—and the second round produced the same results. The department refused to accept the council's choice, and the controversy simmered for years.[13] The department suggested alternate candidates for the position: first, Chief J.W.M. Elliott,[14] then Hilton M. Hill[15] (a Pinetree Chief who worked as the clerk in the Brantford Indian Office). Both of these men had other relatives in the council, so the charge of "too much power in a single family" seems to have been masking the department's real reasons for opposing the Asa Hill hiring. Related to the controversy, the department refused to issue the secretary's salary as well as the chiefs' board money for several months, putting economic stress upon the chiefs both as individuals and as a whole council. The department resorted to this tactic several times between 1915 and 1924, the last record of it appearing in July 1924, when the council ordered payment of $833.35 for twenty months' salary the department had withheld from the secretary.[16] The secretary controversy came to reflect the methods of meddling the Indian Department was willing to resort to in order to control the actions of the Six Nations Council.

The council-department relationship reached a boiling point in the 1920s. The department was asserting authority in internal issues such as estates and membership and supporting impositions on council authority by other branches of Canadian governments, from the Brant County Sheriff to the North West Mounted Police (later known as the RCMP). In June 1924 the Brant County Sheriff threatened to hold a public auction of the property of Mr. and Mrs. Levi General, located on the Six Nations territory.[17] The sale was ordered to cover a judgement against Chief Levi General (Deskaheh) in a case taken to Brant County Court regarding property on Six Nations—a situation over which Brant County had no jurisdiction from the beginning. The visiting superintendent had initially supported the sheriff's actions, but eventually the department notified both the sheriff and Visiting Superintendent Morgan that the county had no jurisdiction in the case. Incidentally, the sheriff had threatened this action while Chief General was in England petitioning for assistance with the Indian Department's assumption of authority. In January 1923, the council sent a protest to Prime Minister William Lyon Mackenzie King regarding the erection of a permanent post for the Mounted Police in the Six Nations community without council approval.[18] In their grievance, they asserted their belief that the police were placed at Six Nations in order to enforce the Soldier Settlement Act of 1919.[19] Less than two years later, the Mounties provided the physical force in the "overthrow" of the Six Nations Confederacy council in October 1924.

Indian Act Impositions

The Six Nations have been protesting the imposition of the Canadian Indian Act since the first act was passed in 1869. The Grand River Haudenosaunee hosted a gathering of Indian nations from across southern Ontario and Quebec in June 1870 to discuss the act's implications for their various territories. While earlier legislation had declared the government's interest in assimilation (following the recommendations of the Bagot and Pennefather commissions) this act was more specific and direct in its "civilizing" intent. Most notable among the communities' concerns were the provision of the act that called for the membership removal of Indian women who married non-Indian[20] men and the provision that allowed the Dominion to replace traditional governments with elected band councils. The 1870 Grand Indian Council called for a repeal of the act, collectively asserting the rights of their nations to govern their own territories and people.[21]

As the federal government grew and developed in the 1870s, it attempted to consolidate the various pieces of legislation directed at addressing the relationship with Indian communities. These efforts resulted in the 1876 Indian Act, which again drew negative Native responses, primarily due to the minimizing of local governance authority for Indian governments and its proclamation of Canadian authority over Indian lands and property. The 1884 Indian Advancement Act pretended to give wider powers for local governing but actually reduced Indian councils' authority by placing the local Indian Affairs superintendent as council chairman.

Beyond the 1870 Grand Indian Council, the Six Nations Council repeatedly notified the Indian Department and the governor general of their concerns with aspects of the various legislation. Most common in these petitions was a reminder of the Six Nations' status as an ally to the Crown (see Table 5).

Table 5. Examples of Six Nations Council Complaints against Provisions of
the Indian Act, 1887–1919.

Date	Issued to	Complaint	Requested Resolution/ Explanation
8 Nov. 1887	Indian Department	1880 Indian Act: provision not allowing illegitimate children to be placed on paylist	Requested Six Nations exemption
25 Apr. 1890	Indian Department	Indian Advancement Act	Requested exemption, stating: "the hereditary system has allowed them to make great achievements and that as they hold their land in common under the seal of the Haldimand Deed that they have the right to select chiefs in the ancient customs and to make their own decisions about officers of the council."
11 Mar. 1898	Indian Department	Indian Act: leases to white men	Request for Six Nations exemption
1 Feb. 1910	Indian Department	Indian Act: interference with estate cases	An imposition of the Indian Act "which does not apply on this Reserve"
18 Oct. 1910	Indian Department	Imposition of liquor laws from the Indian Act	"Act should not apply to the Six Nations because we have By-laws covering the liquor clauses of the Indian Act with penalties, fines etc, which apply to our Reserve, and which have been approved by the Governor in Council."
11 Apr. 1911	Governor General	Proposed amendments to the Indian Act	"Council reiterated their position that they are not under the Indian Act, reserve is not Crown land, etc."
21 Nov. 1911	Indian Department	Departmental interference in the estate of Joshua Williams	"They claim that what they are doing now, they are only carrying out their old customs and usages of the Council and the Department never interfered with until now, and therefore they hope that the Department will be good enough not to insist, and go beyond their jurisdiction."

Date	Issued to	Complaint	Requested Resolution/ Explanation
6 Oct. 1914	Indian Department	Membership transfers to other bands	"They strongly object and protest the transferring of the people of the Six Nations into other Bands which tends to the disestablishment of the Six Nations Confederacy and not only that but it is a violation of the trust imposed on them in taking money from the funds of the Six Nations and placing the same to the credit of other bands."
16 July 1918	Governor General	National Registration	"The Six Nations do not wish to ballot"
25 Feb. 1919	Indian Department	By-Laws for the Taxation of dogs upon the Reserve	"Refuse to accept such taxation on the ground that it would be in direct violation to our treaty rights with the British Crown."
15 Apr. 1919	Dominion Government	Legislation amending the Indian Act in 1918, providing for the taxation of Indian property.	Due recognition of the claims of the Six Nations.
9 Mar. 1920	Speaker of the House of Commons	Proposed amendment to the Indian Act	"We feel as a people amendment must not include the Six Nations neither should our case be made a matter of an order in Council while our said case is pending in the Supreme Court."

Source: SNCM, Nov. 1887; Apr. 1890; Mar. 1898; Feb. 1910, Apr. 1911; Nov. 1911; Oct. 1914; July 1918; Feb. 1919; Apr. 1919; Mar. 1920. SNCM, April 1890. Also appears in WCC Archives, Art Anderson Collection.

As demonstrated in their suggested solutions, the Confederacy Council remained adamant in their assertions of Six Nations sovereignty, as recognized in the treaties with the Crown. The council was willing to work with the Indian Department— just as their ancestors had worked with Sir William Johnson—as representatives of the Crown, but they were not willing to relinquish the relationship of the treaties, which promised the attention, respect, and friendship of the Crown.

In the spring of 1909 a petition against the Confederacy Council was circulated in the Six Nations community and addressed to Visiting Superintendent Smith, who forwarded the petition to the department headquarters. The council heard rumour of the petition and questioned Smith about it at a council meeting. He admitted its existence and said that it had been forwarded to his supervisors but refused to provide details of the grievances.[22] The council wrote to the department requesting the information contained in the petition, but instead the department sent notice that the council had violated the channel of communication in bypassing the superintendent.[23] They failed to acknowledge that Smith was the first to violate the channel of communication by forwarding the petition without first discussing it with the council, as had always been the case in prior grievances brought to the superintendent.

Smith created another controversy ten years later when he circulated a letter charging that the council had mistreated the community's returning soldiers, which led to divisions in the community. The council addressed him regarding the letter:

> After the Chiefs had considered the contents of circular letters signed by Gordon J. Smith which were distributed upon the Reserve containing misstatement concerning the attitude of the Six Nations Council in connection with the reception of its returned soldiers and which caused a division among the people the Council thought best to ask Supt. Smith to explain his reason for sending such letters against the Council, whereupon Supt. Smith claimed he knew the said letters had caused a division and he wished to withdraw all false statements made in the said circular letters and claimed he had only issued about eighteen.[24]

Smith admitted he had provided false information that caused divisions in the community but provided no real offer to make amends for his falsehoods. The council called for his removal[25] but Smith remained in the position until 1923. Undoubtedly, his presence contributed to the growing tensions between the council and the department.

Grievance against the Caledonia Dam

In the spring of 1891 the Caledonia Dam broke, part of it washed out completely, and the Grand River receded almost to the level it had been prior to the navigational developments earlier in the century. As the river levels went down, the Six Nations people were reminded how much land they had lost to

the "improvements"—land for which they had never been compensated. At
a May 1891 council meeting the Rotiyanehson informed Mr. Ed Cameron,
their new visiting superintendent, of their grievances surrounding the dam:

> 1ˢᵗ They are deprived from the use of several hundred acres of choice
> land. 2ⁿᵈ The numerous bridges along River Road are always in
> danger many times the said bridges will get recket [*sic*], turn and
> carried away. 3ʳᵈ The fences along the flats and River Road are often
> washed and carried away and have the occupant or occupants fence-
> less for a time. 4ᵗʰ It prevents the owners of the lots in question to
> build and reside near said road. 5ᵗʰ The great difficulty and expense
> in crossing the river. 6ᵗʰ The great scarcity of good fish. 7ᵗʰ The
> enormous increase of malaria which causes the increase of sickness
> and death as we are [*sic*] often been informed by our physicians and
> others. All to benefit two or three millers in Caledonia. Therefore
> the Council unanimously decided to ask the Indian Department
> to use all its influence, ability and power to prevent the rebuilding
> [of] the said dam upon the grounds and reasons as above enumer-
> ated and many more.[26]

Cameron did forward these concerns to his supervisors in the Indian
Department and communication was returned to the council indicating that the
case would be forwarded to the Justice Department.[27] The dam was rebuilt that
same year before the Justice Department acted upon the complaint.[28] The Indian
Affairs and Justice Departments had a chance to correct a wrong that had been
inflicted upon the Six Nations people by their government, but they neglected
to capitalize on that opportunity. The Six Nations Council did not attempt to
stop the rebuilding, but they did petition the government again for its removal.[29]
They also hired a surveyor to estimate the acreage lost to the twenty-inch rise in
the river as a result of the dam, expecting some form of compensation from the
mill owners who benefited from the dam.[30] Their petition became part of the
Justice Department's file concerning the Six Nations' claims against Canada in
regard to the Grand River Navigation Company, claims that are still pending
between Six Nations and the Government of Canada today.[31]

Council Control over Lands and Accounts

One of the council's greatest concerns with impositions of the Indian Act
centred on control over their territory and accounts. As allies to the Crown,
the Haudenosaunee considered themselves sovereign. They were regularly

reassured by the governor general and others that their treaty rights remained intact, yet the actions of the Indian Department and provisions of the Indian Act made things appear otherwise. The Rotiyanehson continued to govern the Six Nations community, but a great deal of their time was spent on combatting attempts to usurp their authority over the Grand River Territory

When Canadian soldiers returned from the First World War, Parliament passed the Soldier Settlement Act to provide compensation to war veterans and to further Canada's development plans. Much of the land offered through the act was found in the West, but some tracts were made available in the East, often by claiming Indian lands.[32] As soon as the Confederacy Council became aware of the act, they notified their superintendent of their decision against its application at Six Nations. They cited the fact that the community held its land in common and the individual titles accorded through the Soldier Settlement Act would disturb the existing system. Council did, however, offer to assist any Six Nations soldier desiring to farm through the existing loan system.[33] The department ignored the council's decision and began plans to settle Six Nations soldiers on individual allotments of Six Nations land. In 1921, the department declared the Curley farm—Six Nations land held by the council—the property of Mr. Joseph J. Hill, a returned soldier.[34] In April 1922, the council confirmed a previous decision that allowed Gordon Vyse[35] to remain on the property.[36] Since the council would not allow the department to remove Vyse, Duncan Campbell Scott, deputy superintendent of the Department of Indian Affairs, eventually charged the accounts of the Six Nations $869 to compensate Joseph J. Hill for being deprived of the property accorded to him under the Soldier Settlement Act.[37] These actions represented an infringement upon Six Nations autonomy not only in land title issues but also in regard to their finances. The results were far beyond jurisdictional and financial, however. Many of the Six Nations people watched to see what would happen in this situation. Some of these individuals had become concerned about the relationship between the Indian Department and the council and worried about the implications for the community as a whole. John A. Noon, based on interviews with agitators twenty-five years later, determined that the inability of the council to stop the Indian Department from enacting the Soldier Settlement Act fed the dissension of those who eventually protested against the Confederacy Council.[38]

Continued Land Claims

Following in the traditions of the leaders who came before them, stretching back to the times of the Canajohare and Kayadohsera Patents in the Mohawk Valley, the Rotiyanehson of this era continued to lay their land grievances upon the Crown, in hopes of resolution and restitution. The Crown also followed in the footsteps of its predecessors by making empty commitments to investigate the claims and offering a series of promises to "act better next time." Many of the nineteenth- and twentieth-century land claims were rooted in the title problems of the Haldimand Deed, especially the Headwaters Claim. Others originated shortly after settlement on the Grand River Territory and were the result of negligent government decisions and investments, such as claims against the Grand River Navigation Company and the New England Company. In addition, a set of claims came about directly due to government error or fraud, such as those of Innisfil and Hawkesbury townships and the 1847 and 1865 Mississauga agreements, as discussed earlier. Council persisted in asserting the claims during this era, especially with respect to the Grand River Headwaters Claim, the Glebe Lots, and the Mississauga occupation.

Grand River Headwaters Claim

The council, as the voice of the Six Nations people, regularly reminded the Canadian governments and the Crown that they were the rightful owners of the Headwaters based upon the 1784 Haldimand Proclamation. In 1882, the council sent a delegation to Ottawa to meet with the governor general concerning the upper part of the Grand River Territory—refreshing the Crown's memory about earlier visits from other Confederacy leaders such as John Norton and John Brant, who had articulated the same concerns. The delegation was following up on communications they had forwarded several years prior to the governor general, the Marquis of Lorne, and the prime minister, Sir John A. Macdonald.[39] The letter to Macdonald responded to his request seeking explanation of the claim; the council responded as follows:

> Firstly: According to the deed in our possession, issued by Sir Frederick Haldimand, dated at the Castle of St. Louis, Quebec, the 25th day of October, 1784, and which was registered in Lib. A, fol. 8th, on the 20th day of March, 1795, in the secretary's office, Upper Canada, we claim that we are the only proper and rightful owners of a tract of land lying from the north boundary of the township of Nichol to the head or source of the Grand River, a distance of

forty miles, inasmuch as it has never been ceded to the Crown by us. And according to the Royal Proclamation by his late Majesty King George the Third, dated the 24th Day of December 1763, no one other than the Six Nation Indians shall have a right to settle upon such lands on any pretence whatever.

Secondly: That whereas it may be argued that the people now occupying the said lands have established their right to the said lands by lapse of time. We would say that the Six Nations had established their pre-emption right to the said lands long before any white man settled on the said lands by occupation. Our forefathers have occupied the lands in question as their hunting grounds, and have always lived within the limits of the deed referred to, and therefore they have been in occupation before and ever since the deed was issued.

Thirdly. It may be asked why the Six Nations did not make a strong protest against the fact of people taking their lands and settling thereon. The answer to that is, that it was the opinion entertained by the chiefs, that it was the duty of the Indian Department as our guardians to protect our rights in that respect.[40]

The Rotiyanehson effectively articulated not just their claim to the Headwaters but also their grievances against the government for not protecting the interests of the Six Nations as they had continually promised to do. Government investigations into the claim continued, but in 1886 Macdonald deemed the case unworthy of claim. In an internal government communication, Macdonald articulated his rationale for denying the Six Nations' Headwaters claim:

> The introduction of a new practice of submitting Indian claims in the first instance to the Judicial Committee would operate as a complete change in the manner in which the Indian races have hitherto been dealt with, and would establish a distinction between them and the other inhabitants of Canada. This is very objectionable, as the great aim of our legislation has been to do away with the tribal system and assimilate the Indian people in all respects with the other inhabitants of the Dominion, as speedily as they are fit for the change.
>
> The present claim of the Six Nations has no merits, and does not deserve any exceptional consideration.[41]

Macdonald was unwilling to open a potential floodgate of Indian claims litigation. He was willing, however, to bypass justice if it meant furthering the cause of government's assimilation plans. The council received notification of Macdonald's assessment in the fall of 1886, considered going to England regardless, but eventually decided to let the claim rest for a while. They renewed the pursuit of this claim in 1911, as part of other claims investigations.[42] It remains an outstanding claim against the Crown.

Claims against the New England Company

In the 1820s the Colonial Office made an alliance with the New England Company, allowing them entrance to the Six Nations community and offering them financial support for their missionary efforts among the Grand River Haudenosaunee.[43] These efforts eventually included a series of Anglican churches, five day-schools, and the Mohawk Institute residential school. In order to finance these initiatives, the Colonial Office allowed the New England Company an allocation of Six Nations land proceeds as well as sizable land grants for their schools and churches. In the late 1800s, the company often leased these lands, using the profits to pay for their "civilizing" projects and the salaries of their employees. The funding scheme—derived from Six Nations funds and lands—was never approved by the council. Throughout the history of the relationship between Six Nations and the New England Company, the council expressed regular concerns about the cost-benefit balance of the missionary activities in their communities. The chiefs grew especially concerned when the New England Company began claiming Six Nations property as their own and attempted to sell certain parcels in and around the City of Brantford.[44]

In 1913, the council made their first grievance through their lawyer, A.G. Chisholm,[45] regarding the Glebe Lots (also known as the Mohawk Parsonage) near the Mohawk Institute grounds, which the company had attempted to sell.[46] The grievance was debated between the council, its lawyer, the Indian Department, and the New England Company for the next several years.[47] The Six Nations initially hoped to reclaim title to the lands so they could then surrender them to a potential buyer (who had been secured by the New England Company). Once the New England Company realized they did not hold title, they agreed to relinquish their claim to the property in exchange for a portion of the sale, claiming rights of improvement. The council eventually conceded to the company, receiving some of the sale proceeds as outlined in the April 1914 council record:

The Council after careful reconsidering the matter of the Glebe
lot at Brantford originally containing 220 acres, and in view of the
use by the Missionaries, and the New England Company during
the long period of eighty seven years they must have derived
enormous benefits and profits from these lands, moreover they have
disposed some 45 or 46 acres to various companies and got some
$22,598.90, therefore the Council decided to offer the said New
England Company to retain the money they have received from
the sales and rents of the said Glebe lot without prejudice to waive
their rights, and this offer is to be either accepted or refused in two
months, from the time this resolution will be formally laid before
the said New England Company by the Deputy Superintendent
General of Indian Affairs.[48]

Despite the compromise reached between Six Nations and the New England
Company, the Indian Department refused to make the necessary transfer
of funds that would have completed the agreement. As a result, the claim
became a persistent point of contention between the council and the Indian
Department for years. Today, portions of this tract remain in a claim status (as
part of the Eagles Nest Tract), over ninety years after the Six Nations council
reached the settlement with the New England Company.[49]

Mississauga Occupation

The problems between the Six Nations and the New Credit Mississaugas arose
in the 1880s as a direct result of the Indian Department's failure to comply
with the provisions of the 1868 agreement between the Confederacy and the
Mississaugas. The Indian Department failed to transfer the agreed-upon monies from the Mississauga trust accounts to those of the Six Nations, voiding the
previous agreements. Therefore, in the 1880s, the council was aware of three
important facts: their land base was fixed with no immediate opportunities
for expansion,[50] their population was growing, and over one-tenth of their
community was occupied by a people who had never paid for the privilege of
using Six Nations land. The Six Nations council sent repeated invitations to the
Mississauga council to discuss their concerns. After two years of inaction, the
Six Nations council issued an order to the Mississauga council in May 1886
to remove from Six Nations lands.[51] The threat of removal finally inspired the
Mississaugas to respond, and negotiations between the two councils ensued.

In May 1887, the Six Nations Council presented the Mississaugas with five options:

1. Purchase the land from Six Nations and then amalgamate;
2. Amalgamate without any purchase;
3. Pay rent for the use of the land;
4. Purchase land from Six Nations and remain independent; or
5. Six Nations will pay for improvements and Mississaugas will leave.[52]

After lengthy negotiations, offers and counter-offers, the two councils reached an agreement on 25 September 1900, containing the following provisions:

> First. That the tribe nor any member of family of them shall not exchange, sell or convey any part or portion of the said parcel or block of land to any tribe or member or family of any tribe or to any people save and except to members or families of the Six Nations, without the knowledge and consent of the General Council of the Six Nations and sanctioned and approved of by the Governor General.
>
> Second. The door to be open in common, any family on whose lot may be a deficiency of timber, may if convenient have it from lots without the block assigned and set apart for the tribe, and in like manner any family of the Six Nations will be privileged to have timber from off the said block if found necessary, or either of the parties that of making sugar from the maple trees under the general regulations.
>
> Third. The amount paid from the funds of the Six Nations for the improvements to be paid by the Mississauga tribe,[53] the Chiefs of which to be responsible for the amount.[54]

Of critical importance in the agreement is the fact that Six Nations never surrendered the lands. They still retain title while the Mississaugas retain possession. It took the Indian Department three years to process the $10,000 payment.[55] Tensions continued to flare up between the two councils around gas and oil exploration,[56] as well as the proposed surrender of 200 acres to the Village of Hagersville in 1924. Ironically, the Indian Department upheld the Six Nations title in that case, and against the wishes of some of the Mississaugas, but not until after the department had replaced the Confederacy

Council with an elected band council.[57] It is unclear whether or not the Confederacy Council would have consented to the surrender at all.

Throughout, the various Six Nations land claims evidence indicates that government officials knew the Haudenosaunee had been treated very poorly. In essence, many in government realized they were wrong but did nothing to rectify the situation when opportunities arose. As found in the controversy over the Soldier Settlement Act, it was as if the department was simply waiting until the Confederacy Council could be eliminated so they would not have to be held accountable for their problematic land actions.

Assertions of Six Nations Sovereignty

Despite the external pressures placed upon the Confederacy Council during this period, they continued to conduct themselves within the parameters of the values shared in their cultural history. At different times they adopted new structures, attempting to streamline council procedures that had grown in number and complexity as a result of population growth and increased bureaucratic involvement by the Department of Indian Affairs. Some of these adaptations included committee development, hiring council employees, and changes in council deliberation processes. Several times the council attempted to adapt a voting system within their ranks, but such reforms rarely lasted. Either a group from within or a delegation of "the people" would remind the council of the ancient procedures of Confederacy and the fact that those procedures worked best for governing the Haudenosaunee. For example, in June 1884 a petition was sent to the council by a group of "warriors" encouraging the council to continue working "in accordance with the rules and regulations handed down since time immemorial."[58] Similarly, in the 1920s a group called the Mohawk Workers (also referred to as the National Workers) organized in the community in response to the federal government's attempts to remove the hereditary system of governance at Six Nations. In 1923, they sent a delegation to Buffalo to meet with advisors in regard to addressing their grievances with the Indian Department.[59] This group continued its support of the Confederacy long after Canada's imposition of the elected band council in 1924.[60]

The record also demonstrates that the foundational relationship between Yakoyaner and Royaner continued. While most of the business between a Clan Mother and Chief would have been conducted outside of the council, the council minutes do reflect several instances where individual Clan Mothers notified the council of newly selected replacements for their family's male leader.[61] In certain cases, especially those involving charges against the "unbecoming" actions of an individual chief, the council would refer the matter to the relevant Clan Mother, under whose authority the charges would be considered.[62] These examples demonstrate that the family structures established under the Kayaneren'kowa—based upon balance between male and female leadership—remained intact and active during this period.

The council also maintained its connections with and responsibilities to other Haudenosaunee communities. Council members regularly travelled to other Six Nations territories to assist in the "raising" of new chiefs and to counsel on other important matters of the Confederacy.[63] Just as the Six Nations Council maintained its responsibilities to the Crown, it also upheld obligations within the entire Confederacy.

The perpetuation of internal structures was also demonstrated in the council's assertions in favour of continuity of treaty relationship with the Crown. Just as the Royaner knew that their authority came through the fulfillment of duties to their families, nations, and the Confederacy, they also knew that the protection of the rights of their people was based within the treaty relationship. The records of the Confederacy, the Government of Canada, and the Crown all reflect the constant reminders of the promises made at the various treaty councils of the seventeenth and eighteenth centuries. One of the clearest examples of this is recorded in the minutes of the 1870 Grand Indian Council held at Six Nations to discuss the 1869 Indian Advancement Act. The meeting opened with the short form of condolence, then commenced with a recitation of the Two Row Wampum and Covenant Chain treaty belts:

> The wampum having two men standing one at each end, represents the first meeting or treaty with the British Government. They stand on their own rules, which they laid down, the British Government gave a wampum to confirm what the Six Nations had done in their rules and declarations. The marks worked on the wampum shows the British and Six Nations had united by Treaty. They were each to have their own way; not hurting their customs or rules or regulations. If the Indian had his bark canoe, let him have it, let the British have his large vessels. The British gives the wampum to confirm the rules and regulations of the Confederacy.[64]

The relevance of these belts to the 1870 situation was clear and simple: the basis of the peaceful and friendly relationship between the Haudenosaunee and the British was grounded in the agreement of non-interference in each other's internal affairs.

The council again recalled those same treaty agreements when it saw the Dominion interfering with Haudenosaunee sovereignty through legislation such as the 1890 Indian Advancement Act. The following was expressed to the governor general in 1890:

> Brother
>
> ...we will tell you we are disappointed because there never was yet any treaty made between you and Us, the Five Nations Indians, that you would force any kind your laws that we did not like, and now in some cases we see you are doing so.
>
> Brother,
>
> We have kept patience for a long time, because, knowing the Treaty of which our forefathers and your forefathers made in the year 1758 being durable to us. But in the way you have treated us thinking for to ask you if the sun and moon has gone out of your sight. But we see the sun and moon as when our forefathers and your forefathers made the agreement. The treaty, whenever you or us the Indians see anything wrong or dissatisfaction, we are to renew brighten and strengthen the ancient Covenant.
>
> And we want to be always free and satisfied to be governed by our own laws and customs, for we have laws of our own. And those that are in favour of your laws and customs we have nothing to do with suppose they are to be governed by it. But we cannot help them in no way, for they [have] broken our word, rules and customs.[65]

The responsibility to "renew" came directly from the treaty record and spoke to a basic belief of the Haudenosaunee: in order to live up to the agreements one people have made to another, there must be constant dialogue between the two peoples and a regular recounting of the agreements "to keep it fresh in their minds." On several occasions Haudenosaunee leaders compared the oral recollection of treaty promises to the written record of the British (and other Europeans) and noted that the Haudenosaunee methods required them to always have the agreement in their thoughts—and, as a result, always informing their actions.[66]

Canadian government officials became politically savvy about the treaty language of the Six Nations, and, like the imperial officials who preceded them, they would echo the sentiments of their ancestors in an attempt to appease

Haudenosaunee complaints of treaty abrogation. Even Duncan Campbell Scott, who ordered the 1924 Canadian government takeover at Grand River, knew the proper words to say. A speech he presented to the Confederacy Council in October 1920 reflected this:

> The Council decided to ask Chief David John to address the Deputy Superintendent General according to the custom of the Confederacy.
>
> The Deputy Superintendent General after listening to the Fire Keeper responded in a fitting manner expressing with pleasure his being able to be present with the Chiefs. He is always interested in the Six Nations and shall continue to do so. In the words of the Fire Keeper he feels he can see better since he has come and his ears are clear to hear them and his throat is clear so that he can respond. At this juncture he presents the Chiefs with a picture of the great Chief Joseph Brant painting of Romnie as his expression of good will.
>
> The Council accepts with pleasure the gift from DC Scott Deputy Supt General of the likeness of Capt. Joseph Brant.[67]

History would quickly demonstrate that Scott was simply pretending to have "friendship and respect" toward the. Confederacy Council.

As departmental interference grew out of control in the 1920s, the council looked to their speaker, Cayuga Hoyaneh Levi General (Deskaheh), to take up their cause and attract the attention of the Crown to their plight. In 1922, the Confederacy Council instructed him to refer their case to the International Court of Justice.[68] Related to this, in the next year they authorized him to travel to England in the effort. While there, he gave several impassioned speeches about the treaty relationship and the responsibilities of the Crown in regard to the Haudenosaunee. In an August 1923 speech in London, he said, "we would not have consented to take Canada's franchises if she had asked us politely to do so . . . we are very willing to remain allies of the British against days of danger, as we have been for 250 years . . . but we wish no one-sided alliance, nor will we ever be subjects of another people, even of the British if we can help it."[69] While many individual English people were sympathetic to Deskaheh's message, he was unsuccessful at getting the attention of the King.

When Deskaheh returned home, he pushed forward and authored *The Red Man's Appeal for Justice*, a manifesto for Six Nations rights. In it he argued, "The only process known to international law whereby an independent people may yield their sovereignty is either by defeat in war or voluntary abandonment of it formally evidenced. The Grand River people have never yielded their sovereignty by any formal abandonment of it, and they have never been conquered in war by any power on earth of which there is either record or tradition."[70] Deskaheh hoped that the international arena would apply pressure on the British, especially in light of the oppression exposed in other countries through the First World War, but his pleas fell upon deaf ears once again. Deskaheh returned to Europe, this time seeking to address the League of Nations in Geneva, Switzerland. He travelled with George P. Decker, a Rochester, New York, lawyer who provided legal assistance to the chief. Echoing the sentiments of the British government, the League refused Deskaheh's request, despite the support he received from Belgium. The league stated that his was a domestic issue for Canada to address internally. Deskaheh returned to North America near the end of 1924, apparently after the Canadian government takeover at Grand River. Deskaheh was denied entry into Canada based upon his political activities and spent the last few months of his life as a political refugee, staying at the home of Tuscarora chief Clinton Rickard. He died in June 1925, but the assertions of Six Nations sovereignty lived on as a testament of his inspiration.

Political Critics and Confederacy Supporters

As happens in all societies, political dissension has probably always existed among the nations of the Haudenosaunee. It seems, however, that when an Indigenous society, such as the Six Nations, experiences political diversity it is reported by others as if it might represent the complete end of that particular society. When a country like the United States or Canada experiences similar political diversity, it is seen as simply a difference of opinion. Political dissension in those societies is expected and understood to be a reality of human nature; it is rarely seen as a threat to the very existence of the society. Yet the same types of political dissension within Indigenous nations are rarely accorded the same balanced representation. Instead, they are reported as "the beginning of the end." That is certainly the way in which political diversity among the Haudenosaunee has been presented, even before the relocation to the Grand River Territory. Academics such as William Fenton have forwarded the idea that the Confederacy ended when young men from within the Confederacy fought each other in the Revolutionary War. If they applied that same litmus test to the United States, that particular confederacy would have ended in 1861. Why is it that Western nations can have internal disputes yet still exist, but Indigenous nations are said to "disintegrate" at the mere mention of a difference of opinion?

With that in mind, the first report of political dissension on the Grand River—or, rather, the first time a Haudenosaunee citizen took his concerns to an outside body, apparently according it some authority in the matter—came in 1861 through a petition circulated by Isaac Powless regarding the council's inability to achieve redress for the failed Grand River Navigation Company investment.[71] Many ironies were at work in this political act. First, Powless was appealing, without the authority of the council, to the Indian Department, whose governmental predecessors had been instrumental in the navigational investment. Second, the government itself (indirectly) admitted responsibility for the investment, as shown in the recommendations of the 1843 Bagot Commission. Third, it appears that Powless had personal motivations against the council, having been overlooked in his application to serve as council interpreter. Politics do seem to have been at play in this situation, but it appears that at least some of them were more personal than community-minded. Powless did convince 167 individuals to sign the petition calling for a municipal government to replace the Confederacy Council,[72] but it is unclear as to who these agitators were and how much they understood about the petition they signed. An important aspect of this petition, however, was the fact that Powless and several other young men did actively plot an overthrow of their government and were willing to collaborate with the Indian Department to make it happen.[73] Even though their numbers were not a significant portion of the community population, it does indicate that some dissenters were willing to go to any length—even overstepping the system their ancestors helped to create—in order to do so.

Some political critics attempted reform within the system, and their comments have been recorded in the Six Nations Council Minutes. Some suggested voting by the council in order to expedite decision making. Others recommended reducing the number of chiefs, again alluding to the idea that a smaller representative body would be able to govern more efficiently.[74] As Haudenosaunee citizens, these would-be reformers were allowed to address the council and, even if their suggestions were opposed by the chiefs, they were not shunned, nor did they lose their rights. That is probably indicative of the fact that they were not advocating removal of the chiefs nor were they suggesting a complete end to the hereditary system.

Other Confederacy critics followed in the footsteps of Powless, circulating petitions and arousing the fears of their fellow citizens at different points during this period. In 1907, a community group known as the Indian Rights Association[75] sent an anonymous letter to the visiting superintendent asking him to ask the chiefs a series of questions regarding impositions on Six Nations rights through the Indian Act.[76] The chiefs refused to answer until the author was willing to put his name to the letter. A.E. Hill sent a duplicate letter directly to the council, which he signed as association secretary.[77] The questions asked all centred on the Indian Act and ultimately asked why the council often publicly opposed the act, since the council, in their eyes, already operated completely under the act. It seems that this group was in favour of "advancement," as the department had defined it, and were unhappy that the council was working against the total imposition of the act on the community. There had been earlier rumours circulated to the council that the new visiting superintendent, Gordon Smith, had been agitating among the political critics of the council and assisting in the development of a petition.[78]

In the published histories of the Six Nations community, one can find many references to the political opponents of the Confederacy Council, but it is rare to find reference to the council supporters.[79] This misrepresentation might lead one to believe that the agitators were a significant—maybe even a majority—representation of the community's citizenry. While their voices should not be discounted in the community's history, they also should not be overly privileged in recalling the events of the time. Instead, it is important to represent both the critics and supporters. Obviously, the most vocal supporters represented their families in council. But it is important to recall that while those men were the voice of their clan families within the Confederacy system, they did not stand alone. In fact, many of the Royaners' sub-chiefs were active participants in the council, and their names often appear on the chiefs' roll as well as on important committees and other council initiatives. Less often referenced, but still active participants, were the Yakoyaner and the Faithkeepers. These positions were more active within the clan structure and their duties appeared less often in the deliberations of council. After all, working with the council was the Royaners' responsibility.

An unusual source provides an indirect reference to council supporters in the 1880s. In July 1883, the ethnographer Horatio Hale attended a condolence ceremony at the Onondaga Longhouse. He focussed his report on chronicling the ceremonial aspects of the day, but in an offhand manner mentioned that the event was attended by over 200 people. Certainly these people were active supporters of the Confederacy and took time out of their busy schedules—the green bean harvest would have been in full swing at that point in the summer—to travel by foot or wagon to gather for this important Confederacy event. That took much more effort than was expended by Isaac Powless's petitioners two decades prior to this gathering.

During different times of stress for the community (e.g., Indian Act impositions, land claim problems, etc.), individuals often approached the council offering their assistance and support. The "warriors" are commonly noted as having made suggestions regarding specific issues or having recommended a raise in the chiefs' board money (the chiefs would not vote themselves a raise). These "warriors" should not be confused with "Warriors Associations" that sprang up from time to time in opposition to the council.[80] Instead, these "warriors" were the men of the community, the workers. They served the council as citizens of the Confederacy. Some of their ranks accompanied chiefs' delegations to Ottawa. Others assisted as Pathmasters, Forest Wardens, or members of the locating line committee. And still others simply showed up for council meetings in order to stay informed about the issues their government was addressing on their behalf.

As tensions grew in the community because of the impositions of the Indian Department and the reluctance of the Dominion and the Crown to address the land claims, citizen groups formed to support the council and provide encouragement to their traditional leaders. In the early fall of 1920, one of these support groups sponsored a large-scale community picnic as a means of demonstrating their support. A resolution was written and approved by the people at the gathering and the council adopted it into the council records three weeks later:

> Resolved,—
>
> That at this crucial period of our history we unite ourselves as one great family, sinking all differences, and rise unanimously to stand behind our ancient and accepted confederate body of Chiefs in all their dealings with the Dominion Government. Moved by Andrew Scott and seconded by A.H. Lottridge.
>
> Signed
> Thomas A. Miller
> Chairman[81]

Their words were simple and direct but spoke volumes regarding the support that these people had for their council.

The 1924 "Takeover"

The Rotiyanehson understood the danger of their political tensions with the Department of Indian Affairs and other branches of the Canadian governments. They were well aware of the fact that the Crown no longer needed their assistance as allies, but they also knew that the treaty relationship was the only thing they did have in their favour. They continually called upon the conscience of the Crown "to keep their promises."

The council also reaffirmed the values and principles upon which their government was built, especially in regard to the specific issues of the Grand River community. In February 1923, they made a series of proclamations in council—all of which were reported to Indian Affairs through the visiting superintendent—that supported their claims of sovereignty and ultimate authority of the government and lands of the Six Nations. The first proclamation addressed land cessions:

> Re Cession of lands of the Six Nations:—
>
> The Council decided that no cession of the Grand River lands or of any lands forming part of the territory covered by the Haldimand Treaty and which remain unceded, shall be valid unless made with the consent of the men and of the women of the Six Nations given by a two-thirds majority of those of the men voting and a two thirds majority of the women voting on votes to be taken under authority of this council nor shall such cessions be valid unless such consents if given shall be confirmed by this council.[82]

This declaration demonstrated a change in older council policy wherein the chiefs, acting on behalf of their families and nations, were the ones to authorize land cessions. In this, however, the council did maintain ultimate authority over calling such votes. This statement was in direct reaction to the Soldier Settlement Act. The next provision addressed the Six Nations' trust accounts:

> Re funds and other securities held in trust by the Dominion Government
>
> The Council decided that the remainder of all funds and any securities therefor taken by the Dominion Government with the authority of this Council, belonging to the Six Nations of the Grand River, received by or in the custody of the Government of

the Dominion of Canada in trust or otherwise be and are hereby called for and the Dominion Government is hereby requested to deliver the same to the Treasurer of the Six Nations who is hereby authorized to receive and receipt for such funds and securities for funds as shall be so received by him.

The Secretary is directed to forward copy of this decision to the Honorable Dominion Minister of Interior by registered mail.[83]

In essence, the council was articulating the desire to end the financial relationship with the Indian Department. Certainly the controversies surrounding the secretary's salary and the chiefs' board money contributed to this decision. It also reflected the long-standing mistrust resulting from examples of unscrupulous financial management, such as that of Samuel P. Jarvis in the 1830s. The third declaration dealt with the right to hold land on the territory: "The Council decided that all conveyances, leases or mortgages herein made of any private location, allotment or holding within the lands of the Six Nations, and being part or parcel of the Grand River lands described in and by the Haldimand Treaty and claimed by any other than a person enrolled by this Council as a National of the Six Nations or a descendant of such National in the mother's line shall be void, and all such conveyances leases or mortgages heretofore made without the consent of this Council, are and shall remain void."[84] In this provision, the council articulated a return to an ancient principle of the Confederacy: matrilineal descent. This was an obvious reaction to the patriarchal policies of the Indian Act that stood in direct opposition to Haudenosaunee values. Unlike the Department of Indian Affairs, however, the council did not eliminate the rights of non-matrilineal descendants in order to provide for the rights of those born to Six Nations women.

The council minutes of 1924 give no indication, however, that the chiefs allowed their concern for governmental overthrow to inhibit their ability to govern the territory and guide the people. They continued to address estate cases and counselled broken marriages. They celebrated the Queen's Birthday "as usual." They even made plans for a "Six Nations National Day," as described in their minutes: "On the suggestion of friends in England that it would be proper for the Six Nations in Canada to take the 25th of October as a National day being the date on which 'The Grant' was executed by Sir Frederick Haldimand, on behalf of His Majesty King George the Third, granting to them Six Miles on each side of the Grand River from its mouth to its source."[85]

The chiefs were not oblivious to what was going on behind their backs, but they refused to be paralyzed in fear of what *might* occur as a result. Indian Affairs had commissioned Col. Andrew Thompson to investigate the impasse between the council and the department.[86] Thompson was associated with some of the soldiers involved in the Soldier Settlement Act controversy, so the council was not surprised when his report recommended the abolition of the hereditary system. Just before the noon break of the 7 October 1924 council meeting, visiting superintendent Morgan read an order-in-council voiding the authority of the Confederacy Council. The proclamation called for the first election of the new band council. Morgan—along with an RCMP escort—confiscated the council fire wampum strings[87] and several other wampum records from the Council House.[88] They posted a sign on the Council House doors notifying the community about the first election of the band council, scheduled for 21 October. According to the oral record of the community, only twenty-seven people voted in that first election.[89] There were thirteen positions in total being voted upon. Weaver claims that between 20 and 40 percent of those eligible to vote did so in the first and subsequent elections. There is no evidence to support this assertion. Even in contemporary times, the average voter turnout is in the vicinity of 15 percent.

The Confederacy Council refused to recognize the authority of the Canadian government and continued to meet and be recognized by most of the people of the community. However, a small group of dissenters capitalized on the opportunity provided by the Canadian government and elected themselves as the first Six Nations band council. As a creation of their government, this band council was given authority by the Canadians over all financial matters in accordance with the provisions of the Indian Act. While the Government of Canada could not tell the Six Nations people who their leaders were, they could decide who *they* were going to deal with—and who they would allow to access the trust funds of the Six Nations (as set out in the Indian Act).

The 1924 "takeover" represented the lengths to which the federal government was prepared to go in order to gain and maintain control over the Grand River community and lands. It also represented the fact that a small group of political dissidents could rise to power without the backing of the community. The Indian Department had encouraged political dissension in the community for many years. They knew that given enough time and inspiration, the dissenters would provide the department with sufficient complaints to warrant the imposition of Dominion control over the Six Nations.

ooooo

The years 1847 to 1924 witnessed major changes for the Grand River Haudenosaunee in terms of community development and infrastructure as well as the diminished relationship with the Crown. Important cultural values and attitudes persisted through these changes, however, and guided the Six Nations people and their council through the many challenges of the era. Some Six Nations people welcomed the "opportunities" of Indian Affairs' advancement strategies; they became the department's symbols of achievement. Most of the Haudenosaunee, however, agreed with their council and opted against taking the road of "advancement." Instead they kept on their own path, travelling alongside their white neighbours as their respective ancestors had agreed to hundreds of years earlier.

This era has typically been presented in the context of what was done to the Six Nations by the Canadian governments. This chapter has chronicled many of those events as well, but has attempted to represent both the actions and reactions of the Haudenosaunee to these Indian Affairs "inflictions." The Confederacy Council continued to govern the community with their minds on the future at all times. They struggled with the impositions placed upon them by the Department of Indian Affairs. They were saddened and frustrated by the Crown's refusal to become involved. And they were disheartened to see that some of their own people were willing to collaborate with the Indian Department in order to further their own personal causes rather than looking out for the future of the entire community. The Great Law not only requires the Royaner to be mindful of the future but also expects each individual to uphold the same responsibilities. The Rotiyanehson were concerned that these individuals were attacking them, but they were more concerned that these individuals had turned their backs on Haudenosaunee law.

The realities of the consolidated territory forced the council to develop policies and procedures for governing the community, especially around issues of land and membership. The records demonstrate the council's efforts to be consistent and fair in their rulings about property. Their policies were quite consistent but were never applied so strictly as to not allow for uniqueness in each situation. At times, the council used provisions of the Indian Act to determine property ownership when they lacked internal policy and when the act did not conflict with Haudenosaunee values. It is important to realize that the cases that came to council only represented a fraction of the inheritance issues the community would have encountered during those years. As their ancestors had done before them, most Six Nations families continued to govern their property affairs within the family.[90] The only cases taken to council were instances when the family could not agree on property distribution or custodial issues for dependent children. Through their property and membership decisions the council attempted to be fair and consistent. They also attempted to govern in a manner that was consistent with the values and expectations of their people. Their actions represented the collective mind of the community, a mind that continued to view land as an entity that provided sustenance for the people, and in turn the people endeavoured to protect the land and their rights to her in order to provide for the future generations.

Tetitewennonhtonhstha Tsi Niyonkwarihotenhs— We Are Causing Ourselves to Have Control Again, the Way We Do Things

As Haudenosaunee, the people of the Grand River Territory continue to define themselves as sovereign Indigenous people of Turtle Island (North America). For example, when they cross the U.S.–Canada land border, most identify as either "Haudenosaunee/Six Nations" or as "North American Indians."[1] Similarly, Haudenosaunee individuals typically have a relationship with both the Canadian and U.S. governments. Nevertheless, given Canada's proximity and connection to (and claims over) the Grand River Territory, the actions of the Canadian government have a greater effect on the Grand River Haudenosaunee. For over a decade Canada has been talking about reconciling their relationship with Indigenous peoples and in May 2015 found themselves "called to action" by the Truth and Reconciliation Commission (TRC) regarding the impacts of the Canadian Indian Residential School system. Many of Canada's public entities have since been considering ways to reconcile the wrongs of the past, especially the direct and indirect impacts of the residential school system. Certainly, people from Six Nations and entities who have a connection to the community (school boards, local and provincial governments, post-secondary institutions, etc.) are regular participants in those conversations. However, what is often missing from these talks is any consideration of what constitutes reconciliation itself.

In terms of land and land tenure at Grand River, there is a long history of interference by the Canadian state with the Haudenosaunee people. Residential schools did play a part, but they were not the central vehicle of dispossession for the Grand River Haudenosaunee. Instead, it was unscrupulous land thefts, policy impositions, and governance interference that created an unreconciled relationship between the Crown and the Haudenosaunee. Thus, as Canada seeks to reconcile its shared past with the Indigenous peoples of the land, what might reconciliation look like between the Grand River Haudenosaunee and Canada?

Land Claims. When I first heard about reconciliation between Canada and Indigenous peoples, my mind jumped to the financial use of the term reconciliation. I thought, "Yes, it's time that Canada starts reconciling their financial debts to First Nations communities"—and I thought specifically about the unaccounted-for Six Nations Trust Funds. I soon learned, however, that Canada's idea of reconciliation was likely to be more symbolic than literal, at least in direct financial matters. I continue to believe, however, that there cannot be reconciliation without an equitable accounting for lands and monies illegally and unethically seized.[2] That is a huge bill; however, Canadian wealth gained at a cost to Six Nations has created a very unhealthy relationship. The road forward must address this in order to succeed.

Education. The TRC's call understandably emphasizes education and related institutions. For Six Nations, there is certainly a need to address the direct impacts of the residential school system on the community, especially for the remaining survivors and their direct descendants. However, as many Indigenous people across Canada (and beyond) suggest, the effects are much further-reaching, and the mentality that brought about residential schooling also altered fundamental ideas held by Indigenous people about education, particularly in how it relates to Indigenous Knowledge/Original Teachings. The primary conduits for traditional Native education are the Native languages of the people. The attack on Indigenous languages by the residential school system and related policy initiatives is the most measurable in terms of impact. Therefore, upon embarking on reconciliation, the most assessable area of improvement could be language revitalization (for those communities who deem it a key goal of reconciliation). Fewer than 1 percent of all Grand River Haudenosaunee are now fluent in any of their original languages, but there is a great desire to regain fluency.

Alongside clearly articulated goals for Haudenosaunee language revitalization are aspirations for community-controlled education for the Six

Nations community as well as adequate financial support to access quality educational opportunities inside and outside the community; this is relevant for all levels of education, from pre-school through doctoral studies. Many community-based thinkers have suggested this could easily be financed through land claims resolution.

Environmental Responsibility. Many prominent Haudenosaunee philosophers acknowledge Haudenosaunee environmental thought, ethics, and knowledge as among their people's greatest contributions to the world, matched only by Haudenosaunee teachings about peace. True reconciliation would result in a relationship marked by shared values, especially where the environment is concerned. And while it may be lofty to expect Canada to embrace all Haudenosaunee environmental values, it is not unreasonable to expect that in those places of shared environments, those values might serve as a guide for how the environment will be treated. Within the Grand River watershed, as an example, that would mean greater consideration of the river and related ecosystems and how proposed developments might affect those systems. Alternative energy is a huge movement currently in the region and may align well with Haudenosaunee environmental ethics; however, there is concern about whether adequate research regarding potential negative impacts on humans and other life forms will be conducted before large- and small-scale projects are undertaken. In-depth research is equally important for any new commercial and residential projects.[3] Haudenosaunee environmental ethics mandate actions that support life beyond immediate human desires. Planning based upon that philosophy will benefit all life in the Grand River region, including the human lives of the Haudenosaunee and Canadians.

Ultimately, all of this boils down to a recognition of and respect for the treaty relationship between the Haudenosaunee and the Crown, which spans over 350 years (over 400 years when the Dutch promises documented in the Kaswentha—for which the British assumed responsibility in 1664—are included). If Canadians are looking for the path to move forward in their relationship with the Haudenosaunee, they need not look further than the wampum belts that document the treaty history between the two peoples. Some modern political critics—both Indigenous and non-Indigenous—suggest that treaties are irrelevant because they have been broken and perhaps were never meant to be kept (by the Crown) anyway. The Haudenosaunee reading of those treaties and the mutual obligations held within them suggests otherwise, however. Quite simply, it is time to polish the chain and commit to never letting it tarnish again.

Today as always, Six Nations is a diverse and vibrant community with many complexities. The community carries scores of burdens that resulted from the unhealthy relationship with the Crown and Canada, and it grapples with how to address the internal aspects of those burdens while simultaneously attempting to literally and figuratively stand its ground in relation to the ongoing developments within the original Haldimand Tract as well as the larger traditional territory (some of which is acknowledged in the 1701 Beaver Hunting Grounds Treaty). In thinking about a positive way forward, it is essential to recognize that the community has responsibility for internal matters and should be accorded the right to address those matters free of external interference.[4] In terms of external matters, Canada bears a huge responsibility to conduct itself in a far more honourable manner than it has over much of its history as a nation. The Grand River Haudenosaunee of today, much like their ancestors of many previous generations, are willing to travel that river together, in peace and friendship again.

SIX NATIONS CENSUSES

This appendix includes information from eight censuses found in several sources (as noted) that speak to the population of the Six Nations community between 1785 and 1924. It is included here for reference purposes and has been mentioned in several cases in the text.

Census of the Six Nations on the Grand River, 1785

	Persons
Mohawks	448
Onondagas Council fire	174
d° Bear's foot's party	51
Senecas	47
. . . Onondagas from the West	20
Upper Cayugas	198
Upper Tootalies [Tutalos]	55
Oghguagas	113
Delaware Aaron's party	48
Oghguaga Joseph's party	49
Tuscaroras	129
Lower Cayugas	183
St Regis	16
Montours	15
Creeks & Cherokees	53
Lower Tootalies	19
Delawares	183
Senecas from the West	31
Nanticokes	11
	1843

Source: LAC, Haldimand Papers, B 103, 457; Charles M. Johnston, ed., *The Valley of the Six Nations: A Collection of Documents on the Indian Lands of the Grand River* (Toronto: University of Toronto Press, 1964), 52.

An Indian Census, 1810–11

	[1810] Taken	[1811]
Mohawks	436	436–83 Men, 100 Women, 91Children [?]
Upper Cayugas	208	209 a Stout Young Cayuga Man
Lower (Cayugas)	200	203 Tall Shawane lad [?]
Aughhquagas	158	158 no return given
Delawars	216	230 by Delawar Dame [?]
Tuscaroras	141	143 Billy Jack
Onadagas Turkey	180	192 by Turkey & Clear Sky
Delawar Aaron	73	73 no return given
Senecas	41	39 Tahquesca
Upper Tootelies	53	64 By a Young Tootelie lad
Onadagas B:Foot	32	33 Bears Foot
Onyda Joseph	38	47 Onyda Joseph
Montuers	27	31 By George Montuir
Lower Tootelies	29	41 By a Tootelie
St. Regis	15	19 by a Young Man said to be of the Family
Nanticokes	9	10 By Hobkins the White man

Source: LAC, Claus Papers, X, 39–30; Johnston, *Valley of the Six Nations*, 281.

Major General H.C. Darling's Report on the Six Nations, 1834

Quebec, 24th July 1828

[Census conducted by Major General Henry Charles Darling, Lord Dalhousie's military secretary]

...their present possessions in houses, horses, cattle, &c.; viz.	
Dwelling-houses	416
Computed number of acres of land in cultivation	6,872
Horses	738
Cows	869
Oxen	613
Sheep	192
Swine	1,630

Source: Great Britain, Colonial Office, Parliamentary Paper, 1834, no. 617, Aboriginal Tribes, 28–30; Johnston, *Valley of the Six Nations*, 291–292.

Census of Six Nations of Grand River, 1886

	Births	Deaths	Increase	Decrease
1874	118	120		2
1875	128	61	67	
1876	113	71	42	
1877	132	111	21	
1878	118	117	1	
1879	115	86	29	
1880	127	101	26	
1881	75	96		21
1882	84	91		7
1883	99	83	16	
1884	93	109		16
[total]	1209	1046	202	46
Before 1874	118	120		2
[total]	1084	926	202	44
	158	Natural increase in ten years, while in eleven years the increase is only 156		

Source: Six Nations Council Minutes (SNCM), June 1886.

Census for the Six Nations for 1900

	Births
Upper Mohawks	13
Lower Mohawks	10
Oneidas	5
Onondagas	4
Bearfoot Onondagas	1
Upper Cayugas	10
Lower Cayugas	7
Senecas	3
Tuscaroras	5
Delewares	4
	Total 62

Source: SNCM, February 1900.

Population of Six Nations Reserve by Date, 1784–1900

Year	POPULATION	YEAR	POPULATION	YEAR	POPULATION
1785	1843	1876	3069	1899	3929
1800	1856	1877	3134	1900	3968
1810	1856	1878	3152	1901	4023
1811	1928	1879	3152	1903	4050
1814	1748	1880	3204	1904	4132
1824	2220	1881	3205	1905	4195
1835	2236	1882	3195	1906	4267
1836	2330	1883	3416	1907	4315
1839	2149	1884	3216	1908	4286
1840	2210	1885	3216	1909	4236
1841	2172	1887	3320	1910	4275
1843	2223	1889	3384	1911	4466
1851	1584	1892	3440	1912	4510
1855	2330	1893	3474	1915	4606
1871	2916	1894	3531	1916	4716
1872	2992	1895	3557	1917	4776
1874	2952	1897	3667	1922	4491
1875	3069	1898	3703	1924	4307

Source: Doxtator, "Iroquois Clans," 131–32.

Census of 1888

Band	Adult Males	Adult Females	Youth M	Youth F	Children M	Children F	Totals	Births	Deaths	Additions	Removals
Upper Mohawks	192	205	52	42	132	120	743	26	17	2	
Lower Mohawks	127	125	21	30	82	61	446	24	4	1	2
Walker Mohawks	11	9	4	2	8	9	43	2	1		
B of Q Mohawks	21	19	3	6	10	12	71		1		
Oneidas	72	61	15	11	49	28	236	10	2		
Onondaga ClearSky	80	76	13	12	43	47	271	10	7	2	1
Bearfoot Onondagas	21	20	6	4	15	9	75	1	2	1	
Tuscaroras	85	91	30	25	53	45	329	11	7	3	
Upper Cayugas	89	96	27	29	44	51	336	13	10		2
Lower Cayugas	132	132	38	26	70	74	472	11	16		
Kanadaga Senecas	22	17	12	11	18	13	93	4	1		
Nikarondasa Senecas	26	25	11	9	21	21	113	4	4		2
Delewares	37	38	11	5	22	21	134	1	2		
	915	914	243	212	567	511	3362	114	74	9	7

Source: Census Book 1884–1889, Six Nation Indians.

Census of 1889

Band	Adult Males	Adult Females	Youth M	Youth F	Children M	Children F	Totals	Births	Deaths	Additions	Removals
Upper Mohawks	189	204	49	35	139	140	756	29	15	1	1
Lower Mohawks	127	128	18	27	81	65	446	9	5	1	2
Walker Mohawks	10	8	4	1	9	8	40	2	1		
B of Q Mohawks	22	19	2	8	12	9	72	2	1		
Oneidas	69	62	15	10	52	26	234	3	3		
Onondaga ClearSkies	76	72	10	13	43	45	259	8	12		1
Bearfoot Onondagas	22	10	5	4	16	13	79	4	1		
Tuscaroras	87	92	27	23	55	39	323	3	4	1	
Upper Cayugas	93	103	29	29	49	63	368	13	2		
Lower Cayugas	125	134	37	28	76	76	477	12	1		7
Kanadaga Senecas	22	18	11	10	18	14	93	1			
Nikarondasa Senecas	28	19	9	8	18	19	107	2	4		
Delewares	37	37	11	4	25	23	137	6	3		
	907	915	227	200	593	540	3385	94	62	3	11

Source: Census Book 1884–1889, Six Nation Indians.

Six Nations Claims Filed with the Specific Claims Branch

These following claims constitute a significant portion of the over 900,000 acres alienated from the Grand River Haudenosaunee since the Haldimand Proclamation of 1784. More claims could be filed.

Claim
Canadian National Railway Right-of-Way, Oneida Township, 259.2 acres (Resolved, 24 December 1985)
Innisfil Township, 900 acres
Hawkesbury Township, 4,000 acres
Block #5, Moulton Township, 30,800 acres
Hamilton-Port Dover Plank Road, Seneca, and Oneida Townships, 7,680 acres
Welland Canal (Feeder Dam), 2,415.6 acres (Accepted for negotiations, 13 May 1994)
Block #6, Canborough Township, 19,000 acres
Johnson Settlement, Brantford Township – Fed. Gov't responsibility, 7,000 acres
Burtch Tract, Brantford Township, 5,233 acres
Ordnance Reserve – Lots 25 and 26, Con. 4, Port Maitland, Dunn Township
1841 Purported Surrender
Eagle's Nest Tract, Brantford Township, 1,800 acres
Onondaga Township – Lots 10-14, Con. II, and Lots 6-15, Con. III, 2,000 acres
Martin's Tract, Brantford Township, 1,500 acres
Oxbow Bend, Brantford Township, 1,200 acres
Oneida Township

Claim
Canadian National Railway Right-of-Way, River Range, Onondaga Township
Cayuga Township South Side of the Grand River
Grand River Navigation Company (Land Grants), 368.7 acres
Bed of the Grand River and Islands thereon
Tow Path Lands
Exploration of Oil and Natural Gas underlying the Six Nations Reserve
Source of the Grand River, 300,000 acres
Six Nations Investments in Custody of Coutts and Company
Misappropriation of Six Nations Funds by Samuel P. Jarvis
The Right to Hunt and Fish
Compensation for Lands Included in Letters Patent No. 708 (dated 5 November 1851) – Re: Brantford Town Plot
Compensation for Lands Patented to Nathan Gage on 25 February 1840 – Re: Brantford Town Plot (claim refused to be accepted by Specific Claims Branch)
Compensation for Lands Included in Letters Patent No. 910 (dated 12 July 1852) – Re: Brantford Town Plot (claim refused to be accepted by Specific Claims Branch)

Source: Six Nations Elected Council, *Six Miles Deep: Land Rights of the Six Nations of the Grand River* (Ohsweken, ON: Six Nations Elected Council, 2015).

NOTES

Introduction

1   Unless otherwise noted, Haudenosaunee terminology will be given in the Kanyen'keha (Mohawk) language. The Thanksgiving Address is also known in Cayuga as Ganohonyohk.

2   The Cayuga word is sgaihwa:t (note: spellings vary).

3   Deborah Doxtator writes about this linguistic fact in her article "Inclusive and Exclusive Perceptions of Difference: Native and Euro-based Concepts of Time, History and Change," in *Decentering the Renaissance: New Essays on Canada 1500–1700*, ed. Germaine Warkentin and Carolyn Podruchny (Toronto: University of Toronto Press, 2002), 33–47. I discuss it further in Chapter 2.

4   For examples, see Vine Deloria, Jr., *Custer Died for Your Sins: An Indigenous Manifesto* (Norman, OK: University of Oklahoma Press, 1969); James (Sákéj) Youngblood Henderson, "Ayukpachi: Empowering Aboriginal Thought," in *Reclaiming Indigenous Voice and Vision*, ed. Marie Battiste (Vancouver: University of British Columbia Press, 2000), 248–78; and Linda Tuhiwai Smith, *Decolonizing Methodologies: Research and Indigenous Peoples* (Auckland: Zed Books, 1999).

5   James (Sákéj) Youngblood Henderson, "The Context of the State of Nature," in *Reclaiming Indigenous Voice and Vision*, ed. Marie Battiste (Vancouver: University of British Columbia Press, 2000), 11–38.

6   For detailed discussions of this philosophy within a Haudenosaunee context, see Carol Cornelius, *Iroquois Corn in a Culture-based Curriculum* (Albany: State University of New York Press, 1999); and Haudenosaunee Environmental Task Force, *The Words That Come Before All Else* (Akwesasne, Haudenosaunee Territory: Native North American Travelling College, 2000).

7   Smith, *Decolonizing Methodologies*, 34–35.

8   Georges Sioui, *For an Amerindian Autohistory: An Essay on the Foundations of a Social Ethic* (Montreal: McGill-Queen's University Press, 1992), 37.

9   Ibid.

10 Gaiwiyo is the Cayuga term for the Good Message of Handsome Lake. At Grand River, the Cayuga form of the word is more commonly used.

11 Jigonsaseh (Tsikonhsaseh in Mohawk) was the first person to accept the Great Law; see Chapter 1 for a detailed explanation of her role in the formation of the Haudenosaunee Confederacy.

12 He calls them "Sinnekens," but it is believed they were Oneidas as the previous term was often used to refer to all four Haudenosaunee nations west of the Mohawks.

13 Dean R. Snow, Charles Gehring, and William Strarna, eds., *In Mohawk Country: Early Narratives about a Native People* (Syracuse: Syracuse University Press, 1996), 4.

14 Josiah Hill and his brother Richard Hill were both Confederacy Chiefs originally named as representatives of the Nanticoke through their father's lineage (the Nanticoke followed patrilineal descent) but also recognized as Tuscarora leaders

through their mother's lineage (the Tuscarora, like the other Haudenosaunee nations follow matrilineal descent).

Chapter 1: Karihwa'onwe—*The Original Matters*

1   Other major elements also exist, including stories of the formation of clans and the beginnings of various medicine societies, but I have chosen to focus on the four that have been identified in my own personal learning experiences. There is also a general approval of the discussion of these cultural foundations beyond the community. That is not the case for some of the other elements that have not been selected for this study.

2   *Onkwehonweneha* can refer to anything having to do with Indigenous cultures, specific aspects of Haudenosaunee culture, or any/all of the Haudenosaunee languages. In this context it is used to refer to all of the Haudenosaunee languages.

3   Prior to the introduction of glass seed beads, these designs were depicted in a variety of ways, including paint, porcupine quillwork, and moose hair embroidery.

4   For example, see the *Jesuit Relations* and Joseph-François Lafitau's *Customs of the American Indians Compared with the Customs of Primitive Times* (Toronto: Champlain Society, 1977).

5   For a brief discussion of reported Native "devil-worship," see Olive Dickason, *The Myth of the Savage* (Edmonton: University of Alberta Press, 1997 [1984]), 30–31 and 200.

6   Some would argue that an earlier study, published by David Cusick from the Tuscarora Nation, is the first academic undertaking of Haudenosaunee Creation but that short account falls more closely as a literary endeavour. For a discussion of Cusick in relation to other accounts of the Creation Story, see Kevin J. White, "Rousing a Curiosity in Hewitt's Iroquois Cosmologies," *Wicazo Sa Review* 28.2 (2013): 87–111.

7   Lewis Henry Morgan, *League of the Ho-de-no-sau-nee, or Iroquois* (New York: MH Newman, 1851), 152.

8   Most biographical discussions of Hewitt refer to him as "Tuscarora." For example, see: Elisabeth Tooker, "J.N.B. Hewitt," in *Encyclopedia of North American Indians*, ed. Frederick E. Hoxie (Boston: Houghton Mifflin, 1996); Marie L.B. Baldwin, "John N.B. Hewitt, Ethnologist," *Quarterly Journal of the Society of American Indians* 2 (1914): 147–50; and John R. Swanton, "John Napoleon Brinton Hewitt," *American Anthropologist* 40 (1938): 286–90.

9   J.N.B. Hewitt, "Iroquois Cosmology, Part 1," *Annual report of the Bureau of American Ethnology to the Secretary of the Smithsonian Institution* 21 (Washington: Smithsonian Institution, 1903), 137.

10   For examples, see Tooker, "J.N.B. Hewitt," Baldwin, "John N.B. Hewitt, Ethnologist," and Swanton, "John Napoleon Brinton Hewitt."

11   "Iroquoian Cosmology: Part 2," *Annual report of the Bureau of American Ethnology to the Secretary of the Smithsonian Institution* 43 (Washington: Smithsonian Institution, 1928).

12   It is important to note that while Hewitt called these "an Onondaga version" or "a Mohawk version," for example, the versions he recorded were in those languages but do not represent different creation stories attributed to the individual nations. There is only *one* creation story. It exists in all six languages and has been written about in many pieces and forms of its entirety. Therefore, in referencing these Hewitt texts I

refer to them as an "Onondaga language version" or a "Mohawk language version," for example.

13 Of the other three versions, two also were collected at Grand River. An Onondaga language version was shared by Onondaga Royaner John Buck and a Mohawk language version was provided by Seth Newhouse of the Onondaga Nation. The Seneca language version was collected from John Armstrong of the Cattaraugus Territory. The fifth version was not published and its origins are not discussed in the BAE report.

14 For examples, see publications from William Fenton ed., *Parker on the Iroquois* (Syracuse, NY: Syracuse University Press, 1968); Hazel Hertzberg, *The Great Tree and the Longhouse: The Culture of the Iroquois* (New York: Macmillan, 1966); Arthur C. Parker, *The Code of Handsome Lake, the Seneca Prophet* (Albany: New York State Museum, 1918); and *The Constitution of the Five Nations* (Albany: University of the State of New York, 1916); and Elisabeth Tooker, "The Five (Later Six) Nations Confederacy, 1550–1784" in *Aboriginal Ontario: Historical Perspectives on the First Nations*, edited by Edward S. Rogers and Donald B. Smith (Toronto: Dundurn Press, 1994), 79–91; "Women in Iroquois Society" in *Extending the Rafters: Interdisciplinary Approaches to Iroquoian Studies*, edited by Michael K. Foster, Jack Campisi, and Marianne Mithun (Albany: State University of New York Press, 1984), 109–24; and "Iroquois Since 1820" in *The Handbook of North American Indians: Vol. 15: Northeast*, edited by Bruce G. Trigger (Washington: Smithsonian Institution, 1978), 449–65.

15 For example, Cayuga leader Jake Thomas recorded parts of the Creation Story in English and Onkwehonweneha written forms, audio recordings, and video footage. Another well-known English form of the story was published in Barbara K. Barnes, ed., *Traditional Teachings* (Akwesasne, QC: North American Indian Travelling College, 1984).

16 John Mohawk, "A View from Turtle Island: Chapters in Iroquois Mythology, History and Culture" (PhD diss., State University of New York at Buffalo, 1993), 168.

17 Ibid., ix.

18 Carol Cornelius, *Iroquois Corn in a Culture-Based Curriculum* (Albany: State University of New York Press, 1999), 79.

19 Examples of "private texts" would include those used ceremonially or those that exist within the oral record of certain families and individuals who do not wish to have them made public.

20 Hewitt, "Iroquoian Cosmology: Part 2," 475.

21 One of Hewitt's versions asserts that Mature Flowers carried dirt with her from the Sky World—she attempted to grab hold of the earth there before she fell through the hole of the uprooted tree. This alludes, also, to the transformative power of soil in this world as a product of the Sky World.

22 Hewitt, "Iroquoian Cosmology: Part 2," 480.

23 This appears in both the Newhouse and Buck versions. Hewitt, "Iroquoian Cosmology: Part 1."

24 Flint is also known as Sawiskera, a reference to ice or coldness.

25 Hewitt, "Iroquoian Cosmology: Part 1," states that they did not bury her body but kept it wrapped up and later used it to create the sun and the moon. This is not part of the oral records that I am familiar with so I have chosen to refer to the more commonly related story.

26 Some versions (both oral and written) of this part of the story say the plants grew on their own. Those that mention the planting refer to the belief that Mature Flowers grabbed those seeds from the Sky World when she fell.

27 In some cases, this part of the story is told with Flint as the adversary of his brother.

28 In the text, when citing the narration of the 1928 Hewitt publication of the Creation Story, I will reference it as "Gibson and Hewitt" in order to acknowledge Gibson's primary contribution to the publication. When referencing Hewitt's interpretations of the story and its meanings, "Hewitt" will be referenced singly.

29 Hewitt, "Iroquoian Cosmology: Part 2," 498.

30 Ibid., 510–11.

31 Ibid., 511.

32 Raymond R. Skye and Jeff Burnham, *The Great Peace: Gathering of the Good Minds* [CD-ROM] (Brantford, ON: Working World New Media, 1999).

33 Hewitt, "Iroquoian Cosmology: Part 2," 558.

34 Ibid., 559.

35 N. Carol Jacobs, "Presentation to the United Nations, July 18, 1995," *Akwesasne Notes*, Fall 1995, 116.

36 In the Haudenosaunee languages, the Peacemaker is commonly referred to as "the man from the North." At the conclusion of the formation of the Confederacy, the Peacemaker instructed the people that his name was not to be used lightly. In fact, he gave instructions that if the Great Peace ever becomes vulnerable, the chiefs are to gather around a swampy elm tree and call his name, asking for his return in order to save the Great Law.

37 Technically speaking, it is incorrect to refer to the Haudenosaunee by that name prior to the establishment of the Great Peace. The provisions of the Great Law created one people, comprised of five different nations, who were described as the people who build (or make) a house (it is inferred that the "house" is a longhouse'). Thus, the Haudenosaunee came into existence. It is most proper to refer to the people of the Haudenosaunee prior to this time as *Onkwehonwe* ("the first people"), which is the contemporary term used within the languages to speak of humans of that time as well as the word used to refer to Haudenosaunee and other Indigenous people of today.

38 It must be noted that at least two early renditions of the Great Law were written in Kanyen'keha (Mohawk language). Horatio Hale worked from two Native language manuscripts that were supplied to him by John Smoke Johnson (speaker of the council) and John Buck (Onondaga Royaner, Skanawati). The first was a copy of a copy of a text written down by a Mohawk Royaner known as "David" prior to the removal from the Mohawk Valley (pre-1784). The latter is of unknown origin but appears to be related to the first with the exception of the use of Onondaga terminology at times. Hale used these two texts in conjunction with translation assistance from John Buck and George Henry Martin Johnson (a Mohawk Royaner who was the son of John Smoke Johnson) for a chapter in *The Iroquois Book of Rites* (Philadelphia: DG Brinton, 1883; rpt. in Iroquois reprints series, ed. Wm. Guy Spittal, Ohsweken, ON: Iroqrafts, 1989). These renderings are not included in this category of Great Law texts because their original purpose was strictly internal, used to aid later generations in learning the required information in order to conduct the Condolence Ceremony.

39 For examples, see Six Nations Council Minutes [hereafter referred to as SNCM], June 1870, October 1920, and May 1922.

40 Newhouse was originally part of a committee charged with this responsibility but ended up working on the text on his own. He produced a couple of versions before the final 1897 text, including one that received the support of three chiefs but not the entire council. Jacob E. Thomas, *The Constitution of the Confederacy by the Peacemaker, written by Seth Newhouse in 1897* (Wilsonville, ON: Sandpiper Press, 1989).

41 Committee of the [Six Nations] Chiefs, "Traditional History of the Confederacy of the Six Nations," in *Transactions of the Royal Society of Canada*, 3rd Series, Vol. 5, Sec. 2 (Ottawa: Royal Society of Canada, 1912) [hereafter referred to as Chiefs, 1912].

42 There are discrepancies about the nation of origin of the Peacemaker. Within the oral record he is described as having been of the Huron Nation. Others refer to him as a Huron who was adopted by the Mohawks during the formation of the Great Law. The Gibson-Goldenweiser text says he came from a Mohawk village on the northern shore of Lake Ontario, but does not explain this location of a Mohawk village being so far removed from the Mohawk homelands along the Mohawk River. John Arthur Gibson and Hanni Woodbury, *Concerning the League: The Iroquois League Tradition as Dictated in Onondaga by John Arthur Gibson / Newly elicited, edited and translated by Hanni Woodbury; In collaboration with Reg Henry and Harry Webster; On the basis of A.A. Goldenweiser's manuscript* (Winnipeg: Algonquian and Iroquoian Linguistics, 1992) [hereafter referred to as Gibson-Goldenweiser].

43 Here I cite the popular ordering of the Three Principles. Gibson-Goldenweiser refers to the Three Principles as the Good Message, Power, and Peace.

44 "Tsikonhsaseh" is the Mohawk spelling of her name; in Seneca it is spelled "Jigonsaseh." There are two different translations given to her name: "she has a fat face" or "she has a new face." Some say that she was originally of the Erie or Cat Nation—and later adopted by the Senecas—and that her name refers to her nation of origin. Others state that when she accepted the Great Peace the Peacemaker gave her this name in recognition of the new person she had become.

45 The Haudenosaunee Grand Council consists of fifty Royaner who represent the forty-nine families of the Five Nations. The fiftieth representative, Atatarho, is chosen by the other Rotiyaner to serve as the presiding officer of the council.

46 Chiefs, 1912, 200–201.

47 Ibid., 219.

48 Tsikonhsaseh, as the first person to accept the Peacemaker's message, secured the responsibility for women to bestow the Royaner titles from within their matrilineal families. At the confirmation of the Great Law, each Royaner and his Clan Mother were called forward and the Peacemaker instructed the women to join him in placing the antlers of authority on the men's heads. Atatarho is the only Royaner who serves on the Grand Council without a Clan Mother. It is said that he is without a clan or a nation and serves all of the Haudenosaunee people. When the first Atatarho was installed, Tsikonhsaseh was the woman chosen by the Peacemaker to place the antlers on his head.

49 Gibson-Goldenweiser, 342–43.

50 Ibid., 323–24.

51 Some sources refer to the original wampum beads as feather quills cut up and strung together. Others say the first wampum was made of small branches that were hollowed out and strung together. Others yet tell of a story wherein Ayenwahtha

passed by a lake and found shells that he strung together. The commonality in all of these stories is that Ayenwahtha is associated with wampum and wampum was used to assist with the mourning process, to represent the legitimacy of a message, and to record important events. It continues to be used in all of those roles today.

52   When Ayenwahtha was camped outside of the Oneida settlement, he would not accept the invitation to enter the village until it was confirmed by strings of wampum. The wampum served as a sign that the invitation was on proper terms (Gibson-Goldenweiser, 186).

53   Thomas, *Constitution of the Confederacy*, 34.

54   The distinction between older/younger brothers and uncles/nephews is a complication with translation into English. It is further complicated because the plural form of these terms often includes both genders. The inclusion of women within the grouping of these nations is implied within the Haudenosaunee languages. It is also understood that the Royaner stand as representatives of their families, including men, women, and children. See Barnes, ed., *Traditional Teachings*, 37.

55   It has also been suggested that the distinction between "older" and "younger" refers to the theory that the Oneidas were once part of the Mohawk Nation and that the Cayugas were once part of the Seneca Nation; hence, the statements that "you are our younger relative" and "you are our older relative" are supported.

56   There is a more detailed process that follows the same system when one of the sides is unable to reach consensus. For a more detailed discussion of this and general Council protocols see Chiefs, 1912; Gibson-Goldenweiser; or Thomas, *Constitution of the Confederacy*.

57   At Grand River, the Younger Brothers are known as the Four Brothers, referring to the addition of the Tuscarora and Tuteloes. The Delaware, Nanticokes, and others are also represented by this side of the council.

58   Mike McDonald (Akwesasne Mohawk, Wolf Clan) has talked about his understanding of the Ayenwahtha and other wampum belts at conferences such as Trent University's Annual Elders and Traditional Peoples Gathering. Others who have discussed these ideas include the late Jake Swamp (Akwesasne Mohawk Nation Council) and the late Chief Jacob Thomas (Cayuga Nation, Grand River Territory).

59   Woodbury's note says this: "the rule states that the law pertaining to each settlement is a local affair, and that the jurisdiction of the Confederacy Council is confined to matters which relate to the Confederacy as a whole." She does not specifically cite the origins of this statement, but it is assumed to come from either Webster or Henry or both (Gibson-Goldenweiser, 426).

60   In Mohawk, place names are generally noted with a variation of a "ke" ending, while nations are typically denoted with a "haka" ending. "Ke" serves as a location marker while "haka" refers to a nation or group of people—the people of a particular place/land. There are variations to this standard.

61   Chiefs, 1912, 220–22. It must be noted that this passage does not include the confirmation of the name for the Onondagas, but that is discussed in other versions.

62   Gibson-Goldenweiser, 520 and 532.

63   Hale, *Iroquois Book of Rites*, 125.

64   Jacob E. Thomas, *The Great Law* [videorecording] (Brantford, ON: Iroquois Institute, 1992), part 2.

65 Thomas, *Constitution of the Confederacy*, 40.

66 For example, see the case of Jonas Smith (SNCM, January 1902).

67 The Gibson-Goldenweiser manuscript notes that the Oneidas had forgotten their clans so the Peacemaker reorganized the nation into three clans. If, indeed, they were the literal offspring of the Mohawks, that was both a sensible and practical choice.

68 Gibson-Goldenweiser, 307.

69 Ibid., 309.

70 Some note this responsibility as belonging to Atatarho while others attribute it to Skanawati (the Great Wolf).

71 Paul Kayanasenh Williams and Curtis Arihote Nelson, "Kaswentha," January 1995, Research report prepared for the Royal Commission on Aboriginal Peoples, in *For Seven Generations: An Information Legacy of the RCAP* (Libraxus, 1997), unpaginated.

72 Gibson-Goldenweiser, 304–5.

73 Ayenwahtha's three daughters suffered mysterious deaths believed to be caused by Atatarho's sorcery. Some believe that Atatarho killed Ayenwahtha's wife as well. In his grief, Ayenwahtha moved away from the village and lived alone in the bush. Later, while processing his grief, he created the structure behind the Condolence Ceremony.

74 In contemporary times people of adopted nations have joined the Younger Brothers' side. These include the Tuscarora, Delaware, Nanticoke, and Tutelo Nations. Today this side is referred to as "the Four Brothers." The elder nations are often referred to as "the Three Brothers."

75 In an 1892 publication based upon a manuscript prepared in collaboration with John Buck, J.N.B. Hewitt describes "Thirteen Matters" but in subsequent manuscripts he discusses fifteen. Woodbury's translation of the Gibson-Goldenweiser manuscript discusses fifteen. See J.N.B. Hewitt, "Legend of the Founding of the Iroquois League," *American Anthropologist* 5.2 (1892): 131–48.

76 Woodbury's note on the term *ota'hekh'kta'* reads, "Simeon Gibson notes that the expression refers to the place where 'the clearing surrounding a house meets the grass.'" (Gibson-Goldenweiser, 535).

77 Gibson-Goldenweiser, 535–37.

78 This is often referred to as the "Chiefs' Roll Call."

79 "At the Edge of the Woods" is sometimes referred to as *Ohenton Karihwatehkwen* ("the words that come before all else"); the latter term is also used to refer to the Thanksgiving Address.

80 Hale, *Iroquois Book of Rites*, 115.

81 Hale also made the following interpretation of the meaning of this recollection: "The chiefs, in their journey to the place of meeting, are supposed to have passed the sites of many deserted towns, in which councils had formerly been held. Owing to the frequent removals of their villages, such deserted sites were common in the Iroquois country. The speaker who welcomes the arriving guests supposes that the view of these places had awakened in their minds mournful recollections." Ibid., 146.

82 Gibson-Goldenweiser, 613–14.

83 Ibid., 655.

84 Ibid., 458–60.

85 Today, venison, beef, or buffalo meat is substituted for the beaver meat.

86   Gibson-Goldenweiser, 320–23.

87   Ibid., 313–14.

88   Ibid., 447–48.

89   Thomas, *Constitution of the Confederacy*, 30.

90   Gibson-Goldenweiser, 475–78.

91   For examples, see Arthur C. Parker, *The Code of Handsome Lake, the Seneca Prophet* (Albany: New York State Museum, 1918); William Fenton, ed., *Parker on the Iroquois* (Syracuse: Syracuse University Press, 1968); and Anthony F.C. Wallace, *The Death and Rebirth of the Seneca* (New York: Random House, 1972 [1969]).

92   Jacob E. Thomas, *Teachings from the Longhouse* (Toronto: Stoddart, 1994), 46.

93   For examples, see Beth Brant, *Writing as Witness* (Toronto: Women's Press, 1994); and Paula Gunn Allen, *The Sacred Hoop: Recovering the Feminine in American Indian Traditions* (Boston: Beacon Press, 1986).

94   See Deborah Doxtator, "What Happened to the Iroquois Clans? A Study of Clans in Three Nineteenth Century Rotinonhsyonni Communities" (PhD diss., University of Western Ontario, 1996), iii–v.

95   Ibid., 9.

96   Fenton, ed., *Parker on the Iroquois*, 38.

97   This is discussed in greater length in Chapter 4. Also see Kurt A. Jordan, "An Eighteenth Century Seneca Iroquois Short Longhouse from the Townley-Read Site, c. A.D. 1715–1754," *The Bulletin: Journal of the New York State Archeological Association* 119 (2003): 49–63; and Kurt A. Jordan, "Seneca Iroquois Settlement Pattern, Community Structure, and Housing, 1677–1779," *Northeast Anthropology* 67 (2004): 23–60.

98   Fenton, ed., *Parker on the Iroquois*, 38.

99   Ibid., 64.

100   Ibid., 65–66.

101   Ibid., 65–66.

102   Ibid., 66.

103   Ibid., 68.

104   Ibid., 68, note 2.

Chapter 2: Kontinonhsyonni—*The Women Who Make the House*

1   J.N.B. Hewitt, "Status of Women in Iroquois Polity Before 1784," *Annual Report of the Board of Regents of the Smithsonian Institution for the year ending June 30, 1932* (Washington: Smithsonian Institution, 1933), 476.

2   Lucien Carr, "On the Social and Political Position of Woman among the Huron-Iroquois Tribes," *16th and 17th Annual Reports of the Trustees of the Peabody Museum* 3, 3–4 (1884): 207–32; Morgan, *League of the Ho-de-no-sau-nee*.

3   Hale, *Iroquois Book of Rites*, 64–66.

4   Lafitau, *Customs of the American Indians*, I: 69.

5   Ibid., I: 290–94.

6   See Carr, "On the Social and Political Position," 223 and 232; William M. Beauchamp, "Iroquois Women," *Journal of American Folk-Lore* 13, 49 (April–June 1900): 85.

7　　For an example, see Cara Richards, "Matriarchy or Mistake: The Role of Iroquois Women through Time," in *Cultural Stability and Cultural Change*, ed. V.F. Kay, *Proceedings of the 1957 Annual Spring Meeting of the American Ethnological Society*, 1957, 38; rpt. in W.G. Spittal, ed., *Iroquois Women, An Anthology* (Ohsweken: Iroqrafts, 1990), 151.

8　　Hewitt, "Iroquoian Cosmology: Part 2," 475.

9　　For an example, see Hewitt, "Iroquois Cosmology: Part 1."

10　*Indian Time Haudenosaunee Booklet*, "Ancient Clan System," *Indian Time Newspaper*, Akwesasne Mohawk Territory, January 7, 2000, 4.

11　Thomas, *The Great Law*. See also Gibson-Goldenweiser, 340.

12　Ibid., 340.

13　Hewitt, "Iroquoian Cosmology: Part 2," 542.

14　Ibid., 544.

15　For a contemporary scientific discussion of this connection see Winnifred B. Cutler, Wolfgang M. Schleidt, Erika Friedmann, George Preti, and Robert Stine, "Lunar Influences on the Reproductive Cycle in Women," *Human Biology* 59, 6 (1987): 959–72.

16　The term "power" is meant to refer to the metaphysical strengths of femininity within Haudenosaunee philosophy.

17　As noted above, there is sufficient evidence to demonstrate that a matrilineal social structure was already in place among the Five Nations prior to the coming of the Great Law; however, it also appears that men were ascending to leadership positions through warfare rather than through female selections within their clan families.

18　The use of "deputies" here by Lafitau should not be confused with the use of that term in reference to a sub-chief (or runner). It is also important to note that Lafitau's inference that the Clan Mothers are secondary to the chiefs is incorrect.

19　Lafitau, *Customs of the American Indians*, I: 293–94. This is also a much-referenced source by later ethnographers, including Carr, Beauchamp, Hale, Tooker, and Fenton.

20　See Doxtator, "Iroquois Clans," for a longer discussion of the agricultural economy.

21　For example, see Hazel Hertzberg, *The Great Tree and the Longhouse: The Culture of the Iroquois* (New York: Macmillan, 1966), 31.

22　Gibson-Goldenweiser, 419.

23　Thomas, *Constitution of the Confederacy*, 23.

24　Gibson-Goldenweiser, 628.

25　Thomas, *Constitution of the Confederacy*, 24. Newhouse, in an apparent attempt to represent the legitimacy of the Great Law, organized his Great Law text through the categorizing of numbered sections such as "40th Wampum." He may have been attempting to demonstrate that the Great Law was equivalent to the constitutions of Western nations such as Canada and the United States. No actual strings or belts of wampum exist that coincide with Newhouse's ordering of the Great Law. Thomas appears to follow the same system as a means of working through Newhouse's text.

26　Thomas, *Constitution of the Confederacy*, 48.

27　Repeatedly in his text, Thomas reiterates that while "Rarontaron" has been translated into the English "warrior" it actually refers to a man who "protects the tree."

28　Thomas, *Constitution of the Confederacy*, 43.

29   Ibid., 44.

30   Doxtator, "Iroquois Clans," 77.

31   Thomas, *Constitution of the Confederacy*, 19.

32   For example, amongst the Kanyen'kehaka, a matter will be discussed first by the three chiefs representing the Turtle Clan families. They will then pass it across the fire to the three chiefs who represent the Bear Clan families. Once they have considered the matter, they then pass it to the three chiefs of the Wolf Clan families, who will announce the final decision on the matter.

33   Thomas, *Constitution of the Confederacy*, 19.

34   See Chapter 3 for a discussion of this link between adoption and territory.

35   Reuben Gold Thwaites, ed., *The Jesuit Relations and Allied Documents* (Cleveland: Burrows Bros., 1896–1901), XLIV, 37 (hereafter referred to as *Jesuit Relations*).

36   For an example of such a story, see *Jesuit Relations*, XLIII, 225.

37   Unless otherwise noted, the spellings for the names of various villages will follow that which has been documented by the source.

38   Dean R. Snow, Charles Gehring, and William Starna, eds., *In Mohawk Country: Early Narratives about a Native People* (Syracuse: Syracuse University Press, 1996), 4.

39   Robert Venables testified about this event in *Mitchell v. Minister of National Revenue* (2001), using it as evidence of the types of inter-nation trade that existed within the Confederacy in the seventeenth century. See Plaintiff's Memorandum of Fact and Law [Factum], Federal Court of Canada, Trial Division, http://www.usask.ca/nativelaw/factums/view.php?id=251, para. 285 (accessed 16 August 2016).

40   Van den Bogaert used the term "Sinnekens" to refer to the Oneidas. This was a common misnomer in the early historic record.

41   Snow, Gehring, and Starna, *In Mohawk Country*, 5.

42   Beauchamp, "Iroquois Women," 82. The quotation marks in this passage are from his text, but he does not elaborate as to the origins of the quotation.

43   I assume that women travelled less frequently because of child-rearing and agricultural responsibilities that would have required most women to stay close to home.

44   *Relation* of 1671, as quoted by Hale, *Iroquois Book of Rites*, 64–66.

45   See Chapter 3 for further discussion of epidemic impacts.

46   Beauchamp, "Iroquois Women," 86.

47   For a detailed discussion of this, see "Audrey Shenandoah, Onondaga," in Harvey Arden and Steve Wall, *Wisdomkeepers: Meetings with Native American Spiritual Elders* (Hillsboro, OR: Beyond Words Publishing, 1999).

48   Charlevoix, *Letters I*, 317, as quoted in Carr, "On the Social and Political Position," 223.

49   Beauchamp, "Iroquois Women," 86.

50   See Chapter 3 for references to alliances that included protection under the law with Native nations such as the Neutral, the Erie, the Delaware, and others.

51   For a brief discussion of this spokesperson, see Beauchamp, "Iroquois Women," 86.

52   I say that it was not a "regular" part of the council because the women did not have a designated speaker who served as one representative in council. Instead, each Royaner was a spokesperson for both the women and men of his respective clan family. The Royaner and Clan Mothers are expected to work closely together to

support their families and the Confederacy. On certain occasions, however, the women would specify a singular person to express their collective views to the council as a whole—rather than on an individual basis of Clan Mother to chief on a family-to-family basis. In this era, those statements were almost always about land.

53 Examples of these misperceptions can be found in Barbara Mann, *Iroquoian Women: The Gantowisas* (New York: Peter Lang, 2000); J.N.B. Hewitt, "Status of Woman in Iroquois Polity"; and Carr, "On the Social and Political Position."

54 Doxtator, "Iroquois Clans," 77.

55 Johnson made a home with a Mohawk woman, Molly Brant. Their relationship is often described as a common-law marriage, using British descriptions of the relationship.

56 William L. Stone, *Life of Brant* (New York: A.V. Blake, 1838), I: 9; Carr, "On the Social and Political Position," 231. Stone and Carr both date this statement to 1742, but that is not likely to be correct if Johnson was directly involved. Part of the same passage is quoted by Beauchamp ("Iroquois Women," 87), who gives the date as 1758—which is more likely the correct one.

57 William L. Stone was an early historian who wrote biographies and other historical essays on men involved in the history of colonial New York. Included in his publications was a two-volume biography of Joseph Brant. While he provides often detailed accounts of important events, his failure to cite references (common for that period of writing) makes it difficult to substantiate some of his findings. Therefore, he is used with caution here.

58 By this time, European settlers/squatters were pushing further and further into Haudenosaunee territory, in violation of treaty agreements. There are many recorded instances of settlers taking up arms against Haudenosaunee people as they attempted to grab their lands.

59 Stone, *Life of Brant*, I: 10.

60 Ibid., 123. Carr, "On the Social and Political Position," 230–31, also relates this event, but not in as great a detail.

61 Stone, *Life of Brant*, I: 131.

62 Ibid., 132.

63 The British awareness of this is demonstrated in the writings of Sir William Johnson.

64 Beauchamp, "Iroquois Women," 86–87.

65 Beauchamp, "Iroquois Women," 87–88. Doxtator ("Iroquois Clans," 76) attributes this passage to the Pennsylvania Archives, 2nd Series, Vol. 4, 505. Carr ("On the Social and Political Position," 217) also cites William L. Stone, *The Life and Times of Sa-Go-Ye-Wat-Ha, or Red Jacket* (Albany: J. Munsell, 1866), 155.

66 It is unclear whether or not Red Jacket held any official title within the Seneca Nation, but he was well known for his oratory skill and was often selected as a speaker in treaty negotiations.

67 Carr, "On the Social and Political Position," 217.

68 Stone, *Life and Times*, 155. Also quoted by Carr, "On the Social and Political Position," 217.

69 This is often referred to as the Treaty of Big Tree.

70 John N. Hubbard, *An Account of Sa-Go-Ye-Wat-Ha, or, Red Jacket and His People, 1750–1830* (Albany, NY: J. Munsell's Sons, 1886), 182–83. See also Stone, *Life and Times*, 243, and Carr, "On the Social and Political Position," 217–18.

71   James E. Seaver, *A Narrative of the Life of Mrs. Mary Jemison* (Canadaigua, NY: n.p., 1824), 92.

72   Stone, *Life and Times*, 246, as referenced by Carr, "On the Social and Political Position," 230.

73   This is discussed at length earlier in this chapter and in the previous chapter. Also see Doxtator, "Iroquois Clans," 9.

74   Some of these include Barbara Mann, Paula Gunn Allen, and Beth Brant. They often cite Wallace's *Death and Rebirth of the Seneca* on the subject.

75   Stone, *Life of Brant*, II: 442.

76   Usually the nations referred to in this category are the Onondagas, Lower Cayugas, Senecas, and Delawares.

77   Stone, *Life of Brant*, II: 443.

78   Ibid., 443–44.

79   Beauchamp, "Iroquois Women," 87. Unfortunately, he does not give reference to the record of this event.

80   SNCM, November 1834.

Chapter 3: Teyohahá:ke—*Two Roads*

1   Many of these "circles of influence" persist today, but there are shifts caused by the segmenting of our territories through treaties and other losses of land.

2   The term "contact" is usually seen as an event, but in reality it is a process. The Canadian courts fail to understand that and place emphasis on a moment rather than on relationships.

3   In certain instances one clan might have been split among two or more longhouses, depending upon the size and available resources of that clan.

4   The term "harvesting" refers to both the harvest of agricultural products and the harvests of uncultivated foods and animals. It encompasses the activities of hunting, fishing, and gathering.

5   Doxtator, "Iroquois Clans," 113.

6   The oral record notes that visitors with peaceful intentions often approached the village singing songs of peace (like those of the Great Law).

7   Doxtator, "Iroquois Clans," 113–16.

8   O'seronni ("they make axes") is a common Mohawk term referring to all people of European extraction. In Cayuga, they are referred to as Hotinyo'oh.

9   Some historians, such as Cadwallader Colden, *History of the Five Indian Nations Depending on the Province of New York*, Part I (Ithaca, NY: Cornell University Press, 1994 [1727]), assert that the St. Lawrence Iroquoians were also ancestors of some of the seventeenth-century Haudenosaunee.

10   Reportedly, Algonquin, Huron, and Montagnais warriors accompanied Champlain on this expedition.

11   Matthew Dennis, *Cultivating a Landscape of Peace: Iroquois-European Encounters in Seventeenth-Century America* (Ithaca, NY: Cornell University Press, 1993), 72 (he notes "2 chiefs" were killed); Francis Jennings, ed., *The History and Culture of Iroquois Diplomacy: An Interdisciplinary Guide to the Treaties of the Six Nations and Their League* (Syracuse, NY: Syracuse University Press, 1985), 233.

12 Tuscarora historian Richard W. Hill, Sr., has noted, "Previously, they had met in an open field, and hand to hand combat determined the victor. When a force was overcome, the fighting stops and the weaker forces were made prisoners. With the introduction of guns, open field fighting made no sense, so the Iroquois turned to guerrilla style warfare, with surprise attacks, swift hit-and-runs" (Richard Hill, "The Cultural History of Iroquois Sovereignty" [unpublished manuscript, 1999]).

13 *Mitchell v. Canada (Minister of National Revenue)*, [1999] 1 C.N.L.R. 112. Paul Williams, an attorney for Mike Mitchell, has called this the "bullet to the head school of first contact." Personal communication.

14 There are also reports of a Frenchman, Étienne Brûlé, visiting western Haudenosaunee territory in 1615 (Hill, "Cultural History"). These are not well documented. Similarly, it is quite likely that other Dutchmen visited Mohawk villages close to Fort Orange before van den Bogaert, but no written or oral record of their visits is presently known. In 1626, a French Recollet missionary visited the Neutral Nation along the Grand River; he is the first recorded European to visit the Grand River Territory.

15 The Dutch paper document of this treaty was recently discovered after being lost for nearly four centuries (Hill, "Cultural History").

16 In some descriptions the three elements are described in the order of "mutual respect, friendship (or trust), and peace."

17 For example, see Oren Lyons, "The American Indian in the Past," in *Exiled in the Land of the Free*, ed. Oren Lyons and John Mohawk (Santa Fe, NM: Clearlight Publishers, 1992), 40–42.

18 For example, the Covenant Chain between the Haudenosaunee and British was built upon the principles of the Kaswentha. The British also extended the Covenant Chain to other Native nations in many of their peace treaties. For further discussion of this, see Williams and Nelson, "Kaswentha."

19 Williams and Nelson, "Kaswentha."

20 Dennis, *Landscape of Peace*, 137.

21 Ibid.; Daniel K. Richter, *The Ordeal of the Longhouse: The Peoples of the Iroquois League in the Era of European Colonization* (Chapel Hill: University of North Carolina Press, 1992), 59.

22 Richter, *Ordeal*, 59. Richter notes that it is unknown why this tends to be the case with the impact of "childhood" diseases on previously unexposed populations, but it has been the common trend in many places around the world.

23 Many of the refugees were the remnants of villages and nations decimated by disease and/or warfare. Often these people would come to the Haudenosaunee seeking refuge under the provisions of the Great Law that allowed them to be integrated into the Haudenosaunee as adopted people.

24 In the competition to control the fur trade, many of the Nations "kidnapped" citizens of other nations in an attempt to rebuild their populations. A French man's experiences as a Mohawk captive are included in Snow, Gehring, and Starna, *In Mohawk Country*.

25 Richard Aquila, *The Iroquois Restoration: Iroquois Diplomacy on the Colonial Frontier, 1701–1754* (Detroit: Wayne State University Press, 1983).

26 Daniel K. Richter and James Merrell, eds., *Beyond the Covenant Chain: The Iroquois and their Neighbors in Indian North America, 1600–1800* (Syracuse: Syracuse University Press, 1987).

27 Dennis, like myself, also takes the position that the Haudenosaunee did not seek an imperial role. See Dennis, *Landscape of Peace*, 258n3.

28 For example, the Roman Catholic Church is presently experiencing major growth in several Third World nations of Africa and Latin America, but in more developed countries, like Canada, they are closing some parishes due to a lack of priests to service those congregations.

29 These include the Sulpicians and the Recollets. Protestant missionaries came later, especially amongst the Haudenosaunee, but they followed patterns similar to their Catholic predecessors.

30 The Jesuits received permission from the Grand Council to set up missions in each of the five national territories of the Confederacy. The missions among the Oneidas, Cayugas, and Senecas were short-lived and relatively unsuccessful.

31 Since that time, Kateri's example has been used to influence missionary activities among many different Indigenous peoples worldwide. In 2012, Kateri was canonized as a saint within the Roman Catholic Church.

32 They utilized the same name of Caughnawaga for their new village as well as several other relocation sites in the area many years later. The contemporary Mohawk community of Kahnawake, near Montreal, is the final site for this mission village.

33 The claims of "religious persecution" are documented in many places, including within the *Jesuit Relations* and at the Kateri Shrine, near Fonda, New York.

34 It is also possible that Huron refugees may have already been Catholic before coming to the Mohawk Valley, providing additional incentive for them to move to the St. Lawrence with the Jesuits.

35 Caughnawaga on the St. Lawrence also attracted Odawas, Ojibwas, and Abenakis who eventually assimilated into the Mohawk core of the community.

36 Ronald Wright, *Stolen Continents* (Toronto: Penguin Books, 1992),14.

37 Haudenosaunee medicines and religious beliefs are more closely interwoven than were European medicine and religion of the seventeenth century, when Western "science" and religion began to separate.

38 Put simply, it is difficult to console someone else when you yourself are in grief. Haudenosaunee condolence procedures are based upon the idea of "clear minded" people consoling those who have experienced death. With death all around, no one would have been "clear minded."

39 As noted, most of these lands were already accessed by the Haudenosaunee in shared hunting relationships, but when many of their neighbours became Haudenosaunee their prior competition for furs ceased to exist. For further discussion, see Francis Jennings, *The Ambiguous Iroquois Empire* (New York: Norton, 1984).

40 Doxtator, "Iroquois Clans," 62.

41 It is estimated that 30 percent of longhouses of this period showed evidence of expansion after they were built—literally "expanding the rafters"—indicative of quick population increases (Doxtator, "Iroquois Clans," 62).

42 Hill, "Cultural History."

43 As noted previously, in the early colonial period variations of the name "Seneca" were typically applied to any or all of the four western Haudenosaunee Nations. It was a decade after this treaty before the British finally realized that there were four Haudenosaunee Nations, rather than one, in addition to the Mohawks.

44 E.B. O'Callahan, *Documents Relative to the Colonial History of the State of New York* (Albany: Weed, Parsons and Co., 1853–1887), I: 67–68 [hereafter referred to as NYCD].

45 For a detailed discussion of this, see Paul Williams, "The Chain" (LLM thesis, University of Toronto, 1982).

46 Williams and Nelson, "Kaswentha."

47 It has been noted that in treaty making, Indigenous peoples generally sought to build a relationship with the allied nation. For example, Jean Friesen makes the following assertion regarding Cree treaty making philosophy: "[the treaties] represented the beginning of a continuing relation of mutual obligation." Jean Friesen, "Magnificent Gifts: The Treaties of Canada with the Indians of the Northwest 1869–76," *Transactions of the Royal Society of Canada* 5,1 (1986): 49. In other words, the treaty is really about the ensuing relationship rather than the event.

48 [British] Public Records Office [PRO], Kew, England, Colonial Office Papers [CO] 1/40; see also NYCD, XIII: 510.

49 For a discussion of this, see Francis Jennings, "Iroquois Alliances in American History," in Jennings, *Iroquois Diplomacy*, 37–65.

50 Williams and Nelson, "Kaswentha."

51 Corlaer was the first governor of New York, and his name became a title by which all subsequent governors of the colony became known by the Haudenosaunee.

52 4 June 1691, NYCD, III: 779; as quoted by Williams and Nelson, "Kaswentha."

53 For a detailed discussion of the White Roots of Peace during the colonial era, see Paul A.W. Wallace, *The White Roots of Peace* (Port Washington, NY: Ira J. Friedman, 1946).

54 There were periods when the relationship weakened and the meetings did not happen.

55 This follows Haudenosaunee protocols. For example, when a new Royaner is to be condoled, the process begins with a recollection of the beginning of the Confederacy (the Peacemaker's journey). The idea of "refreshing" one's memory of the past is seen to be critical before one can make decisions for the future with a good mind.

56 Emphasis added.

57 Library and Archives Canada [LAC], RG 10, Vol. 1822, 22.; as cited by Williams and Nelson, "Kaswentha."

58 LAC, RG 10, Vol. 1822, 22–29; also cited by Williams and Nelson, "Kaswentha."

59 Williams and Nelson, "Kaswentha."

60 Aquila terms this the "Twenty Years War," following the years 1680–1701, but recognizes that it was not a single war in the formal sense. Aquila, *Iroquois Restoration*, 43.

61 There is contemporary speculation that Denonville had exaggerated this amount, but Ganondagan was known to be a corn repository for the Seneca Nation, serving both as a storehouse for the nation and a stockpile for trading with others (Natives and Europeans). The actual amount of corn is not as important as the fact that the French made a major economic hit against the Senecas with the corn destruction.

62 Today, the site of Ganondagan has been made into a New York State Historic Site, with a recognition of the impact of Denonville's attack. For a detailed discussion of the campaign, see John Mohawk, *War Against the Seneca* (Canandaigua, NY: Ganondagan State Historic Site, 1987).

63 Onontio—"nice/good hill"—is the Haudenosaunee title given to the French governor. It has been erroneously translated as "big mountain," which would be "Onontawenen."

64 As cited in Hill, "Cultural History."

65 Ibid.

66 Jennings, *Iroquois Diplomacy*, 163.

67 The historic record often refers to this nation as the "Ottawas," but I use the contemporary spelling, which is a better match for the name these people are known by in their own language.

68 Jennings, *Iroquois Diplomacy*, 164–65.

69 Williams and Nelson, "Kaswentha."

70 Williams and Nelson discuss this in-depth in "Kaswentha."

71 NYCD, IV: 908-11, as cited in Williams and Nelson, "Kaswentha."

72 *Calendar of State papers, Colonial Series, America and West Indies, Preserved in the Public Record Office,* Vol. 1701.1896; as cited in Hill, "Cultural History."

73 In fact, Seneca historian John Mohawk asserts that Haudenosaunee traditional philosophy is an example of progressive pragmatism. He explains this in a discussion of the Great Law: "'Now we put our minds together to see what kind of world we can create for the seventh generation yet unborn.' ... [It lays] out the idea that we are now going to put our minds together to create some kind of desirable outcome. And pragmatism is entirely about outcome. To begin with, you lay out the outcome and then you step back and negotiate the steps to go from here to the outcome that you want." John Mohawk, "What Can We Learn from Native America about War and Peace?: The Progressive Pragmatism of the Iroquois Confederacy," *Lapis Magazine Online,* http://www.lapismagazine.org/what-can-we-learn-from-native-america-about-war-and-peace-by-john-mohawk.

74 While British subjects, the ethnic background of these colonists varied from Dutch to English to German to Scottish.

75 NYCD, I: 345–47.

76 Ibid., 346.

77 Ibid.

78 Doxtator, "Iroquois Clans," 116.

79 Julian Boyd, ed., *Indian Treaties Printed by Benjamin Franklin, 1736–1762* (Philadelphia: Historical Society of Pennsylvania, 1938), 78; as cited in Wright, *Stolen Continents,* 128.

80 Pennsylvania Archives, Ser. 4, 2, 698–707; as cited in Timothy Shannon, *Indians and Colonists at the Crossroads of Empire: The Albany Congress of 1754* (Ithaca, NY: Cornell University Press, 2000), 166.

81 Treaty Minutes, Pennsylvania Council Minutes, 16 June 1744, 4, 706–9; as cited by Wright, *Stolen Continents,* 129–30.

82 This section refers to the Mohawks of the Mohawk Valley. I have not attempted to address the village patterns of the northern Mohawk communities at this time.

83 For example, Doxtator ("Iroquois Clans," 24) simply asserts that the Mohawks were living in cabins by this time, leaving the impression that bark structures had become totally obsolete.

84 This "Brant" is the grandfather of Joseph Brant.

85 Christian Daniel Claus and Conrad Weiser, "A Journey to Onondaga, 1750"; as cited in Snow, Gehring, and Starna, *In Mohawk Country*, 239.

86 François-Jean de Beauvoir described a Mohawk house in 1780: "These huts are like our barracks in time of war, or like those built in vineyards or orchards, when the fruit is ripe and has to be watched at night. The framework consists of only two uprights and one crosspole; this covered with a matted roof, but is well lined within by a quantity of bark." Snow, Gehring, and Starna, *In Mohawk Country*, 293–94.

87 The Tuscarora language belongs to the Southern Iroquoian linguistic family.

88 As cited in Hill, *Cultural History*.

89 Not all of the Tuscaroras fled north at the end of the war. Many attempted to stay in their southern homelands. In the decades that followed, those who had moved north returned home to entice their relatives to migrate back with them to Haudenosaunee territory.

90 As cited in Hill, "Cultural History."

91 Ibid. While the Tuscarora are seen as the sixth nation, they do not have their own representation in the Grand Council. Originally their interests were voiced by the Oneidas as their host nation. Today, their chiefs sit with the Royaner of the Younger Brother nations, but officially their issues are raised by the Tonawanda Seneca Royaner.

92 Hill, "Cultural History." These nations were closely related to the Tuscarora and had been neighbours to them in the Carolina-Virginia region.

93 John Bartram, *Travels in Pennsylvania and Canada* (Ann Arbor, MI: University Microfilms, 1966), 42; as discussed in Doxtator, "Iroquois Clans," 124.

94 Hill, "Cultural History."

95 Officially the Tutelo Nation no longer exists, but many Grand River families (especially within the Cayuga Nation) continue to identify as Tutelo descendants and maintain some of their major ceremonies.

96 For a description of Seneca villages of this period see Kurt A. Jordan, "Seneca Iroquois Settlement Pattern, Community Structure, and Housing, 1677–1779," *Northeast Anthropology* 67 (2004): 23–60.

97 Tooker, "Iroquois Since 1820," in *The Handbook of North American Indians: Vol. 15: Northeast*, ed. Bruce G. Trigger [Washington: Smithsonian Institution, 1978], 449–65); and Wallace, *Death and Rebirth of the Seneca*, 194, note that the Clinton-Sullivan Campaign of 1779 destroyed all of the longhouses in the Onondaga, Cayuga, and Seneca villages.

98 Doxtator, "Iroquois Clans," 125.

99 Cited in Doxtator, "Iroquois Clans," 55.

100 Johnson reported his participation in this ceremony in his papers: "Then I marched at the Head of the Chiefs singing the condoling song which contains the names, laws, and customs of their renowned ancestors, and praying that their deceased brother might be blessed with happiness in his other state." NYCD, VII: 1330.

101 Council, Onondaga, 25 April 1748, *The Papers of Sir William Johnson* [SWJP], I (Albany: University of the State of New York, 1965), 158; see also Jennings, *Ambiguous Iroquois Empire*, 145.

102 NYCD, VI: 781–83; as cited in Wright, *Stolen Continents*, 132.

103 NYCD, VI: 788; as cited in Wright, *Stolen Continents*, 132–33.

104 Aquila, *Iroquois Restoration*, 105.

105 Jennings, *Iroquois Diplomacy*, 187.

106 As cited in Aquila, *Iroquois Restoration* ,107.

107 SWJP, I: 530.

108 SWJP, XIII: 40. British Public Record Office, PRO 95, Chatham Papers.

109 Emphasis added. SWJP, II: 234.

110 Emphasis added.

111 SWJP, I: 854–55.

112 NYCD, XXXIII: 18, as cited in Williams and Nelson, "Kaswentha."

113 Williams and Nelson, "Kaswentha."

114 These are some of the patents within the Mohawk Valley which the Haudenosaunee considered to be illegal based upon both Haudenosaunee and British law. These are among the patents referenced by many Haudenosaunee speakers at various treaty councils (some of which are cited within this text). They are also among patents which Sir William Johnson considered to be illegal (referenced above).

115 Ibid.

116 SWJP, XI.

117 As cited in Williams and Nelson, "Kaswentha."

118 SWJP, X: 977–85.

119 SWJP, X: 974–76.

120 LAC, RG 10, Vol. 1825, 61.

121 Williams and Nelson, "Kaswentha."

122 SWJP, XI.

123 For example, see *Seneca Nation v. State of New York*, United States Court of Appeals for the Second District, decided 9 September 2004, http://caselaw.findlaw.com/us-2nd-circuit/1033184.html. On 5 June 2006 the United States Supreme Court refused without comment to hear the appeal.

124 Williams and Nelson, "Kaswentha."

125 SWJP, IV: 513.

126 SWJP, XII: 617–31; also in NYCD, VIII: 113–34.

127 SWJP, XII: 617–31.

128 Hill, "Cultural History."

129 PRO, CO 42, Vol. 44, 133–35.

130 The discussion of the American Revolution here is only an overview, with an emphasis on Haudenosaunee territorial impacts only. For a detailed discussion of Haudenosaunee participation in the war, see Barbara Graymount, *The Iroquois in the American Revolution* (Syracuse: Syracuse University Press, 1972).

131 The specific colonies involved were Massachusetts, New York, and Pennsylvania; however, "colonists" from many different British colonies crossed the Fort Stanwix line and homesteaded in Haudenosaunee Territory.

132 This is sometimes also referred to as the "Sullivan Campaign" or the "Sullivan-Clinton Expedition." For a discussion of the impact of the campaign, see Wallace, *Death and Rebirth of the Seneca*, 141–44; Tooker, "Iroquois", 449–65; Doxtator, "Iroquois Clans," 124; and Barbara Graymont, *Iroquois*, 192–222.

133 LAC, RG 19, F1, Vol. 2, 89–90.

134 In the 1990s, the Oneidas of New York purchased lands within their land claim area of their traditional homeland territory. Some of that land was transferred into "trust status" by the U.S. Bureau of Indian Affairs, but the recent *Sherrill v. Oneida* decision in U.S. Federal Appeals Court calls into question the legality of other lands owned by the Oneida Nation of New York—primarily the land where the Turning Stone Casino is built—as being eligible for reservation status. *City of Sherrill v. Oneida Indian Nation of New York*, 544 U.S. 197 (2005).

135 PRO, CO 42, Vol. 44, 133–35.

Chapter 4: Shotinonhsyonnih—They Built the Longhouse Again

1 It could be argued that in actuality the final surrender of Six Nations land was in 1957 with the Cockshutt Surrender agreed to by the Six Nations Elected Band Council. It is also important to note that the 1847 Mississauga Settlement was not a surrender but rather an agreement to share a portion of the Six Nations lands (4,800 acres) with the Mississauga who had surrendered the last of their lands near Lake Ontario. In 1865, the Six Nations added to that tract another 1,200 acres of their land. The Six Nations Elected Band Council was also instrumental in allowing the Government of Canada to define this as a formal surrender of 6,000 acres in 1929.

2 The term "dependent nations" is used in reference to Native nations who were taken in by the Grand River Haudenosaunee but who retained a separate national identity. Most notable of these nations are the Tuteloes (Tutulies), Nanticokes, and Delawares. The Tuscaroras held a similar status to these "dependent nations" but received a more formal recognition, becoming officially the sixth nation of the Confederacy in the early 1700s. Among the Grand River Haudenosaunee all of these "dependent nations"—including the Tuscarora—are considered to be "Younger Brothers" in the council structure, and collectively these nations, under the Oneidas and Cayugas, are referred to as the "Four Brothers" or the "Four Brothers' side."

3 The Beaver Hunting Tract (from the 1701 Beaver Hunting Grounds Treaty) is referenced here.

4 When the British courted Haudenosaunee military support at the onset of the war, they promised to replace any lands forfeited upon the possibility of defeat. This promise also echoed the promises of the 1664 Treaty at Albany.

5 "The Rev. John Stuart's Report to the S.P.G., July 4, 1783," LAC, Society for the Propagation of the Gospel (SPG), Journals, XXIII, 169–70; cited in Charles M. Johnston, ed., *The Valley of the Six Nations: A Collection of Documents on the Indian Lands of the Grand River* (Toronto: University of Toronto Press, 1964), 232.

6 Many other nations also took refuge at Fort Niagara, including the Tuteloes and Delawares, who later made their way to the Grand River Territory under the conditions of the Haldimand Agreement.

7 LAC, Haldimand Papers, B 103,175–82, Allan Maclean to Sir Frederick Haldimand, Niagara, 18 May 1783; as cited in Johnston, *Valley of the Six Nations*, 36.

8 Those men who participated in American campaigns against other Haudenosaunee villages did so in violation of the Great Law.

9 "A Census of the Six Nations on the Grand River, 1785" lists the Oneidas as part of the "Oghguaga Joseph's party," numbering forty-nine (LAC, Haldimand Papers, B 103,457; as quoted by Johnston, *Valley of the Six Nations*, 52). By 1810, the Oneidas are separated out and numbered thirty-eight (LAC, Claus Papers, X, 39–30; as quoted in ibid., 281).

10 Today, many Grand River families are in regular contact with their extended relatives (blood relations as well as clan families) in the communities that still exist in the original homelands.

11 Such as the long-standing connections between the Brant family and the Johnson family, most notably the marriage of Joseph Brant's sister Molly to Sir William Johnson, the first imperial representative to the Six Nations.

12 LAC, Haldimand Papers, B 103, 175–82; as quoted in Williams and Nelson, "Kaswentha." The letter also appears in Johnston, *Valley of the Six Nations*, 35–38.

13 Haldimand carried the Mohawk name of "Asharekowa" ("the Big Knife"), as many other colonial leaders had before him. This was also the title given to the governor of Virginia after Lord Effingham gave a cutlass to the Haudenosaunee in 1690.

14 "Bostonians" was the term used by the Haudenosaunee to refer to the Americans. The Mohawk version of the word, "Wastonrohno" ("the people of Boston"), today remains the Grand River Mohawk dialect term for contemporary U.S. citizens.

15 PRO, CO 42, Vol. 44, 133–35; as cited by Williams and Nelson, "Kaswentha."

16 British Museum, Haldimand Papers, Addtional Manuscripts 21705, ff. 154–55; as quoted by Williams and Nelson, "Kaswentha," Part III; also cited by Johnston, *Valley of the Six Nations*, 42.

17 These options included tracts near Cataraqui and the Bay of Quinte. For further discussion, see Johnston, *Valley of the Six Nations*, xxxvi–xxxvii.

18 This site was also close to Cataraqui, the chosen resettlement site of Molly Brant, who was accorded her own personal land as replacement for the war losses of her inherited lands and estate from her deceased common-law husband, Sir William Johnson. Cataraqui, first settled by the French as one of their three trading posts (along with Niagara and Detroit), controlled the entrance to Lake Ontario (Cataraqui Lake) from the St. Lawrence River.

19 Johnston, *Valley of the Six Nations*, xxxvi.

20 As it had been a part of the western hunting territories of the Haudenosaunee, members of the Six Nations were familiar with the Grand River area. Johnston also notes that Brant and several Chiefs had extensive knowledge of the Grand River lands and based their selection upon those experiences (Johnston, *Valley of the Six Nations*, xxxvi–xxxvii).

21 Ibid., xxxviii.

22 "The Report of the Rev. John Stuart, May 25, 1784," LAC, SPG, Journals, XXIII, 379–82; as quoted in Johnston, *Valley of the Six Nations*, 49.

23 Doxtator, "Iroquois Clans," 134.

24 While it is not a well-documented aspect of the Grand River Haudenosaunee, there remain today several families who trace their lineage to the Neutral Nation, who had made their homes along the Grand River until the mid-seventeenth century. Those who survived devastating flu epidemics and the "Beaver Wars" of that era sought refuge among the Senecas to the east but never forgot their Neutral heritage. Upon the relocation to the Grand River, many of those families affiliated themselves with the Cayuga Nation—the most common host to the "dependent nations"—where they remain to this day.

25 A similar idea could explain some of the rationale behind the Bay of Quinte selection for some Mohawk families. Many of the eighteenth-century Mohawks were descended from refugee nations originating from the east and north, including

St. Lawrence Iroquoians, Hurons, Mahicans, etc. It is entirely possible that some of the Fort Hunter Mohawks who preferred the Bay of Quinte option may have recalled that territory as part of their former homelands. It should also be noted that the Bay of Quinte is considered the birthplace of the Haudenosaunee Peacemaker, which may have also influenced that selection.

26   For example, a General Council of the Six Nations was held at "Onondagua Council House 29ᵗʰ June 1835." A March 1835 council meeting was recorded to have taken place at "the Mohawk village." SNCM, 1835.

27   "Proceedings of a council of the Six Nations Indians held at the Onondaga Council fire at the Grand River on the 14ᵗʰ October 1829," University of Western Ontario [UWO] Archives, John Brant Letterbook.

28   PRO, CO 42, Vol. 46, 224–25; as cited in Johnston, *Valley of the Six Nations*, 47–48. The parentheses and brackets within this passage belong to the Johnston text. This passage is also cited by Williams and Nelson, "Kaswentha."

29   These statements were most likely specifically referring to what is known as the "Iroquois-Ojibwa" Friendship Belt, wherein the two sides agreed to live in peace and friendship as neighbours and to share their common hunting grounds. Williams and Nelson, "Kaswentha," also discuss this idea of the "former and mutual agreement."

30   For a discussion of this see Williams and Nelson, "Kaswentha."

31   Lord North to Haldimand, 8 August 1783, British Museum, Haldimand Papers, Additional Manuscripts 21705, ff. 154–55; as cited by Johnston, *Valley of the Six Nations*, 42.

32   British troops from Sir John Johnson's disbanded Royal Regiment of New York had been granted land along the north shore of the St. Lawrence from Lonquiel to Kingston starting in April 1784. Brant was fully aware of this as he had met with the Akwesasne chiefs in their territory in May 1784.

33   Allan Maclean to Sir Frederick Haldimand, LAC, Haldimand Papers, B 103, 175–82; as cited in Johnston, *Valley of the Six Nations*, 35.

34   Ibid., 38.

35   Haldimand, along with Sir John Johnson, spent the summer of 1784 settling Loyalists along the north shore of Lake Ontario and along the St. Lawrence River (the Royal Townships). It was not until fall that Haldimand made time to address the Six Nations resettlement needs.

36   LAC, Haldimand Papers, B 222, 1061; also cited in Johnston, *Valley of the Six Nations*, 1964; Williams and Nelson, "Kaswentha"; and various LAC RG 10 files.

37   "Uncle" is the familial term for the Haudenosaunee used by those of the Delaware Nation who settled on the Grand River under the protection of the Six Nations.

38   Emphasis added.

39   David and Aaron Hill to Johnson, Nassau, 15 April 1790, PRO, CO 42, Vol. 69, 249; as quoted in Johnston, *Valley of the Six Nations*, 55.

40   This is listed as "Source of the Grand River" in the claims submitted by the Six Nations Elected Council's Land Claims Research Office—see Appendix 2.

41   Dorchester to Johnson, PRO, CO 42, Vol. 69, 249; as cited in Johnston, *Valley of the Six Nations*, 55.

42   Haldimand had used his personal seal-at-arms rather than the Great Seal of the Province. For a detailed discussion of this see *Doe dem. Jackson v. Wilkes* (1835), 4 UCKB (OS)) 142; and *Doe dem Sheldon v. Ramsay* (1852), 9 UCQB 105.

43 Joseph Brant to Lord Dorchester, 24 March 1791, PRO, CO 42, Vol. 73, 144; as quoted in Williams and Nelson, "Kaswentha."

44 Public Archives of Ontario, Crown Land Papers, Surveyors' Letters, 1766–1800; as quoted in Williams and Nelson, "Kaswentha." In *Haida Nation v. British Columbia*, the Supreme Court of Canada stated, "It is always assumed that the Crown intends to fulfil its promises" (2004 SCC 73, para. 20, 18 November 2004). One would expect that this ruling will have implications on the Six Nations land claims under the Haldimand Proclamation (as well as impacting other Native claims across Canada).

45 Emphasis added.

46 Henry Motz to Johnson, Quebec, 9 May 1791; PRO, CO42, Vol. 73, 147; as cited in Johnston, *Valley of the Six Nations*, 58.

47 Report of Committee Investigating Indian Claims, 24 December 1791; PAO, Crown Land Papers, Surveyor's Letters, 1788–1791; as cited in Johnston, *Valley of the Six Nations*, 59. Part of the issue, as seen later in *Jackson v. Wilkes*, was whether an Indian Nation had the legal "personality" to be able to hold land.

48 The surveyor was Augustus Jones, father of the Mississauga leader Rev. Peter Jones.

49 *Extract from the Minutes of the Nassau District Land Board*, Niagara, 1 February 1791, PAO, Crown Land Papers, Surveyors' Letters, 1766–1800; as quoted in Johnston, *Valley of the Six Nations*, 56–57. Johnston also notes that the map described "is believed lost or destroyed."

50 Brant's Address to William Claus on the Subject of the Indian Lands, 24 November 1796, PRO, CO 42, Vol. 321, 49–53; as quoted in Johnston, *Valley of the Six Nations*, 83.

51 Ibid., 73.

52 This recognition was reiterated by the British in 1755 as part of their drive to recruit Haudenosaunee military help in the Seven Years' War.

53 In treaty dealings with Indigenous nations, the honour of the Crown is always at stake. See *R. v. George*, [1960] SCR 871.

54 Johnston, *Valley of the Six Nations*, xlv.

55 Brant is noted as explaining this based upon the belief that the Six Nations would have white neighbours regardless, but through these land grants they would have the ability to select people they already knew and trusted.

56 Johnston, *Valley of the Six Nations*, xlvi.

57 Brant and Simcoe also clashed over the issue of whether or not Crown courts had jurisdiction over a murder that had occurred between Mohawks.

58 Simcoe's Patent of the Grand River Lands to the Six Nations, 14 January 1793, LAC, Q329, 91; as cited in Johnston, *Valley of the Six Nations*, 73–74.

59 Simcoe had probably borrowed Sir John Johnson's Indian Affairs records—two of the "four great volumes" Sir William alluded to.

60 Speech by Simcoe to the Indian Confederacy, Navy Hall, Niagara, 22 June 1793; as cited in John Graves Simcoe, *The Correspondence of Lieut. Governor John Graves Simcoe* (Toronto: Ontario Historical Society, 1923–1931), Simcoe Papers, I: 364.

61 For an example of Six Nations' complaints against the Simcoe Deed, see "Brant to Alexander McKee," LAC, Claus Papers, VI, 25 February 1793; as cited in Johnston, *Valley of the Six Nations*, 75.

62 Proceedings of an Indian Council at Hamilton, 4 July 1819; LAC, Claus Papers, XI,

238–41; as quoted in Johnston, *Valley of the Six Nations*, 67. Also quoted in Williams and Nelson, "Kaswentha."

63 This relationship—long in existence before the 1784 negotiations—guided both Native nations in their land dealings with each other, including the Haldimand Purchase and Proclamation as well as the 1847 Mississauga settlement on Six Nations land.

64 Norton was born of Scottish and Cherokee parentage but was adopted by the Mohawks after he came to the Grand River Territory as an interpreter. Because of his military skill and oratory gifts, he was made a Pinetree chief and given the responsibility to assist the council when called upon. He was a successful military strategist, leading Six Nations warriors and British troops in campaigns such as the Battle of Beaver Dams, during the War of 1812.

65 John Norton, *The Journal of Major John Norton, 1816*, ed. C.F. Klinck and J.J. Talman (Toronto: Champlain Society, 1970), cxii. Also referenced in Johnston, *Valley of the Six Nations*, 174.

66 McDonell to Selkirk, York, 28 November 1808, LAC, Selkirk Papers, McDonell MSS, X (Baldoon Settlement Letterbook); as quoted in Johnston, *Valley of the Six Nations*, 177.

67 The terms "Upper" and "Lower" Mohawk refer to the home villages of particular clan families in the Mohawk Valley, before coming to the Grand River. Those clans, through their Royaner, continued to distinguish themselves as "Upper Mohawk" and "Lower Mohawk," as evidenced in the council records through the 1830s. Some scholars have erroneously assumed that these designations were also indicative of the later "Upper-end/Down-below" distinction made in the Grand River Territory. Weaver and Harring have both erroneously reported that the Upper-Lower political conflicts at Grand River had their origins with this internal Mohawk conflict.

68 As recounted by John Smoke Johnson, SNCM, February 1838.

69 Lord Bathurst to the Chiefs of the Six Nations, LAC, Claus Papers, XII, 131–36; as quoted in Johnston, *Valley of the Six Nations*, 69.

70 For an example of this representation of Brant, see the film *The Broken Chain* (1993).

71 These authors include Kelsay, Harvey Chalmers, and Helen Robinson.

72 In the eighteenth century, the distinction between "sachems" and "chiefs" was often used to differentiate between Confederacy leaders (Royaner) and more local or informal ones.

73 While some English translations of the Great Law refer to one "war chief" for each nation, there is no consensus as to whether this position is really a "war chief" or an assistant with special duties to his nation.

74 "Speaker" in this sense—and as it is used within formal Haudenosaunee governance—is used to refer to someone who has been "given the voice" of the entire brotherhood ("Elder Brothers" or "Younger Brothers") of chiefs or the entire council. This designation was typically reserved for the most skilled orators among the Royaner.

75 Brant's Address to William Claus on the Subject of the Indian Lands, 24 November 1796, PRO, CO 42, Vol. 321, 49–53; as quoted by Johnston, *Valley of the Six Nations*, 83.

76 Brant to James Green, Grand River, 10 December 1797, Cruikshank and Hunter, eds., *Russell Correspondence*, II, 39; as quoted by Johnston, *Valley of the Six Nations*, 92–93.

77 For example, in several cases, Brant had negotiated personal grants of land for himself and his family (such as the property on Burlington Bay) and/or sums of money for his efforts in leases and sales.

78 Sir John Johnson was Joseph Brant's sister's stepson, probably a factor in Brant's openness to him through this letter.

79 Brant to Sir John Johnson, Grand River, 10 December 1797, LAC, Indian Affairs, Civil Control, Upper Canada, I (1798–99), 178–85; as quoted in Johnston, *Valley of the Six Nations*, 93–94.

80 For examples see SNCM, January 1832; July 1834; and January 1835.

81 Robert Liston was British foreign secretary Lord Grenville's envoy to the United States.

82 Brant to Liston, Grand River, 29 December 1797, LAC, G 53, Part 1, 140–45; as cited in Johnston, *Valley of the Six Nations*, 96.

83 William Dummer Powell to John Askin, 7 May 1798, Quaife, ed., *John Askin Papers*, II, 139–40; as quoted in Johnston, *Valley of the Six Nations*, 103.

84 In these less-than-selfless actions, one could compare Brant to his mentor, Sir William Johnson. For example, Johnson often personally gained from his role in treaty negotiations, such as the "gift" of the Niagara Islands he received from the Senecas while negotiating the 1764 Niagara Strip Treaty.

85 Grant of Block No. 1 to Philip Stedman, 1795, *Waterloo Historical Society*, Second Annual Report (Berlin, Ontario, 1914), 7–8; as quoted in Johnston, *Valley of the Six Nations*, 148.

86 Francis Gore to Lord Castlereagh, York, 4 September, 1809, PRO, CO 42, Vol. 349, 88; as quoted by Johnston, *Valley of the Six Nations*, 112–13.

87 Brant's Power of Attorney to Sell the Indian Lands, 2 November 1796, PRO, CO 42, Vol. 321, 35–36; as quoted by Johnston, *Valley of the Six Nations*, 79–80.

88 By this time the Confederacy had "rebuilt their house" in terms of the head titles of the Confederacy (the Rotiyanehson) so this number should represent thirty-five of the fifty titles that would have comprised the entire council. It is possible, however, that some of those who signed held other titles such as sub-chief or Pinetree chief. This number is unusual in that it does not represent the full council, and it is too many to have been single (or even double) representatives from each nation of the community.

89 Indian Treaties and Surrenders, I, 27. Also quoted in Johnston, *Valley of the Six Nations*, 129.

90 "Report of the Executive Council on Indian Land Sales, May 14, 1830" [Upper Canada, House of Assembly, Journals, 1836, Appendix 37, Report on Petition of N. Cozens, 28–31]; as cited in Johnston, *Valley of the Six Nations*, 142 (emphasis in original).

91 Simcoe used that as one of his reasons for issuing an alternate "deed" in 1793, which reduced the acreage of Haudenosaunee lands under the Haldimand Proclamation by one-third.

92 SNCM, Brantford House, 8 November 1834, Six Nations Letterbook, 1832.

93 For a more extensive look at Joseph Brant from a Six Nations perspective, see Rick Monture, *We Share Our Matters: Two Centuries of Writing and Resistance at Six Nations of the Grand River* (Winnipeg: University of Manitoba Press, 2014).

94 Brant also worked hard for the Western Confederacy of the Native nations of the Great Lakes, protecting the Ohio country from 1786 to 1794.

95 Claus Papers, as referenced in Isabel Kelsay, *Joseph Brant, 1743–1807: Man of Two Worlds* (Syracuse: Syracuse University Press, 1984), 625.

96 The source does not reveal the motivations for this change, so it can only be assumed.

97 The poor relationship with Simcoe was due in part to Brant's close association with the Johnson family. Sir John Johnson, the acknowledged leader of the Loyalists, sought for several years to be appointed lieutenant governor of Upper Canada. Simcoe rightly saw him as a political rival and Brant as his associate. As well, Simcoe saw the Six Nations as subjects of the Crown, and Brant's sovereignty stance offended him. This is discussed in Williams and Nelson, "Kaswentha."

98 Johnston, *Valley of the Six Nations*, 173.

99 As quoted by Williams and Nelson, "Kaswentha."

100 Charles M. Johnston, "The Six Nations of the Grand River Valley, 1784–1847," in *Aboriginal Ontario: Historical Perspectives on First Nations*, ed. Donald B. Smith and Edward S. Rogers (Toronto: Dundurn Press, 1994), 173.

101 Johnston, *Valley of the Six Nations*, xliii; Johnston, "Six Nations," 174–76; John A. Noon, *Law and Government of the Grand River Iroquois* (New York: Viking Fund Publications, 1949); and Sally M. Weaver, "Six Nations of the Grand River, Ontario," in *Handbook of North American Indians, Vol. 15: Northeast*, ed. Bruce G. Trigger (Washington: Smithsonian Institution, 1978), 525–36.

102 SNCM, Brantford House, 8 November 1834, Six Nations Letterbook, 1832.

103 Johnston and others refer to these transactions as "deeds," but I assert that since the Six Nations retained ownership in the case of a grantee vacating the property this was not a transfer of title to the individual Loyalists.

104 A Deed from the Six Nations Inhabiting The Grand River, 26 February 1787, LAC, Indian Affairs, Indian Records, Six Nations & Niagara, 1763–1810, XV, 201–4; as quoted in Johnston, *Valley of the Six Nations*, 71. Similar grants can be found in ibid., Section D, 120–92.

105 SNCM, November 1834.

106 Earlier Council records discuss specific cases of grantees "passing the limits" of their leases:

Brothers,

The next place we come to, is that of John Nelles, we were not generally acquainted with the quantity or the manner in which it was granted by our late Chief [Joseph Brant]; but we imagine that he has caused the survey to pass the limits and he has behaved very improper to some of our people, therefore we leave it to the consideration of our Dy Supert General if he shall be removed or if he shall be constrained to reform. Mr Anderson agreed to keep a mill in order when 200 acres of land was granted him—but he has extended his limits, left the Mill, which seldom does any. . . and rents it to people that in general are not agreeable to us—We also lay this before him.

Brothers,

The lands given to John Young . . . [and] Warner Nelles, we mean to be held by them on condition that they pay three bushels for every two hundred acres and that none of their lands shall exceed 122 acres. One objection we have to John Nelles is that he persists in selling liquor contrary to our desire. We intend William Nelles to hold his land on the same terms as his brother—but we hope that if he does not like to live here himself that he send good peaceable people stay on his place, lest some disagreeable accident might happen.

107 For example, see SNCM, July 1836.

108 Proceedings of a Six Nations' Council at Onondaga, 9 November 1806, LAC, Indian Affairs, Records and Correspondence of the Deputy Superintendent General, XXVI; as quoted in Johnston, *Valley of the Six Nations*, 137.

109 Johnston, *Valley of the Six Nations*, lv.

110 Resolutions of a Six Nations' Council at the Onondaga Village, 1 March 1809, LAC, Indian Affairs, Records and Correspondence of the Deputy Superintendent General, XXVII, 511 ff.; as quoted in Johnston, *Valley of the Six Nations*, 111.

111 This name has been spelled many different ways amongst the Haudenosaunee descendants of this family. Some spellings include Dochsteder, Dockstetter, Doxtador, Dockstader, and Doxtator.

112 "Clear Sky Onondagua Chief said Brother the Chiefs of the Six Nations are unanimous and will now speak to their Superintendent we have decided that the Children of old Kate Dockstetter and likewise hereby should have two Hundred Acres of Land each as Children of an Indian Woman by a White Man. John Burnham a Cayuga Indian child by a white Man we likewise wish should have two Hundred acres of land. Old Kate Dockstetters' Children are seven in Number." SNCM, August 1835. It appears that because of their family's land grant, these children were not fully integrated members of any of the Six Nations villages, but the council continued to recognize their rights to land as Haudenosaunee citizens. It also appears that Kate Dockstetter was the wife of William Dockstetter, who, like John Dochsteder, sold his land grant for personal gain and not for the benefit of his wife and children.

113 As noted on census materials, the Mohawks were divided into two prominent bands at the time of settlement on the Grand River (the Bay of Quinte Mohawks came later). The designations of "Upper" and "Lower" refer to their village positions on the Mohawk River, the "Upper" Mohawks being from Canajohare and the "Lower" coming from Schohare (Fort Hunter). In some cases, the two sides spoke through one representative in council but on occasion they selected separate speakers. They also, at different times, comprised the "conflicting groups" among the Six Nations that are often referred to as "factions." Ironically, by Grand River standards they were both "upper" nations, yet their internal disputes are often cited as evidence of an "upper"/ "lower" split between the nations.

114 SNCM, April 1835.

115 SNCM, July 1835.

116 A Six Nations' Council at Fort George, 8 October 1803, LAC, Upper Canada State Papers, VII, 33–45; as quoted in Johnston, *Valley of the Six Nations*, 104.

117 Ibid., 105.

118 Williams and Nelson, "Kaswentha."

119 Letter from (Tekarihoken) John Brant to Z. Mudge, Esq., York, 20 January 1831, John Brant Letterbook, UWO Archives.

120 For a detailed discussion of this, see Sidney L. Harring, "The Six Nations Confederacy, Aboriginal Sovereignty and Ontario Aboriginal Law: 1790–1860," in *Earth, Water, Air and Fire: Studies in Canadian Ethnohistory*, ed. David T. McNab

(Waterloo, ON: Wilfrid Laurier University Press, 1998), 181–230; Sidney L. Harring, *White Man's Law: Native People in Nineteenth-century Canadian Jurisprudence* (Toronto: University of Toronto Press, 1998).

121 For example, see SNCM, July 1836. Also, see Harring, *White Man's Law*, 43.

122 Proceedings of a Council of the Six Nation Indians held at the Onondaga Village Council fire at the Grand River on 31 January 1833, John Brant Letterbook, UWO Archives.

123 David Kanatawakhon, *Akwekon Tetewakhanyon—Let's Put It All Together* (London, ON: University of Western Ontario, 2002), 166.

124 Proceedings of a Council of the Six Nation Indians held at the Onondaga Village Council fire at the Grand River on 31 January 1833, John Brant Letterbook, UWO Archives (emphasis added).

125 Proceedings of an Indian Council held at the Onondaga Council House, 4 February 1834, John Brant Letterbook, UWO Archives.

126 SNCM, April 1835.

127 Reports by Stuart and the Rev. Robert Addison to the S.P.G., 1788–95, (i) Stuart, 2 July 1788; LAC, SPG, Journals, XXV, 120–21, 321, 393, 425–26; XXVI, 77, 167, 199–200; XXVII, 37–38, 114; as quoted in Johnston, *Valley of the Six Nations*, 236.

128 For example, Sir John Johnson wrote the following to Claus in October 1787: "Independent of the first Object of Extending the Gospel to those remote Parts of His Majesty's Possessions it would be highly beneficial in a Political point of View." LAC, Claus Papers, IV, 167–68; as quoted in Johnston, *Valley of the Six Nations*, 236. Peter Russell shared similar sentiments with Bishop Jacob Mountain in 1798: "the placing of a discreet & respectable Clergyman of the Church of England among the five Nations would be a most usefull measure in every point of view, whether religious, Moral, or Political." PRO, CO 42, Vol. 322, 153–54; as quoted in Johnston, *Valley of the Six Nations*, 240.

129 The Rev. John Douse to the Rev. Richard Reece; in Clark, "Earliest Missionary Letters of the Rev. John Douse, from the Salt Springs Mission on the Grand River in 1834 and 1836," Ontario Historical Society, Papers and Records, XXVIII (1932), 42–45; as quoted in Johnston, *Valley of the Six Nations*, 261. While there is no way of supporting this missionary's claims, it does demonstrate the persistence of Longhouse beliefs among the Mohawks who had been reported to be completely Christian for decades prior to this report.

130 Johnston, *Valley of the Six Nations*, 246 and 262.

131 For example, see Report by the Rev. Alvin Torry, 1823, *Methodist Magazine* (US), VI (November 1823), 232–34; as quoted in Johnston, *Valley of the Six Nations*, 246.

132 "A Description of the Confederacy, 1817," in Hall, *Travels in Canada, and the United States in 1816 and 1817*, 219–26; as quoted in Johnston, *Valley of the Six Nations*, 286.

133 Ibid.

134 Survey Diary of Augustus Jones, 1797, PAO, Crown Land Papers; as quoted in Johnston, *Valley of the Six Nations*, 126.

135 Proceedings of a Council of the Six Nations Indians held at the Onondaga Council fire at the Grand River on 14 October 1829, John Brant Letterbook, UWO Archives.

136 McDonell to Selkirk, York, 28 November 1808, LAC, Selkirk Papers, McDonell MSS, X (Baldoon Settlement Letterbook)]; as quoted in Johnston, *Valley of the Six Nations*, 174.

137   Norton to an Unknown Correspondent, Grand River, 10 August 1808, LAC, Indian Affairs, Civil Control, II (1808); as quoted in Johnston, *Valley of the Six Nations*, 277–78.

138   In the original homelands, the Six Nations had established extensive stores of food. For example, when the French burned the Seneca village of Ganondagan in 1687, it was estimated that they destroyed over a million bushels of corn (although this may have been an exaggeration on the part of the French). Similar storages of corn were ravaged during the Clinton-Sullivan Campaign as well as other battles during the Revolutionary War. The Oneida corn supply contributed to the survival of George Washington and his troops during one of the harsh winters of the war. Supplies such as these require several decades to accumulate.

139   While some leasing did exist in the Mohawk Valley, this economic endeavour was completely new to the other Haudenosaunee nations who settled the Grand River.

140   The annual presents from the King were promised by Sir William Johnson in the 1764 Treaty of Niagara.

141   Proceedings of a council of the Six Nations Indians held at the Onondaga Council fire at the Grand River on 14 October 1829, John Brant Letterbook, UWO Archives. Part of these proceedings also describe the Brantford town tract and revoke Claus's position as Six Nations Trustee.

142   The Six Nations remain sensitive to the difference between the Crown and its governments. The Crown, in traditional British law, has the obligation to protect those under it from abuses by the government. That is why so many Haudenosaunee addresses to the governor general are in the form of "petitions of right"—and why the chiefs continue to visit the governor general and not the prime minister.

143   One must be careful in referencing John Brant because he held both the Mohawk Royaner title of Tekarihoken (beginning in 1830) and that of the superintendent of Indian Affairs for Six Nations (beginning in 1828). Generally in council he spoke on behalf of the imperial government. Sometimes his fellow Royaner would reply to him as "Superintendent" and sometimes he would be referenced as "Brother" or "Cousin," depending upon the nation of the one addressing him. In his written communication, John Brant typically wrote as the superintendent, but certainly his views and opinions in that role were informed and impacted by the Confederacy responsibilities he held on behalf of his clan and nation.

144   The legislature had authority over settlers, so they were the government responsible for addressing the squatter issue; in 1838 they passed the Act for the Protection of Indian Reserves. The imperial government retained responsibility for Indian affairs throughout this period.

145   Proceedings of a Conference of the Six Nations Indians held at the Onondaga Council fire at the Grand River, 22 March 1830, John Brant Letterbook, UWO Archives.

146   For a detailed discussion of several court cases that arose from these breaches of the Crown's promises, see Harring, "Six Nations Confederacy."

147   Proceedings of a council held at the Onondaga council fire at the Grand River on 19 April 1830, John Brant Letterbook, UWO Archives.

148   This was the beginning of yet another present-day claim of the Six Nations against Canada (in right of the Crown). The government's promise of compensation is discussed in SNCM, April 1831.

149 At an 1832 council meeting, Chief Oneida Joseph stated, "We see by every day's experience that we cannot protect our property from the constant aggressions of the White people." John Brant Letterbook, UWO Archives.

150 Proceedings of a Council of the Six Nation Indians held at the Onondaga Village Council fire at the Grand River on 31 January 1833, John Brant Letterbook, UWO Archives.

151 Johnston, *Valley of the Six Nations*, 298.

152 SNCM, July 1834.

153 The New England Company was the North American successor to the Society for the Propagation of the Bible. They were instrumental in establishing both land development schemes and Native residential schools across the continent.

154 Jacob H. Busk to Sir George Grey, 13 December 1838, Great Britain, Colonial Office, British North American Provinces, Parliamentary Paper, 1839, No. 323, 115–17; as quoted in Johnston, *Valley of the Six Nations*, 301.

155 SNCM, February 1833.

156 Charles M. Johnston, "A Report on the Six Nations Land Surrender of 1841" (unpublished research report for the Government of Ontario, 1991), 7.

157 In a restructuring of the Indian Department, the trustees were relieved in 1839, with Jarvis picking up those duties.

158 Jarvis was allowed to resign instead (reportedly due to his connections with the "Family Compact"); see Harring, "The Six Nations Confederacy," 208. The financial accounts of the Indian Department during his tenure were in complete chaos.

159 The majority of source material for this section comes from a research report by Charles Johnston written for the Ontario government in 1991. It has not been published, but is by far the most exhaustive study to date regarding the 1841 "Surrender."

160 Johnston, "Report," 11.

161 Several of the seven were described as "junior" chiefs, probably meaning they were sub-chiefs or possibly Pinetree Chiefs.

162 Johnston, "Report," 21.

163 Ibid.

164 Johnston notes that Jarvis had once been reprimanded for applying on a surrender document the signature of a northern chief who had not authorized him to do so. Johnston, "Report," 29.

165 Ibid., 28–29.

166 Ibid., 32.

167 Ibid.

168 Ibid., 45.

169 1847 Agreement as described in SNCM, February 1896.

170 SNCM, February 1896.

171 For further discussion of this, see Williams and Nelson, "Kaswentha."

172 For a listing of current Six Nations lands claims, see Appendix 2.

CHAPTER 5: Skanata Yoyonnih—*One Village Has Been Made*

1   The term village is used here to denote the entire community, not the later developed "Village of Ohsweken."

2   Doxtator, "Iroquois Clans," 56.

3   Six Nations men continued to hunt on surrendered and other lands, in order to supplement the community economy as well as to assert their rights to hunt across southern Ontario under the 1701 Beaver Hunting Grounds Treaty.

4   Proceedings of a Council of the Six Nations Indians held at the Onondaga Council fire at the Grand River on 14 October 1829, John Brant Letterbook, UWO Archives.

5   SNCM, July 1835.

6   For example, a family of five would have received at least 1,000 acres under the council's plan (chiefs were to have been allotted 300 acres to help provide for their extended clan families—part of their duties under the Great Law), but under the 1840s compromise they would have only received 100 acres, or 10 percent of what the Confederacy had desired to allot to a family of that size.

7   See SNCM, November 1834 (Speech of Henry Brant), or SNCM, July 1835 (Speech of Isaac Locke).

8   See Map 1 for the village locations.

9   Chun-fen Lee, "Land Utilization in the Middle Grand River Valley of Western Ontario," *Economic Geography* 20, 2 (1944): 130–51.

10   Sally M. Weaver, "The Iroquois: The Consolidation of the Grand River Reserve in the Mid-Nineteenth Century, 1847–1875," in *Aboriginal Ontario: Historical Perspectives on the First Nations*, ed. Edward S. Rogers and Donald B. Smith (Toronto: Dundurn Press, 1994), 186.

11   Scholars such as Weaver, Harring, and Doxtator all rely upon this theory to explain the origins of political diversity in the community throughout the latter half of the nineteenth century.

12   During the early years on the Grand River, smaller communities were built and served as "satellites" to the main villages. Some of these smaller communities contained a significant Christian population, such as Davisville, a mixed Mohawk and Mississauga village located upriver from the Mohawk Village. It was abandoned by the early 1830s.

13   These Tuscarora families also included Nanticokes—who were often grouped together with the Tuscaroras—such as brother chiefs Richard and Josiah Hill.

14   Specific report findings and recommendations regarding Six Nations were included in Appendix EEE of the Bagot Commission Report.

15   Province of Canada, *Journals of the Legislative Assembly of Canada*, Sessional Papers, Appendix 21, "Report of the Special Commissioners" (Toronto, 1858).

16   Ibid.

17   For further discussion, see Canada, *Report of the Royal Commission on Aboriginal Peoples*, Vol. 1, Section 9, Part 4. In *For Seven Generations: An Information Legacy of the Royal Commission on Aboriginal Peoples* [CD-ROM]. Ottawa: Libraxus, 1997.

18   Peter S. Schmalz, *The Ojibwa of Southern Ontario* (Toronto: University of Toronto Press, 1991), 174–75. The specific protests of Six Nations against this act are discussed later in this chapter.

19   This assembled group, under the leadership of the Grand River Haudenosaunee, published the minutes of this council. This section is an analysis of those minutes. "The General Council of the Six Nations, and delegates from different bands in Western and Eastern Canada, June 10, 1870" (Hamilton, ON: [Six Nations Council] Spectator Office, n.d.)

20   Williams and Nelson, "Kaswentha."

21   SNCM, January–June 1885.

22   There are no known prosecutions against Haudenosaunee practising traditional ceremonies under this act, but the threat existed and was known among the various Haudenosaunee communities.

23   Williams and Nelson, "Kaswentha."

24   SNCM, March 1898.

25   See Section 9, An Act to amend and consolidate the laws respecting Indians, 1876. www.aadnc-aandc.gc.ca/eng/1100100010252/1100100010254.

26   SNCM, March 17, 1882.

27   For example, in 1891 a total of five estate cases were raised in council (four involved a will and one did not). Similarly, in that same year a total of ninety-six deaths were recorded in the annual census. While not all of the deceased would have been property owners, if it is assumed that at least one-fourth (based upon the idea that at least half were adults and half of them being property owners—I believe this to be a very conservative estimate) were, that would have meant at least twenty-four estates would have been settled that year. The five that were addressed by the council would represent just over 20 percent of the total.

28   SNCM, December 1890.

29   For example, the council refused to place Thomas Good on his wife's estate on the grounds that he had left her and was living with another woman at the time of his wife's death (SNCM, May 1888). For further evidence of this, see the section below regarding the council's interpretations in marriage disputes.

30   Further discussions of marriage guidelines are included in the published accounts of the Good Message of Handsome Lake. It should also be noted that many Christian marriage values are similar to those of the Longhouse.

31   SNCM, July 1896.

32   The council determined that the youngest son should purchase the shares of his brothers, an aspect of the agreement that the two older sons did not favour. Despite their misgivings with that part of the settlement, there is no record of complaint regarding the property division into six equal shares.

33   A search of the Department of Indian Affairs files pertaining to Six Nations (RG 10 Collection) was conducted to determine if a grievance had been filed directly with the Indian Department in this case. None was discovered.

34   SNCM, March 1886.

35   SNCM, July 1915.

36   Officially, wills should have been confirmed at the time of their writing; however, there are only a handful of instances in the council records where an individual had their will confirmed prior to death. That resulted in the "confirmation" process being one of both validation and interpretation following the death.

37   Communication recorded in council records of July 1912. The Communications Committee was charged to respond to the "insult." SNCM, July 1912.

38   SNCM, January 1887, *Aaron S. Johnson v. Mrs. Peter Davis.*

39   SNCM, August 1908.

40   For examples of marriage disputes, see SNCM, *Joseph Kick v. Winnie Kick,* July 1880; *Mr. Isaac Claus v. Mrs. Isaac Claus,* December 1899; and Mr. and Mrs. Simeon Hess, June 1916.

41   For example, see SNCM, Mr. & Mrs. T.A Cusick, November 1880; Mr. and Mrs. William Claus, February 1894; and James Monture and Julia Dixon, September 1916.

42   This category includes both married and common-law relationships. The council would reference the difference in their description of the case but considered people in both types of relationships equally—unless one or both had legal marriage partners.

43   SNCM, September 1916.

44   As noted previously in the case of Lucius Henry; see also SNCM, Mr. and Mrs William K Lewis, December 1881; Mrs. Charles Burning, November 1887; and Mrs. Deborah Claus, August 1919.

45   SNCM, June 1924.

46   SNCM, March 1880.

47   For example, see SNCM, November 1887, regarding a desired exemption in the Indian Act (1880) for "illegitimate" children.

48   SNCM, February 1881.

49   SNCM, March 1915.

50   SNCM, November 1901.

51   For examples, see: SNCM, December 1887; March 1915; and September 1923.

52   SNCM, February 1881.

53   It is unknown whether or not Lucy Brant was left on the Six Nations paylist after the council agreed to have her reinstated. Her case does not appear again in the council records, which leads me to believe that Superintendent Gilkison may have been successful in having her re-transfer upheld.

54   For further examples, see SNCM, Hannah Skylar and Mary Sickles, December 1885; and Henry Farmer, March 1894.

55   For example, see SNCM, Joseph Farmer, December 1884; Justus and Thomas Isaac, March 1898; and Jonas Smith, January 1902.

56   For examples, see SNCM, November 1887; January 1899; and May 1909.

57   SNCM, November 1894.

58   SNCM, January 1898.

59   SNCM, September 1897.

60   The Oneida Nation is part of the Haudenosaunee and, in traditional governance terms, the communities all fall under the Confederacy; however, for the purposes of band lists maintained by the Indian Department, each community was seen as separate for the purposes of local "rights" such as annuity payments and land holdings. This is another example of departmental interference that negatively impacted traditional governance systems.

61   SNCM, January 1902.

62   A separate chiefs' superannuation fund provided retirement assistance for chiefs

aged seventy and over who wished to access it and withdraw from the list of active chiefs. At different times, this account was referenced as a pension fund as well, but it is a different fund completely from the regular "pension list."

63 SNCM, February 1901.

64 SNCM, January 1906.

65 SNCM, January 1917.

66 For example, in March 1916, the council requested the Indian Department "to draw both spring and fall's distribution at the same time due to crop failures in the fall (esp potatoes)." SNCM, March 1916.

67 In February 1922, the council decided to advance $80,000 from the capital account, "as times are hard upon the Reserve" (this would have amounted to twenty dollars per capita). The department refused this allocation. The council counter-requested a ten-dollar per capita allotment (SNCM, 1922). See also the later discussion in this chapter regarding the loan fund.

68 Schmalz, *Ojibwa*, 174–75.

69 Weaver, "Consolidation," 200.

70 Nearly all of these records are classified as "restricted" by Library and Archives Canada under the Privacy Act.

71 SNCM, January 1907.

72 Peter Kulchyski, "'A Considerable Unrest': FO Loft and the League of Indians," *Native Studies Review* 4, 1–2 (1988): 107.

73 SNCM, December 1915.

74 For a discussion of this, see Doxtator, "Iroquois Clans," 56.

75 For example, see SNCM, case of John Sydney Brant, October 1914.

76 SNCM, August 1906.

77 SNCM, August 1912.

78 For examples, see SNCM, Sand pit, October 1893; Anthony Barnes, November 1908; and Mrs. Mary Lape (née Isaac), January 1920.

79 SNCM, April 1884.

80 SNCM, September 1916.

81 SNCM, October 1914.

82 For a discussion, see SNCM, December 1885.

83 SNCM, November 1914.

84 SNCM, March 1898.

85 SNCM, May 1888. In this case also, the husband was a white man found to be living "immorally" with another woman in the community. This may have influenced the decision of the council to confirm the mother's purchase.

86 SNCM, June 1882.

87 SNCM, May 1897.

88 SNCM, February 1906.

89 SNCM, November 1913.

90 An example of this occurred in the case of Sarah Burnham: SNCM, June 1911.

91 SNCM, February 1914.

92 SNCM, September 1906.

93 SNCM, October 1909.

94 SNCM, August 1912.

95 SNCM, October 1894.

96 SNCM, June 1909.

97 At this time, the council seemed to be liquidating any assets they could in order to meet their financial obligations as well as to finance the legal costs of their several land claim cases. See SNCM, 1922–1924.

98 SNCM, February 1914.

99 SNCM, April 1881.

100 SNCM, January 1883. The reference to "labour" may have meant the labour involved in removing the stones or it may have referenced statute labour requirements.

101 This summary is compiled from the reviewed Six Nations Council Minutes.

102 SNCM, February 1884. See also Horatio Hale, "Chief George HM Johnson, Onwanonsyshon," *Magazine of American History* 13 (1885): 129–41. Martin was beaten nearly to death in 1865 and shot in 1873 while working to protect the community from timber exploitation.

103 It is known that Six Nations people also continued to harvest plants in their traditional territory, although no specific mention of it appears in the documents of the council or Indian Affairs.

104 SNCM, May 1891.

105 SNCM, March 1898.

106 *Consolidated Regulations of the Six Nations Indians of the Grand River* (1910).

107 This growth in responsibilities is evident in the increased number of meetings (sometimes the council met up to ten days in a month). Council's recognition of increased responsibilities was discussed on several occasions, including January 1923 (SNCM, January 1923).

CHAPTER 6: Te Yonkhi'nikònhare Tsi Niyonkwarihotenhs—*They Are Interfering in Our Matters*

1 SNCM, February 1881.

2 SNCM, July 1912.

3 SNCM, September 1916.

4 SNCM, March 1917.

5 For example, in 1881 the department attempted to change the selection process for chiefs to elections rather than hereditary rule. The council deliberated the issue and informed the department that they would remain in the original form of government. The department acceded to the council's decision (SNCM, May 1881).

6 SNCM, October 1914.

7 For examples, see Estate of Joshua Williams, SNCM, 21 November 1911; and Estate of the Jos. Martin, SNCM, July 1924.

8 SNCM, August 1908.

9 SNCM, June 1912.

10 The property had been purchased by the department from an individual landowner in the Village of Ohsweken. The purchase price was not reported. The council requested the opportunity to repay the department for the land so that the entire hospital situation could be resolved (SNCM, June 1914).

11   SNCM, March 1915.

12   Asa R. Hill was the brother of Seneca Royaner David Hill. Based upon personal knowledge of the Josiah Hill family, it is very unlikely that Asa Hill was in any way related to his predecessor.

13   The council initially offered Asa Hill a two-year appointment. He applied for and was granted reappointment in 1917, which the department again attempted to overturn. Every time the position came up for renewal the department meddled in the decision of the council.

14   SNCM, May 1915.

15   SNCM, August 1915.

16   SNCM, July 1924.

17   SNCM, June 1924.

18   A complaint was filed with the council in July 1924, wherein the children of Richard Hill complained that their father had sold his home to Deputy Superintendent General D.C. Scott so a permanent barracks could be built to house the RCMP. The children objected as this was the only home for their father; the council objected as Scott had completely usurped their authority in this sale. SNCM, July 1924.

19   SNCM, January 1923.

20   Specifically, a "Status Indian" woman would lose her status if she married a man who was not recognized by the Canadian government as a "Status Indian." In other words, if a Six Nations woman married a Seneca man from Tonawanda (in New York State) she would lose her status just as if she had married a white man from Caledonia. The same was true of marriages between "Status Indian" women and Indigenous men who were mixed-blood (non-Status Native), Métis, or from non-recognized communities (e.g., several Algonquin bands did not have formal government recognition).

21   "The General Council of the Six Nations, and delegates from different bands in Western and Eastern Canada, June 10, 1870" (Hamilton, ON: [Six Nations Council] Spectator Office, n.d.).

22   SNCM, March 1909. A review of Indian Affairs files did not produce a copy of this petition.

23   SNCM, March 1909.

24   SNCM, June 1919.

25   SNCM, July 1919.

26   SNCM, May 1891.

27   SNCM, June 1891.

28   SNCM, December 1891.

29   SNCM, December 1891.

30   SNCM, February 1892.

31   In 1894, the federal government found that the responsibility in the Grand River Navigation Company issue belonged to the imperial government, not the Dominion. SNCM, January 1894.

32   Many of the western lands were also carved from existing Indian reserves.

33   SNCM, June 1919.

34   SNCM, October 1921.

35 There is evidence that indicates Gordon Vyse may have also served in the First World War. His name appears on a list of "Six Nations Indians coming within Class 1 [first WWI conscription draft]." See LAC, RG 10, Vol. 6768, File 452-20, Reel C-8513.

36 SNCM, April 1922.

37 Letter from D.C. Scott to Levi General, 29 May 1923; copy reproduced in the SNCM, July 1923.

38 Noon, *Law and Government*, 64.

39 Williams and Nelson, "Kaswentha."

40 Return to an Order of the House of Commons, 2 May 1887, by command of the Secretary of State, 15 June 1887, 17; as cited in Williams and Nelson, "Kaswentha."

41 Ibid.

42 SNCM, November 1911.

43 They followed in the footsteps of previous missionaries, including those from the Society for the Propagation of the Gospel in Foreign Parts.

44 SNCM, December 1887.

45 Chisholm represented First Nations communities from across the province in various cases against the government.

46 SNCM, September 1913.

47 See SNCM, 1913–1922.

48 SNCM, April 1914.

49 Additional information for this section came from the Six Nations Lands and Resources Office file, "The Glebe Farm/Lot, Eagles Nest Tract, 1800 acres, Brantford Township," reviewed 12 September 2005; and LAC RG 10, Indian Affairs, Vol. 6829, File 503-8-2, Reel C-8548.

50 While the chiefs must have had hope that their land claims might eventually be recognized, they probably knew better than to count on it.

51 SNCM, May 1886.

52 Adapted from SNCM, May 1887.

53 This reference is in regard to the payments made by the Six Nations Council in the 1840s for squatter improvements on the tract later inhabited by the New Credit Mississaugas.

54 SNCM, September 1900. Also included in "Six Nations Agency Correspondence," LAC, RG 10, Vol. 2358, File 72,566 pt. 2, C-1107.

55 "Six Nations Agency Correspondence," LAC, RG 10, Vol. 2358, File 72,566 pt. 2, C-1107.

56 SNCM, September 1911.

57 "Six Nations Agency Correspondence," LAC, RG 10, Vol. 2358, File 72,566 pt. 2, C-1107.

58 SNCM, June 1884.

59 SNCM, April 1923. The records do not indicate who they were working with, but it is likely that they met with Rochester-based lawyer George Decker, who had offered assistance in their claims against the Canadian government.

60 Annemarie Shimony, *Conservatism Among the Iroquois at the Six Nations Reserve*, Yale University Publications in Anthropology 65 (New Haven, CT: Department of Anthropology, Yale University, 1961), xxxiv.

61 For example, see SNCM, May 1904; March 1915; and January 1917.

62 For example, see discussion of charges against Chief Harry Martin, SNCM, March 1910.

63 This included words of encouragement sent to the Akwesasne Mohawk Council in 1899, after that community's hereditary Chiefs' Council was raided by the RCMP (SNCM, October 1899). One chief had been killed in the incident. This action was the impetus for the creation of the elected band council on the "Canadian" side of the Akwesasne Territory.

64 Minutes, Council, Willow Grove, 1870; as cited in Williams and Nelson, "Kaswentha."

65 LAC, RG 10, Vol. 1826; also quoted in Williams and Nelson, "Kaswentha."

66 For example, see SNCM, January 1908.

67 SNCM, October 1920.

68 SNCM, May 1922.

69 Deskahe (Levi General), speech given in London, August 1923; as cited in Williams and Nelson, "Kaswentha."

70 *The Red Man's Appeal for Justice* (Six Nations, Grand River Territory: March 1924), 23.

71 LAC, RG 10, Indian Affairs, Series A, Vol. 402, Reel C-9611; as cited in Weaver, "Consolidation," 202.

72 The Six Nations' population at that time was around 2,500. If all the signatories were men over the age of twenty-one, this number would still have represented less than 25 percent of what would have become the electorate if they had gotten their way and a municipal government had been imposed at Six Nations. Of the total population, it represented less than 7 percent. See also Weaver, "Consolidation," 202.

73 LAC, RG 10, Vol. 402; as cited by Weaver, "Consolidation," 202.

74 An example of this is found in the recommendations of the "Warrior Elem Bearfoot," SNCM, March 1899.

75 Not to be confused with the later national organization of the same name.

76 SNCM, March 1907.

77 SNCM, March 1907.

78 SNCM, February 1907.

79 For example, Weaver makes repeated references to the "Dehorners" (in reference to the different groups who petitioned against the Confederacy Council at various times from 1904 onward) in her 1994 essay on Six Nations history, but completely leaves out the Mohawk Workers (who supported the council). She perpetuates the same imbalance in her other publications. One of the only published sources to accord discussion of Confederacy supporters is Shimony's *Conservatism*.

80 SNCM, February–March 1907; April 1908; April 1909. Weaver also refers to these dissident "warrior associations" as "Dehorners."

81 SNCM, October 1920.

82 SNCM, February 1923.

83 Ibid.

84 Ibid.

85 SNCM, September 1924.

86 Sally M. Weaver, "The Iroquois: The Grand River Reserve in the Late Nineteenth and Early Twentieth Centuries, 1875–1945," in *Aboriginal Ontario: Historical Perspectives on First Nations*, ed. Donald B. Smith and Edward S. Rogers (Toronto: Dundurn Press, 1994), 248.

87 The actual wampum Morgan confiscated was a "spare set" of the strings.

88 The council had been meeting in the Agricultural Building due to renovations in the Council House, but the wampum belts and strings were still stored there at that time.

89 The records of the Indian Department only report the names of those elected.

90 Typically, the distribution of property is addressed through the ten-day mourning process in the case of a death. In situations of marriage separation, the couple would be expected to reach an amicable arrangement, especially in regard to their children.

Conclusion: Tetitewennonhtonhstha Tsi Niyonkwarihotenhs— We Are Causing Ourselves to Have Control Again, the Way We Do Things

1 When crossing in areas within traditional Haudenosaunee territory (New York–Ontario, New York–Quebec, Vermont–Quebec) people will usually articulate Haudenosaunee citizenship, but when crossing at other ports farther away (i.e., Washington–British Columbia, North Dakota–Manitoba, Maine–New Brunswick, etc.) they are likely to articulate identity as a North American Indian/Native American.

2 In addition to the documented matters discussed in this book, further evidence and discussion can be found in *Land Rights: A Global Solution for the Six Nations of the Grand River*, available at http://sixnations.ca.

3 Haudenosaunee activists who initiated the reclamation of a residential development site near Caledonia, Ontario, in 2006, regularly cited an inadequacy of Caledonia environmental and municipal services to address the population influx of that development. This topic was discussed in several radio interviews aired on CKRZ 100.3 FM.

4 For a detailed discussion of this, see Theresa McCarthy, *In Divided Unity: Haudenosaunee Reclamation at Grand River* (Tucson: University of Arizona Press, 2016).

GLOSSARY

Atatarho (Mohawk)	name for one of the Onondaga Chiefs, also known as Tadodaho; "entangled"
Aton:wah (Mohawk)	the Men's Chant (one of the Four Ceremonies)
Awen'ha'i (Onondaga)	Mature Flowers, also known as Sky Woman (from the Creation Story)
Ayenwahtha (Mohawk)	Hiawatha; Mohawk Chief title; "he who combs"
De'haonhwendjiawa'khon (Onondaga)	Earth Grasper (from the Creation Story)
Gaende'so'k (Onondaga)	Zephyr (from the Creation Story)
Gaiwiyo (Cayuga)	the Good Message; Code of Handsome Lake
Ganohonyohk (Cayuga)	Thanksgiving Address; "acknowledgement, thanks, and appreciation"
Ganyodaiyo/Sganyodaiyo (Seneca)	Handsome Lake; Seneca Chief title
Gayo'goho:no' (Cayuga)	Cayuga Nation; "people of the marshy area"
Goyani (Cayuga)	Clan Mother
Guswentha (Cayuga)	wampum belt; specifically, the Two Row Wampum
Haudenosaunee (Onondaga)	"people who make a house"; "people of the longhouse"
Hodiyanehson (Cayuga)	Confederacy Chiefs
Hoyanih (Cayuga)	Confederacy Chief
Kahwatsire (Mohawk)	family
Kane:hon (Mohawk)	Drum Dance
Kanikonhri:yo (Mohawk)	a good mind
Kanonhsa (Mohawk)	house
Kanyen'keha (Mohawk)	Mohawk language
Kanyen'kehaka (Mohawk)	Mohawk Nation; "people of the flint"
Karihwiyo (Mohawk)	the Good Message; Code of Handsome Lake
Kasehstenhsera (Mohawk)	power
Kaswentha (Mohawk)	wampum belt; specifically, the Two Row Wampum
Kayaneratsherakowa (Mohawk)	the Great Law; "the great, proper path"
Kayaneren'kowa (Mohawk)	the Great Law; "the great, proper path"
Kayentowa:nen (Mohawk)	the Peach Stone Game, one of the Four Ceremonies

Kayeri Niyorihwa:ke (Mohawk)	the Four Ceremonies or Four Dances
Kontenhnoteronh (Mohawk)	sister clans, a term used in the context of the Great Law
Kontinonhsyonni (Mohawk)	"the women who make the house"
Ohenton Karihwatehkwen (Mohawk)	Thanksgiving Address; "the words that come before all else"
Ohenton Thonhtenti (Mohawk)	"before they came"
Ohswe:ken (Mohawk)	the Grand River Territory; refers to the willow trees along the river
Ohswekenhronon (Mohawk)	the people of the Grand River Territory
Ogwehowe (Cayuga)	"first people" or "real people"
Onhwentsakon:shon Taienkonsohtonnion:tie' (Mohawk)	"those yet unborn"
Onhwentsya (Mohawk)	Earth
Onkwehonwe (Mohawk)	"first people" or "real people"
Onkwehonweneha (Mohawk)	Haudenosaunee languages
Onodagega (Onondaga)	Onondaga Nation; "people of the hills"
Onondawa:ga (Seneca)	Seneca Nation; "people of the great hills"
Onyata'a:ka (Oneida)	Oneida Nation; "people of the standing stone"
Oswe:gę (Cayuga)	the Grand River Territory
Otara (Mohawk)	clay, clan, or pottery
Otsire (Mohawk)	fire
Rotinonhsyonni (Mohawk)	"people who make a house," "people of the longhouse"
Rotiyanehson (Mohawk)	(all of the) Confederacy Chiefs
Royaner (Mohawk)	Confederacy Chief(s)
Sgaihwa:t (Cayuga)	one mind
Sganyadaiyo' (Cayuga)	Handsome Lake
Shonkwaya'tihson (Mohawk)	the Creator; "he completed our bodies"
Skanyatariyo (Mohawk)	Handsome Lake
Skanikonhra (Mohawk)	one mind
Skaru:reh (Tuscarora)	Tuscarora Nation; "shirt wearers"
Skennen (Mohawk)	peace or health
Tehatirihoken (Mohawk)	plural of Tekarihoken, used in reference to the entire Mohawk Nation
Tekarihoken (Mohawk)	"between two matters," one of the Mohawk Chief titles
Yakoyaner (Mohawk)	Clan Mother
Yethi'nihstenha Onhwentsya (Mohawk)	"she-to-us, our mother, the earth"
Yeya'takweniyo (Mohawk)	female leader, often "Clan Mother"

BIBLIOGRAPHY

Primary Sources and Manuscripts

D.B. Weldon Library, University of Western Ontario, London, Ontario

Brant, John. John Brant Letterbook, Six Nations Council Minutes, 1828–1834.

Norton, John. John Norton Letterbook, 1805–1810.

Library and Archives Canada, Ottawa, Ontario

Canada, Government of. RG 10, Department of Indian Affairs, Vols. 712, 715, 716, 717, 893, 894, 895, 896, 1738, 1739, 1740, 1741, 1742, 1743, 1744, 1745, 1746, 1747, 1748, 1749, 1750, 1751, 1752, 1753, 1754, 1755, 1756, 1863, 1879, 1881, 1886, 1894, 1897, 1949, 2063, 2064, 2968, 2069, 2070, 2075, 2077, 2078, 2082, 2083, 2523, 2525, 2529, 2550, 2627, 2737, 2778, 2792, 2802, 2560, 2562, 2563, 2569, 2572, 2573, 2584, 2585, 2586, 2589, 2590, 2596, 2614, 2717, 2619, 2623, 3162, 3163, 3164, 3167, 3168, 3169, 3175, 3218, 6768, 7132, 7154, 7577, 7578, 7755, 7930, 8281, 8731.

Canada, Government of. RG 6, Secretary of State, Vols. 91, 112, 127, 139.

Canada, Government of. RG 13, Justice Department, Vols. 87, 106, 928, 1042, 1856, 1860, 1873.

Six Nations [Elected Band] Council

Six Nations Lands and Resources. File: "The Glebe Farm/Lot, Eagles Nest Tract, 1800 acres, Brantford Township."

Woodland Cultural Centre Archives, Grand River Territory via Brantford, Ontario

Bomberry, Evelyn. Papers.

General Ethnology Files.

Harris, Judy. Papers.

Hill, Birdie. Papers.

Jamieson, Robert. Papers.

Six Nations Council Minutes and Records: 1832–1924.

Published Documents, Narratives, Letters, and Papers

Canada, Government of. *Indian Treaties and Surrenders, 1680–1890.* 4 vols. Toronto: Coles Publishing, 1971.

Canada, Government of. Department of Indian Affairs and Northern Development. *Annual Reports, 1870–1915.*

Cheshire, F.J. *Account of the Proceedings… Settlers on Indian Lands in Townships of Tuscarora and Oneida, 1846, 1847.* Hamilton, ON: Cheshire, 1847.

Johnson, William, Sir. *The Papers of Sir William Johnson.* Albany: University of the State of New York, 1921–62.

Johnston, Charles M., ed. *The Valley of the Six Nations: A Collection of Documents on the Indian Lands of the Grand River.* Toronto: University of Toronto Press, 1964.

Norton, John. *The Journal of Major John Norton, 1816,* edited by Carl Klinck and James Talman. Toronto: Champlain Society, 1970.

O'Callaghan, E.B. *The Documentary History of the State of New York.* Albany: Charles Van Benthuysen, 1851.

Province of Canada. *Journals of the Legislative Assembly of Canada.* Sessional Papers, Appendix 21, "Report of the Special Commissioners." Toronto, 1858.

Simcoe, John Graves. *The Correspondence of Lieut. Governor John Graves Simcoe, with allied documents relating to his administration of the government of Upper Canada.* Toronto: Ontario Historical Society, 1923–26.

Six Nations Council of Chiefs. "The General Council of the Six Nations, and delegates from different bands in Western and Eastern Canada, June 10, 1870." Hamilton, ON: [Six Nations Council] Spectator Office, 1980.

———. *Consolidated Regulations of the Six Nations Indians of the Grand River.* 1910.

Thwaites, Reuben Gold, ed. *The Jesuit Relations and Allied Documents.* Cleveland: Burrows Bros., 1896–1901.

Upper Canada. *Report on the Affairs of the Indians in Canada, Laid before the Legislative Assembly.* March 1845.

———. *Report on the Indians of Upper Canada.* 1839.

Secondary Sources

Abler, Thomas S., ed. *Chainbreaker: The Revolutionary War Memoirs of Governor Blacksnake.* Lincoln: University of Nebraska Press, 1989.

Abler, Thomas S. "Factional Dispute and Party Conflict in the Political System of the Seneca Nation (1845–1895)." PhD diss., University of Toronto, 1971.

———. "Longhouse and Palisade: Northeastern Iroquoian Villages of the 17th Century." *Ontario History* 62 (1970): 17–40.

Abler, Thomas S., and Elizabeth Tooker. "Seneca." In *Handbook of North American Indians, Vol. 15: Northeast,* edited by Bruce Trigger. Washington: Smithsonian Institution, 1978.

Alfred, Gerald R. *Heeding the Voices of Our Ancestors: Kahnawake Mohawk Politics and the Rise of Native Nationalism.* Toronto: Oxford University Press, 1995.

Allen, Paula Gunn. *The Sacred Hoop: Recovering the Feminine in American Indian Traditions.* Boston: Beacon Press, 1986.

Aquila, Richard. *The Iroquois Restoration: Iroquois Diplomacy on the Colonial Frontier, 1701–1754.* Detroit: Wayne State University Press, 1983.

Arden, Harvey, and Steve Wall. *Wisdomkeepers: Meetings with Native American Spiritual Elders.* Hillsboro, OR: Beyond Words Publishing, 1999.

Baldwin, Marie L.B. "John N. B. Hewitt, Ethnologist." *Quarterly Journal of the Society of American Indians* 2 (1914): 147–50.

Barnes, Barbara K., ed. *Traditional Teachings*. Akwesasne, QC: North American Indian Travelling College, 1984.

Battiste, Marie, ed. *Reclaiming Indigenous Voice and Vision*. Vancouver: University of British Columbia Press, 2000.

Beauchamp, William. *A History of the New York Iroquois: Now Commonly Called the Six Nations*. Long Island, NY: Ira J. Friedman, 1962.

Beauchamp, Wm. M. "Iroquois Women." *Journal of American Folk-Lore* 13, 49 (1900): 81–91.

Beaver, George. *Mohawk Reporter: The Six Nations Columns of George Beaver*. Ohsweken, NY: Iroquois Publishing and Craft Supplies, 1997.

Brant, Beth. *Writing as Witness*. Toronto: Women's Press, 1994.

Campisi, Jack. "National Policy, States' Rights, and Indian Sovereignty: The Case of the New York Iroquois." In *Extending the Rafters: Interdisciplinary Approaches to Iroquoian Studies*, edited by Michael K. Foster, Jack Campisi, and Marianne Mithun, 95–108. Albany: State University of New York Press, 1984.

Canada. Royal Commission on Aboriginal Peoples. *Report of the Royal Commission on Aboriginal Peoples*. In *For Seven Generations: An Information Legacy of the Royal Commission on Aboriginal Peoples* [CD-ROM]. Ottawa: Libraxus, 1997.

Carr, Lucien. "On the Social and Political Position of Women among the Huron-Iroquois Tribes." *16th and 17th Annual Reports of the Trustees of the Peabody Museum* 3, 3–4 (1884): 207–32.

Chadwick, Edward M. *The People of the Longhouse*. Toronto: Church of England Publishing Co., 1897.

Chafe, Wallace. *Onodowa'ga:' Gawe:no' Oiwa'sho'oh Words of the Seneca Language*. Salamanca, NY: Seneca Bilingual Education Program/Salamanca Central School District, 1983.

Colden, Cadwallader. *The History of the Five Indian Nations Depending on the Province of New-York in America*. 1727 (Part I) and 1747 (Part II). Ithaca: Cornell University Press, 1994.

Committee of the [Six Nations] Chiefs. "Traditional History of the Confederacy of the Six Nations." *Transactions of the Royal Society of Canada*, 3rd Series, Vol. 5, Sec. 2. Ottawa: Royal Society of Canada, 1912.

Cornelius, Carol. *Iroquois Corn in a Culture-Based Curriculum*. Albany: State University of New York Press, 1999.

Cutler, Winnifred, et al. "Lunar Influences on the Reproductive Cycle in Women." *Human Biology* 59, 6 (1987): 959–72.

Deloria, Vine, Jr. *Custer Died For Your Sins: An Indigenous Manifesto*. Norman: University of Oklahoma Press, 1969.

Dennis, Matthew. *Cultivating a Landscape of Peace: Iroquois-European Encounters in Seventeenth-Century America*. Ithaca, NY: Cornell University Press, 1993.

Deserontyon, John. *A Mohawk Form of Ritual of Condolence, 1782*. New York: Museum of the American Indian, Heye Foundation, 1928.

Deskaheh [Levi General]. *The Red Man's Appeal for Justice.* Grand River Territory, March 1924.

Dickason, Olive. *The Myth of the Savage.* Edmonton: University of Alberta Press, 1997.

Doxtator, Deborah. "Inclusive and Exclusive Perceptions of Difference: Native and Euro-based Concepts of Time, History and Change." In *Decentering the Renaissance: New Essays on Canada 1500–1700*, edited by Germaine Warkentin and Carolyn Podruchny, 33–47. Toronto: University of Toronto Press, 2002.

———. "Godi'nigoha': The Women's Mind and Seeing through to the Land." In *Godi'Nigoha': The Women's Mind,* 29–41. Brantford: Woodland Cultural Centre, 1997.

———. "What Happened to the Iroquois Clans? A Study of Clans in Three Nineteenth Century Rotinonhsyonni Communities." PhD diss., University of Western Ontario, 1996.

Fenton, William ed. *Parker on the Iroquois.* Syracuse, NY: Syracuse University Press, 1968.

Fixico, Donald L. "Methodologies in Reconstructing Native American History." In *Rethinking American Indian History*, edited by Donald L. Fixico, 117–30. Albuquerque: University of New Mexico Press, 1997.

———. "Ethics and Responsibilities in Writing American Indian History." *American Indian Quarterly* 20, 1 (1996): 29–39.

Foster, Michael, Jack Campisi, and Marianne Mithun, eds. *Extending the Rafters: Interdisciplinary Approaches to Iroquoian Studies.* Albany: State University of New York Press, 1984.

Friesen, Jean. "Magnificent Gifts." *Transactions of the Royal Society of Canada* 5, 1 (1986): 41–51.

George-Kanentiio, Doug. *Iroquois Culture and Commentary.* Santa Fe, NM: Clear Light Publishers, 2000.

Gibson, John Arthur, and Hanni Woodbury. *Concerning the League: The Iroquois League Tradition as Dictated in Onondaga by John Arthur Gibson / Newly elicited, edited and translated by Hanni Woodbury; in collaboration with Reg Henry and Harry Webster; on the basis of A.A. Goldenweiser's manuscript.* Winnipeg: Algonquian and Iroquoian Linguistics, 1992.

Graymont, Barbara, ed. *Fighting Tuscarora: The Autobiography of Chief Clinton Rickard.* Syracuse, NY: Syracuse University Press, 1973.

———. *The Iroquois in the American Revolution.* Syracuse: Syracuse University Press, 1972.

Greene, Andrea. "Land, Leadership, and Conflict: The Six Nations' Early Years on the Grand River." MA thesis, University of Western Ontario, 1984.

Hale, Horatio. "Chief George HM Johnson, Onwanonsyshon." *Magazine of American History* 13 (1885): 129–41.

———. *The Iroquois Book of Rites.* Philadelphia: DG Brinton, 1883. Rpt. in Iroquois Reprints Series, edited by Wm. Guy Spittal. Ohsweken, ON: Iroqrafts, 1989.

Harring, Sidney L. "The Six Nations Confederacy, Aboriginal Sovereignty and Ontario Aboriginal Law: 1790–1860." In *Earth, Water, Air and Fire: Studies in Canadian Ethnohistory*, edited by David T. McNab, 181–230. Waterloo, ON: Wilfrid Laurier University Press, 1998.

———. *White Man's Law: Native People in Nineteenth-century Canadian Jurisprudence.* Toronto: Osgoode Society for Canadian Legal History, University of Toronto Press, 1998.

Haudenosaunee Environmental Task Force (HETF). *The Words That Come Before All Else.* Akwesasne Haudenosaunee Territory: Native North American Traveling College, 2000.

Hauptman, Laurence M. *Conspiracy of Interests: Iroquois Dispossession and the Rise of New York State.* Syracuse, NY: Syracuse University Press, 1999.

———. *The Iroquois in the Civil War.* Syracuse, NY: Syracuse University Press, 1992.

———. *Formulating American Indian Policy in New York State, 1970–1986.* Albany: State University of New York Press, 1988.

———. *The Iroquois Struggle for Survival.* Syracuse, New York: Syracuse University Press, 1986.

———. *The Iroquois and the New Deal.* Syracuse, NY: Syracuse University Press, 1981.

Henderson, James (Sákéj) Youngblood. "Ayukpachi: Empowering Aboriginal Thought." In *Reclaiming Indigenous Voice and Vision,* edited by Marie Battiste, 248–78. Vancouver: University of British Columbia Press, 2000.

———. "The Context of the State of Nature." In *Reclaiming Indigenous Voice and Vision,* edited by Marie Battiste, 11–38. Vancouver: University of British Columbia Press, 2000.

Hertzberg, Hazel. *The Great Tree and the Longhouse: The Culture of the Iroquois.* New York: Macmillan, 1966.

Hewitt, J.N.B. "Status of Woman in Iroquois Polity Before 1784." *Annual Report of the Board of Regents of the Smithsonian Institution for the year ending June 30, 1932.* Washington: Smithsonian Institution, 1933.

———. "Iroquoian Cosmology: Part 2." *Bureau of American Ethnology, Forty-third annual report, 1925/26.* Washington: Smithsonian Institution, 1928.

———. "Iroquois Cosmology, Part 1." *Annual report of the Bureau of American Ethnology to the Secretary of the Smithsonian Institution* 21. Washington: Smithsonian Institution, 1903.

———. "Polysynthesis in the Languages of the North American Indian." *American Anthropologist,* October 1893.

———. "Legend of the Founding of the Iroquois League." *American Anthropologist* 5, 2 (1892): 131–48.

Hill, Richard W. "The Cultural History of Iroquois Sovereignty." Unpublished manuscript, 1999.

Holm, Tom. "Peoplehood: A Model for the Extension of Sovereignty in American Indian Studies." *Wicazo Sa Review* 18, 1 (2003): 7–24.

Hubbard, John N. *An Account of Sa-Go-Ye-Wat-Ha, or, Red Jacket and his People, 1750–1830.* Albany, NY: J. Munsell's Sons, 1886.

Hurley, J.D. *Children or Brethren: Aboriginal Rights in Colonial Iroquoia.* Saskatoon, SK: University of Saskatchewan Native Law Centre, 1985.

Indian Time Haudenosaunee Booklet, "Ancient Clan System," *Indian Time Newspaper,* Akwesasne Mohawk Territory, 7 January 2000.

Jacobs, N. Carol. "Presentation to the United Nations, July 18, 1995." *Akwesasne Notes*, Fall 1995, 116–17.

Jemison, Peter, and Anna M. Schein. *Treaty of Canandaigua 1794: 200 Years of Treaty Relations between the Iroquois Confederacy and the United States.* Santa Fe, NM: Clear Light, 2000.

Jennings, Francis. *The Ambiguous Iroquois Empire.* New York: W.W. Norton, 1984.

Jennings, Francis, ed. *Iroquois Indians: A Documentary History of the Six Nations and Their League.* Woodbridge, CN: Research Publications, 1985.

———. *The History and Culture of Iroquois Diplomacy: An Interdisciplinary Guide to the Treaties of the Six Nations and Their League.* Syracuse, NY: Syracuse University Press, 1985.

Johnston, Charles M. "The Six Nations of the Grand River Valley, 1784–1847." In *Aboriginal Ontario: historical perspectives on First Nations*, edited by Donald B. Smith and Edward S. Rogers, 167–81. Toronto: Dundurn Press, 1994.

———. "A Report on the Six Nations Land Surrender of 1841." Unpublished research report for the Government of Ontario, 1991.

———. "An Outline of Early Settlement in the Grand River Valley." *Ontario History* 54, 1 (1962): 43–67.

Jordan, Kurt A. "Seneca Iroquois Settlement Pattern, Community Structure, and Housing, 1677–1779." *Northeast Anthropology* 67 (2004): 23–60.

———. "An Eighteenth Century Seneca Iroquois Short Longhouse from the Townley-Read Site, c. A.D. 1715–1754." *The Bulletin: Journal of the New York State Archeological Association* 119 (2003): 49–63.

Kanatawakhon, David. *Akwekon Tetewakhanyon—Let's Put It All Together.* London, ON: University of Western Ontario, 2002.

Kelsay, Isabel. *Joseph Brant, 1743–1807: Man of Two Worlds.* Syracuse: Syracuse University Press, 1984.

Kulchyski, Peter. "'A Considerable Unrest': F.O. Loft and the League of Indians." *Native Studies Review* 4, 1–2 (1988): 95–117.

Ladner, Kiera L. "When Buffalo Speaks: Creating an Alternative Understanding of Traditional Blackfoot Governance." PhD diss., Carleton University, 2000.

Laenui, Poka [Hayden F. Burgess]. "Processes of Decolonization." In *Reclaiming Indigenous Voice and Vision*, edited by Marie Battiste, 150–60. Vancouver: University of British Columbia Press, 2000.

Lafitau, Joseph-François. *Customs of the American Indians Compared with the Customs of Primitive Times.* Toronto: Champlain Society, 1977.

Lee, Chun-fen. "Land Utilization in the Middle Grand River Valley of Western Ontario." *Economic Geography* 20, 2 (1944): 130–51.

Lyons, Oren, and John Mohawk, eds. *Exiled in the Land of the Free.* Santa Fe, NM: Clearlight Publishers, 1993.

Mann, Barbara. *Iroquoian Women: The Gantowisas.* New York: Peter Lang, 2000.

McCarthy, Theresa. *In Divided Unity: Haudenosaunee Reclamation at Grand River.* Tucson: University of Arizona Press, 2016.

McKeown, Justice William P. *In the Matter of an Appeal pursuant to section 135 of the Customs Act, S.C. 1986, c. 1 and In the Matter of an Action for declaratory relief between: Grand Chief Michael Mitchell, a.k.a. Kanantakeron, Plaintiff, and The Minister of National Revenue, Defendant.* Federal Court of Canada, 27 June 1997.

McNab, David T. *Circles of Time: Aboriginal Land Rights and Resistance in Ontario.* Waterloo: Wilfrid Laurier University Press, 1999.

Mitchell, Michael. "Akwesasne: An Unbroken Assertion of Sovereignty." In *Drumbeat: Anger and Renewal in Indian Country*, edited by Boyce Richardson, 105–36. Toronto: Summerhill Press (for Assembly of First Nations), 1989.

———. Plaintiff's Memorandum of Fact and Law, Federal Court of Canada Trial Division, *In the Matter of an Appeal pursuant to section 135 of the Customs Act, S.C. 1986, c. 1 and In the Matter of an Action for declaratory relief between: Grand Chief Michael Mitchell, a.k.a. Kanantakeron, Plaintiff, and The Minister of National Revenue, Defendant.* Federal Court of Canada, 8 December 1996.

Mohawk, John C. *Utopian Legacies: A History of Conquest and Oppression in the Western World.* Santa Fe, NM: Clearlight Publishers, 2000.

———. "A View from Turtle Island: Chapters in Iroquois Mythology, History and Culture." PhD diss., State University of New York at Buffalo, 1993.

———. *War Against the Seneca.* Canandaigua, NY: Ganondagan State Historic Site, 1987.

———. "What Can We Learn from Native America About War and Peace?: The Progressive Pragmatism of the Iroquois Confederacy." *Lapis Magazine Online*, n.d. http://arnieegel.blogspot.ca/2006/12/john-mohawk-what-can-we-learn-from.html (accessed 15 March 2017).

Monture, Rick. *We Share Our Matters: Two Centuries of Writing and Resistance at Six Nations of the Grand River.* Winnipeg: University of Manitoba Press, 2014.

Morgan, Lewis Henry. *League of the Ho-de-no-sau-nee, or Iroquois.* New York: M.H. Newman, 1851.

Myers, Merlin G. *Houses and Families of the Longhouse Iroquois at Six Nations Reserve.* Lincoln, NE: University of Nebraska Press, 2006.

Noon, John A. *Law and Government of the Grand River Iroquois.* New York: Viking Fund Publications, 1949.

O'Callahan, E.B. *Documents Relative to the Colonial History of the State of New York.* Albany: Weed, Parsons and Co., 1853–1887.

Parker, Arthur C. *Parker on the Iroquois.* Syracuse: Syracuse University Press, 1968.

———. *The Code of Handsome Lake, the Seneca Prophet.* Albany: New York State Museum, 1918.

———. *The Constitution of the Five Nations.* New York State Museum Bulletin 184. Albany: University of the State of New York, 1916.

Reville, F. Douglas. *History of the County of Brant.* Brantford, ON: Brant Historical Society, 1920.

Richards, Cara. "Matriarchy or Mistake: The Role of Iroquois Women through Time." In *Cultural Stability and Cultural Change*, edited by V.F. Kay, 36–45. Proceedings of the 1957 Annual Spring Meeting of the American Ethnological Society.

Richter, Daniel K. *The Ordeal of the Longhouse: The Peoples of the Iroquois League in the Era of European Colonization.* Chapel Hill: University of North Carolina Press, 1992.

Richter, Daniel K., and James Merrell, eds. *Beyond the Covenant Chain: The Iroquois and their Neighbors in Indian North America, 1600–1800*. Syracuse: Syracuse University Press, 1987.

Rogers, Edward S., and Donald B. Smith, eds. *Aboriginal Ontario: Historical Perspectives on the First Nations*. Toronto: Dundurn Press, 1994.

Rudes, Blair A. *Tuscarora Roots, Stems, and Particles: Algonquin and Iroquoian Linguistics; Memior 3*. Winnipeg: Algonquin and Iroquoian Linguistics, 1987.

Rudes, Blair A., and Dorothy Crouse. *The Tuscarora Legacy of J.N.B. Hewitt: Materials for the Study of Tuscarora Language and Culture/J.N.B. Hewitt w'a ekhirihway'e O skarur'e: yerihety 'a khw'a h'a uwe the tihsn'e urihwaka y'e skarur'e*. Ottawa: Canadian Museum of Civilization, 1987.

Schmalz, Peter S. *The Ojibwa of Southern Ontario*. Toronto: University of Toronto Press, 1991.

Seaver, James E. *A Narrative of the Life of Mrs. Mary Jemison*, Canandaigua, NY: 1824.

Shannon, Timothy. *Indians and Colonists at the Crossroads of Empire: The Albany Congress of 1754*. Ithaca, NY: Cornell University Press, 2000.

Shimony, Annemarie. "An Analysis of an Iroquois Uprising." In *Extending the Rafters: Interdisciplinary Approaches to Iroquoian Studies*, edited by Michael K. Foster, Jack Campisi, and Marianne Mithun, 153–64. Albany: State University of New York Press, 1984.

———. *Conservatism among the Iroquois at the Six Nations Reserve*. Yale University Publications in Anthropology 65. New Haven, CT: Department of Anthropology, Yale University, 1961.

Sioui, Georges. *For an Amerindian Autohistory: An Essay on the Foundations of a Social Ethic*. Montreal and Kingston: McGill-Queen's University Press, 1992.

Six Nations Elected Council. *Six Miles Deep: Land Rights of the Six Nations of the Grand River*. Ohsweken, ON: Six Nations Elected Council, 2015.

Skye, Raymond R., and Jeff Burnham. *The Great Peace: Gathering of the Good Minds* [CD-ROM]. Brantford, ON: Working World New Media, 1999.

Smith, Linda Tuhiwai. *Decolonizing Methodologies: Research and Indigenous Peoples*. Auckland: Zed Books, 1999.

Snow, Dean R., Charles Gehring, and William Strarna, eds. *In Mohawk Country: Early Narratives about a Native People*. Syracuse: Syracuse University Press, 1996.

Snyderman, George S. "Concepts of Land Ownership Among the Iroquois and Their Neighbors." In *Symposium on Local Diversity in Iroquois Culture (1949)*, edited by William N. Fenton, 15–34. Washington, DC: US Government Printing Office, 1951.

Spittal, W.G., ed. *Iroquois Women: An Anthology*. Ohsweken, ON: Iroqrafts, 1990.

Starna, William A. "Aboriginal Title and Traditional Iroquois Land Use: An Anthropological Perspective." In *Iroquois Land Claims*, edited by Christopher Vecsey and William A. Starna, 31–48. Syracuse, NY: Syracuse University Press, 1988.

Stone, William L. *The Life and Times of Sa-Go-Ye-Wat-Ha, or Red Jacket*. Albany: J. Munsell, 1866.

———. *Life of Brant, Vols. I and II*. New York: A.V. Blake, 1838.

Sturtevant, William C., ed. *Handbook of North American Indians.* Washington: Smithsonian Institution, 1978.

Surtees, Robert J. "Land Cessions, 1763–1830." In *Aboriginal Ontario: Historical Perspectives on the First Nations,* edited by Edward S. Rogers and Donald B. Smith, 92–121. Toronto: Dundurn Press, 1994.

Swanton, John R. "John Napoleon Brinton Hewitt." *American Anthropologist* 40 (1938): 286–90.

Sweetgrass First Nations Language Council, Inc. *English/Cayuga Language Dictionary.* Draft edition. Brantford, ON: Sweetgrass, 1996.

Thomas, Jacob E. *Teachings from the Longhouse.* Toronto: Stoddart, 1994.

———. *The Great Law* [videorecording]. Prod. Robert Rooney and Brenda Rooney. Dir. Robert Rooney. Brantford, ON: Iroquois Institute, 1992.

———. *The Constitution of the Confederacy by the Peacemaker, written by Seth Newhouse in 1897.* Wilsonville, ON: Sandpiper Press, 1989.

Tooker, Elisabeth. "J.N.B. Hewitt." In *Encyclopedia of North American Indians,* edited by Frederick E. Hoxie. Boston: Houghton Mifflin, 1996.

———. "The Five (Later Six) Nations Confederacy, 1550–1784." In *Aboriginal Ontario: Historical Perspectives on the First Nations,* edited by Edward S. Rogers and Donald B. Smith, 79–91. Toronto: Dundurn Press, 1994.

———. "Women in Iroquois Society." In *Extending the Rafters: Interdisciplinary Approaches to Iroquoian Studies,* edited by Michael K. Foster, Jack Campisi, and Marianne Mithun, 109–24. Albany: State University of New York Press, 1984.

———. "Iroquois Since 1820." In *The Handbook of North American Indians: Vol. 15: Northeast,* edited by Bruce G. Trigger, 449–65. Washington: Smithsonian Institution, 1978.

Tuck, James. *Onondaga Pre-history.* Syracuse: Syracuse University Press, 1971.

Vecsey, Christopher, and Robert W. Venables, eds. *American Indian Environments: Ecological Issues in Native American History.* Syracuse, NY: Syracuse University Press, 1980.

Vecsey, Christopher, and William A. Starna, eds. *Iroquois Land Claims.* Syracuse, NY: Syracuse University Press, 1988.

Wallace, Anthony F.C. *The Death and Rebirth of the Seneca.* New York: Random House, 1972 [1969].

Wallace, Paul A.W. *The White Roots of Peace.* Port Washington, NY: Ira J. Friedman, 1946.

Waugh, Frederick Wilkerson. *Iroquois Foods and Food Preparation.* Ottawa: Government Printing Bureau, 1916.

Weaver, Sally M. "The Iroquois: The Consolidation of the Grand River Reserve in the Mid-Nineteenth Century, 1847–1875." In *Aboriginal Ontario: Historical Perspectives on the First Nations,* edited by Edward S. Rogers and Donald B. Smith, 182–212. Toronto: Dundurn Press, 1994.

———. "The Iroquois: The Grand River Reserve in the Late Nineteenth and Early Twentieth Centuries, 1875–1945." In *Aboriginal Ontario: Historical Perspectives on the First Nations,* edited by Edward S. Rogers and Donald B. Smith, 213–57. Toronto: Dundurn Press, 1994.

————. "Six Nations of the Grand River, Ontario." In *Handbook of North American Indians, Vol. 15: Northeast*, edited by Bruce G. Trigger. Washington: Smithsonian Institution, 1978.

————. *Medicine and Politics Among the Grand River Iroquois: A Study of the Non-conservatives*. Ottawa: National Museums of Canada, 1972.

Weaver, Sally M., and Virginia Cooper. "An Early History of the De-horners." Unpublished paper, 1970.

White, Kevin J. "Rousing a Curiosity in Hewitt's Iroquois Cosmologies." *Wicazo Sa Review* 28.2 (2013): 87–111.

Williams, Paul. "The Chain." LLM thesis, University of Toronto, 1982.

Williams, Paul, and Curtis Nelson. "Kaswentha." January 1995. Research report prepared for the Royal Commission on Aboriginal Peoples. In *For Seven Generations: An Information Legacy of the RCAP*. Libraxus, 1997.

Wright, Ronald. *Stolen Continents*. Toronto: Penguin Books, 1992.

Zeisberger, David. *Zeisberger's Indian Dictionary: English, German, Iroquois (the Onondaga), and Algonquin (the Delaware)*. Cambridge, MA: J. Wilson and Son, 1887.

INDEX

Gore, Francis, 160–61
Goyani. *See* Clan Mother
Grand Council: belief in continuity of
treaty relationship with Crown,
227–30, 234; and Brant leases,
167; and Caledonia Dam, 218–19;
Canada pushes for replacement of,
28, 187, 191–92, 215, 218, 226; and
ceded land, 170, 176, 234; choice
of Grand River as homeland, 134,
137; and Condolence Ceremony,
40; consolidation of Grand River
community, 188; dealing with
Indian Affairs, 237; development
of policies by, 174, 186, 187, 194–
211, 237; and 1847 Mississauga
Settlement, 183–84, 204; and 1842
Surrender, 180–81; and flooding,
177; and Indian Act, 191–92,
219–20; interdependence of, 38–39;
issues of disagreement with Indian
Affairs, 28, 187, 196, 213–15, 218,
237; and Joseph Brant, 155–56,
158, 161–62, 275n106; keeping
with old traditions, 226–27; and
land grants, 165–67; and loss
of investments, 178–80; and
Mississauga occupation, 226;
and New England Company,
223–24; petitions against, 218, 231;
referenced in Great Law of Peace,
29, 30, 31, 33–35; reform ideas
for, 226, 231–32; responsibility
of keeping peace, 43–44; setting
up permanent fund, 167; shifts
meetings to Ohsweken, 189; special
nation names for, 36–37; and
squatters, 169; support for, 232–33;
takeover of 1924, 215, 234–36;
and territorial expansion, 91; W.
Johnson addresses, 115; and War
of Independence, 127–28; women
addressing, 67, 73–75
Grand River: British government secures
title to, 143–45, 146; and 1847
Mississauga Settlement, 182–84;
and 1841 Surrender, 180–82;
establishing social structures at,
139–42; flooding of, 177, 178,
179–80; government, 171, 174;
maps of Six Nations' settlement,
140–41; missionaries at, 172; and
mixed-nation villages, 175–76; Six
Nations establishes consolidated
community at, 188–90; Six Nations
selects as new homeland, 129–30,
136–39; social structure at, 170–71;
surveying of, 147, 149–50; women's

role at during 19th century, 73–76.
See also Grand Council; Six Nations
Grand River Navigation Company, 178–80,
191, 209, 219, 231
Great Law of Peace: academic study of,
27–29; and adoption, 200; and
Condolence Ceremony, 39–42,
88; and connection between land
and identity, 35–38; connection
to Creation Story, 45–46; early
renditions of, 254n38; its parts
described, 30–35; and kinship
system based on interdependence,
38–39; referenced in Covenant
Chain, 96, 97, 99, 100; and refugees,
112; on rights and responsibilities,
42–45; role of women in, 58–63; on
territories and boundaries, 35
Great League, 37
Great Peace of Montreal, 102–3
Great White Mat, 31
Green, James, 157
Green, Peter, 182
Greenhalgh, Wentworth, 91–92
grief, 88, 139, 153, 264n38
Guswentha. *See* wampum
Gwynne, John, 181

H
Haldimand, Frederick, 128, 129, 130, 135–
36, 143–44, 145–46, 163
Haldimand Proclamation, 148–49, 150–51,
152, 153, 156–57, 161
Hale, Horatio, 54, 65, 232
Handsome Lake, 46–52, 73
Hardy, Charles, 117–18
Haudenosaunee. *See* Grand Council; Six
Nations
Headwaters Claim, 148, 150, 152, 154–55,
221–23
Henry, Reg, 28
Hewitt, J. N. B., 17–19, 21, 28, 54
Hill, A. E., 232
Hill, Aaron, 147, 173
Hill, Asa R., 214, 285n13
Hill, Catherine, 204
Hill, David, 147
Hill, Elias, 202
Hill, George W., 205
Hill, Hilton M., 214
Hill, John, 204
Hill, Joseph J., 220
Hill, Josiah, 211
Hodiyanehson. *See* Rotiyanehson
hospitals, 213
Hoyanih. *See* Rotiyanehson
Huff, John, 165–66
hunting, 49, 167, 173, 208–9, 280n3